Apartheid City
in Transition

Editors:
Mark Swilling, Richard Humphries,
and Khehla Shubane

Contemporary South African Debates

1991
Oxford University Press
Cape Town

Oxford University Press
Walton Street, Oxford OX2 6DP, United Kingdom

Oxford   New York   Toronto
Delhi   Bombay   Calcutta   Madras   Karachi
Petaling Jaya   Singapore   Hong Kong   Tokyo
Nairobi   Dar es Salaam   Cape Town
Melbourne   Auckland

and associated companies in
Berlin   Ibadan

ISBN 0 19 570585 8

Published by Oxford University Press Southern Africa
Harrington House, Barrack Street, Cape Town, 8001,
South Africa

DTP conversion in 10 on 12 point Garamond by
Theiner Typesetting (Pty) Ltd of Bellville
Printed and bound by Belmor Printing, Cape Town

Contents

Contributors

Doreen Atkinson is a researcher at the Centre for Policy Studies, University of the Witwatersrand.

Simon Bekker is Director of the Centre for Social and Development Studies, University of Natal, Durban.

Ann Bernstein is Executive Director of Urbanization at the Urban Foundation, Johannesburg.

Rob Cameron lectures in the Department of Political Studies, University of Cape Town.

Fanie Cloete is Professor of Development Studies at the Rand Afrikaans University and a research associate with the Centre for Policy Studies, University of the Witwatersrand.

William Cobbett is a local government specialist at Planact, Johannesburg.

Cas Coovadia is the Assistant General Secretary of CAST and the Publicity Secretary of Actstop.

Gerhard Croeser is the Director General of the Department of Finance.

Rodney Davenport is a former head of the Department of History, Rhodes University.

Paul Hendler is a specialist housing researcher and development consultant based in Johannesburg. He is at present employed by Planact.

Chris Heymans is a political analyst at the Urban Foundation, Johannesburg.

Richard Humphries is a researcher at the Centre for Policy Studies, University of the Witwatersrand.

Roland Hunter is an economist with Planact, Johannesburg.

Alan Mabin is an Associate Professor in the Department of Town and Regional Planning, and is Director of the Programme for Planning Research, University of the Witwatersrand.

Nigel Mandy is an urban affairs consultant based in Johannesburg.

Jeff McCarthy is Professor of Geography at the University of Natal, Pietermaritzburg.

Colleen McCaul is a senior researcher at the South African Institute of Race Relations, Johannesburg.

Deborah Posel lectures in the Department of Sociology, University of the Witwatersrand.

Louwrens Pretorius is an Associate Professor in the Department of Sociology, University of South Africa, and a research associate with the Centre for Policy Studies, University of the Witwatersrand.

Lawrence Schlemmer is Director of the Centre for Policy Studies, University of the Witwatersrand.

Jeremy Seekings is currently employed at the Research Unit, Sociology of Development, University of Stellenbosch.

Khehla Shubane is a researcher at the Centre for Policy Studies, University of the Witwatersrand.

Mark Swilling is a local government specialist with Planact, Johannesburg, on secondment from the Centre for Policy Studies, University of the Witwatersrand.

Tony Wolfson is a development planner at Planact, Johannesburg.

Acknowledgements

The editors would like to thank various persons for their help in making this collection of essays possible:

- Glenda Younge, at Oxford University Press in Cape Town, for her encouragement, advice, and forbearance during the entire process.

- Wendy Powell, also at OUP, for editing the lengthy manuscript.

- Fiona Higginson, at the Centre for Policy Studies, for her general assistance over many months in various capacities. An enormous debt of gratitude is due to her.

- To all the contributors for having agreed to participate, completing their chapters against often severe work pressures.

- To all our colleagues, past and present, at the Centre for Policy Studies, who helped to create such a congenial research atmosphere.

Introduction

Wherever they exist, cities are always changing because they are the product of constantly shifting and usually unpredictable socio-political and economic dynamics. Cities, however, are not always undergoing a fundamental transition from one urban regime to another. In the history of societies, it is possible to identify moments when the function of the city in the social system as a whole undergoes a fundamental transition on every level.[1] At issue during these periods is the reorganization and re-articulation of the three most basic components of industrial society: industrial time, urban space, and political citizenship.[2]

During the 1980s, the South African city was thrown into an urban transition that had its roots in the 1976 uprisings, continued through the 1980s, and is set to reach a climax during the 1990s as the intense struggle over the terms of urban reconstruction culminates in a new set of urban pacts based on a post-apartheid articulation of time, space, and citizenship. The contributions in this book attempt to capture the complexities of these processes and point to possible directions for the future.

Time, space, and citizenship in the 1980s

Urban apartheid was premised on a very specific conception of the articulation between industrial time, urban space, and political citizenship. Under classic apartheid, industrial time was seen as the exclusive perogative of South Africa's white managerial class. All formal rights to regulate the length of the working day and its value lay in the hands of employers until 1979. This class managed the consolidation of South Africa's manufacturing base for the purposes of meeting the needs of a predominantly white domestic market[3] of well housed and completely serviced largely urbanized consumers.

The organization of industrial time was supported rather than subverted by the racially based spatial structure of the city that the apartheid state enforced via a gamut of urban regulations, such as influx control and the Group Areas Act.[4] The system of differentiated labour power reproduction that these laws entrenched produced the classic apartheid labour market and reduced to a minimum the costs of labour power reproduction.[5] This was based on the division between 'migrants' with their rural bases linked to urban hostels, and the 'urban insiders' with their rented 'matchbox' houses and formal 'temporary' status. The urban system this gave rise to underpinned, and was a necessary precondition for, the formal disenfranchisement of the black majority from the nation-state. This effectively meant the 'nation-state' that depended on urban apartheid was reserved exclusively for the beneficiaries of the urban system. In other words, whites were the only citizens that qualified for full political, industrial, and urban citizenship.

But as South Africa's rich social history tradition has forcefully demonstrated, what policy-makers and administrators planned to achieve rarely occurred in reality. It was not simply that the planners who carved up the society into racial categories had a mistaken assumption about the nature of the society. It was more to do with the fact that the people whose communities they were carving up had their own capacities to think, associate, and organize. The result, therefore, was the constant struggle between a wide range of contradictory and cross-cutting interests over the control of industrial time, the structure and regulation of urban space, and the definition of political citizenship. Put another way, the apartheid concept of citizenship generated a popular societal reaction that held up an alternative concept of democracy that defined South Africa's citizens as the equal bearers of rights in the workplace, the city, and polity. From a global comparative perspective, this is a far more radical conception of citizenship than traditional liberalism envisages.

The most enduring image from the 1980s of the way urban apartheid was contested will surely come from East London. During the course of the 1983–5 bus boycott, the trains that transported the black labour force from their 'homeland' town of Mdantsane wound their way every morning through the sleepy white suburbs. Inside the trains the long 25 kilometre journey was relieved by political meetings as these moving protected spaces became the means of communication for the organizers of social movements that were committed to dismantling the apartheid state system, starting with the Ciskei. In other words, the racially based separation between home and work that underpinned a 'homeland' state formation is what politicized a workforce that, in turn, joined trade unions that challenged the structure of production in East London, not least because the working day was artificially lengthened by the time needed to travel to work for wages that never took this into account. The means of transport became the means of organizational cohesion and the Ciskei state used coercion to break a boycott of a bus company that it partly owned. If one dwells for a moment on the causes of this bewildering mix of complex conflictual interests, then some of the flavour and texture of urban politics can be appreciated.

The first pillar of classic apartheid began to crumble the moment Durban's workers downed tools in 1973 and hit the streets with their red flags and faceless leaders. Out of this was born a trade union movement that had, by 1979, won the right to free association. By 1982 the unions had won a firm base on the factory floor and in so doing brought an end to the era of industrial time management controlled exclusively by white managers. The black working class had won industrial citizenship and hence the right to a say in the length and value of the working day.[6] Black workers, however, were also part of urban communities and so the struggle over time in the workplace came to be closely tied to the struggle over the nature and control of urban space.

It is now the accepted wisdom of the 'New South Africa' consensus that the granting of industrial citizenship to urban workers in 1979 (including migrant workers after an initial attempt to leave them out) was the first fundamental break from apartheid. One consequence was to bring South Africa's managers into direct contact with organized interests who wanted more than simply the right to bargain for better wages and working conditions. This, in turn, contributed to the increasingly coherent organization of business during the course of the 1980s around major policy initiatives.[7] At the heart of this effort was the Urban Foundation which, not surprisingly, identified the city and the need to deracialize its spatial structure and controls as the key to securing a politically stable, democratic, and market-based economic future.[8] Its lobbying efforts complemented the impact of the social movements which resulted in the abolition of influx control in 1986 and the adoption by the state in 1990–1 of a non-racial urban policy framework designed largely by the think-tanks of big business.[9]

The state, however, did not make the link between industrial citizenship and urban citizenship in the same way that business did in the early 1980s. Instead, by accepting the Riekert Commission recommendations in 1979 at the same time as it implemented the Wiehahn Commission's recommendations on labour reform, the state launched itself into a contradiction that only resolved itself when it accepted the need to abolish influx control in mid-1986. With the scrapping of influx control, the state accepted in theory that industrial and urban citizenship should be premised on the same inclusive principle. This was complemented by the simultaneous acceptance at the National Party's 1986 Federal Congress of the need for a new constitutional dispensation based on the principles of a 'united South Africa' and 'universal suffrage'. In short, apartheid was theoretically dead by the end of 1986. In reality, the state tried to achieve the old objective of domination under the guise of a new anti-apartheid discourse. This was what the 1986–90 state of emergency was all about and at the centre of this perverse last-ditch attempt to hang on to the old order was, of course, the urban system.

The 'winning-hearts-and-minds' (WHAM) strategy was the cornerstone of the state's 'counter-revolutionary warfare' programme during the emergency period. As has been demonstrated elsewhere,[10] the WHAM strategy was premised on the assumption that the black majority was more interested in urban services than in democracy. It followed that the state needed to meet a range of urban demands for services, land, and housing if the political demands for a majoritarian state were to be deflected. In other words, urban citizenship was conceded on condition this was accepted by the black majority as a substitute for political citizenship. Significantly, this strategy was based on the assumption that the urban social movements were politically inspired and would disappear if urban demands were (partly) met and the liberation movements suppressed.

In the end this strategy failed because the trade-off between political citizenship and urban upgrading was roundly rejected by the majority. It was also rejected because the state's recession-induced fiscal crisis made the costs of buying off the majority prohibitive.

The failure of WHAM intensified the political crisis faced by the state and prepared the way for a new approach that F. W. de Klerk eventually emerged to implement after he won his power struggle with chief 'securocrat' P. W. Botha in 1989. This intensifying political crisis was reflected in South Africa's increasingly isolated international position, the declining support for state strategy among black 'moderates', the deepening political differences between the state and capital, the politically overdetermined recession and, most importantly, the continued survival of the social movements. The eventual unbanning of the liberation movements on 2 February 1990 was premised on an acknowledgement that nothing would be achieved if the social movements — and their political expression in the liberation movements — remained excluded from the process of reconstituting political citizenship. The result was the initiation of a 'non-revolutionary regime transition'.[11] Although it is broadly accepted that regime transition in South Africa is going to take 10 years, what is not adequately understood at a popular level is that this political transition is going to depend heavily on the nature of the urban transition. In other words, like previous phases in the struggle for political power, the political transition that began on 2 February 1990 is already playing itself out in new struggles, conflicts, and pact formations at local level that are centred on the nature and function of the city in society.

Transition and the city

In many 'non-revolutionary regime transitions' that have taken place elsewhere over the last 20 years in Latin America, southern Europe, eastern Europe, and more recently in Africa (albeit only beginning), transition has tended to revolve around political citizenship. There were, of course, cases where the pacts that drove the transition related to the nature of industrial time and urban space (e.g. Spain).[12] What is significant about the South African transition is that it is not simply about the (well known) deracialization and reconstitution of the polity.[13] It is also about the changing nature of industrial time and urban space.

As far as time is concerned, on 20 September 1990 the cabinet accepted a proposal that an amended Labour Relations Act as set out in the bill jointly formulated by COSATU, NACTU, and SACCOLA (South African Consultative Committee on Labour Affairs) should be submitted to parliament. This probably marks the first 'state-capital-people' pact in the post 2 February 1990 era that is both a product of previous struggles and a bid to put into place a set of post-apartheid rules for the game. This does not in and of itself challenge the economic power of the corporations; but it does provide the legal framework within which trade unions can organize to mount a challenge to these interests. It is widely accepted by both capital and labour, however, that the way the workplace struggle is waged will be directly affected by the pace, intensity, and nature of the struggles over urban space. In other words, it is recognized that where people live, how far they travel, the services they receive, the houses they live in, the health care they receive, and how their children get educated are all issues that the entire society must face and deal with as part of the overall process of transition.

All the major players moved forcefully and decisively during 1990–1 to kick-start the urban reconstruction process. As far as the social movements were concerned, they escalated the rent boycotts, especially in the Transvaal, OFS, and northern Cape. These boycotts were the final death blow to the black local government system, and as these structures crumbled, the local urban actors came together to negotiate the full range of alternatives. The basic demand of the social movements that came to be accepted by everyone was for a 'non-racial and democratic municipality based on a single tax base'. There is little doubt that the local-level negotiations are helping drive the transition from 'below' — another unique feature about South Africa's transition and a statement once again about the centrality of the city in the South African social formation as a whole.

The state also moved on a range of fronts, with the establishment of the Independent Development Trust with a R2 billion grant to finance the reconstruction being the most significant initiative. This was complemented by moves to replace the existing local authorities with a new non-racial local government system, the scrapping of Group Areas and separate amenities, the abolition of the land acts, provisions for 'less formal' township establishment, the initiation of mass housing schemes, etc.

Organized business also surged forward at the policy level when the Urban Foundation released its series of urban policy documents after completing a five-year policy research exercise.[14] This was complemented by efforts such as those initiated by the Perm's Bob Tucker to build a transition 'scenario' based on:
- a political 'compact' to establish a new constitution;
- an urban 'compact' based on the annual erection of 200 000 houses, 400 000 serviced sites, and a million electrified sites; and

- an economic 'compact' premised on a manufacturing-based export-led growth path.[15]

The most useful way of conceptualizing the urban transition is by using a systems approach to break up the city into a series of sub-systems.[16] These sub-systems have their own histories and dynamics and lock the matrix of urban interests together in complex ways that often result in cross-cutting alliances and conflicts. They are the following:

The spatial system The apartheid spatial system, as it manifested itself within the urban system as a whole, was premised on policies aimed at decentralizing and deconcentrating employment at the macro level and dividing the city itself into racial residential areas at the micro level. Until 1986, entry into the city itself was regulated by influx control, i.e. the dividing line between 'town and countryside' was secured by repressive racially based legislation. This division was complemented, however, by economic constraints that blocked access for the poor to spaces that were too costly for the in-migrating populations.[17] Underpinning this racial and class-based exclusion was the regional integration of labour markets that undercut constitutional and racial boundaries.[18] The result has been a massive waste of resources and the net spatially based redistribution of wealth from the poor to the rich as a result of divided tax bases, constraints on small business development, limits on agglomeration in the inner cities, the subsidization of transport to counteract the costs of subsidized deconcentration/decentralization, and costly misuse and non-use of land. Out of this has emerged the need for what the Urban Foundation has called the 'compact city', i.e. a city that maximizes the use of its resources and ensures access to its services for the poor. Although legislative deracialization is a necessary condition for building the compact city, the built environment is spatially fixed. How the compact city will be built in a way that simultaneously utilizes the deconcentrated urban infrastructure that already exists will emerge as the main challenge.

The urban services system Over the decades, an enormous investment has been made in the urban infrastructure. The basic infrastructure is there with respect to roads, mass transit, electrification, water supply, sanitation, and waste disposal. However, for reasons related both to the class structure of the society that results in low levels of remuneration for employment, and the racial structure of the apartheid city that forbid until 10 years ago certain residential areas from being serviced, these bulk services are, on the whole, denied to the urban poor because the cost of the service and what is 'affordable' cannot be reconciled by the level of subsidization. It follows from this that at the policy level a commitment to services for all is required that is premised on a distribution-focused (as opposed to bulk supply side) subsidization formula that is capable of bridging the gap between affordability and cost. The once-off capital subsidy for upgrading and site-and-service schemes that the Independent Development Trust will be financing is a step in this direction. This does not, however, subsidize operating costs which are the costs that could lead to large-scale exclusion of the poor if they have to be carried exclusively by the poor. Intra-urban cross-subsidization and central-local subsidization formulae are going to be needed if a 'basic services for all' policy has any chance of working.

The housing system In crude terms, the subsidized market has met the housing needs of the white population and a subsidized state delivery system has met some of the most basic shelter needs of the black population. After 1968, however, very little housing was provided for urban Africans. Instead, what houses were built were constructed during the 1980s by the private sector for the upper levels of the housing market. The subsidization that did occur was for infrastructure and for owners that qualified for state housing subsidies of one form or another. The result is that by 1990 the construction industry was declining, the upper levels of the housing market were saturated, the state was not providing mass housing, and the market could not respond to the housing needs of the urban poor. The result has been the massive proliferation of shack settlements. The state and business are united in saying that the solution lies in subsidizing infrastructure and leaving housing construction to the family 'self-help' systems and the private developers. To finance this, complex new mechanisms have been created that place the financial institutions and structures like the South African Housing Trust and Independent Development Trust at the centre of the new housing delivery system. The basic problem with this approach from the perspective of the social movements is that this could simply lead to the servicing of shack settlements rather than a genuine mass housing programme. This will be the result if the underlying structural causes of low-income households are not dealt with. This is why the 'housing as a growth path' policy framework has become increasingly appealing because it could use the process of meeting housing needs to stimulate economic growth in a way that decreases unemployment and, hopefully, raises household incomes. This, in turn, will place resources in the hands of those who need to pay for what they need. For all this to happen, the construction industry and cartelized building materials industry may well need to be restructured.

The land system The identification of appropriate land for development, its acquisition, and ownership have emerged as key factors in resolving the urban crisis. To date, the Land Acts and Group Areas Act have regulated the use of land in favour of whites at the macro and micro level. For the state, business, and social movements, legislative deracialization is a necessary precondition for reordering the land system. Major disagreements have emerged, however, with respect to what some of the sufficient conditions for land redistribution may be. These are with respect to:

- compensation for past racially based expropriations effected through forced removals; and
- the role of the market in reallocating land.

The fact of the matter is that the best urban land has been used for white settlement and what is left are either developed areas that are too costly for the poor to penetrate, or undeveloped land that is itself either too expensive if it is strategically located, or, if it is located far from centres of employment, is also effectively too expensive if transport costs are calculated into the equation. This suggests that either land must be removed from the market and/or transport costs must be subsidized. What is certain is that if the market becomes the primary allocator, the compact city will remain an illusion as the poor get steadily squeezed out into the new urban dumping grounds on the metropolitan peripheries.

The local government system Local government structures have always been designed to reproduce the urban system in accordance with the policy objectives of the state. The result has been the bewildering proliferation and duplication of local authority structures along both horizontal and vertical axes to enforce, primarily, a racially based governmental system at local level. To create a new system, every aspect of the old system will have to be reorganized. The redefinition of boundaries, the reallocation of powers and functions between different levels of government, the reconstitution of the legislative and executive structures in accordance with nationally negotiated constitutional principles, the introduction of a new redistributive local fiscal system, and the integration and rationalization of the administrations are just some of the more fundamental tasks that will have to be tackled. Given the centrality of the city during transition and its role during reconstruction, how the cities are governed and managed will critically affect their performance and their ability to meet the needs of the urban poor. This is why decentralization to empower local government so that it can be interventionist rather than simply reactive will become increasingly necessary.

Urban reconstruction will involve the resolution of problems within each of these sub-systems. How successful this will be will depend to a large extent on how economic and urban policy approaches are integrated. Clearly the task of a future economic policy must be to resolve the structural economic crisis that is currently resulting in massive unemployment, recession, inflation, manufacturing stagnation, alarming levels of financial speculation, and poor productivity levels. In other words, how macro-economic policy approaches intend reorganizing production and hence the nature of industrial time, will directly affect the nature of consumption and hence the resources available for urban reconstruction. There is a growing consensus between certain business think-tanks and the approach of economic planners in the liberation movement around the need for a 'growth through redistribution' strategy. It is proposed that resources should be focused on a housing and services programme in order to stimulate the expansion of the domestic market which, it is hoped, should stimulate economic growth. For people like Tucker of the Perm, this could even provide the basis for an export led growth model once the basic conditions of urban existence have been put in place. Whether or not this neo-inward industrialization programme is linked at a later stage to an export-led growth model, the fact remains that tax incomes will become increasingly important in the financing of an economic strategy that will have as its key focus the reorganization and reconstruction of the South African city. Without a full democracy, this economic model would be unworkable. And so the time-space-citizenship circle completes itself.

The politics of city futures

Cities are not simply the product of technocratically conceived plans. Nor are they the anarchic outcome of 'the struggle'. All the major interests want to ensure that industrial time, urban space, and citizenship are articulated in ways that suit their particular interests. To achieve this they organize, plan, and above all, seek out others to form alliances to achieve common objectives. This, in essence, is the stuff of city politics.

All major urban stakeholders have already begun to reposition themselves to secure advantageous positions in the emerging development alliances. In every local-level negotiation process under way in some 50 localities in the Transvaal, this repositioning and pact formation is evident. At the centre of it all are players who in one way or another are primarily part of one of three basic social forces: business, the state, and the social movements. The development professionals (engineers, architects, planners, economists, etc.) tie themselves to one or more of these three categories and ply their trade by constructing the concepts through which the urban environment is comprehended and replanned in accordance with the interests they represent.

At this stage it is impossible to predict where city politics are going. Ideally, the 'just city' should be premised on a concept of citizenship that is not limited simply to the political realm. If this occurred, it would have meant that a political transition had taken place without a simultaneous urban transition. To arrive at the 'just city', in addition to political citizenship, citizenship in the workplace and city will need to be the policy objective. This will involve the institutionalization of the means whereby the length and· value of industrial time, the quality and cost of urban living space, and the entitlements of full citizenship can be negotiated. In practice this should facilitate the reconciliation of productivity and wages in the workplace, affordable access to the city and the cost of services, and maximum citizen participation in decision-making and effective urban management. The interconnections are obvious: if the value of the working day is less than what the average homeless family would need to invest in formal shelter, then the housing programme will fail; if productivity does not match this value, then public revenues will become increasingly dependent on deficit financing and international loans; if subsidization levels are inadequate and urban services become too costly, access to the city will be denied to those who need it most; and if political citizenship is granted without a substantial improvement in the material conditions of the urban poor, the result will be a highly unstable post-apartheid political democracy.

Another (more pessimistic) direction is what could be called the 'deracialized apartheid' option. To date, the so-called 'First World' standards in the white cities have been made possible by the 'colonization' of the townships that, in turn, facilitated the transfer of wealth from the latter to the former. Because employers linked wages exclusively to productivity and not to social conditions of existence, the consequences of urban underdevelopment were ignored until it was too late. Legislative deracialization will not in and of itself solve the problem. Instead, race divisions could well become class divisions as economics rather than racial controls come to regulate the spatial mobility of the urban poor. In this scenario, access to the city for the urban poor will not substantially improve. Inequalities will deepen which, in turn, will undermine the economic performance of the local urban economies. If local government structures operate like they do now and have the same limited powers (albeit all within a non-racial mould), then they will be powerless to deal with the problems. This could lead to unstable local government and, in all likelihood, a return to violent confrontation. In this context, the entitlements of citizenship may well come to be perceived as meaningless.

Whether we are heading towards 'deracialized apartheid', the 'just city', or some mixture of the two cannot be determined from conditions at the moment. What is needed, however, is a clear and crisp vision of the 'just city' that is capable of cementing development alliances that are centred on the organizations of the urban poor. Some of these have already emerged from business think-tanks and have been favourably received by a range of major urban stakeholders. There are, however, alternatives in formation: the civic associations involved in leading the social movements are, for example, forming a national 'civic charter' to guide grassroots development approaches, and the trade union movement has mounted its own policy project to investigate the relationship between housing and economic growth. So, in sum, as the struggle for the cities drives the urban transition, the first vague outlines of where some powerful stakeholders would like our cities to go are beginning to emerge. Hopefully this book will assist these stakeholders and the public at large to understand the problems in all their complexity so that adequate solutions can be debated and implemented before it is too late for the South African city to negotiate the transition successfully.

Notes

1 The word 'city' will be used as a generic term to refer to all urban concentrations, including what should more accurately be called 'towns' that either form part of metropolitan agglomerations, or stand alone at the centre of rural economies.

2 This analysis borrows certain ideas from the seminal analysis of the African city developed by Fred Cooper in his introduction to Cooper F. *Struggle for the City:*

Migrant Labour, Capital and the State in Urban Africa (Beverley Hills: Sage 1983).

3 For an analysis of these processes see Webster E. *Cast in a Racial Mould: Labour Process and Trade Unionism in the Foundries* (Johannesburg: Ravan Press 1986).

4 The notion that racial domination was functional to capitalist economic rationality has been questioned by, among others, Lipton M. *Capitalism and Apartheid* (Aldershot: Gower 1985). However, as the rest of the chapter will reveal, the author is in agreement with those who have argued that although apartheid and capitalism have, on the whole, been functional, there is no inherent structural necessity for why this should be the case. This conjunctural conception of apartheid's functionality *vis-à-vis* capitalism is reflected in Wolpe H. *Class, Race and the Apartheid State* (London: James Curry 1988).

5 See Hindson D. *Pass Controls and the Urban African Proletariat* (Johannesburg: Ravan 1987).

6 For the best account of this period of the union movement up to the mid-1980s see Friedman S. *Building Tomorrow Today: African Workers in Trade Unions, 1970–84* (Johannesburg: Ravan Press 1987).

7 See Lee R. and Buntman F. 'The Business Sector's Involvement in Policy Change, 1986–89' in Centre for Policy Studies *South Africa at the End of the Eighties: Policy Perspectives* (Johannesburg: University of the Witwatersrand, Centre for Policy Studies 1989).

8 Urban Foundation *Policies for a New Urban Future* (Johannesburg: Urban Foundation 1990/1).

9 See Swilling M. 'Deracialized Urbanization: a Critique of the New Urban Strategies and Some Policy Alternatives from a Democratic Perspective' *Social Dynamics* 1 ii (1990).

10 See Boraine A. 'Wham, Sham or Scam? – Security Management, Upgrading and Resistance in a South African Township', paper presented to the Centre for African Studies Africa Seminar, University of Cape Town, 2 August 1988.

11 This is the process studied by O'Donnell G. et al. *Transitions from Authoritarian Rule* (Baltimore and London: Johns Hopkins University Press 1988) vols. 1–4.

12 On Spain see O'Donnell G. et al. *Transitions from Authoritarian Rule: Southern Europe* (Baltimore and London, Johns Hopkins University Press 1988); Castells M. *The City and Grassroots* (Berkeley and Los Angeles: University of California Press 1983) part 5.

13 See Swilling M. 'Political Transition, Development and Civil Society' *Africa Insight* (1991).

14 See Urban Foundation, op. cit.

15 See Swilling M. and Bond P. 'Scenario of an Unlikely Deal' *Work in Progress* (1991) 73.

16 In line with what happens in most systems approaches, these are heuristic devices for understanding the 'flow' of social phenomena rather than fully-fledged conceptual tools.

17 For this argument see Mabin A. 'Struggle for the City: Urbanization and Political Strategies of the South African State' *Social Dynamics* (1989) 15 i.

18 See Cobbett W. et al. 'A Critical Analysis of South Africa's State Reform Strategies in the 1980s' in Frankel P. et al. (eds.) *State, Resistance and Change in South Africa* (London: Croom Helm 1988).

1 Historical background of the apartheid city to 1948

Rodney Davenport

It requires an effort of the imagination to grasp the point that mandatory urban segregation in southern Africa is a development of the last hundred years. In a number of instances, local authorities previously made provision for the separate residence of Africans; but with the exception of the Orange Free State (OFS) Volksraad, which took such a step in 1893, no South African legislature carried a general law controlling the ownership and occupation of property in urban areas before the end of the Anglo-Boer War.[1]

From 1902 onwards there was a change in the official approach, inspired by the Milner regime's Teutonic concern for orderliness in the face of increasing African urbanization in an era marked by industrial growth and dominated by a fear of health hazards.[2] The Lagden Commission recommended the segregation of Africans, but where the towns were concerned, this objective was only roughly sketched out.[3] The commission wanted separate residential locations occupied by Africans whose employment entitled them to be in town, where they could either build homes of an acceptable standard, or live in council houses in supervised locations purged of vagrants, alcoholics, and prostitutes. Specific legislation accompanied this ideological vision: the Native Reserve Locations Act in the Cape (1902), the Native Locations Act in Natal (1904), and the Orange Free State Municipal Ordinance of 1903, which took the 1893 legislation further by tightening restrictions on Africans who could not prove gainful employment. In the Transvaal, many urbanized Africans were housed in mine compounds and were therefore outside municipal control. The town regulations of 1899 had prohibited 'coloured persons' (including Africans) from living 'in places abutting on the public streets in a town or village', as opposed to their employers' backyards; but a municipal ordinance of 1903 authorized town councils to lay out locations, regulate 'the housing of natives by their employers', and license casual labour. Authority over all locations was placed in town councils in 1905.[4]

Milner's governments thus tightened urban segregation by giving the native location regular status on the South African landscape, justifying it in terms of a currently acceptable ideology, and limiting residential rights to healthy temptation-resisting employees. By 1919 the Union's Department of Native Affairs could take it for granted that 'the ideal to be arrived at is the territorial separation of the races'.[5]

The making of the Natives (Urban Areas) Act, 1923

The main object of public policy during the Botha–Smuts era (1910–24) was to bring under control the growing instability of town and country at a time when the legitimacy of the South African political system was being challenged from many quarters.[6] The government was concerned about a major immigration of Africans and whites to town, in view of the unrest among Afrikaners, English-speaking immigrant workers, and Africans in town and country, which led to industrial confrontations in 1913–14, 1920 and 1922, the rebellion of 1914, and the sensational violence at Bulhoek and among the Bondels of South West Africa in 1921–2. The Assaults on Women and the Tuberculosis Commissions of 1913 and 1914 gave further food for thought, especially the latter, with its graphic generalizations about the appalling health and housing conditions in South African urban locations.[7]

The Department of Native Affairs drafted its first Urban Areas Bill in 1912, but decided not to go ahead with it because the Natives Land Bill and the Native Affairs Bill, which were not presented until 1913 and 1917 respectively, had a logical priority, and because the public was not yet sufficiently 'educated' on key policy aspects.[8] Despite the initial rejection of the Native Affairs Bill, which was only passed in amended form in 1920, the government published a new urban bill in December 1918, incorporating the principle of compulsory segregation without removing exemptions allowed in existing provincial laws. It also introduced several new ideas, such as the creation of separate native revenue accounts (to counter exploitation by white local authorities, which had been criticized by the Tuberculosis Commission), and structures through which Africans could advise local authorities on any matters which might affect them. The bill explicitly recognized such African leasehold rights in urban locations as existed in the Cape, Natal, and Transvaal and the rights of African shopkeepers. It also, however, envisaged restrictions on the right of unemployed Africans to remain in town.

By the time the government was ready to test its proposals in public through the statutory Native Affairs Commission (NAC), set up under General Smuts's Native Affairs Act of 1920, it had already had to deal with African strikes on the Rand and in Cape Town, as well as racial disturbances in Port Elizabeth. All these actions were manifestations of a new restlessness brought about by the decline in African living standards during the war years,[9] and the serious influenza epidemic of 1918, which hit South African migrant workers particularly hard.[10] The commissioners toured widely, discussing the bill with municipal bodies, representatives of African communities, and welfare societies. They also held a meeting with Colonel Stallard's Transvaal Local Government Commission in Johannesburg. Each body recorded a consensus which needs to be noticed[11] in the light of the legislation which eventually emerged, for there are signs that the Urban Areas Act, as passed, was a product of divided counsels rather than of a clear agreement between these official bodies.[12]

Location administrators wanted control over people and that, in short, meant passes; but passes had already begun to cause great resentment among Africans for the indignity and unequal hardships which they caused.[13] Opposition to the carrying of passes had led to open confrontations with the police by African women in the OFS in 1913, which a select committee under General Botha had investigated,[14] and by male workers on the Rand in 1919, soon after F. S. Malan, the acting Prime Minister, had told a delegation of the South African Native National Congress that he would try to ameliorate the pass laws but could not abolish them.[15] After the 1919 disturbances, the investigating magistrate, G. J. Boyes, recommended the urgent appointment of a commission on account of the intense hostility of Africans to passes, and the government responded by asking a committee, chaired by acting Under-secretary for Native Affairs, Colonel G. A. Godley, to examine the whole question of controls.

The Godley Committee[16] travelled to all the main centres, as well as to the Transkei and Ciskei. It took evidence from all the main African political movements; African women's organizations; clergy and teachers; clerks and workers; as well as from white officials of the Department of Native Affairs; police and army officers; mining, commercial, and agricultural interests; churches and inter-racial organizations. Its interrogations were well directed towards the clarification of opinions, black and white, with the aim of reaching a compromise acceptable to all parties.

The committee recommended radical reform in the light of the doubtful efficacy of existing pass systems, and the extremely critical tone of most African evidence, even though some African witnesses accepted the need for registration. It favoured the repeal of all existing pass laws, and the substitution of a 'registration certificate' to be carried by African males of 18 upwards, with full particulars of personal identity and domicile, and the signature of the holder (or his left thumb print, as distinct from both hand prints normally taken for criminal record purposes). The right to demand production of these certificates was to be restricted to white police officers of sergeant's rank or above, justices of the peace, and special appointees of the minister, but only on suspicion of lawbreaking. Service contracts were to be recorded in registration books and a special court, including 'two native assessors as advisers', was to deal with urban misfits, who could be rusticated, or in serious cases sent to a labour colony. The committee proposed to limit curfew hours to between 11 p.m. and 4 a.m. They insisted on the exemption of African women from pass bearing; and they recommended, for exemption, all males with standard five education, those on the voters' roll, certificated artisans, reputable employees with 10 years' service, and chiefs recognized by the government.

In the light of these recommendations, the Department of Native Affairs drew up a Native Registration and Protection Bill to be introduced simultaneously with the Natives (Urban Areas) Bill in 1923. It proposed to give the African a chance 'to improve his surroundings by providing for the establishment of Native villages where fixity of tenure can be secured', with the right to build his own house subject to local regulations. This was in the spirit of the Godley Report, rather than of the Stallard Commission's emphasis on urban

Africans as merely temporary sojourners. It was at one with Stallard in insisting that such villages had to be segregated; but segregation was not the wish of the Native Conference which met (in terms of Smuts's Native Affairs Act of 1920) in Bloemfontein in May 1922. That body made it clear that Africans 'do not admit it as a principle', even if people often found it 'convenient to live apart' and 'tended to gravitate to a particular quarter for residence' in towns.[17]

Smuts's speech introducing the second reading of the Urban Areas Bill on 7 February 1923 echoed the desire of Godley and the department to ameliorate urban controls, and endorsed the departmental plan for individual tenure in segregated 'native villages', with temporary residential rights for others in locations. He also announced that the Registration and Urban Areas Bills would be sent to a select committee after the second reading.

But Smuts soon lost the initiative. General Hertzog immediately protested that to allow Africans to own property in the white area was an infringement of the Natives Land Act. A phalanx of Nationalist speakers backed him, and very few others spoke up for African urban titles. Smuts concluded the debate by lamely commenting that he was 'not wedded to any particular method of giving effect to the idea', and the legislation went to the select committee without any firm government directive.

The select committee threw out not only individual tenure, but also the Godley proposals for pass amelioration in the Registration Bill, and then reincorporated the control provisions in the urban areas measure, including the compulsory registration of service contracts, rules governing casuals and unemployed, and punishments for document dodgers. No explanation was given in the report for the abandonment of the Godley proposals, but the debate on the new clause 12 of the Urban Areas Bill, dealing with the pass laws, revealed much disagreement among speakers who had sat on the select committee.[18] Whatever the explanation, the chief reason given for not proceeding with the Registration Bill — that African opinion had not been consulted — made nonsense in view of the exhaustive attention paid to African evidence by the Godley Committee; and even if valid, it was an argument which applied equally to other sections of the bill which were incorporated in the Urban Areas Act. This was a major rebuff to responsible African opinion over urban areas legislation, and it was by no means the last. The Native Conference, meeting in Pretoria in September after the act had passed into law, carried by 15 votes to

10 a motion which almost exactly reproduced the Godley Committee's proposal for a uniform registration certificate, with safeguards against victimization.[19]

The question of African title to urban property did raise problems. Smuts, in abandoning his earlier position, was influenced by the Cape Municipal Association and by the argument of the Vos Report of 1922 on the application of the Glen Grey system, both of which argued that rural Africans had shown themselves unable to handle the intricacies of title.[20] Those witnesses who testified against individual tenure in urban areas before the select committee were moved by other arguments: that title would make the African town dweller too independent of the municipality; or that the result would be a wholesale buying up of property by Africans 'throughout the country' which would necessitate their municipal enfranchisement everywhere; or that the Estates Act made no provision for the estates of Africans or for polygamous marriages.[21]

The case for African title had, in fact, been made by Selby Msimang, who insisted that Africans should enjoy the same rights as whites in their own areas; by Dr A. W. Roberts of the NAC (though he would later weaken in the senate); and by his colleague C. T. Loram, who may have thought that some aspects of Glen Grey title, like forfeiture for rebellion, should be applied to urban Africans, but at least made up for this by insisting on safeguards against fraudulent alienation. He also opposed the idea that loss of employment should involve the loss of residential rights. 'If the native is not given freehold,' Loram said, 'he will not take that interest in his property that he would if he knew that on his death the Town Council could not expropriate it. No freehold would destroy the idea of a village.'[22] But on 16 April, the select committee resolved, by six votes to one, with three abstentions, to omit the word 'ownership' from the first clause. W. H. Stuart moved for rescission in Committee of the Whole, with a little support from South African Party and Labour Party members, but he was defeated by 69 votes to 18 in a debate marked by the absence of rigid party divisions.[23]

Between the passage of the bill through the assembly on 16 May and its second reading in the senate on the 30 May, the African National Congress (ANC) met in Bloemfontein. Its anger at the rejection of property rights and the omission of protective clauses against pass indignities was great. The ANC sent a 10-man deputation under its president, J. T. Gumede, to Cape Town. They met

Smuts, in company with Sir Walter Stanford and Godley, on 1 June. R. V. Selope Thema read the congress resolution and protested that his people had a 'right and a claim' to their ancestral land where they had since dug for minerals, built cities, and constructed railway lines. Complimenting the delegates on their moderation, Smuts found the Bloemfontein resolution too inflammatory, and played down the need for freehold rights, arguing now that they were unnecessary, and even that African evidence to the Godley Committee had constituted adequate consultation. The bill, he said, had to be enacted that session. Gumede then counter-attacked, demanding that Smuts advise the governor-general to withhold his assent. Smuts refused with some asperity, and the deputation withdrew.[24]

On the previous day, Smuts had denounced 'vague formulae which do not work' during the Native Affairs vote debate. 'The large principles we must leave to the future,' he said, 'however much a policy of going step by step may be criticized.' But Stallard's segregationist doctrine was hardly a 'vague formula'. Linked to a denial of residential rights, it was a 'large principle', and it had been adopted before its implications had been thought through, at the expense of the pragmatic approach which Smuts had first recommended.

The Natives (Urban Areas) Act of 1923 was not, by the standard of its later amendments, a harsh measure.[25] It empowered local authorities to set aside land for African occupation in defined locations, or to house them, or require their employers to do so. It stopped whites from acquiring or occupying premises in locations, and prevented unexempted Africans from living outside them; although their right to buy property outside locations, which still existed in the Cape, was not taken away until 1937, and the ban on African residence in white areas only took effect with the Group Areas Act of 1950. African residence in peri-urban areas was also restricted. Municipalities were required, under governmental scrutiny, to keep separate native revenue accounts, into which all moneys from rents, fines, and beer hall profits had to be paid, and then spent only on the location. The act also provided for an advisory board in each location, to contain at least three elected or appointed African members, with a chairperson who was to be white; but these bodies never acquired administrative, legislative, or financial power, and were phased out from 1968.[26]

New emphases, 1923–37:
the enforcement of influx control

Although attempts were made in the 1930s to establish more effective representation by dividing some locations into blocks, each returning elected members, no attempt was made to increase the power of advisory boards by integrating them politically into the wider municipalities, so that they remained unpopular and elections continued to be marked by low polls. The act also entrusted urban local authorities with the registration of service contracts. Africans arriving in the area, or being discharged from service, had to report accordingly, while the local authority could deport the 'idle, dissolute or disorderly'. No serious attempt, however, was made to control the influx of Africans into town before 1937. Strict conditions were laid down in the 1923 act for the brewing and sale of 'kaffir beer', which came increasingly to be regarded as a means of raising location revenue. The local authority could also control location trading, and trade on its own account; but the minister was given power to intervene if he was not satisfied that the needs of the residents were being met.

Municipalities could adopt the legislation at will. Some acted without delay — Bloemfontein in November 1924 and Johannesburg in December — but Port Elizabeth delayed until 1935. Registered urban locations numbered 234 in 1937, but the need to finance housing schemes deterred the introduction of compulsory segregation until very low interest loans were made available in the 1930s. The introduction of service contract registration was also sluggish, only 76 municipalities having taken on this responsibility by 1937, while many local authorities neglected to set up advisory boards. There was rather more response to a recommendation by the Stallard Commission for the setting up of Native Affairs committees on white town councils, to whom the location superintendent or (in richer towns) the manager of Native Affairs would report. Managers were often former police officers. Few possessed ideal qualifications, which for J. R. Cooper of Bloemfontein meant 'a knowledge of Native Law, customs and psychology and of civil law', in addition to all the human virtues. But the best of them improvised their way through the difficulties of a complex law, sometimes effecting improvements, even making the advisory board system work fairly satisfactorily, and frequently plying the

Secretary for Native Affairs with suggestions for improving the law. This added greatly to the law's complexity, as shown by the weight of the official manual for the guidance of managers, which increased from 200 grams in 1923, to 470 in 1945, to 1 360 in 1959.

Various administrative weaknesses in the law were responsible for the changes made in 1930. One was the difficulty of persuading Africans living in white suburbs to move into locations prepared for their use. Another was the difficulty of controlling the influx of women, which led to the introduction of a permit system at both ends of the journey by two stages, in 1930 and 1937. The difficulty of persuading some local authorities to allow Africans to trade in their own locations led the minister to assume greater powers (which he was often reluctant to use) in 1930. Again, the need experienced by some managers to make it harder for individuals or groups to hold political gatherings was met in 1930 by a related tightening of controls.

But one policy which did not commend itself to thoughtful administrators was influx control, despite the general support among whites for the Stallard doctrine. Some, including Hertzog, who said as much during the 1930 debate, doubted whether the African influx could indeed be stopped at all.[27]

Hertzog's final attempt to 'solve' the racial problem in the mid-1930s was put together behind the doors of the joint select committee on the 'native bills' at a time when South Africa was recovering from the Depression of 1929–32. The Representation of Natives and the Native Trust and Land Bills of 1936, did not, as is often supposed, comprise the total 'new deal'. In the following year, an inconspicuously titled Native Laws Amendment Bill, 32 of whose 42 clauses dealt with Africans in urban areas, passed into law. This measure had no place in Hertzog's original vision of a segregated South Africa. Its origins go back to the deliberations of the joint select committee on 4 March 1932, when Stallard moved the insertion of a new clause in the Native Land Bill to require each urban local authority to make an annual estimate of 'the number of natives required to minister to the wants of the non-native population' and 'the number of natives in excess of that number resident in such areas', together with a detailed estimate of labour needs, so that the minister could require the local authority to remove those in excess of the number required. The proposal was defeated, but a sub-committee was appointed to 'give effect to the purpose of [Stallard's] Draft Bill'. It failed to reach agreement; but on 11 October, after the joint committee had been converted into a commission, some of its members resumed discussions in Pretoria and drew up a bill which incorporated Stallard's proposals.[28] The joint select committee, however, decided instead to prepare an amended version for submission to parliament the following session,[29] and to that end a fact-finding committee was appointed, consisting of J. M. Young and A. L. Barrett, two senior officials of the Department of Native Affairs, the former with mainly rural experience, the latter with urban.

Young and Barrett toured South Africa and produced a report which trounced Stallardism in no uncertain terms.[30] They rejected the doctrine that the towns were the special creation of the whites, dismissed the notion that unemployment was a sufficient reason for the rustication of Africans, and disagreed with the argument (which the Native Farm Labour Committee of 1939 would also throw out) that there were surplus Africans in the urban areas. They took exception to 'the proposition that every municipal location ought to be regarded as a reservoir for native labour from which the worn-out labourer must be required to depart when he no longer ministers to the needs of the white man', and claimed to have found widespread opposition to such an idea.[31]

G. Heaton Nicholls, a committed segregationist on the NAC, explained in parliament that this committee had been set up by Richard Stuttaford, acting Minister of Native Affairs, who 'knew nothing about the arguments and discussions which had taken place'.[32] But Young and Barrett were very senior officials in the department concerned, and for that reason the discrepancy between their report and government policy can only be seen as extraordinary. The wonder is that its thrust was so effectively parried. By 1936 both Nicholls and Young were members of the NAC, whose job it was to reconcile the bill and the report. They considered the bill in September 1936, but did not complete their report till September 1937, which was too late for it to be discussed in the parliamentary session during which the legislation was debated. Their findings were full of the eloquence of Nicholls, and sought to present the recommendations of the report as a coherent part of Hertzog's land and franchise deal, ironing out the differences in a way which could hardly have been done had one party to the deliberation not been a very artful politician, and the other a discreet civil servant.

The Native Laws Amendment Bill was presented to parliament two months before the Native Representative Council (NRC), created under the Representation of Natives Act, had been elected. This timing evoked strong criticism in parliament, which the government turned by arguing that as the NRC was itself a creature of the legislative package of which the 1937 bill was a part, it had no *locus standi*. But the Transkeian General Council had explicitly asked for it to be consulted, and the Location Advisory Boards Congress, which had become an increasingly effective forum for urban African leaders since 1929, had reacted with anger to the bill.[33] This was another conspicuous evasion of African viewpoints at a crucial moment in the development of urban policy.

The clause of the act dealing with worker redundancy was similar to Stallard's original proposal, save that the minister, instead of the local authority, now had the power to decide which individual Africans in any municipality should be rusticated, from a list supplied by the local authority once the biennial census to correlate numbers of Africans and numbers of available jobs, had been taken. There were strong reactions to the arbitrary power thus assumed, but the government was able to ride the criticism of what Tommy Boydell, once a Labour Party member of the Pact cabinet of 1924, described as this 'scruff-of-the-neck' clause. It responded to the anxiety of the larger municipalities by agreeing to pay half the costs of the census, but was not hard pressed on the larger question of principle. Furthermore, the assumption of a new initiative by the government led to an immediate increase in the number of urban areas into which African entry was restricted.[34]

Yet, the strategy was thoroughly ineffective. Not surprisingly, at a time of rapid industrial recovery, there was a labour shortage in the large towns, as revealed in the Farm Labour Report of 1939.[35] The real demand, to which the government was responding by tightening influx control, was from people with farming interests who wished to prevent a townward drift of their own labour force. But influx control was not the way to solve that particular problem.

The 1937 bill also contained a clause to empower the minister to close down any 'church, school or other institution' for Africans in the white part of an urban area, and also prohibit the starting of others.[36] On this occasion, though, the government was sensitive enough to exclude existing churches from the embargo.

Relaxation and confrontation during World War 2

Whatever justification there was for tightening up on segregation, by the start of the war the policy no longer served the needs of the economy.[37] Social and economic conditions were transformed during the 1930s as a result of the industrial boom following the devaluation of the South African pound. Poor whiteism, the leading justification for the colour bar, was on the way out, assisted by state action. Dilution of labour, the mixing of skilled and unskilled on the same shop floor, was the unofficial answer given to the shortage of skilled workers during the war years.[38] Politically, the breakdown of the colour bar was in contention during the war, being opposed by the purified Nationalists on the one hand, and energetically promoted by African representatives on the other. Officials had begun to change their tune in 1938. Douglas Smit, for example, the Secretary for Native Affairs from July 1934 to March 1945, an honest, humane administrator with the mind of a faithful civil servant, defended the policy of the Native Laws Amendment Act consistently during 1937–8; but by 1942, when he chaired the important Interdepartmental Committee on Urban Africans, he had radically changed his standpoint. Smuts, too, had moved a long way from the segregationism of his 1929 Oxford lectures when he addressed the Institute of Race Relations in January 1942, confessing that the history of influx control reminded him of Dame Partington's famous conflict, broom in hand, with the Atlantic ocean on her doorstep.

The Smuts government, although preoccupied with the war, paid a lot of attention to post-war reform. The Smit Committee pointed to a new direction in social policy for urban Africans.[39] It introduced pensions, health and housing schemes, and vocational training for Africans, and promoted their right to run businesses in urban areas. It was prepared to consider the recognition of African trade unions, and even the repeal of the pass laws, trusting in the retention of a mild curfew and the improved registration of service contracts as a means of preserving urban control. The effective implementation of its proposals in these areas is to be explained largely by the joint efforts of Smit himself, the Natives' Representatives in parliament, and other members of the cabinet. But the point at which it intervened most controversially in urban areas policy was the pass laws.

From its inception, the NRC attacked the pass laws, carrying resolutions nearly every year from 1937 to 1946.[40] Taking up the NRC
initiative, W. T. Welsh moved in the senate in 1938 for their 'substantial modification and simplification throughout the Union'.
Senator H. A. Fagan, Hertzog's Minister of Native Affairs, referred
the question to the NAC, whose report, over Young's signature,[41]
met the objections to passes based on the complexity of the system, but not those based on the argument of inequity, above all the
capacity which they had for filling the jails with short-term non-
criminal offenders. But questions to the Minister of Justice by the
Natives' Representatives, Margaret Ballinger and G. K. Hemming, in
1941 and 1942 respectively, elicited such disturbing figures with
regard to these imprisonments that the minister directed the police
in May 1942 not to demand the pass of any African unless there
were good grounds for believing that he was involved in crime.[42]
The number of arrests in the main urban centres fell dramatically
from 13 641 in the period February to April 1942, to 1 808 in the
period June to August.[43]

But by April 1943, the police were again making routine
demands for passes. A crime wave had prompted the appointment
of the Elliot Committee to look into it. It concluded that, although
the incidence of crime was bad, it was not possible at that stage to
draw any connection between the crime rate and the relaxation of
pass demands by the police. But the committee also picked up a
decline in the number of work-seeking permits asked for at the
municipal reception depots. They calculated that without rigorous
enforcement of the pass laws, the whole machinery of worker registration under the Urban Areas Act was threatened. Amelioration of
urban conditions, they argued, would be defeated by unregulated
influx; so instead, they recommended a tightening of influx control.

The Elliot Committee had unfortunately fallen foul of the ANC,
for although it co-opted African members, it inadvertently failed to
publish their minority report. This fact, linked to the resumption of
pass raids in 1943, provided a pretext for the launching of a large-
scale 'anti-pass campaign, of which Dr A. B. Xuma became the
chairperson in Johannesburg in April 1944. At the height of the
campaign, Xuma tried and failed to get an interview with Smuts,
who was about to leave for San Francisco. Further failures to make
contact with members of the government resulted in an escalation
of the conflict, until the campaign had come close to flash point by
November 1945. Early in the new year the Reef Advisory Boards

took up the cause, and in 1946 the campaign erupted in a spate of pass burnings which failed to move the government to abolish the system, but did lead to the appointment of the Fagan Commission.[44]

Confrontation over the pass laws, however, was not the only development to build up tension between the African urban communities and the government. Of great significance was the housing crisis of 1944–7. According to the Fagan Report on the Moroka riots of 1947[45] the African population of Johannesburg had increased between 1936 and 1946 by 68 per cent, from 229 000 to 384 000. During the 1930s the Johannesburg City Council, as part of its earlier policy of clearing and rehousing slum dwellers, established Orlando township, and in fact built more houses in its locations than it could persuade Africans living in its 'white' suburbs to occupy. After 1937, however, the increased population pressure filled the vacant houses to overflowing just at a time when the shortage of workers and materials precluded the possibility of further building. The housing shortage in Johannesburg rose to 16 195 in 1947. The upshot was a succession of spontaneous, generally well-led squatter movements on municipal commonage, of which the best known was that of James 'Sofasonke' Mpanza, who defied the municipal regulations and eventually forced the Johannesburg municipality, under pressure from the government, to provide the squatters with amenities and, eventually, breeze-block homes on the Moroka commonage.[46]

With influx control in ruins, the pass laws in strong contention, and the housing policy in crisis owing to the squatter problem, the Urban Areas Act by the mid-1940s seemed moribund. Yet it remained the core of government urban policy. It was amended in 1944, consolidated in 1945, and its reform or refinement occupied much of the time of the NRC, however much that body might disagree with the principles on which it was based. Nor were the NRC's criticisms necessarily ignored. The 1944 bill, for example, contained 28 clauses. Of these, one was initiated by the NRC, 15 were accepted by it, 5 were amended as a result of NRC criticisms, 3 were withdrawn for that reason, and only 5 were carried in the face of NRC criticism.[47] Of all the issues which occupied the councillors, and the leaders of the Advisory Boards Congress too, the most serious was the problem of access to power, without which effective reform had quite simply become impossible for African leaders to imagine.

In 1946 and 1947 the Smuts government tried hard to breathe new life into the legislation. After the miners' strike and the adjournment *sine die* of the NRC in August 1946, which created a crisis situation, the government attempted to democratize the advisory board system downwards so as to make it more representative without making it more powerful.[48] From a government which was, at the same time, closing the door on trade unions, such a policy was unacceptable; but the government itself would not bend, preferring 'practical social policy away from politics' in Smuts's words.[49] This was despite the plea of Ballinger, who urged that 'the Natives want rights, and not improvements', adding that 'if the pressure of the pass laws were replaced by a genuine effort to provide better economic opportunity, and if the leaders of the people were drawn into consultation ... we would get possibly ten years in which to prepare the country for the political changes that should and must come'.[50]

The appointment of the Fagan Commission was the best the government could do, and its two symbolically simultaneous reports, one on the Moroka riots and the other handling the reform of laws for Africans, were the swan song of the Smuts government. Fagan's proposals for a Union-wide network of labour bureaux, which might eventually provide a substitute for influx control, can be traced via Ballinger to the Smit Report. His proposals for the stabilization of African labour, which meant (as he stressed in the Moroka Report) encouraging those who worked in town to bring their families with them, was likewise an idea the Natives' Representatives had been pushing. Fagan did not think that migrant labour could be legislated out of existence, or stopped by administrative decree, or forced on employers; but he urged experimentation in the new OFS goldfields. He walked the same tightrope as Godley (1920), Holloway (1932), and Young (1939) over the pass laws, trying to reduce their role as control devices while promoting them as a means of ensuring contact between the urban worker and his rural base. His published report, appearing as it did on the eve of the 1948 general election, had little chance of applying the brakes to an electorate already lurching in the direction of a renewed and irrational Stallardism; but this is merely to state that the South African voting public, after failing to learn from its mistakes, was setting off on the uphill road of learning the same lesson all over again.

Notes

1 Baines G. F. 'The Origins of Urban Segregation: Local Government and the Residence of Africans in Port Elizabeth c. 1835–1865' *South African Historical Journal* (1990) 70–6.
Davenport T. R. H. 'The Beginnings of Urban Segregation in South Africa: the Natives (Urban Areas) Act of 1923 and its Background' (Institute for Social and Economic Research: Rhodes University 1971) occasional paper 15.
Maylam P. 'The Rise and Decline of Urban Apartheid in South Africa' *African Affairs 89* (1990) 57–84.
Saunders C. C. 'Segregation in Cape Town: the Creation of Ndabeni', Collected Papers (Centre for African Studies: UCT 1978) 1, 43–63.
Van Aswegen H. J. 'Die Verstedeliking van die Nie-blanke in die Oranje-Vrystaat, 1854–1902' *SAHJ* (1970) 25–8.
2 Baines (1990) 76–7.
Davenport (1971) 6–7.
Saunders (1978) 47–8.
Swanson M. W. 'The Sanitation Syndrome: Bubonic Plague and Urban Native Policy in the Cape Colony, 1900–9' *Journal of African History* (1977) 18, 387–410.
3 Report of the South African Native Affairs Commission (5 vols., 1905) i 46–8.
4 Davenport (1971) 2–6.
5 U.G. 7 — 1919 p. 17.
6 See Yudelman D. *The Emergence of Modern South Africa: State, Capital and the Incorporation of Organized Labour on the South African Goldfields, 1902–39* (Cape Town: 1984).
7 Davenport (1971) 6–8.
Davenport T. R. H. and Hunt K. S. *The Right to the Land* (Cape Town: 1974) 69.
Kallaway P. 'F. S. Malan, the Cape Liberal Tradition, and South African Politics, 1908–1924' *Journal of African History* (1973) 14, 119–23.
U.G. 39 — 1913, U.G. 34 — 1914 pp. 234–71.
8 Davenport (1971) 8.
Lacey M. *Working for Boroko: the Origins of a Coercive Labour System in South Africa* (Johannesburg: 1981) 86–94.
Tatz C. M. *Shadow and Substance in South Africa* (Pietermaritzburg: 1962) 17–26, 29–37.
UG (1919) 17, 16.
9 Bonner P. 'The 1920 Black Mineworkers' Strike: a Preliminary Account' *Labour, Townships and Protest* (ed.) Bozzoli B. (Johannesburg: 1979) 273–97.
10 Phillips H. 'South Africa's Worst Demographic Disaster: the Spanish Influenza Epidemic of 1918' *SAHJ* (1988) 20, 70–4.
11 Allison J. S. 'Urban Native Legislation' *Race Relations* (1940) 7, 56–7.
T.P. 1 — 1922 app. 7.
U.G. 15 — 1922 pp. 25–8, 34–6
12 Davenport (1971) 13.
13 Africans arrested increased from an average of 6 049 a year in 1912–18 U.G. 7 — 1919 app. 9. to 161 477 in 1941–50 (Khan E. 'The Pass Laws' *Handbook on Race Relations* (ed.) Hellmann E. (1949) 275–91; Savage M. 'The Imposition of Pass Laws on the African Population in South Africa, 1916–1984' *African Affairs 85* (1986) 185–6; Wilson F. *Migrant Labour* (Johannesburg: 1972) 232–3).
14 U.G. 7 — 1919 pp. 5–6, U.G. 41 — 1922 pp. 3–4.

15 Kallaway (1973) 124–5.
16 Davenport (1971) 10–12.
U.G. 41 — 1922 'Report of the Inter-departmental Committee on the Native Pass Laws, 1920' 41. I am indebted to Richard Humphries for access to the evidence collected by this body which is sometimes erroneously referred to as a commission.
17 Davenport (1971) 13–15.
Imvo Zabantsundu 23, 30 May, 6 June 1922.
S.C. 3 — 1923 pp. 178–9.
U.G. 36 — 1923 pp. 4–5.
18 *Cape Times* 8 May 1923.
SC (1923) 3 — 1923, dated 20 April.
19 U.G. 47 — 1923 pp. 34–7.
20 *Cape Times* 5 May 1923.
U. G. 42 — 1922, 'Report of Native Location Surveys', read in association with E. R. Gathorne's minutes of a conference on land tenure, 17 November 1922, in the J. F. Herbst Papers, University of Cape Town, printed in Davenport and Hunt (1974) 49–51.
21 For example S.C. 3 — 1923 pp. 46 (Gardiner W. C.); 78 (Hill F. G.); 122–3, 128–9 (Van Coller C. M.); 132–4 (Layman C. F.); 154 (Nicholson M. G.).
22 S.C. 3 — 1923 pp. 16–17 (Jabavu D. D. T.); 113–6 (Pim H., Msimang H. S.); 129 (Morris G. A.); 175–8 (Loram C. T.).
23 *Cape Times* 5 May 1923.
Davenport (1971) 18–20.
24 *Cape Times* 2 June 1923.
Davenport (1971) 21–2.
25 For fuller summaries of the act and its amendments, see Davenport T. R. H. 'African Townsmen? South Africa's Natives (Urban Areas) Legislation through the Years' *African Affairs* 68 (1969) 95–109; and 'The Triumph of Colonel Stallard: the Transformation of the Natives Urban Areas Act between 1923 and 1937' *SAHJ* (1970) 77–96.
26 See the present author's unpublished 'Urban African Self-government: the First Abortive Phase', given at the first Conference on the History of Cape Town (UCT: 5 June 1981).
27 Davenport (1970) 83.
House of Assembly Debates (1930) col. 221.
'The Native Economic [Holloway] Commission' U.G. 22 — 1932 pp. 72–4. This commission was in complete accord, stating that 'no good purpose' was served by disregarding the fact 'that a considerable number of Natives have become permanent town dwellers, or by acting on the assumption that it is not a fact … To continue employing Natives in urban areas, but to treat them as if they should not be there, is both illogical and short-sighted'.
28 Accounts of the origins of the bill are in *H. of A. Deb.* (1937) cols. 4218–20, 6181–6; *Senate Deb.* (1937) cols. 1186–91, 1229–36 (Grobler), 6174–80 (Christopher), 6096–6111, 6179–81 (Nicholls).
29 Joint Select Committee (1935) 1, 3.
30 'Report of the Departmental Committee Appointed to Inquire into and Report upon the Question of the Residence of Natives in Urban Areas and Certain Proposed Amendments of the Native Urban Areas Act no. 21, of 1923'. The report was not published, although key sections were printed as an appendix to the Fagan Report, U.G. 28 — 1948. I have used a typescript copy in the D. L. Smit Papers, Settlers' Museum, Grahamstown. See also Davenport (1970) 84–9.
31 Young-Barrett Report, para. 15.

32 *H. of A. Deb.* (1937) cols. 6179–81.
33 Davenport (1970) 91–2., *H. of A. Deb.* (1937) cols. 3701–16.
34 According to a typescript in pamphlet box 30 N–Z, in the J. H. Hofmeyr Library, SA Institute of Race Relations, Johannesburg, the number of municipalities to adopt influx control regulations increased from 3 per annum in 1930–7 to 205 in 1938, 10 in 1939, and 74 in 1940, subsequently tailing off again to very small figures.
35 'Report of Native Farm Labour Committee' An. 520 — 1939, paras. 138–40.
36 Davenport (1970) 94–6. This apparent move into the sphere of cultural apartheid was inspired by a nuisance-based argument rather than political ideology, such as was in large part the case with the more famous 'church clause' controversy of 1957. It had a precedent in the OFS dating back to 1903 (see Van Aswegen, 29).
37 From this point the ground is more fully covered in my seminar paper 'The Smuts Government and the Africans, 1939–48' *The Societies of Southern Africa in the 19th and 20th centuries* Collected Seminar Papers no. 18 (University of London Institute of Commonwealth Studies: 1974) 5, 80–91. Footnote references not supplied in the seminar paper are, where necessary, given here.
38 See the *Union Year Book, 1956–57* 858–67 for details on the wartime dilution of labour. Of 21 136 persons working on government plant and annexed factories in October 1944, 2 314 were skilled whites and 13 794 were unticketed non-whites. Dilution of labour had the support of the Van Eck Commission (UG (1941) 40, paras. 168–75, 188–92) and of the Board of Trade and Industries *Report 282* (1945) 46.
39 'Report of the Inter-departmental Committee on the Social, Health and Economic Conditions of Urban Natives' An. 47 — 1943.
40 Native Representative Council Verbatim Proceedings (1937) 204–10; (1939) 513–32; (1940) 304–20, 342; (1941) 197–200; (1943) 106–25, 252, 285; (1944) 381–93; (1945) 152–64, the ninth session 116–37; (1946) 16–25. No verbatim proceedings were taken in 1938.
41 For the Young Report, as modified and endorsed by the other members of the Native Affairs Commission, see U.G. 42 — 1941 app. H pp. 61–3.
42 *H. of A. Deb.* (1941) cols. 3165–6 (Mrs Ballinger's question); (1942) col. 4204 (Hemming's question). For Reitz's reaction see his senate speech on 26 March 1942. There is a copy of the Minister of Justice's order in the A. B. Xuma papers (ABX 420405), University of the Witwatersrand.
43 Figures calculated from the report of the committee appointed to investigate the position of crime on the Witwatersrand and in Pretoria (chairperson: S. H. Elliot), para. 30. A copy of the report is in the A. B. Xuma Papers at ABX 421231a. For other figures, see footnote 13.
44 'Report of the Native Laws Commission', U.G. 28 — 1948.
45 An. 145 — 1948 paras. 8–16. (This is not to be confused with the better-known Report on Native Laws.)
46 Full details are given in An. 145 — 1948.
    See also Stadler A. W. 'Birds in the Cornfield: Squatter Movements in Johannesburg, 1944–7' *Journal of Southern African Studies* (1979) 6, 93–123; Davenport (1974) 85.
47 NRC verbatim proceedings (1944) adjourned session, iii, annex. B.
48 Davenport (1974) 89. There is full documentation of the government proposals in the D. L. Smit Papers.
49 Smuts to Hofmeyr in the Hofmeyr Papers (University of the Witwatersrand: 28 August 1946).
50 M. Ballinger to Smuts (Smuts Archive: 14 February 1947).

2 Curbing African urbanization in the 1950s and 1960s

Deborah Posel

It is common cause that by the time of the 'reform' era (from the late 1970s), the apartheid system was wracked by a series of failures and contradictions which the state was unable to resolve. Less conspicuous, perhaps, is the fact that debilitating failures and contradictions have been endemic to apartheid since its inception, even during the heyday of 'grand apartheid' in the 1960s. It is true, of course, that the pre-reform period was marked by a number of spectacular successes on the part of the state — the smashing of black opposition, forced removals on a vast scale, and the proliferation of a massive and powerful state bureaucracy, to name a few. By the late 1960s, the state was thus sufficiently strong and resourceful to have reshaped the South African city in particularly brutal ways, dumping large numbers of African inhabitants beyond the urban boundary. But the enormity of this process of social engineering can blind one to the weakness, uncertainties, and sheer muddles of apartheid. Even at the zenith of its power, the apartheid state still lacked control in several key policy areas. The development of apartheid has been shaped by *ad hoc* responses to the unintended consequences of particular policies, as much as by the foresight and control of its leading architects. Integral to the perpetuation of apartheid, therefore, has been an ongoing process of adaptation, during which the state has had to react to the exigencies of the moment and revise old methods and goals in the light of new and unforeseen challenges.

This chapter focuses on the state's efforts to contain the size of the African presence in the city during the 1950s and 1960s. It argues that the state's capacity to realize its aims during the 1950s was hindered by an unwitting internal contradiction in the formulation of apartheid policy, which widened the space for resistance on several fronts. Moreover, the perceived weaknesses of the urban policies of the 1950s played a major role in prompting an unforeseen policy shift during the 1960s. The ambitious and ruthless urban removals programme of the 1960s would not have been possible without a massive enlargement of the state's bureaucratic resources and repressive machinery, which the Nationalists achieved during the 1950s. But the decision to embark on such aggressive policies was also a response to the fact that less interventionist, more pragmatic attempts to reduce the urban African presence during the 1950s, were a resounding failure.

African urbanization and labour regulation in the 1950s

Thrust to power unexpectedly in 1948, the Nationalist government regarded a solution to the 'urban Native problem' as one of its first priorities. The size of the urban African population had rocketed during the 1940s, boosted by expanding employment opportunities in the cities and desperate rural poverty. (Between 1936 and 1946, the urban African population had grown by 57.2 per cent, from 1 141 642 to 1 794 212, as compared with a 31.5 per cent growth in the white urban population, from 1 307 386 to 1 719 338.)[1] Whites' anxieties about being 'swamped' by Africans in the cities were heightened by rising levels of political turbulence and often militant protest in urban African communities, provoked largely by appalling living conditions.[2] A dire housing shortage meant that at least 58 per cent of the urban African population were squatters on unserviced land.[3] To make matters worse, average wages for Africans in urban areas were well below the breadline, at the same time as war-time shortages pushed up the price of basic foods and transportation.[4]

Accelerating African proletarianization was not only politically inflammable; it was also considered by the Nationalists to be economically 'irrational'.[5] White farmers suffered serious labour shortages, while the cities contained large 'surpluses' of African labour, symptomatic of widespread unemployment and under-employment. Moreover, many urban employers — especially those paying particularly low wages for unskilled work — spurned the reserve army of labour on their doorsteps, choosing to recruit so-called 'raw' migrant workers from the reserves. While the journals of organized commerce and industry sang the praises of a 'stable' urbanized workforce, individual employers often preferred the services of rural recruits, particularly for unskilled work, on the grounds that 'rural labour' was less 'job choosy', more 'docile' and disciplined, and prepared to work for lower wages, than urbanized workers.[6] Once new rural recruits were more familiar with the urban job market, however, many moved on to better-paying jobs, leaving vacancies which the employers filled with 'rural labour' once more. The result was a high labour turnover in the cities, coupled with rising levels of urban unrest and under-employment.

A large part of the solution, according to the Nationalists, was to curtail the growth of the urban African population, and eliminate urban unemployment, by means of an influx control policy[7] which would restructure the urban labour market in accordance with an 'urban labour preference principle'.[8] A policy of urban population resettlement was not part of the original apartheid strategy devised during the late 1940s and early 1950s. The state's remedy to the rampant proletarianization of the 1940s was initially less aggressive, due partly to a misplaced faith in the state's power to orchestrate and control urban employment patterns. The architects of apartheid were confident that once urban employers' access to workers recruited from rural areas was restricted, these employers would be forced to make 'better use' of a smaller (urbanized) labour pool, which would cut labour turnover and reduce unemployment in the urban areas.[9] Reducing the number of workers drawn into the cities from rural areas in turn promised to curb the growth of the urban African presence. And, with urban labour demands more fully catered for by the resident African population, substantial numbers of work seekers from the reserves could be deflected to white farms to redress labour shortages there.[10]

The 'urban labour preference policy' would be complemented by an immediate urbanization freeze: any migrants who were permitted access to urban employment would be prohibited from settling permanently in the urban area. Their right to be in the area would lapse once their employment contract ended.

This strategy for regulating the size and composition of the urban African population was grounded in a clear ideological and administrative division, between the 'detribalized' core of the urban African population and other city-dwellers who were still 'tribalized', retaining a permanent base in a rural area. During the 1950s, the architects of apartheid conceded that 'detribalized' Africans had become fully urbanized, having made the city their permanent home. This earned them the 'residential right' to remain there, whether or not they were employed there.[11] For the rest, the city was merely a 'temporary' base for the purposes of taking up employment. Any labour 'surplus' among the 'tribalized' group could be eradicated by expelling the unemployed back to their areas of origin. The 'urban labour preference policy' would provide the means for mopping up unemployment within the 'detribalized' population, by 'channelling' urbanized work seekers into all available jobs ahead of their 'tribalized' counterparts.[12]

As suggested earlier, the Nationalists were well aware that the 'urban labour preference policy' conflicted starkly with economic realities. Indeed, one of the principal aims of the Nationalists' urban strategy was to restructure prevailing employment patterns by legal and administrative fiat. For this reason, the implementation of the 'urban labour preference policy' was seen to depend on developing the appropriate administrative machinery, in the form of a national system of labour bureaux, to establish systematic and comprehensive control over the allocation of African labour to urban areas. Denied the right to recruit labour independently, urban employers would be compelled to accept the workers allocated to them by labour bureaux officials, who could then ensure that local work seekers had first claim on all available jobs.

Any superficial semblance of rationality in this policy shatters with the exposure of a fundamental internal contradiction. On the one hand, the allocation of 'residential rights' to 'urbanized' people was seen as the essential instrument of the 'urban labour preference policy'. These rights would identify the Africans who, if unemployed, would be placed in employment ahead of 'tribalized' work seekers. On the other hand, the concept of 'residential rights' thoroughly undermined the logic of the 'urban labour preference policy', by giving urbanized people the right to refuse employment, if they so wished. Whereas the 'urban labour preference policy' was premised on the state's power to force urbanized Africans into particular jobs, the allocation of residential rights gave urbanized Africans the freedom to resist any such pressure.[13]

This contradiction was entrenched, and indeed exacerbated, by the legislation passed in 1952 to enact the Nationalists' influx control strategy. The architects of this strategy had proposed to confer residential rights extremely narrowly, limiting their acquisition to people who had been born and continuously resident in one particular urban area — thereby excluding hundreds of thousands of people who had lived and worked in an urban area for several years, despite having been born elsewhere. Confronted by a broad front of opposition to this proposal, Dr H. F. Verwoerd (as Minister of Native Affairs at the time) made two concessions which enlarged the scope of residential rights. Thus, in terms of section 10 (1) (b) and (c) of the 1952 Native Laws Amendment Act, Africans who had lived and worked in one urban area continuously for 10 years (if for one employer) or for 15 years (working for several employers), as well as their wives and dependent children, were also recognized as 'urbanized' people entitled to residential rights. These new conditions, although conceded grudgingly, were by no means generous. Yet they deepened the contradiction within the 'urban labour preference policy', by enlarging the numbers of people legally entitled to refuse work allocated to them by the labour bureaux.

The 1952 Native Laws Amendment Act also jabbed a spoke in the wheel of the proposed urbanization freeze. The implication of section 10 (1) (b) and (c) of this law (as described above) was that Africans who had been born in rural areas, but had spent long periods of time living and working in urban areas, were accepted as new members of the urbanized population who were legally entitled to raise children there.

The limits of the NP's powers in the legislative process were small, however, compared to the gaping holes in the labour bureaux's control over the urban labour market. By 1961, a conference of Chief Bantu Commissioners had to acknowledge that the performance of the labour bureaux system to date had been a 'complete failure'.[14] Large numbers of urban employers simply ignored the labour bureaux system, refusing to surrender their choice. Thousands of work seekers shared a similar disdain for the labour bureaux, risking arrest by taking work illegally. Ironically, even those employers who did patronize the labour bureaux often succeeded in persuading the bureaux's officials to waive the terms of the 'urban labour preference policy', in order to make 'rural labour' available when specifically requested.[15]

The failure of the labour bureaux system in the 1950s illustrates the powerful effects of unorganized resistance on the development of apartheid — resistance which was facilitated, in part, by the contradictory formulation of state policy. The state proposed to restructure the urban labour market in a manner which took no account of workers' or employers' preferences, the specific labour requirements of different jobs, or workers' prior training and level of skill. As a vacancy arose, it was to be filled by the urbanized work seekers at the head of the job queue, irrespective of the nature of the job, or the workers' particular abilities or preferences. This proposal conflicted starkly with both employers' and workers' interests. Despite the continuing trend towards capital intensification within the manufacturing sector, the overwhelming urban demand for African labour during the 1950s was for unskilled labour.[16] And the stereotypes which had moulded employment patterns during previous decades still prevailed: rural recruits were generally preferred, particularly for unskilled work, on the grounds that they were more disciplined and less 'job choosy' than urbanized workers. Steeped in prejudice, these stereotypes were also grounded in reality to some extent. Migrants did tend to take what employers recognized as the 'obnoxious' jobs which urbanized workers disdained.[17] Lacking the security of residential rights, migrants were in constant danger of arrest unless employed, while the pressure of rural poverty often precluded the option of waiting for a better-paid job to come up. Moreover, new arrivals in the city tended to find employment through informal migrant networks which colonized particular places of work, as a means of keeping migrants from the same village or clan together.[18] 'Obnoxious' work was sometimes the price paid for solidarity and security.

Vulnerable, and yet able to protect themselves to a degree against the insecurities of their position, migrant workers were therefore doubly threatened by the 'urban labour preference policy', which endangered their access to jobs ('obnoxious' or otherwise) and thereby threatened to undermine the job clustering which preserved their sense of solidarity. Urbanized work seekers, for their part, also had little to gain from the labour bureaux system, which altogether ignored their preferences and abilities in the allocation of work. And, protected by their residential right to remain in an urban area whether employed or not, most urbanized workers could legally resist any uninvited pressures from labour bureaux officials.

The majority of urban employers and work seekers alike, therefore, had compelling reasons to resist the labour bureaux system, which threatened to deprive them all of their freedom to negotiate employment contracts independently. And throughout the 1950s, when the labour bureaux system was still relatively new and unpractised, the authorities could do little to curb 'illegal' employment on a vast scale.[19] This is not to say that the labour bureaux system was wholly toothless. Large numbers of workers, and small numbers of employers, were prosecuted for violating the Labour Bureaux Regulations; indeed, the threat of arrest pervaded Africans' experience of city life. But ubiquitous policing of the employment process in the cities was an impossibly onerous task.

The minority of employers who did patronize the labour bureaux found that 'few if any labour bureaux are operating strictly according to the Bureaux Regulations'.[20] The 'urban labour preference policy' was rarely applied, having become impaled on the horns of its internal contradiction. Because the labour bureaux officials lacked the power to coerce urban work seekers into unwanted jobs, or indeed to participate in the labour bureaux system at all, the labour bureaux functioned to the extent that they did largely by relying heavily on the ready supply of labour in rural areas. Ironically then, the contradiction within the 'urban labour preference policy' ensured that the labour bureaux system reproduced employers' preference for, and reliance on, 'raw' labour, regardless of the existing level of urban unemployment.

The overall result, as an interdepartmental inquiry into Idleness and Unemployment among Urban Bantu (hereafter referred to as the Botha Report, 1962) pointed out, was a perpetuation of the original problem which the 'urban labour preference policy' had been designed to solve: 'the anomaly exists that (African) work seekers from outside the urban areas are admitted in, despite the fact that there is already a surplus in the towns'. At the same time as labour bureaux officials admitted the 'persistent underutilization' of the urban labour reservoir, industrialists noted that 'the percentage of migratory workers ... is increasing annually'.[21]

Another serious loophole in the labour bureaux system during the 1950s, was the near-complete absence of control over the employment of African women in the urban areas. During the 1940s, the United Party government had resisted often vehement calls from local authorities for stricter controls over the movements of African women, largely for fear of inflaming widespread protests. The local authorities found a more sympathetic audience in the Nationalist government, however, which stressed the importance of curbing women's migration to urban areas. Women's settlement in urban areas meant a new generation of urban-born children, pushing the size of the urban African population up exponentially. Ignoring an angry uproar, the Nationalists therefore proposed to apply the same influx control laws to women as men — that is, apart from the women accepted as 'urbanized', in the state's strict sense of the term, women's presence in urban areas would be contingent on securing employment through the labour bureaux, and in accordance with the 'urban labour preference policy'.[22] Successful in his effort to entrench these measures on the statute book, Verwoerd then made an important concession to popular pressure. 'Notwithstanding the fact that these provisions are applicable to native women,' he stated, 'it is not our intention to proceed with its [sic] practical application at the moment because we do not think that the time is ripe.'[23] This meant, *inter alia*, that women were administratively exempt from the labour bureaux regulations — in other words, they were not legally obliged to seek work through the offices of the labour bureaux, which were therefore completely unable to control women's employment patterns. Women's right to live in urban areas did not depend, therefore, on their securing employment there. Instead, Verwoerd delegated the authority to control women's movements to local authorities, most of whom — fearing outbreaks of protest — were relatively lenient. The Botha Report thus found that 'as a rule, Bantu women entered and settled in the cities unhindered'.[24]

With the 'urban labour preference policy' largely a dead letter, widespread illegal employment of African men in urban areas, and very little control over the movements and employment of African women, the urban African population continued to mushroom during the 1950s. According to the 1960 population census, the resident urban African population increased from 2 328 534 in 1951, to 3 443 950 in 1960 — an increase of 47 per cent. By 1960, the urban African population comprised 31 per cent of the total African population, as compared with 24.3 per cent and 27.9 per cent in 1946 and 1951 respectively.[25] These figures, however, did not reflect untold numbers of illegal city-dwellers, who had obvious reasons to elude census-takers. The proportion of 'illegals' varied between regions and between different types of residential areas. 'Model townships' constructed during the 1950s, with starkly parallel and perpendicular streets and regularly spaced houses, made for a far greater degree of municipal control than could be exercised in older, more rambling townships. Also, the energetic implementation of the Prevention of Illegal Squatting Act (1951) saw the destruction of many shanty towns which had been home to thousands denied permission to live legally in urban areas. Despite such measures, however, municipal administrators generally assumed, as a rule of thumb, that 15 per cent to 25 per cent of the communities under their jurisdiction was 'illegal'.[26]

New measures in the 1960s

These gaps in the state's control in urban areas were starkly spotlighted at the turn of the decade, by an upsurgence of urban resistance. During 1959, the sprawling shanty town of Cato Manor (outside Durban) exploded, ignited by the Durban City Council's proposal to level the settlement. By August, the city council admitted outright defeat, its authority in Cato Manor having been wholly overthrown.[27] The shooting by police of anti-pass demonstrators in Sharpeville in 1960 then provoked a storm of criticism, in the country and abroad, about the plight of Africans in urban areas. The clamour persuaded the ruling regime, too, of the need for a fundamental reassessment of its urban policies.

Diagnoses of, and remedies for, the 'unrest' varied, the ruling Afrikaner Nationalist alliance itself divided. The verdict which prevailed within the state, and which shaped the development of apartheid for the decade to come, was that the unrest had been fuelled by the manifest failures of existing urban policies. Mounting unemployment, in the midst of persistent accommodation shortages and grinding poverty, had turned the townships into political tinder boxes. More drastic measures were now considered necessary to curb the size of the urban African population, and to tackle the problem of urban unemployment. In the words of Blaar Coetzee (as Deputy Minister of Bantu Administration and Development): 'How are we to deal with the increase of Bantu labour [in the cities]? ... It is clear that influx control can never be more than an instrument to make the flow of labour more orderly. It can never be a solution.'[28]

The state's new strategies were premised on a fundamental redefinition of the city. The architects of apartheid now denied that there was, or ever had been, a 'detribalized' community in the urban areas. This change of tack swiftly overturned the basis of the state's existing influx control policy. State ideologues now stressed that all Africans were thoroughly 'tribalized' at heart, and therefore spiritually and culturally anchored in ethnically defined 'homelands'.[29] Townships in 'white' cities were now to be treated as mere outposts of these homelands, providing 'temporary sojourn' for all Africans irrespective of their place of birth or the duration of their stay in the city.

'Residential rights' were identified as an anomaly, which had mistakenly conferred a degree of permanence and protection on the allegedly 'detribalized' group.[30] The status of all Africans was now to be levelled, making all equally vulnerable to expulsion from the urban areas once unemployed.

This ideological and policy shift opened the way for a newly aggressive strategy for reducing the size of the urban African presence: the resettlement of urban inhabitants who were 'superfluous' to white needs, in ethnically defined 'homelands'. First mooted by the Department of Bantu Administration and Development (BAD) in 1959, the prospect of mass removals from urban areas was originally tied in with plans for infrastructural and agricultural development in the homelands.[31] The 'surplus' urban population was to be resettled in homeland villages, built at the central state's expense. This proposal was enthusiastically received by many local authorities, who saw it as a means of shifting financial responsibility for 'unproductive' Africans in their areas to the BAD.[32] Long lists of 'superfluous' residents were dutifully compiled, in anticipation of a rapid drive to trim the urban community down to its 'productive' core.

But the BAD's progress was tardy, hampered in part by the slow pace of its 'development' drive. It was only in the mid-1960s that the BAD created an internal resettlement branch, to manage the ambitious urban removals programme.[33] And its work only began in earnest once the BAD had released the resettlement project from its dependence on the pace of homeland development. By 1980, this policy had led to the removal of at least 730 000 Africans from allegedly 'white' urban areas.[34]

Another new strategy introduced in the 1960s to lessen the pace of African proletarianization, was the imposition of urban labour quotas. Having failed to restructure urban employment patterns by means of the 'urban labour preference policy', the BAD now set out to impose a maximum permissible ratio of African to white workers in certain labour-intensive industries.[35] This proposal, however, encountered fierce opposition from organized commerce and industry, which defeated attempts to introduce the necessary legislation in 1960 and 1963. It was only in 1970, following the Report of the Inter-departmental Committee on the Decentralization of Industries, that the Nationalists succeeded in pegging the ratio of African to white industrial workers in urban areas (initially only on the Witwatersrand) to 1:2.5 (until 1973) and thereafter at 1:2. Any industry exceeding the quota would be compelled to decentralize to a border area or homeland.

In the meantime, the labour bureaux system was refined and extended, reducing the scale of illegal employment to some extent. Also, by 1963, African women felt the full brunt of the Labour Bureaux Regulations, which led to thousands being arrested and 'endorsed out' of urban areas. The state also renewed its commitment to the 'urban labour preference policy', but set out to eradicate the contradiction within this policy by abolishing urban residential rights.[36] In this instance, however, the state's plans were thoroughly defeated by fierce opposition from local authorities and the urban business community. Repeated and strenuous efforts throughout the 1960s to scrap section 10 (1) of the Urban Areas Act, which conferred urban residential rights, consistently failed. The internal contradiction in the 'urban labour preference policy' thus remained intact.

Facilitated partly by the persistence of this contradiction, resistance to the state's urban policies continued (albeit on a lesser scale than during the previous decade). By 1968, state officials were still complaining of a 'terrific problem' of illegal residence and employment in the urban areas. 'Despite all our laws,' the BAD confessed, 'in practice we all know that there are literally thousands of Bantu who are illegally employed.'[37] By 1978, the Commission of Inquiry into Legislation Affecting the Utilization of Manpower (the Riekert Commission) reported the very same problem which the state had set out to eradicate in the 1950s: the preference for 'rural labour' was still widespread, giving rise to 'unemployment in urban areas and housing and … [other] social problems'.[38] This is not to suggest that the labour bureaux system had changed nothing. As the system grew more sophisticated, employers encountered more resistance to their requests for 'raw' labour. And, continuing capital intensification within the manufacturing sector reduced the degree of demand for unskilled labour. The point is rather that nearly three decades after the institution of the 'urban labour preference policy', the state had failed to 'persuade [urban employers] to make optimal use of the available labour living on a permanent basis in urban areas'.[39]

Conclusion

The effects of the state's urban policies during the 1960s on the size of the urban African population are controversial. According to the 1970 population census, the number of Africans living in 'white'

urban areas had risen to 4 475 356, which represented an increase
of 30 per cent over the comparable 1960 figure. By 1970, the proportion of the African population in urban areas had risen from 31.8 per
cent to 33 per cent.[40] Charles Simkins' calculations, however, show
that between 1960 and 1970, there was a net outflow of 203 000
Africans from the urban areas,[41] so that by 1970 the proportion of the
African population living in urban areas had dropped to 28.1 per
cent.[42] The discrepancies between these figures are obviously crucial,
and prevent a final verdict on the efficacy of the state's strategies.
But both sets of data imply that during the 1960s, the state succeeded in trimming the rate at which the urban African population
expanded — despite an economic boom which was concentrated in
the cities.

This chapter has shown, however, that the interpretation of these
demographic changes is more complex than at first sight. On one
level, they indicate a noteworthy degree of success on the part of the
apartheid regime in taming the pace of African urbanization. Indeed,
the resettlement drive, a major contributor to this result, is often cited
as a measure of the ruthlessness of the apartheid state at the acme of
its power, and a symbol of the unswerving rationality of 'separate
development'. However, on another level, the population statistics in
general, and the urban removals programme in particular, also bore
testimony to some of the ongoing failures and contradictions of
apartheid. Unable to subordinate the urban labour market fully to
the dictates of the law, it was only by physically relocating whole
communities beyond urban boundaries that the state succeeded in
containing the growth of the African population in 'white' urban
areas.

Notes

1   Union of South Africa *Report of the Native Laws Commission, 1946–48* (UG
    28/1948) 6.
2   Lodge T. *Black Politics in South Africa After 1945* (London and New York:
    Longman 1983).
3   Posel D. *Influx Control and the Construction of Apartheid, 1948–1961* D.Phil. the-
    sis (University of Oxford 1987) 45.
4   Walker C. *Women and Resistance in South Africa* (London: Onyx 1982).
5   Union of South Africa *Report of the Department of Native Affairs for the Year
    1951/2* (UG 37/1955).
6   Posel D. *The Making of Apartheid, 1948–1961: Conflict and Compromise* (Oxford:
    Oxford University Press, 1991).

7 'Influx control' policy stipulates the conditions under which Africans could legally live and work in proclaimed urban areas.

8 A discussion of influx control obviously does not exhaust the scope of the state's urban strategy. The Group Areas Act and the Prevention of Illegal Squatting Act were also cornerstones of that strategy, but are not dealt with in this paper.

9 Eiselen W. 'The Demand for and the Supply of Bantu Labour' *Bantu 5* (1958) 5.

10 *House of Assembly Debates* (1952) 77 col. 749.

11 *House of Assembly Debates* (1952) 77 col. 1310.

12 Posel (1991).

13 Posel (1991).

14 Department of Co-operation and Development Library (now rehoused) 'Konferensie van Hoof Bantoesakekommissarisse te Pretoria, 16 tot 18 November 1961'.

15 Posel (1991).

16 According to economist J. L. Sadie, by 1960, 84 per cent of the African workforce in manufacturing was unskilled (Kleu n.d. 120). This proportion was higher in commerce, and even more so in services.

17 Posel (1991).

18 Delius P. 'Sebatakgomo: Migrant Organization, the ANC and the Sekhukhuneland Revolt' *Journal of Southern African Studies* (1989) 15 iv.

19 Department of Bantu Administration and Development 'Verslag van die Interdepartmentele Kommittee Insake Ledige en Nie-werkende Bantoes in Stedelike Gebiede', unpublished (1962).

20 Federated Chamber of Industries (FCI) Unsorted Files on Non-European Affairs (NEAF), 'Memorandum on the Results of the Survey on the Availability of Native Labour', (21 June 1956).

21 FCI, NEAF, 'Native Labour Problems of the Urban Areas Act' (1956) 3.

22 *House of Assembly Debates* (1952) 78 col. 2953.

23 *House of Assembly Debates* (1952) 78 col. 2955.

24 Department of Bantu Administration and Development (1962) 45.

25 Republic of South Africa *Official Yearbook for 1980/1* (Johannesburg: Chris van Rensburg Publishers 1980) 32.

26 Posel (1987) 180.

27 Killie Campbell Library (KCL), Bourquin Papers, KCM 55218, 'Notes for Meeting with Minister of BAD', 3 August 1959.

28 (WRAB), West Rand Administration Board Archive Johannesburg Municipal Records A78/2) 7, B. Coetzee "Effective Bantu Employment".

29 See, for example, Senate Debates (1967) col. 2830.

30 Union of South Africa *Memorandum Explaining the Background and Objects of the Promotion of Bantu Self-Government Bill 1959* (1959) N.P. 3–1959.

31 KCL, Bourquin Papers, KCM 55476, Institute of Administrators of Non-European Affairs (IANA), 'Record of Proceedings of First Biennial Meeting of Officials' (1966) 40–3.

32 IANA (1966) 51, 67 and 99.

33 IANA (1966) 41.

34 Platzky L. and Walker C. *The Surplus People: Forced Removals in South Africa* (Johannesburg: Ravan 1985) 10.

35 See, for example, the *Rand Daily Mail* 6 October 1962.

36 Department of Bantu Administration and Development (1962).

37 KCL, Bourquin Papers, IANA, 'Record of Proceedings of Second Biennial Meeting of Officials' (1968) 88.

38 Republic of South Africa *Commission of Inquiry into Legislation Affecting the Utilization of Manpower (Excluding the Legislation Administered by the Departments of Labour and Mines* (RP 32/1979) 170.

39 Republic of South Africa (1979) 170.

40 Republic of South Africa (1980) 32.

41 Simkins C. *Four Essays on the Past, Present and Possible Future Distribution of the Black Population of South Africa* (Cape Town: SALDRU 1983) 62.

42 Platzky and Walker (1985) 18.

3 The dynamics of urbanization since 1960

Alan Mabin

Introduction

As exiles who left South Africa in the early 1960s began to return during 1990, many exclaimed in Rip van Winkle-like amazement at the changes which the passage of a generation had wrought in our cities. The fabled Rip van Winkle slept through a revolution. South African exiles who left in the 1960s have not missed the long-awaited political revolution, but their absence during a time of tremendous change allows them to remind those of us who have spent all or most of the last 25 years inside the country of the enormity of the changes that have taken place.

This chapter seeks to survey the changes in urbanization processes and policies since the mid-1960s, to explore how they have come about, and to consider implications of present trends for planning. The central theme of the chapter is that urbanization is a far more complex and less tractable process in analytical terms than much of the existing literature would allow. Urbanization is a long-term process and is multidirectional, and urbanization policy is less certain and usually less successful than those who wish to reshape society might like to believe.

The apartheid urban regime

Amid the rapid economic growth of the 1960s, during which the cities grew along with the economy, strains began to emerge in the urban regime constructed under apartheid. That regime had been modified during the 1960s (see Posel's chapter above), but it was some time before strains began to emerge which would ultimately result in the end of the apartheid urban model. In the mid-1960s, what seemed in various ways a successful national and urban growth model appeared to have emerged.

Industrial growth in the cities was served by three kinds of labour pools: city, township,[1] and circular migrant. City-based labour included many literate to highly skilled workers, most of whom had jobs and housing. The city workforce found itself increasingly segregated along race classification lines, as the application of the Group Areas Act to places like South End in Port Elizabeth proceeded. But it also found itself highly in demand, generally in workplaces where strict segregation of jobs among the city-based workers tended to decay. Those city-based workers lived in everything from rented flats to paid-off houses in suburban tracts, and the latter grew rapidly. White workers made up a large proportion of the city-based labour force, together with some Indians and coloureds in areas such as Bosmont (Johannesburg), Sydenham (Durban), and Athlone (Cape Town). Most African, coloured, and Indian workers found themselves in (or looking for) accommodation in the townships.

In the townships, generally located on the peripheries of the cities, a small but growing proportion of the potential workforce shared the characteristics of those in the city proper. More and more students received the rudiments of education in the expanding school systems, however imperfect their conditions and performance.[2] Many households lived in council-owned, rented township housing. Townships were sometimes well serviced, like Daveyton near Benoni (electricity, water-borne sewage, streetlights, paved roads), and sometimes poorly serviced, like Duduza near Nigel (bucket sewage, unfinished streets, communal water). Wages were low, but so were rents and travel costs. Between township and city lay the huge numbers of commuters travelling by subsidized rail and bus services. These were sometimes planned entirely to serve industry (e.g. the rail service from Daveyton to Dunswart bypasses central Benoni and travels straight to the heart of a major industrial area).

Also in the African townships, and to a considerable extent within the working districts of the cities too, many workers lived in hostels. The term 'hostels' includes older compounds associated with private employers, and more recent municipal as well as employer-built accommodation. These places share a history of being intended to house workers of one gender, usually male, without their families and friends, and usually with collective use of kitchens, bathrooms, and bedrooms. Most of their inmates found cheap urban housing in the hostels while maintaining one or more rural bases. Thus the hostels provided the urban base for many such circular migrants.[3]

These three elements structured the urban environment of the mid-1960s. A few anomalies still remained in this system from the 1950s. Some smaller, older, mainly black[4] areas persisted in very central localities of some towns (like Kroonstad) and even cities (like Cape Town). But the Group Areas pattern had largely been set, and together with the even more significant pattern of the new large African township, with their Verwoerdian hinterlands, formed the major building blocks of urban residential environments.

Indeed, the pace of house building had slowed in the African townships, and no longer predominated as an urban concern as it had done in the early 1950s. Planners were more concerned with upmarket urban expansion and intensification than with the housing of the mainly poor black masses. The urban regime of the 1960s provided for expansion of planned schemes affecting African people in the bantustans[5] rather than in the established urban areas.[6] Bantustan townships like Ga-Rankuwa, Mdantsane, or Seshego illustrate this.[7] So planning continued, replicating township forms in new localities rather than contributing innovative urban ideas.

This urban regime rested on a variety of other state policies and practices intended to restrict entry to the cities and to provide for African people to live in the reserves.[8] These oppressive policies may even have been relatively successful in the 1960s, while political organization against oppressive policies affecting mobility and place of residence remained at a minimum. Thus the urban regime of the 1960s acquired what appeared to be stability, and if it did not in itself foster the form and pace of economic growth during that era, it certainly co-existed with it. This is not to say, of course, that the urban regime could maintain long-term stability; and indeed, pressures were already present which would fatally undermine it.

Contradiction in the apartheid urban regime

In addition to those actually living in the townships and elsewhere in urban South Africa, there were those trying to reach the cities. Since the 1940s, people — Africans in particular — moved to town because of the better economic opportunities there.[9] But a primary feature of South Africa in the 1960s was the extent of eviction from rural areas outside the reserves which drove people from their rural homes to seek accommodation and a livelihood elsewhere. Those evictions took three main forms:

Expropriation of 'black spots' i.e. privately held land owned by Africans in areas deemed to be white, and the forced removal of their residents to reserve areas, e.g. from black spots around Ladysmith to Limehill.

Excision of some reserve areas from those scheduled and released under the 1913 and 1936 Land Acts, and the forced removal of their residents to other reserve areas, in the interests of the 'consolidation' of bantustans, e.g. the complete removal of communities from the Gathlose and Maremane reserves south of Kuruman in 1976–7 and their forcible relocation to areas on the fringe of the Kalahari in districts of the Tswana territorial authority (now Bophuthatswana).

Private eviction of 'squatters', tenants, sharecroppers, and, most importantly, labour tenants, from privately and publicly owned land, often aided or accelerated by state action. This included the proclamation of the abolition of labour tenancy area by area which was eventually completed in the 1970s, only to be reversed by the repeal of chapter four of the 1936 Land Act in the 1980s. Such evictions began to accelerate dramatically during the 1960s and continued throughout the quarter century reviewed here — indeed, they continue today. In most cases those evicted had no specific place of refuge, although the allocation of sites in the reserves accelerated and allowed many such people to acquire places to live, even if without much in the way of rights to land for farming or grazing.

The numbers affected by these processes in the 1960s were very high indeed. Expunging black spots and consolidating reserves cost a few hundred thousand people their places of residence, and eviction from private farms was twice that number.[10]

Both evictions from private farms and a variety of measures adopted in the reserves, including the replanning of agricultural communities known as 'betterment', had already created a large landless population by the time the NP government of D. F. Malan came to power in 1948. In many reserve areas, 'miserable', 'bleak and bare' settlements of the landless began to develop,[11] from which, inevitably, most households had to send members to participate in the urban economy. During the 1950s the pace of rural eviction began to increase, and it accelerated greatly in the 1960s and 1970s, until literally millions of people had directly experienced eviction from land on which, in most cases, their family histories were much longer than those of the titular owners.[12]

It should not be assumed that these evictions affected Africans alone. Still less well documented are the many thousands of coloured households that experienced eviction, while others lost their small land holdings under adverse economic conditions. As Zietsman put it, 'in the case of coloureds, the trek to the cities is continuing'.[13] In the southern Cape for instance, even white farm labourers met a similar fate, while many smaller white farmers lost their land to creditors. In Natal, Indians suffered likewise. Unlike Africans, in most cases these rural households could not repair to the reserves; but they were not legally discouraged from moving to the towns where jobs, housing, and welfare could in many cases be secured, even if at bare survival levels.

So while very large numbers of people were pressured off the land, they found themselves face to face with the oppressive urban regime, which, together with the material problems of life in the cities, forced them into mainly non-formal, usually bantustan, settlements. In the 1960s and for much of the 1970s, the state managed the migration of Africans so that it allocated those forced off the farms to closer settlements of various kinds in the reserves.

State policy remained committed to increasing urban control while allowing a little more flexibility in allocating labour within urban areas, as evidenced in the creation of Bantu Affairs Administration Boards (BAABs) from 1969 to 1971.[14] It might be inferred that these boards, which took over the administration of affairs affecting Africans from (white-elected) local authorities, were intended to shore up the urban regime. In fact, since they continued all the more vigorously to implement existing urban policy without alleviating (except to a minor extent) the pressures on the lives of those excluded, they only exacerbated the contradictions of policy, with the result that animosity towards authority increased rapidly.

A key problem in the urban regime was that it failed to provide for significant expansion of the urban African population outside the reserves. In the official mind, this was justified by the notion that a combination of bantustan/border development and influx control would cope with the growth of the African population. But in reality the population of Africans in urban areas showed a considerable propensity to grow, and the underlying problems began to express themselves in disturbing ways.

The problems of the system became manifest in the explosion of informal residences which began in the late 1960s. In the reserves, this took the form of extending the pattern of unapproved, unsurveyed allocation of sites and erection of buildings. Such allocation and building took both 'tribal' and market forms. The result was the beginning of rapid unregulated settlement growth, especially in areas closer to the towns and cities, e.g. Winterveld near Pretoria, the reserve areas close to Pietersburg, and Inanda outside Durban.

In the formal urban areas this growth of informal residence took the form of letting rooms (and in fewer instances to begin with, other spaces) to lodgers. These subtenants, mostly subletting from township house tenants, were not necessarily of a particular social class or category of geographical origin. But they shared the lack of access to housing. Internal population growth alone, coupled with a lack of new house construction, would have brought about overcrowding; but the increasing density of population was also caused by inward migration to the cities of both 'legals' (e.g. contracted migrant workers) and 'illegals' (e.g. passless rural people).

Instead of expanding the housing available in non-reserve urban environments, the state continued to demolish urban housing (e.g. in Marabastad and Kroonstad) and also drastically reduced funds available to local authorities (including BAABs) to build housing despite increases in the size of the urban population. By 1973, many township and hostel residents faced deteriorating living conditions and rising rents in informal markets for residential space. These problems created an environment conducive to strikes by African workers, such as those which rolled across the Durban and East Rand industrial areas in 1973.

Within government there were different views on urban policy. Punt Jansen, Deputy Minister of Bantu Administration and Development, suggested (and raised hopes of) reforms; and some BAABs even tried to secure house building in their own, far-from-reserve, areas — as the Orange-Vaal Board did.[15] But the trajectory of state involvement in the early 1970s continued away from the expansion of township housing. In African areas particularly, the vacuum created by the lack of state developmental activity was hardly filled by the minimal private sector involvement which otherwise might have altered conditions materially. In a few places some private sector firms had begun to involve themselves in house construction for employees, such as Southern Life at Pimville in the Soweto complex. But it was only after the escalation of violence from June 1976 that first private and then public sector thinking began to change.

By the end of 1976, Anglo-American and Rembrandt brought together a wide range of business interests and created the Urban Foundation (UF) with the intention both of piloting projects to alleviate oppressive urban conditions, and of attempting to influence urban policy. Both the widening cracks in existing policy and the disarray resulting from 1976 onwards provided opportunities to do so. The state also recognized the decay of the once-stable urban regime. Numerous commissions of inquiry were appointed, but the pace of urban change eclipsed minimal reform recommendations such as those of the Riekert Commission.[16]

Meanwhile, a veritable mushrooming of informal residence had occurred during the 1970s. No longer was that phenomenon a relatively minor adjunct of formal urbanization. In the reserves, the closer settlements — which had been a minor phenomenon in the mid-1960s — reached 3.7 million people by 1980, according to Simkins's[17] probably low estimate. One effect of this massive population growth was to strain beyond any capability the meagre resources of the new (but rapidly growing) bantustan administrations of the era. The results included desperate conditions such as extreme infant mortality rates. The formally planned, and properly serviced, residential areas within the reserves were completely overshadowed by informal, non-rural, population concentrations. These peculiar features of the landscape prompted the view prevalent in the literature that specific and conscious state actions, underpinned by an ideology called apartheid, 'contained' African urbanization — or, in later views, 'displaced' urbanization.[18]

Increasing bantustan populations delivered large numbers to the job queues at the rural labour bureaux. But, as labour demand stagnated in the late 1970s, rural labour bureaux ceased to have any substantial recruiting function at all, to the point where 'for many blacks in the rural area there is no labour market'.[19] For sheer survival, supposedly 'rural' households — huge numbers of which had no prospect of supporting themselves solely through rural activities — had to find access to urban economies.

Chaskalson[20] puts the consequence starkly: 'the African population … ignored influx control for over a decade'. Different households and different individuals found varying means of doing so, with implications ranging from backyard shacks in formal townships, to squatter communities beyond easy commuting distance from city labour markets.

The state's refusal to build houses in sufficient numbers to meet needs, and the exclusion of 'illegals' from official tenancy in formal townships, forced people to build for themselves. The poverty of the great majority meant that the results were often massively inadequate. The overcrowding of township houses may not have been as serious as some believe, but was in some cases reaching more than 40 persons per four-roomed house in some areas of the eastern Cape. The most serious overflow was reflected in the growth of shack populations in backyards and on open spaces in and around formal townships (35 000 people in Katlehong, for example, in 1980). In short, booms in domestic mine migrant labour recruitment, and often remote bantustan housing construction, could not shore up a crumbling regime of population management. A regime that had produced numerous bureaucratic problems and material difficulties for urban as well as rural people. It had also coexisted with the development of the quite unintended consequence of massive 'informal' population concentrations.

Urbanization and political crisis

In the late 1970s, the main state response to informal settlement by Africans outside the reserves was still to bulldoze. But as the enormity of the 'squatter' or informal residence problem began to impress itself on officialdom, increasing numbers of people established a measure of longevity of residence in shacks. Crossroads on the Cape Flats, for example, survived, grew, and developed a defiant and uncontrolled culture which challenged the bases of an earlier urban regime.

The massive growth of informal settlement in the 1980s demonstrated the failure of state policy towards urbanization over the preceding decades. But the condition and location of those settlements demonstrated the failure of the economy to provide for the basic needs of what has become a non-rural, but not always truly urban, population. This situation is most obvious in the shack areas around Durban and other cities, but prevails in further-flung 'rural slums' such as Botshabelo (45 kilometres east of Bloemfontein) and Kwandebele,[21] and even further afield. Hundreds of kilometres from the Pretoria-Witwatersrand-Vereeniging (PWV) triangle heartland of the highveld lie almost countless settlements which in their broad social character appear very similar to the better known, more centrally situated rural slums. Examples include the tentacles of settlement extending from Mafikeng, and the extraordinary growth of informal urbanism in districts like Nsikazi (Kangwane), or the area around Bushbuckridge. In Graaff's[22] view, by the start of the 1980s, many people had already moved to places where they will probably remain, even with substantial changes in constraints on their movement 'to town'.

The state, of course, has attempted to respond at various stages to these changes which constitute the core of recent urbanization in South Africa. Despite the consumption of many pages by academic literature on the subject, the development of state policy on urbanization in the late 1970s and early 1980s is still not well understood outside the corridors of power. The Riekert Commission's ideas of using access to approved housing as a specific control on urbanward movement were overwhelmed by material reality,[23] although some authors have persisted in treating the Riekert Commission's report as though it became policy. Riekert was indeed successful in rooting the notion of 'orderly urbanization' in government thinking, but considerable internal conflict lay between that stage and the repeal of the pass laws in 1986.

Contrary to the view espoused by Cobbett *et al.*,[24] the Department of Constitutional Development and Planning's system of 'development regions' would appear to have originated in competition with, rather than as a successor to, some of the ideas put forth by the Riekert Commission.[25] Other alternatives to influx control, which the state's planners recognized as a failure, were certainly considered. Along the lines pioneered by the administration board system in the 1970s, the idea that 'labour' might be free to move within development regions but constrained from moving between them, generated discussion in the early 1980s.[26] That application of the regional concept seems not to have taken root, however, and the suggestion of Cobbett *et al.* that the state incorporated such aspects into a comprehensive regional policy seems to have been 'overdrawn'.[27] In the event, influx control was abolished with no new policy to substitute for it, and despite the serious concern over such questions as the position of residents of the nominally independent bantustans — its abolition could, with a little hindsight, be taken as the start of the removal of the major features of apartheid.

This is not to say, however, that the abolition of the pass laws granted complete freedom of movement. An analysis of urbanization in the absence of influx control suggests that other political and material factors greatly affected the migration of Africans particularly.[28] A population constrained by racist and restrictive land allocation and private ownership of land found it nearly impossible to settle in most of South Africa. Fundamental to the growth of informal settlements is usually the question of finding places to live. The kinds of households which find informal residence the best option at present in South Africa would seem in very many cases to be those involved in patterns of circular migration, maintaining a variety of urban and rural bases.[29] Urbanization is not yet thoroughly understood as a result of this and other factors.

The essential point is that entire households have frequently not migrated as whole units, and while a base has been maintained by some members in rural (more recently simply non-formal urban) areas, other household members have moved to town, or indeed other rural areas, for longer or shorter periods. Many 'urban' households combined resources from both urban and rural activities.[30] Furthermore, the nature of the rural households from which migrants, short or long term, go to seek work in industry or town has always varied greatly — a variation which is crucial to understanding the past, present, and future pattern of settlement.[31] Recent research suggests that many households have every intention of persisting in their present circular patterns of migration,[32] but little policy or planning thought is yet being directed to the accommodation needs of this enormously significant section of South African society. The difficulties of the issues have begun to be faced largely through the strength of the union movement, both in the mines[33] and in some other industries (as evidenced in the joint hostel upgrading plans initiated by the National Union of Metalworkers of South Africa).

The seriousness of ignoring the social character of urbanization in policy formulation is underlined by the extent to which violence has come to be associated not only with the informal areas of various South African urban complexes, but also with the hostels. Tensions over access to limited material resources create a volatile environment. For example, in the Central Witwatersrand township of Thokoza, residents of a peripheral shack area known as Phola Park depended on taps at the adjacent male hostel for water, usually carried home by women. Hostel residents made much use of shebeens in Phola Park. In each situation tensions around female-male relationships, among other things, ensured a continuing high level of mutual suspicion. Whatever agency was responsible for provoking the conflicts of August and December 1990, that background allowed violence to escalate rapidly, with devastating results: much of Phola

Park was destroyed within days. Similarly, in parts of Soweto, parties of formal area residents as well as divided hostel communities participated in the destruction of many hostel facilities. The net result has been to leave many circular migrants with even more precarious access to affordable urban space than they had previously enjoyed. Half a decade of conflict in other informal settlements, whether in the western Cape or Natal,[34] speaks of a need to understand the urbanization processes producing those places much more closely than is currently the case, especially if planning is actually to contribute to securing improvement in their material conditions.

Community and state responses

In some townships, community organizations have responded to the pressing demand for relief of these oppressive material conditions by fostering invasions of open land. As in the experience of Latin America, the degree of political opening which characterizes South Africa in the early 1990s has encouraged such events. Civic associations in places as diverse as Mangaung (Bloemfontein) and Wattville (Benoni, east Witwatersrand) have planned and executed land invasions in which members of the township communities concerned have taken over land adjacent to the townships, and erected settlements. Through a variety of tactics, they have encouraged authorities such as local white town councils, development agencies such as the UF, and branches of the state such as provincial administrations to negotiate on their security, and even more significantly, on the provision of basic services to these new urban communities.[35]

Such disciplined reshaping of the urban environment through collective struggle renews the patterns of four or five decades ago, when movements like Sofasonke established new communities by land invasion adjacent to nascent Soweto and in the industrial areas of the Witwatersrand.[36] But these movements are not without their problems. Among other things, they tend to reinforce the broad apartheid geography of the cities rather than fundamentally challenging it. By establishing themselves next to the large townships created in the 1950s, the land invaders reinforce the pattern created under Verwoerd in the 1950s — the pattern of peripheral, segregated African residential areas — a pattern still vigorously enforced in the state's allocation of large tracts of land for legalized informal residence since the mid-1980s.

Using the provisions of section 6a of the amended Prevention of Illegal Squatting Act, minimally serviced areas have been opened to settlement in the hinterlands of the established townships. Orange Farm in the area between Soweto and Sebokeng, Motherwell across the Zwartkops river from the sprawling Port Elizabeth townships, and parts of Khayelitsha on the Cape Flats provide well-known illustrations, while many smaller towns and cities reveal similar patterns. Apartheid in this sense of the broad allocation of segregated, remote land to black urban residents is very much alive, although it is continuously challenged by 'squatters' who occupy land far from the approved townships. Through the actions of 'squatters', support groups, and even officials in places such as Hout Bay and Noordhoek in the Cape, Midrand in the Transvaal, and a few instances in Natal, processes are evident that may at last begin to break down the apartheid land allocation pattern.[37]

Conclusion

Moving into the 1990s, it appears that some social processes affecting urbanization, such as circular migration, may persist for substantial periods and prove little affected by policy changes. At the same time, informal urbanization has challenged authority and altered the make-up of the cities — it may yet challenge their whole structure.

In response to the emerging conditions of urbanism in South Africa, increasing numbers of actors attempt to influence policy over both the short and longer terms. Race no longer plays the central role in the formulation of policy that it once did,[38] and there is probably a greater diversity of approaches to urbanization now entering public debate than at any time since dreams of reconstructing South African society were debated in the closing years of World War 2 and its aftermath.

The 1990s seem set to be an epoch of conflict over urbanization. The critical question which confronts the country is whether that conflict will be conducted through negotiation, debate, election, even land invasion, and other relatively peaceful means, or whether violence — hitherto confined to some parts of the urban environment — will become all-consuming.

Notes

1 'Township' will mainly be used hereafter to refer to formally planned areas, usually separated by significant distances from the cities and towns in which their residents work and shop, intended by the authorities for African and other black occupation.

2 Hyslop J. 'Schools, Unemployment and Youth: Origins and Significance of Student and Youth Movements, 1976–87' (eds.) Nasson B. and Samuel J. *From Poverty to Liberty* (Cape Town: David Philip 1990) 82.

3 Gaffane M. 'Planning Implications of Persistent Circulatory Migration in a Development Environment: Focus on Northern Transvaal Migrants Working in Johannesburg', unpublished M.Sc. (development planning) discourse (Johannesburg: University of the Witwatersrand 1990).
Maluleka K. 'Migration, Urbanization and Development Policy: a Case Study on Implications for Planning in South Africa', unpublished B. Sc. (town planning) discourse (Johannesburg: University of the Witwatersrand 1990).

4 Including all those deemed other than white by the state.

5 The term 'bantustan' was current in the mid-1960s when the concept of creating and extending autonomous (racial) areas within South Africa was fairly new. In this paper the term 'reserves' will generally be preferred to 'homeland', 'national state', etc.

6 Hendler P. 'Capital Accumulation and the Residential Building Industry in the Townships 1980–85', unpublished M.A. dissertation (Johannesburg: University of the Witwatersrand 1986).

7 Mokobane P. 'Towards an Incremental Strategy for Housing in Seshego', unpublished M.Sc. (TRP) dissertation (Johannesburg: University of the Witwatersrand 1989).

8 Hindson D. *Pass Controls and the Urban African Proletariat* (Johannesburg: Ravan 1987).

9 Social and Economic Planning Council (1948) 21–2.

10 Platzky L. and Walker C. *The Surplus People: Forced Removals in South Africa* (Johannesburg: Ravan 1985).

11 Walker O. *Kaffirs Are Lively: Being Some Backstage Impressions of the South African Democracy* (London: Gollancz 1948).

12 Platzky and Walker (1985).

13 Zietsman H. L. 'Regional Patterns of Migration in the Republic of South Africa 1975–80' *South African Geographical Journal* (1988) 70 ii 97.

14 Bekker S. and Humphries R. *From Control to Confusion: the Changing Role of Administration Boards in South Africa, 1971–1983* (Pietermaritzburg: Shuter and Shooter 1985).

15 Chaskalson M. 'Apartheid with a Human Face: Punt Janson and the Origins of Reform in Townships Administration, 1972–1976', African Studies Institute seminar paper (Johannesburg: University of the Witwatersrand 1988).

16 Hindson (1987).

17 Simkins C. *Four Essays on the Past, Present and Possible Future Distribution of the Black Population of South Africa* (Cape Town: Southern Africa Labour and Development Research Unit, University of Cape Town 1983).

18 Fair T. J. D. and Schmidt C. 'Contained Urbanization: a Case Study' *South African*

Geographical Journal (1974) 56.

Letsoalo E. 'Displaced Urbanization: the Settlement System of Lebowa' *Development Studies Southern Africa* (1983) 5. Murray C. 'Displaced urbanization: South Africa's Rural Slums *African Affairs* (1987) 86.

19 Greenberg S. and Giliomee H. 'Managing Influx Control from the Rural End: the Black Homelands and the Underbelly of Privilege' (eds.) Giliomee H. and Schlemmer L. *Up Against the Fences* (Cape Town: Oxford University Press 1985).

20 Chaskalson (1988).

21 Murray (1987).

22 Graaff J. 'The Current State of Urbanization in the South African Homelands' *Development Southern Africa* (1987) 4 i.

23 Adam A. and Moodley K. *South Africa Without Apartheid: Dismantling Racial Domination* (Cape Town: Maskew Miller Longman 1986) 204.

24 Cobbett W., Glaser D., Hindson D., and Swilling M. 'South Africa's Regional Political Economy: a Critical Analysis of Reform Strategy in the 1980s' (ed.) *South African Research Service South African Review 3* (Johannesburg: Ravan Press 1986).

25 Thus the directorate of physical planning in the DCDP complained in 1984 that they had tried to convince other departments of the value of a regional approach since the early 1970s, 'Hersiening van die grense van die nasionale ontwikkelingstreke', annexure C to agenda for the meeting of the National Regional Development Advisory Council (2 August 1984) 9. The terms of reference of the Riekert Commission forced the commission to accept one regional boundary: that of the coloured labour preference area in the western Cape, which was regarded as inviolate at that stage.

26 SA Federated Chamber of Industries *Regional Development in South and Southern Africa* (Pretoria: 9 July 1984) 2.

27 McCarthy J. and Wellings P. 'The Regional Restructuring of Politics in Contemporary South Africa' *Social Dynamics* (1989) 15 i.

28 Mabin A. 'Struggle for the City: Urbanization and Political Strategies of the South African State' *Social Dynamics* (1989) 15 i.

29 Cobbett W. 'Trade Unions, Migrancy and the Struggle for Housing' (eds.) Moss G. and Obery I. *South African Review 5* (Johannesburg: Ravan Press 1989).

Mabin A. 'Limits of Urban Transition Models in Understanding South African Urbanization' *Development Southern Africa* (1990) 7 iii.

Simkins C. 'Population Policy' (ed.) Schrire R. *Critical Choices for South Africa: an Agenda for the 1990s* (Cape Town: Oxford University Press 1990) 223.

30 Martin W. and Beittel M. 'The Hidden Abode of Reproduction: Conceptualizing Households in Southern Africa' *Development and Change* (1987) 18.

31 Mabin (1989).

32 Gaffane (1990).

Mabin (1990).

Maluleka (1990).

Seekings J., Graaff J., and Joubert P., and Joubert P. *Survey of Residential and Migration Histories Of Residents of the Shack Areas of Khayelitsha* occasional paper 15 (Cape Town: Research Unit for the Sociology of Development, University of Stellenbosch 1990).

33 Crush J. 'Accommodating Black Mineworkers: Home-ownership on the Mines' (eds.) Moss G. and Obery I. *South African Review 5* (Johannesburg: Ravan Press

1989).

34　Cole J. *Crossroads* (Johannesburg: Ravan 1987).

　　Hughes H. 'Violence in Inanda, August 1985' *Journal of Southern African Studies* (1987) 13.

　　Kentridge M. *Unofficial War* (Cape Town: David Philip 1990).

35　Mabin A. and Klein G. 'Victories in the Struggle? Land Invasions and the Right to the City in South Africa' *Transformation* (forthcoming).

36　Bonner P. 'The Politics of Black Squatter Movements on the Rand, 1944–1952' *Radical History Review* (1990) 46 vii.

37　In these new African communities, the overwhelming majority of residents would appear to come from existing townships rather than directly from rural areas. It is common cause that most population growth in South African urban communities is supplied internally. Indeed, the peak era of African migration from rural areas to the cities, which probably began in the late 1970s, seems to have subsided by the time influx control was abolished in 1986 (Urban Foundation, 1990).

38　Swilling M. 'Deracialized Urbanization: a Critique of the New Urban Strategies and Some Policy Perspectives from a Democratic Perspective' *Urban Forum* (1990) 1 ii.

4 Managing the coloured and Indian areas

Rob Cameron

Introduction

This chapter looks at the structure and functioning of management committees (MCs) and local affairs committees (LACs), which are advisory coloured[1] and Indian local bodies. Most of the attention will be focused on coloured local authorities, seeing that this 'racial' group consists of about 11 per cent of the country's population, as opposed to the Indian total of about three per cent.

Three phases can be identified in the evolution of these structures. The first phase is the genesis and development of MCs/LACs, a period in which these bodies struggled to be recognized by their mother white local authorities (WLAs), and accordingly had little input into policy. The second phase is that of the tricameral system from 1984 to 1989. Co-option of coloureds and Indians was an important part of the state's strategy in this period, and accordingly measures were introduced to improve their position *vis-à-vis* their mother WLAs. This led to a rise in their status and powers. The third phase is what can be termed the demise of MCs/LACs. The unbanning of previously prohibited organizations has unleashed a new political dynamic which has swept the ground out from under these racially based bodies. This final section will also discuss alternative forms of representation that could be adopted in a post-apartheid South Africa.

History and development

The struggle for recognition

When the NP was elected to power in 1948, the different racial qualifications for coloureds and Indians in the various provinces were as
follows:
- In the Transvaal and OFS, only whites were able to vote and
  stand for election at municipal level;[2] in the Cape, coloureds and
  Indians had technically been on the same legal footing since 1836.
  They appeared on the same voters' roll as whites, and had to fulfil
  the same voting qualifications.
- In Natal, both coloureds and Indians were on the voters' roll and
  could stand for election. However, the system of electoral representation was property ownership of a certain value. This effectively debarred the majority of coloureds and Indians from eligibil-
  ity to vote. There were further restrictions affecting the ability of
  Indians to vote in Natal.[3]

Racially integrated local authorities were contrary to the Nationalist
policy of having separate political structures for different racial
groups. The genesis of separate local government structures was the
Group Areas Act of 1950, which made provision for separate residential areas and for the eventual introduction of separate local government structures for coloured and Indian areas. However, no active
steps were taken to introduce separate local government structures
until 1961, when the Niemand Committee of Investigation was
appointed to investigate the development of local government for
coloureds in urban areas. As a result of its recommendations, the
Group Areas Amendment Bill of 1962 was introduced, which made
provision for three phases in the development of coloured and
Indian local government. The three phases were:
- Consultative committees, which consisted of nominated members
  having advisory powers only and functioning under close official
  guidance from the WLA where they were geographically situated.
- MCs, which were partly elected and partly nominated, also having
  advisory powers, but in addition certain powers could be dele-
  gated to them by their mother WLAs. (MCs were called LACs in
  Natal.)
- Fully-fledged municipal status equivalent to WLAs.
  Before this happened, an investigation was needed by a special

committee which recommended whether or not an MC should become a local authority. Certain essential prerequisites, such as sufficient revenue, trained staff, minimum area size, and a capacity for geographical consolidation, had to be fulfilled before an MC could take this step.

Although the Minister of Community Development[4] was ultimately responsible for the development of coloured and Indian local government, its practical application was the responsibility of different provinces, each of which adopted its own ordinances and framed regulations for this purpose.

The consultative stage was soon dropped, and MCs/LACs were created for most coloured and Indian communities under the tutelage of their mother WLAs from 1964 onwards. MC/LAC administrative staff are employed by their mother WLA.[5] This new form of coloured representation co-existed with direct representation on WLAs in the Cape until 1971 when a provincial ordinance changed the voting requirements, so that only those who were registered as parliamentary voters (i.e. whites) could now register as municipal voters.

Coloured citizens who were registered municipal voters in October 1971 in the Cape could, however, retain their franchise provided that an MC had not yet been created in their area. In Natal, it was decided in 1956 that no new coloured names could be added to the voters' roll. This, together with the already mentioned restrictions on Indian voters dating back to 1924, effectively disenfranchised coloured and Indian voters.[6]

Only four Indian LACs — Verulam, Isipingo, Marburg, and Umzinto North — in the whole country have evolved into independent local authorities. No coloured MC or LAC has ever evolved into an independent local authority.[7] Various commissions into coloured local government highlighted the reasons for this lack of evolution. The Roussow Report of 1960 found that no coloured area in greater Cape Town was in a position to become an independent local government. The most important reasons for this were their lack of viability because most coloured and Indian areas are characterized by little or no rate-generating commercial and industrial areas. In addition, they are dominated by low-rateable, low-cost housing, a shortage of trained staff, a lack of suitable candidates for elected office, and the fact that for town planning reasons local authorities treated coloured areas as an integral part of their jurisdiction. The Botha Report of 1971 came to the same conclusion. Indian local areas were subject to the same constraints.[8]

The mandate of the Theron Commission was to investigate all facets of coloured life, including local government. The commission found that MCs, as a system, had largely been a failure. The main reasons for this were:

- A lack of executive powers. This meant that such bodies were toothless and, as a result, ineffective.
- Especially in the more educated urban areas, coloureds were opposed to apartheid structures and wanted direct representation on WLAs.
- There were jurisdictional and structural problems, such as geographical fragmentation of coloured areas, that were impediments to such bodies becoming viable entities.
- There was often a lack of mutual goodwill between WLAs and their MCs.
- The fact that the Coloured Persons' Representative Council (CPRC)[9] and provincial administrations had concurrent jurisdiction led to ineffective co-ordination of the system.[10]

The Schlebusch Commission was appointed by the Cape Provincial Administration (CPA) in 1978 to investigate the functioning of the MC system in the Cape province, with a view to delegating extra powers to these bodies. This was a response to complaints by ASSOMAC (Association of Management Committees, the representative body for coloured and Indian MCs in the Cape) that local authorities were ignoring their legitimate requests. Coloured members on this commission argued that the system had been imposed upon them and lacked effective powers. The commission also found that the system was being used for political motives, which was a hindrance to its proper functioning, and that members of such bodies were inadequately trained.[11]

Finally, another reason for this lack of progress was that MCs/LACs, through their various provincial representative bodies as well as major coloured and Indian political parties who controlled most of these bodies, have always rejected separate representation. They argue that participation in these structures is a short-term strategy in order to achieve their ultimate goal, namely non-racial representation on white city councils.[12]

The tricameral system, 1984–9

The rise of management committees

The formation of the House of Representatives and House of Delegates (for coloureds and Indians respectively) after the 1984 elections gave MCs/LACs much greater clout in their negotiations with local authorities. These local structures for coloureds and Indians have MPs at central level, and at one time had members in the cabinet taking up the cudgels on their behalf. However, access *per se* is not sufficient to ensure greater influence. It is contended that the reason for this greater influence is due to the fact that the interests of the government and the coloured and Indian political parties converged on the issue of giving these representatives greater say in the running of their own areas.

From the state's side, one of the major aims of its 'total strategy' was to strengthen the powers of the white minority government by incorporating significant elements of the coloured and Indian sectors into the ruling fortress. The promotion of coloured and Indian representatives at all levels of government accordingly became an important objective.

More specifically, MCs/LACs were a critical element in the whole 'own affairs' policy. In addition, the MCs/LACs became the building blocks of the Regional Services Councils (RSCs) and have consequently been promoted by the state.

To understand the perspective of the major coloured and Indian political parties, one has to examine the close relationship between national MPs and MCs/LACs that are dominated by the Labour Party (LP). The latter's policy is 'to keep a tight grip on MCs to derive maximum political benefit for the party'.[13] The committees were the power base of the party after the dissolution of the CPRC and many of its MPs graduated from their ranks. Minister of Local Government in the House of Representatives, D. Curry, was also president of ASSOMAC for a number of years. Similarly, a number of House of Delegates' MPs graduated from the ranks of LACs. For a while, a number of coloured and Indian MPs — including the chairpersons of the Ministers' Councils of both the House of Representatives and House of Delegates, A. Hendrickse and A. Rajbansi respectively — were simultaneously members of MCs/LACs. All these factors ensured that most of these bodies were controlled by the major coloured third-tier structures in the country, while both the National People's Party (NPP) and Solidarity had a number of Indian local bodies under their informal control.

The thinking of these coloured and Indian political parties was that any increase in the powers of the MCs/LACs would give the latter bodies greater scope to promote patronage and increasingly broaden their support. This, it was hoped, would lead to greater legitimacy for all coloured and Indian participants in government structures, given the fact that most MCs/LACs were controlled by the major political parties.

Constitutional parameters

One of the guidelines that underpinned the new constitution was that 'separate local authorities be constituted for the various population groups wherever possible, but subject to the requirement that effective financial arrangements should be made to ensure the viability of these authorities'.[14] This was encapsulated in the RSA Constitution Act of 1983 which made provision for a tricameral system with white, coloured, and Indian chambers deciding exclusively on matters of 'own affairs', subject to the existence of any general policy on general law, and jointly on matters of 'general affairs'.

Local government was one of the functions that was decreed an 'own affair'. Accordingly, local government now became the responsibility of central government. In each chamber a department of local government was created to control constitutionally these ethnic local authorities. The Houses of Representatives and Delegates have thus far refused to assent to the transfer of these powers, seeing this arrangement as an extension of 'own affairs' and apartheid.

Management committee powers

Until 1984, WLAs were obliged to consult MCs/LACs on a number of matters affecting their areas, but were under no obligation to accept their advice. This led to a great deal of frustration within MCs/LACs. For years they felt their requests were ignored by WLAs. Eventually a change was made in the legislation to give MCs/LACs a greater say. Directives issued in 1984, in terms of the Promotion of Local

Government Affairs Act of 1983, made provision for interim regulations to improve communications between white councils and
MCs/LACs, and to allow the latter greater participation in their own
areas. This act did not confer decision-making powers on the committees; it listed seven regulations, of which it was obligatory for
white councils to adopt at least one.[15]

However, certain local authorities dragged their heels in implementing these measures. MCs/LACs now had support at central level
in the form of the Houses of Representatives and Delegates, which
put pressure on the government to give MCs/LACs decision-making
powers, with Curry arguing that obstructionism by WLAs could lead
to the sabotaging of the new constitutional deal.[16] Accordingly, the
Local Government Affairs Amendment Act of 1985 was promulgated.
This made provision for MCs/LACs to acquire certain final decision-
making powers. This was not a conferment of separate municipal
status. It in no way nullified existing provincial legislation, which
gave Administrators power to set up MCs/LACs. It was intended to
be only an interim measure until the impediments to setting up
coloured and Indian local governments had been addressed. Nor
were these powers granted automatically. If an MC/LAC wanted
these powers, it had to petition the Administrator, who in turn had to
conduct an investigation to determine the feasibility of such a
request. Among the powers that MCs/LACs could acquire were:

• the allocation of business licences;
• the allocation of houses and eviction of tenants;
• the approval and planning of new housing schemes and the final
  say in the leasing and utilization of immovable property.[17]

A number of MCs/LACs requested these powers in 1986. However,
matters then reached a standstill. The problems were that, firstly, the
decisions of MCs/LACs could have financial and legal consequences
which could involve their mother local authorities; and secondly,
there was concern about the effect this fragmentation would have on
the rendering of municipal services. The matter was investigated by a
special Action Committee of the Co-ordinating Council for Local
Government Affairs, and as a result 106 functions which could be
delegated to MCs/LACs were listed in the Government Gazette in
May 1988. This list comprises a comprehensive set of functions
which, if delegated to MCs/LACs, would give them powers almost
comparable to WLAs without being divorced *in toto* from the mother
municipality. These powers included the power to allocate new
houses and evict tenants, appoint coloured and Indian staff, make

grants-in-aid, approve building plans, levy tariffs for municipal services and property rates, etc. These powers were not delegated automatically. They depended on the willingness and capability of the respective MCs/LACs to perform such functions.[18]

The LP was in favour of MCs/LACs acquiring these extra decision-making powers. Curry said that 'until direct representation on local government becomes a reality the transfer of final decision-making powers to MCs is the name of the game'.[19] In particular, he saw MCs/LACs having decision-making powers in respect of development, namely housing and urban upgrading, but he rejected the creation of separate administrations and infrastructures for these communities. This arrangement enabled these bodies to utilize their respective WLAs' staff in development projects. It would not involve taking over local authorities' traditional functions such as water and electricity supply.[20]

The enthusiasm for those 106 powers was not shared by all at coloured and Indian local government level. A previous attempt to foist extra decision-making powers on to LACs was rejected by the Natal Association of Local Affairs Committees (NALAC) because it viewed this as a step towards eventual independent ethnic local authorities. Solidarity, in particular, was fiercely opposed to these powers, seeing them as a way of entrenching racial separateness.[21] In the western Cape, a number of urban MCs have so far shied away from accepting these extra powers. MCs which have accepted such powers are generally the smaller, rural areas such as Danielskuil, Hawston, and Victoria West.[22]

This opposition to the 106 powers is, however, perhaps grandstanding to counter left-wing criticism that the MCs/LACs are moving towards racially based independent local authorities. Many local authorities have already informally delegated extensive powers to their MCs/LACs.

A possible reason for the formal rejection but the informal acceptance of greater decision-making powers is that the formal acceptance of these powers would lead to MCs/LACs being given their own budgets within their broader mother local authority's budget. This would entail a measure of financial self-sufficiency. Seeing that most committees are subsidized by their mother WLA, it could put the members in the politically unenviable position of having to reduce the standard of services, or to increase rent charges. The informal acceptance of powers means that these bodies still have the best of both worlds, namely a great deal of say over the running of their areas, as well as subsidization from the general rates fund within the WLAs.

Co-ordinating council for local government affairs

The primary function of the co-ordinating council (CC) is to advise the government on the co-ordination of local authority functions of general interest. The 'own affairs' ministers of local government, as well as the secretary of the National Ad Hoc Committee of the Association of Coloured and Indian Consultative, Local Affairs and MCs, have *ex-officio* representation on the CC.[23]

All local government issues requiring legislative changes are first referred to the CC for recommendation. The CC has generally operated in a top-down fashion, being dominated by minister Chris Heunis. Notwithstanding this, because of the convergence of interests between the government and the major coloured and Indian political parties, the council generally has been rather susceptible to the demands of coloured and Indian representatives. Issues such as the delegation of the 106 powers, greater remuneration and pension benefits for MC/LAC members, and prior votes for the 1988 municipal elections, all originated from coloured and Indian representatives.[24]

The role of the 'own affairs' ministries

There is what a senior official in the Department of Local Government, House of Representatives, called a 'wailing wall' section of the department where complaints from MCs/LACs are heard. These are mostly problems dealing with their relationships with WLAs. The House of Representatives and the provinces attempt to play a peacemaking role in these disputes.[25] This arrangement gives these local bodies a certain amount of leverage in their deliberations with the mother WLAs.

Another manifestation of this greater access is that the minutes of meetings of coloured MCs/LACs are forwarded to the House of Representatives for scrutiny.

Problems which are identified are referred to the relevant authorities for attention.[26] Some local authorities, in the spirit of the government's evolutionary reform policy, have willingly involved these bodies in policy-making to a greater extent than before. Other local authorities have been forced, due to these new structural arrangements, to give greater recognition to these committees.

In a number of local authorities such as Port Elizabeth, Stellenbosch, Johannesburg, the western Cape RSC (in respect of ex-divisional council local areas), WLAs delegated powers down to local authorities. Even anti-apartheid local authorities like Cape Town, which have traditionally regarded MCs as an extension of the apartheid policy that has been imposed upon the council, have had to give these bodies greater recognition. Although there has been no formal delegation of any powers, local authorities have greater input into their budgets and are consulted more adequately about activities in their areas than was previously the case. If the Cape Town City Council (CCC) will not allocate House of Representative funds in accordance with MC wishes, the funds are withheld by the government department. Furthermore, certain council decisions have to go to the Administrator for final approval, e.g. township development. Although the CCC can legally reject a committee's advice in respect of these items, the Administrator would not approve the items unless the MC has agreed with the recommendations.[27]

Service delivery

Coloured and Indian housing is now constitutionally controlled by the Houses of Representatives and Delegates respectively. Each house has created its own Housing Board. All local authorities that receive funds for coloured and Indian housing have to go through these Housing Boards. Functional control of housing is carried out by local authorities on an agency basis for these departments which also have money available for urban upgrading. It means that there are more channels open to coloured and Indian areas to get funds for development (although the amount available is still hopelessly inadequate, given the backlog of housing and facilities). This structural relationship also gives MCs/LACs greater influence in their deliberations with WLAs. A good example of this greater access was when Curry threatened to withdraw financial support from councils which did not involve their MCs in the planning, construction, and allocation of housing.[28]

Free settlement areas

A late development during this era was the promulgation of the Free Settlement Areas Act which established the principle of open residential areas, subject to an investigation of the Free Settlement Board. This was partially due to the fact that certain white areas had become *de facto* mixed, owing to an influx of people from other so-called race groups. A related act makes provision for multiracial bodies to represent residents in free settlement areas. They are identical in status and power to existing MCs, except that they are multiracial in nature. To date, no such bodies have been created.[29]

The demise of MCs/LACs and future options

Although the demise of MCs/LACs was characterized as from 1990 onwards, evidence of their decline was already apparent in 1989. While the results of the 1988 municipal elections represented a stand-off in the sense that there was no clear victor when it came to the issue of participation, they must nevertheless be considered the apogee of both MC/LAC existence and LP participation in government structures in the 1980s.[30] On the other hand, the 1989 general election was clearly a major setback for the LP. Although it won 69 of the 80 House of Representative seats, the average poll had dropped from 30.9 per cent in 1984 to 17.6 per cent in 1989. While the electorate did not necessarily vote on national issues in the 1988 election, given the symbiotic relationship between MCs and the LP, it was felt that a setback for the latter at national level could quite feasibly have adverse implications for its local power base.[31]

This became evident in 1990. The major reason for this decline was the unbanning of hitherto prohibited organizations which unleashed a new political dynamic in the country. A new degree of assertiveness was evident in black townships throughout the country. Demands for the resignation of MCs and the creation of non-racial municipalities became the clarion call in a number of coloured areas, including previously unpoliticized rural areas in the Boland.[32] In some towns, MCs resigned under political pressure from protesting groups in local communities.[33] These attacks on the MC system began to erode traditional LP support. According to a poll by the Human Rights Trust, support for the LP in its northern areas stronghold in Port Elizabeth dropped to about 8 per cent, and 70 per cent of the people who supported the party in the 1989 election switched allegiances. Further, 41 per cent of the respondents now support the ANC/MDM alliance.[34]

The current degree of support for collaborationist Indian parties is less clear. However, it is likely that their support has also been eroded by recent developments.

While the main characteristic of the tricameral system, namely greater access, still remains, MCs are having their feet whipped out from under them by both developments at national level and resistance from below. It seems clear that these little-loved bodies are likely to be scrapped, at least in most of the country. Under State President F. W. de Klerk, the state is moving beyond racially segregated municipalities. It has already committed itself to allowing representatives of all 'population' groups at all levels of government. According to reports, 'own affairs' departments are being downgraded and will eventually be scrapped,[35] and on 13 December 1990, De Klerk announced his support for the 'one city, one tax base' policy.

Given that MCs are ready to be largely confined to the dustheap of history, what does the future hold for local representation in coloured and Indian areas? The CC recommended in May 1990 that five models of local government should receive further discussion and negotiation:

- Separate local authorities for the population groups with own areas of jurisdiction, with the provision that racially separate cities would be allowed where financially viable.
- A mini-RSC, with a joint administration constituted by autonomous local authorities and local bodies, which takes some decisions together.
- A Joint Local Authority constituted by neighbourhood MCs on a non-racial basis.
- A simple majoritarian model with or without protection for minorities.
- Any other locally negotiated model.[36]

This recommendation has been accepted in principle by the government. How does this affect coloured local government, and which are democratically and economically the most viable options?

The first option is likely to be widely rejected as an extension of apartheid, with the possible exception of a few smaller local authorities.

The second option is an extension of the general affairs principle to primary level authority level, namely, separate racial local authorities will continue to exist but a joint administration will carry out some tasks on behalf of all areas. This option is also likely to be given short shrift by representative coloured leaders. However, such an option is likely to make more finance and qualified staff available to coloured areas, which in turn is likely to improve the quality of service provision.

The third option is a non-racial local government with certain powers devolved to sub-municipal units called neighbourhood committees. The CC does not deal with this model adequately, proposing a system that would perpetuate racial inequalities. It is, however, suggested that consideration be given to adopting a more progressive variant of this model, whereby such units have control over certain functions and budgetary powers, as well as having the right to veto developmental proposals for their area. (There would, however, be one common tax base in cities which such sub-municipal units would share.) This participatory option should be considered precisely because of the shortcomings of the fourth option, namely, the city-wide majoritarian model. These are: firstly, larger local authorities are structured around the committee system, which in turn is centred on the operational requirements of services rather than the needs and problems of the community.[37] Although councillors are elected on a ward basis, there is often not enough scope to represent such neighbourhood interests once represented on council. Councillors tend to get sucked into city-wide issues at the expense of their ward concerns.

Secondly, there are problems with centralized bureaucratic service delivery. The traditional bureaucratic principles on which departments are structured are:
• the principle of hierarchy, ensuring clear lines of accountability and control;
• the principle of uniformity, ensuring that policies and procedures of the authority are applied on the same basis throughout the area of the authority;
• the functional principle by which the work of the authority is divided up according to the staff expertise.

Internationally, these principles have come under fierce criticism. It has been argued that traditional forms of service delivery showed a lack of elasticity and a focus on procedure rather than substantial delivery. This has led to unresponsive and uncaring bureaucracies. Decentralized modes of delivery challenge these traditional modes of representation. Decentralization permits a diversity of response, rather than uniformity of practice. Decentralization of decision-making lessens the need for hierarchical control. Organization by area challenges functional organization.[38]

What about the tax base, given the backlog of housing and facilities in many coloured and Indian areas? Although the non-racial cities are up for negotiation among all 'race groups', a shared tax base is a *sine qua non* for any locally negotiated settlement. This will ensure a certain amount of intra-city redistribution. However, most WLAs have only limited resources to undertake development. Furthermore, RSC funds are insufficient to undertake all the necessary upgrading, and housing is not a regional function. Some form of central subsidization still seems necessary for most local authorities. This could be done on a needs-based formula. Furthermore, in terms of this model, qualified staff would be made available to both non-racial city governments and sub-municipal units, which should improve the nature of the service delivery.

Concluding then, it is suggested that the way forward, not only for coloured and Indian local structures but also for local government generally, is to pursue a decentralized model which also makes provision for extensive subsidization of areas where the greatest development is needed.

Notes

1 The use of the term 'coloured' is for the sake of brevity. It does not imply the acceptance of such an ethnic category.
2 Indians were denied rights of residence in the Orange Free State.
3 Republic of South Africa. 'Structure and Functioning of Local Authorities in South Africa'. Unpublished report submitted to joint report of the committee for economic affairs and the constitutional committee of the President's Council on local and regional management systems (Cape Town: Government Printer 1982a) 18–23.
4 These powers were later transferred to the Minister of Coloured Affairs.
5 Cloete J. J. N. *Central, Regional and Local Government Institutions of South Africa* (Pretoria: Van Schaik 1988) 44–6.
Evans S. *New Management Committees in Local Government: an Introduction* (Cape Town: Juta 1969) 97–9.
Republic of South Africa (1982a) 19–25.
Van Rooyen A. 'A History of Local Government in South Africa'. Paper presented at the Institute of Social and Economic Research Seminar 'Does Local Government Really Matter?' (Grahamstown: Rhodes University 1987) 3–4.
6 Craythorne D. L. 'Metropolitan Local Government for Greater Cape Town'. Unpublished Ph.D. thesis (Cape Town: University of Cape Town 1982) 46.
Republic of South Africa (1982a) 18–23.
7 There is one independent coloured local authority, namely Pacaltsdorp, but it did

not arrive at this position via the MC route. It had been under the control of its own village management board since 1886 and became independent in 1975. Republic of South Africa (1982a) 20.

8　Craythorne (1982) 35–60.

9　The CPRC was a representative body for coloureds at a central level, having merely advisory powers. With its dissolution in 1979, these powers reverted to the provincial administrations.
See the joint report of the Committee for Economic Affairs and the Constitutional Committee of the President's Council on local and regional management systems (Cape Town: Government Printer 1982) 28.

10　Theron Commission 'Report of the Commission of Inquiry into Matters Relating to the Coloured Population Group' (Pretoria: Government Printer 1976) 440–3.

11　President's Council (1982) 33–41.

12　See Hansard (17 June 1987) 986–9 for the Labour Party's policy in this regard.

13　*Cape Times* 24 June 1985.

14　Republic of South Africa 'Constitutional Guidelines: a New Dispensation for Whites, Coloureds and Indians' (Pretoria: Government Printer 1982) 9.

15　Cameron R. G. 'The Cape Town City Council. A Public Policy Analysis 1976–1986' *Politikon* (1988a) 15 i 56.

16　Cameron (1988a) 56.

17　Cameron R. G. 'The Administration and Politics of the Cape Town City Council, 1976–1986'. Unpublished Master of Public Administration thesis (Cape Town: University of Cape Town 1986) 121–2.

18　Republic of South Africa 'Delegation of Powers to Coloured and Indian Management and Local Affairs Committees by Local Authorities' *Government Gazette* (Pretoria: Government Printer 13 May 1988) 11298, 317.

19　Correspondence between D. Curry and the Cape Town City Council on the shortage of land for housing (Cape Town: 1988).

20　Hansard (20 March 1989) 3433–6; (17 June 1989) 948.

21　*Network* 18 October 1988.

22　See the House of Representatives' annual report (Pretoria: Government Printer 1987).

23　See the annual report of the Council for the Co–ordination of Local Government Affairs (Pretoria: Government Printer 1986) 1–3.

24　Cameron R. G. 'Local Government Policy–making in the 1980s. The Formation and Adoption Process'. Unpublished paper (Cape Town: 1990).

25　See the annual report of the House of Representatives (Pretoria: Government Printer 1985).

26　House of Representatives (1985) 1.

27　Cameron R. G. 'The Structure and Functioning of Coloured Local Authorities under the Tricameral System'. Unpublished paper (Cape Town: 1988b).

28　Cameron (1988b).

29　Republic of South Africa 'Free Settlement Areas Act' (Pretoria: Government Printer 1988) 152.
Republic of South Africa 'Local Government Affairs in Free Settlement Areas Act' (Pretoria: Government Printer 1988) 133.

30　Cameron R. G. 'An Analysis of the 1988 Coloured Municipal Elections in the Western Cape'. Unpublished paper (Cape Town: 1988c).

31　Cameron R. G. 'The House of Hard Labour. Counting the Non–vote 1984–1989'

Indicator (1989) 6 iv 30–2.

32 *The Argus* 2 June 1990.

33 *The Argus* 23 June 1990.

34 *South* 29 May 1990.

35 *Sunday Star* 20 May 1990; *Cape Times* 29 May 1990.

36 *The Argus* 29 May 1990.

37 Stewart J. 'The Changing Organization and Management of Local Authorities' in Stewart J. and Stoker G. (eds.) *The Future of Local Government* (Hampshire: MacMillan 1989) 171–84.

38 Stewart J. 'Has Decentralization Failed?' *Local Government Policy–making* (1987) 14 ii 49–50.

5 Black local authorities: a contraption of control

Khehla Shubane

The 1980s represent a decade which witnessed the beginning of the decline of apartheid. An examination of local government for the African population best illustrates this. In the 1980s, new forms of local government for the urban section of the African population were conceded. The black local authorities (BLAs), introduced in 1982, represented a significant, but insufficient, improvement in the forms of local government for the African communities in the urban townships. Although introduced within the framework of apartheid, for the first time the BLAs offered a measure of control of the institutions of local government to African urban communities.[1] The contradiction which arose from conceding a municipal franchise to urban Africans while tying them to bantustans for the exercise of a national franchise, served to heighten the already rising tide of radical anti-apartheid struggle and gave it a focus. Civic associations which started emerging in various townships in the late 1970s mobilized increasing numbers of people in opposition to the introduction of BLAs and the nature of the apartheid city. Many civic associations were formed in response to the introduction of BLAs.

This chapter focuses on the foregoing issues and seeks to account for why the institutions of local government for township communities are essentially part of the apartheid system. The argument advanced in the first section aims to show that institutions of local government for the urban African community are historically a product of the country's colonial past. The second section periodizes the short but tumultuous history of the BLAs. The final section looks at community organizations whose struggles have, in part, determined the course of these institutions.

Township local government

Local government for the African population was historically conceived and implemented chiefly as a control mechanism.[2] Initially this control was exercised directly through officials appointed by white municipalities under whose administrative aegis local government for Africans existed.[3] Later, this control was shifted to the government.[4] Until 1982 with the introduction of BLAs, institutions of local government for the African townships were run by these officials. The control function of these institutions is historically rooted in the colonial framework within which they originated. In turn this framework is a legacy of the way in which South Africa was 'decolonized'. South African decolonization followed a similar pattern to that of Australia and Canada — it took the form of the colonial power giving political power exclusively to the white population. For the indigenous populations in all three colonies, power relations remained essentially unchanged. The local white communities which had held political power anyway, albeit for the colonial power, formed the new governments.[5]

It is in this context that institutions of local government for the African population were conceived. This was the case, too, with other political, social, and economic institutions for Africans. These institutions have never escaped their historical origins. The BLAs still bear the scars of their colonial origins. This is manifest in the role townships play in relation to white areas. The former remain essentially labour reservoirs for the labour needs of industries located within the boundaries of white municipalities. In the past 15 years, townships have also increasingly played a role in providing a market for the manufacturing sector of the economy. The location in the white areas of all the major commercial and industrial businesses serves to perpetuate the colonial relationship between townships and white towns, where the latter are centres of power, both economic as well as political. This colonial relationship originated in colonial conquest and has been maintained through deliberate policies pursued by successive white governments, reflecting the broader politico-power relations between whites on the one hand, and the rest of the population on the other.

It is the nature of this relationship which lies at the root of the revenue problems which confront the BLAs. Township local government finances its operations from a limited revenue base.[6] The location of major business concerns within the boundaries of white municipalities, and the resultant lack of these facilities in the townships, have given rise to the virtual absence of a tax base. Thus township municipalities depend largely on rents and service charges levied on residents. This has placed an intolerable financial burden on poor township residents[7] and is undoubtedly the most significant cause of the rent boycotts which seek to redress the inequalities imposed on the townships by the nature of the apartheid city. The apartheid logic imposed municipal boundaries which separated functionally united areas along racial lines.

The belated inclusion of BLAs (announced in late 1984) into the RSCs — which were initially designed for groups in the tricameral parliament — was aimed at alleviating the revenue crisis that they were experiencing. Although their inclusion into the RSCs brought some relief to the BLAs, it failed to resolve the basic problem. The long-term solution to the revenue problems of township municipalities lies in a solution which breaks with the colonial framework within which local government in South Africa has historically remained trapped.

Politically, apartheid in local government functioned through BLAs to create institutions which provided the government with a forum to enlist the support of conservative sections of the township communities. The BLAs, like the bantustans earlier, made available potentially powerful institutions within which some sections of the township communities could express themselves politically, and at the same time it offered a vehicle for upward social mobility for aspirant business people. The introduction of the BLAs coincided with the relaxation of regulations which prohibited ownership of houses. This latter measure opened the way for the emergence of a class of entrepreneurs associated with that industry. It also facilitated corruption among councillors who began to appreciate opportunities available to them as land and houses became commercialized. This came to be a particularly sore point with community organizations which embraced anti-corruption struggles within their broad opposition to BLAs.

Fundamentally, however, BLAs were politically unacceptable to the majority of people they were meant to serve. This rejection rested on the unacceptability of apartheid-creating structures in which the participation of the oppressed could be secured. In the view of many people in the townships and anti-apartheid organizations, legitimate institutions of power could only rest upon the will of all the people of South Africa. BLAs reflected only the will of the white government which had legislatively created them. Those who served in them and purported to be representing the will of the people were rejected and treated with the utmost contempt. Herein lies the critical motivating factor which has driven those who have not stopped at anything in their desire to rid township communities of the BLAs.

Any discussion of BLAs must also take into account the role they played in the accelerated class fragmentation which occurred among township communities.[8] Together with broader restructuring processes introduced by the state in the late 1970s, the advent of BLAs facilitated an important process of class stratification among urban Africans. The middle classes which formed as a result of these processes had an impact on social as well as political developments in the townships. The BLAs played a role in this process by providing institutions around which a new type of middle class formed. Individuals whose rise to middle-class positions was facilitated by the BLA tended to be hostile to radical programmes of local community organizations which rejected BLAs. This middle class is typically a bureaucratic petite bourgeoisie.[9] Individuals within it have the least chance of increasing their wealth because of the hostile environment in which this group has to conduct their business. The growth of township struggles has impacted negatively on business generally in these areas, but has been singularly devastating on business people with links to the BLAs. Boycott campaigns, as well as the actual destruction of their businesses, have ruined many within this sector of the middle class. These limitations, together with those structurally determined by apartheid, set serious constraints particularly on this sector of the township middle class. Resignations from the BLAs, which have become endemic in the history of these institutions, have been accelerated by the desire of some councillors to save their businesses from physical destruction by communities calling for the dissolution of BLAs.

Periodization of the BLAs

In the period during which the BLAs have existed, three distinct phases can be identified. This periodization is linked to and has influenced the history of these structures considerably:

- 1982–4 was the period during which the BLAs were introduced. Vigorous campaigns against these structures were led by civic associations, many of which were formed during this time.

- 1985–9 was marked by the increased use of force to protect BLAs from community struggles which had gained momentum.
- 1989–90 was characterized by a political thaw in the country which saw negotiations between some civic associations and state officials. Hopes of constructing a new local government policy increased. The rejection of BLAs, however, continued unabated.

1982–4

From the time of their emergence, BLAs were faced with a strong movement calling for people not to avail themselves for participation in these structures. When the first BLA elections were held in 1983, the same movement campaigned for boycotts of the elections. The new forms of local government for townships, and the introduction of the tricameral parliament, were the most important steps taken by a government whose rise to and subsequent stay in power rested on a commitment to the maintenance of apartheid.

The first phase in the life of the BLAs was characterized by boycott campaigns which, nevertheless, failed to prevent the election of the councils in many townships. Polls were, however, low. In Soweto it was 10.7 per cent of registered voters in wards which were contested. The figure for Evaton in the Vaal Triangle was 5.9 per cent. A 36.6 per cent poll in Kagiso in the West Rand was the highest attained for any township in the election.[10] With elections over, the various councillors were then faced with demands for their resignation. The first resignations occurred in Lingelihle in Cradock. Although the councillors who resigned denied it, those resignations followed after strong pressure from the Cradock Residents' Association (CRADORA) which had led the way in the country in the formation of street committees. Faced with escalating costs of running townships, many councils raised rents. This goaded community organizations into intensifying their campaigns for the resignation of councillors. It was one such steep rent increase effected by the Lekoa Town Council which resulted in marches in the townships of the Vaal Triangle on September 1984.[11] That action marked the end of one phase and the start of a new phase in the relations between councillors and various community organizations.

1985–9

From late 1984, the townships were fast becoming places in which normal government was impossible. State structures and the individuals serving in them were increasingly subjected to considerable pressure in a campaign which aimed to make apartheid unworkable. Increasing numbers of township councils were run by Administrators following the resignations of elected councils. Campaigns for the resignation of councillors were also increasingly assuming a violent character. In 1985 the 'necklace' method of executing people suspected of working with the government was introduced. First used against the mayor of Langa in Uitenhage, Mr Kinikini, the necklace method was used in different townships throughout the country and attained international notoriety.

This was also the time during which the campaign to render South Africa ungovernable got under way in earnest. The campaigns which had been taking place until then suddenly took on a new meaning. The state interpreted all radical anti-apartheid campaigns as part of an orchestrated move to make the country ungovernable. By placing this interpretation on all anti-apartheid campaigns emanating from radical organizations, the government found it easy to employ the harshest of repressive strategies against all radical opposition. The imposition in 1985 of a state of emergency affected 36 magisterial districts and lasted five years. The state of emergency and the measures which accompanied it characterized the next era in the life of the BLAs. The government had clearly decided to shore them up by force if need be. The deployment of security forces in the townships was to be a key measure employed to crush radical anti-apartheid opposition and safeguard the authority of state institutions in the townships. The systematic incorporation of BLAs into the security system, used by the government to secure tight control over the townships, occurred during this period. BLAs formed a key link in the state security network. The Joint Management Centre (JMC) was the local version of a security network which was controlled from the State Security Council, a key cabinet committee chaired by P. W. Botha, the country's then State President.[12] This incorporation of BLAs into the state security system worsened their already deep legitimacy problems and, together with their apartheid characteristics, fuelled people's resolve to rid their communities of them.

This period also witnessed the spread of rent boycotts to more than 60 townships country-wide. Beginning in 1983 in small eastern Transvaal and eastern Cape townships, the boycott received wide publicity and support after it started in the Vaal townships in September 1984. In the Vaal it was transformed from a campaign involving a few townships with local significance, into a movement which engulfed townships in all the provinces of the country and was to acquire a national importance. This campaign was maintained throughout the state of emergency which was renewed annually until 1990. The rent boycotts were initiated largely as a result of burdensome increases levied by different BLAs. They thus were mostly aimed at forcing a decrease of rents to affordable levels. After the boycotts started, however, many other demands were added by various communities, including the dissolution of BLAs. Consequently rent boycotts were used, *inter alia*, to attempt to force the dissolution of the BLAs and the unification, on a non-racial basis, of functionally integrated areas.

In 1988 municipal elections were held simultaneously for all racial groups in the midst of the state of emergency. Anticipating a boycott of the elections, the government promulgated stringent regulations which, *inter alia*, provided for the elections to take place over a 10-day period. Those who wanted to cast prior votes could do so away from the glare of the organizers and supporters of the boycott. This, it was thought, would protect people who were prepared to vote from the supporters of the boycott. In spite of these measures and the detention of numerous leaders of various community organizations, a vigorous boycott campaign was organized resulting in an average national poll of some 25 per cent. The elections failed to bestow any legitimacy on the BLAs.[13]

Perceiving the boycotts as part of the general onslaught against its authority, the government, through the provincial authorities, stepped in to provide finances to councils denied their major source of revenue due to the rent boycott. This intervention, like the security intervention of the mid-1980s, saved the BLAs from certain collapse. The state was clearly not prepared to stand by and watch one of its structures collapse under popular pressure. In the Transvaal alone, by July 1990 the government had poured in R1.1 billion to 49 townships experiencing rent boycotts.[14]

1989–90

By 1989 the ravages, particularly on organizations, of the preceding years of repression were visible. Organizations which had been once strong were reeling under the effects of the emergency regulations. A new way in which organizations could preserve themselves had to be found. This 'new' way was provided by the Soweto Civic Association (SCA) when it formed the Soweto Peoples' Delegation (SPD) whose task was to explore the possibility of ending the rent boycott in Soweto through negotiations with the councillors. A range of changed circumstances had made this possible. The SCA was one of the community organizations which had held the view that it would not meet with councillors and had consistently called for their resignation.[15]

When state structures accepted that resolving rent boycotts needed the participation of community organizations, permission was granted for those organizations to meet and consult their membership. Thus the SCA was in a position to hold a meeting openly for the first time since February 1988, when it was declared a restricted organization in terms of the state of emergency regulations.[16] Agreeing to attempt to resolve the boycott through negotiations was made possible by the realization of both parties in the negotiations that a clear victory was not possible.

During this period there was an increase in the number of townships boycotting rent. This increase could have resulted from the widespread perception that townships which had boycotted rent were going to benefit from the negotiations which were under way. This period also witnessed a gradual reassertion of radical popular organizations as a result of a relaxation in the application of the state of emergency. Chiefly this was the outcome of the hunger strikes by emergency detainees which resulted in the release of all people detained in terms of the emergency. These developments marked the beginning of a re-emergence of struggles focused on the BLAs. No sooner had organizations regained some space than councillors were reminded of the earlier campaigns aimed at their resignation.

A new co-ordinating body of civic associations was founded in the southern Transvaal. The Civic Associations of the Southern Transvaal (CAST) has been a leading voice in calling for the resignation of councillors and has attributed an increased rate to its activities.[17] By the end of 1990, campaigns aimed at the resignation of councillors had led to the collapse of 40 per cent of the 262 BLAs in the country,[18] and had revived the restiveness which characterized the townships in the mid-1980s. A major difference this time was that some of these councillors joined the ANC after resigning, thus publicly adding their voice to those condemning participation in BLAs.[19] Concomitantly, a flurry of activity focused attention on developing policies for a post-apartheid local government system. Community organizations, as well as the government, released interesting studies which revealed their respective thoughts on the post-apartheid city. Both sets of studies seemed to accept that BLAs were unsustainable.[20]

A major development during this period was the final acceptance by the government that the unification of South African cities would soon be a reality. Speaking at a graduation ceremony at the University of Stellenbosch, the State President admitted this much. He urged those who were campaigning for the resignation of BLA councillors to stop their campaign, for their goal would soon be conceded by the government.[21] This statement signalled an important landmark. A white government had finally conceded that apartheid local government policies were inadequate. The cities of the future would have to be cities whose boundaries departed radically from those racially determined boundaries imposed by apartheid. This was significant because although some white municipalities supported the notion of non-racial cities, this support aimed to preserve existing municipal boundaries by insisting that black people should be allowed to live within white cities if they chose to. The effect of this, if it were accepted, would be to shut the door forever on townships since the tax base would remain locked away in white cities. Thus, in effect, the power relations embodied in the nature of apartheid cities would be perpetuated.

Civic organizations

To be complete, a discussion of BLAs must include a consideration of civic associations, organizations which have played a key role in shaping them, albeit as antagonists. Civic associations predate BLAs, having first emerged in 1977 with the formation of the Committee of Ten in Soweto (CoT) in the aftermath of the 1976 uprisings. That organization was followed by the formation of the Cape Housing

Action Committee (CAHAC) and of the Port Elizabeth Black Civic Organization (PEBCO). Although other civic organizations existed elsewhere in the country even before the formation of the CoT, the present-day civic movement owes its origins to the formation of these three organizations. It was not until 1983 that the civic movement was transformed into a truly mass movement. This transformation was led by CRADORA when it enlisted the vast majority of local township residents into the street committees. Thereafter street committees proliferated in various townships and became a characteristic feature of civic associations throughout the country.

It is this transformation into mass organizations which empowered township communities to lead campaigns which played a critical role in transforming the course of South African politics in the 1980s. Campaigns like consumer boycotts, stayaways, and rent boycotts became possible only after these structures had emerged. The near total consumer boycott which was implemented in Port Elizabeth in July 1985[22] indicated just how powerful these structures had rendered townships, and it also inspired activists elsewhere in the country to follow suite and form street committees. Although the South African security forces seemed to succeed in controlling the infiltration of armed ANC combatants, they certainly were confronted with a much better organized resistance movement inside the country. Images of a country on the verge of collapse on world television screens in the mid-1980s were the result of communities which through street committees had managed to create enclaves which were increasingly becoming impossible for the government to police and control.

Civic organizations played no small part in driving the country to this point. Although they had been formed to contest local issues, it soon became impossible to separate local from national political issues. Due to the pervasive nature of apartheid, opposition to what constitutes a local problem thrusts one into opposition to highly political issues which directly involve the state. Civic organizations were therefore thrust into opposition roles which involved the state from the time they were founded. This explains why most became affiliated to the United Democratic Front (UDF) when it was formed in 1983. This position of straddling two areas, namely the local and the national, has occasioned some tensions in the civic organizations. As local groups focusing their struggles primarily on the improvement of conditions of life in the townships, civic organizations have always set themselves the goal of enlisting into their ranks all residents on a non-partisan political basis. This, however, has not been achieved because of the political partisanship of virtually all civic organizations.

The political thaw resulting from the measures undertaken by the government since February 1990 has created a situation in which civic organizations are focusing on whether they are local structures concerned with local problems, or whether they are national formations concerned with constitutional issues. This debate also focuses attention on whether civic organizations are local government structures of the future non-racial South Africa, or organizations located in civil society. The dominant viewpoint sees civic organizations as the latter.[23] That, however, remains an assertion rather than a well set-out programme in which the place, role, and nature of civil society is clearly articulated.

The role for civic organizations in civil society in apartheid, as well as post-apartheid South Africa, has until now been defined imprecisely. This imprecision raises a number of problems with regards to the nature of civil society in societies like South Africa where the vast majority of the population is excluded from participation in institutions of government. Thus, it is not clear what it means for a people already excluded from the institutions of government, to persist in working independently from those institutions. Even if this persistence is an indication of the future role of civic organizations, it still seems to need careful elucidation. A role for civic organizations in the future must be predicated on the assumption that they will find it hard to retain their single most crucial resource, namely experienced personnel. It seems likely that their personnel will be a resource over which civic organizations will have to compete with other institutions which will inevitably include the state. A post-apartheid state will open the way for entry into state structures for hitherto excluded groups, some of whom are currently part of civic organizations. An influx of such personnel into other social institutions might be so large that in effect it will lead to the demise of civic organizations.

The very existence of a vibrant civil society in a post-apartheid South Africa may have to be striven for. Historically, civil society has been achieved following intense struggles by sections of the bourgeoisie who felt hemmed in by the feudal lords. More recently, civil society has been preserved by groups who actively oppose statism. Many such groups in western societies have not only preserved the right of civil society to exist independently, but have also succeeded in securing funding for their work from the national budget in the same way that institutions of government receive funding. This funding, however, is on the basis of the independence of those groups.

South Africa may take time to become a fully-fledged democracy in the sense of going beyond extending a franchise to all on a non-racial basis, by placing as much power as possible in the hands of the people in their various organizations and institutions. This type of democracy also goes beyond a multi-party form of government into multiplicity of institutions of power both within and without government institutions. To sustain it would require the building of appropriate institutions in the whole society. The emergence of inevitable competing interests in a post-apartheid society will make this undertaking a very difficult task, even if there is preparedness on the side of the government to go ahead with it.

Governments in developing countries tend towards centralizing control of the process of development. All this is done in an attempt to maximize the use of limited resources. In reality this translates into direct control of far too many processes in society, a development which even if it leads to some developmental gains, is bound to result in an omnipresent state. It can be such benign objectives which create conditions for a concentration of power in government giving rise to statism which invariably emasculates democracy.

South Africa already has the advantage of being richly endowed with a variety of organizations, some of which have survived considerable state hostility. These, and a host of other non-political formations, could form the basis for the growth of a sector outside government which would provide a forum for people to express themselves. If this is achieved, it would contribute immensely to enhancing the quality of democracy in a post-apartheid future, and thus ensure the existence of a civil society.

Conclusion

The 1980s were a decade of intense struggles against apartheid. Part of those struggles were focused on local government. The government has come to accept that all should participate in the formulation of a new South Africa which will be based on the rejection of apartheid. This acceptance signals the start of a process which might prove far more difficult than opposing apartheid.

Constructing a viable democratic alternative in a society so long divided by rigid racial divisions will require the strongest of wills and determination. The glib answers which in the past have been offered by many groups, some of them part of the anti-apartheid movement, may be inadequate to resolve practical problems which will inevitably arise on an ongoing basis. The task of levelling the playing field so that everyone can realistically be given more or less equal access to resources will be a task fraught with problems. Local government will continue to be an arena in which innovative strategies will have to be sought. The energy and enthusiasm with which apartheid was opposed will hopefully be channelled into developmental work and building democratic structures of local government.

Notes

1 Murray M. *South Africa: Time of Agony, Time of Destiny. The Upsurge of Popular Protest* (London: 1987) 123.

2 Proctor A. 'Class Struggle, Segregation and the City: a History of Sophiatown, 1905–1940' *Labour, Townships and Protest* (ed.) Bozzoli B. (Johannesburg: Ravan Press 1979) 49–83.

3 Grest J. 'The Crisis of Local Government in South Africa' *State, Resistance and Change in South Africa* (eds.) Frankel P., Pines N., and Swilling M. (Johannesburg: Southern Book Publishers 1988) 89.

4 Humphries R. G. 'The Origins and Subsequent Development of Administration Boards', unpublished MA thesis (Grahamstown: Rhodes University 1983) 156–62.

5 See SACP *Path to Power* for a rendition of a thesis rooted in a colonial understanding of South African society.

6 Development Bank of Southern Africa 'Final Report of the Working Group on the Finances and Economy of Soweto', unpublished report (1988) 3.

7 Chaskalson M., Jochelson K., and Seekings J. 'Rent Boycotts and the Urban Political Economy' *South African Review 4* (Johannesburg: Ravan Press 1987) 55–6.

8 Saul J. *Socialist Ideology and the Struggle for Southern Africa* (New Jersey: Africa World Press 1990) 159.

9 Bureaucratic petite bourgeoisie is intended to carry the same sense as in Mare G. and Ncube M. 'Inkatha: Marching from Natal to Pretoria' *South African Review 5* (Johannesburg: Ravan Press 1989).

10 South African Institute of Race Relations *Race Relations Survey* (Johannesburg: 1984) 258–9.

11 Rantete J. *The Third Day of September: an Eye Witness of the Sebokeng Rebellion of 1984* (Johannesburg: Ravan Press 1984).

12 Swilling M. and Phillips M. 'The Emergency State: its Structure, Power and Limits' *South African Review 5* (Johannesburg: Ravan Press 1989) 68–89.

13 Humphries R. and Shubane K. 'A Tale of Two Squirrels: the 1988 Local Government Elections and their Implications' in *South Africa at the End of the Eighties: Policy Perspective 1989* (Centre for Policy Studies: 1989) 90–110.

14 Transvaal Provincial Administration *The Scope of the Problem* (Pretoria: 1990).

15 Swilling M. and Shubane K. 'Negotiating Urban Transition: the Soweto Experience' *Transition to Democracy* (Cape Town: Oxford University Press 1990).

16 Webster D. and Friedman M. 'Repression and the State of Emergency: June 1987–March 1989' *South African Review 5* (Johannesburg: Ravan Press 1989) 26.

17 *Financial Mail* 7 December 1990.

18 *The Star* 5 December 1990.

19 An example of this is Mr Tom Boya who holds the record of being the longest serving mayor in South Africa. He was mayor of Daveyton for some 10 years, 9 of which were unbroken. He resigned from the BLA and joined the ANC.

20 Examples of such policy documents are:
Centre for Development Studies and ANC Discussion *Report on the ANC National Consultative Conference on Local Government* (Johannesburg: October 1990).
Council for the Co-ordination of Local Government Affairs. Report and Recommendations of the Investigating Committee into a System of Local Government for South Africa. Compiled by Thornhill C.
Planact *The Soweto Rent Boycott* (Johannesburg: 1989).

21 *Business Day* 14 December 1990.

22 Murray (1987) 241.

23 Mayekiso M. *Report on the ANC National Consultative Conference on Local Government*, summary of the keynote address at the ANC National Consultative Conference on Local Government (Cape Town: Centre for Development Studies, University of the Western Cape 1990).

6 Whither Regional Services Councils?

Richard Humphries

Introduction

Historically, South Africa's core institutions of local government have never been subject to periodic grand and fundamental recasting and reorientation. In general, and despite the effects of apartheid policies, there has been more of a continuity of institutions and their roles over time. This began to change in the 1980s. Having introduced a new constitution and parliamentary system in 1984, the NP proceeded to re-examine the roles and functions of various local government or third-tier institutions in the light of the principles contained in the new constitution. As part of this process RSCs were established in the late 1980s. Essentially the RSCs were designed to do two things: to allocate new sources of income for local authorities; and to preside over the provision of certain services within their region of jurisdiction. In addition RSCs were seen by the government as fulfilling an important function within the wider reform and security programme of the period.

Given the NP government's acceptance that a new system of local government has to be introduced and the various recommendations of the Thornhill Committee[1] on the possible parameters of a new system, the future of RSCs within a revised system of local government has to be considered. Put another way, RSCs are a product of the politics of the 1980s; how will they survive the new dynamics of the early 1990s? This chapter explores some of the issues around this topic. The first section situates the introduction of RSCs within the context of the changes brought about to the local government system during the 1980s, while the second section examines some debates around the future of RSCs given the acceptance that a new local government system is necessary. No attention is given in this chapter to the views of extraparliamentary organizations to RSCs since they have not yet shown any sign of softening their total opposition to RSCs.

RSCs and local government policy during the 1980s

Government policy towards local government in the 1980s was shaped by two interacting issues or dynamics. The first was the 1983 constitution and its distinction between own and general affairs in relation to the functions and decision-making process of public or state institutions. This constitutional distinction was used primarily to regulate the terms on which the participant white, coloured, and Indian groups in the tricameral parliament related to one another at a variety of levels of government. Own affairs meant that on issues deemed sensitive to a specific ethnic group or community, decisions on these issues were taken by the community through their own representatives. General affairs, on the other hand, acknowledged that certain other issues affected, for whatever reason, more than one community. Decisions on these issues had to be taken by representatives of all race groups together.

Local government — with the important exception of RSCs — was defined by the constitution as an own affair. Thus the government, during this period, was concerned to secure and entrench the acceptance of autonomous, racially segregated local authority institutions among Africans, whites, coloureds, and Indians.

The second dynamic shaping government policy was the way in which the reform programme generated an almost dialectical response from sections of the African community who were excluded from the tricameral parliament. As the 1980s progressed, this response found expression in the ungovernability programme of the ANC which, among other goals, sought to destroy the BLA system.

The consequences and impact of this programme on the government's local government policy, including RSCs, during the second half of the 1980s need to be briefly considered. Perhaps the most interesting account of this relationship is to be found in a speech by the then Minister of Constitutional Development and Planning, to a meeting of directors' general of government departments in April 1987.[2]

Heunis began by arguing that one should accept that in certain parts of the country the ungovernability programme had achieved such success that a 'revolutionary climate' no longer existed, but rather a 'revolution'. Ungovernability meant that township residents were no longer under the full control or authority of legally constituted authorities; instead they listened to, and obeyed, calls made by another authority. 'This means that their comings and goings are no longer controlled by legislation and regulations and by norms which previously held.'[3]

Heunis noted that it was at the local level that the country was being rendered ungovernable; thus it was at this level that the battle against ungovernability had to be fought. Further, the degree to which the government could control issues at the local authority level was equivalent to the extent to which the country was governable or not. Heunis thus firmly elevated events and dynamics at the local level to a position of critical importance for the government during this period. Having accepted this, Heunis outlined what the response by the government ought to be at local government level, and at higher tiers of government.

First, he argued that the 'normalization' of local authorities had to be a high priority for the government and all government departments. Second, and at the same time, developments on the constitutional terrain had to continue to ensure a consensus between moderate groups over new structures. This consensus could only be achieved through dialogue; if not, only a 'house of cards' would be constructed. In this context Heunis mentioned RSCs, among other structures, as a means of institutionalizing discussion and dialogue at the local level. It was one of the 'basic aims' of RSCs.

Here Heunis was pointing to the role of RSCs as general affairs institutions bringing together representatives of participating white, African, coloured, and Indian local government structures. Although the most important decision-making process within RSCs was to decide on the allocation of levy income and the establishment of regional services, government spokespersons during the late 1980s often argued that the 'success' of the RSCs in performing these functions would have a beneficial effect on the progress of constitutional reform generally.

What they meant was that if representatives of all race groups (and by implication these were representatives of moderate political interests) could establish a consensus about the issues with which RSCs were charged, it would imply that the same could be done at higher levels of government. For example, a Bureau for Information publication argued that RSCs were a 'significant stepping stone towards a negotiated constitutional settlement' and if they could show that consensus politics could work effectively, RSCs 'would certainly facilitate power sharing at higher levels of government'.[4] The same publication held that the establishment of RSCs was a practical step to broaden democracy and to eliminate domination and discrimination.

A related political goal was that of upgrading socio-economic conditions, particularly in the African townships. Heunis, in the speech referred to above, noted that while it would be naive to expect upgrading to eliminate political demands, it could help to direct such demands to 'non-revolutionary channels'. RSCs were involved in this upgrading through their allocation of the income generated by the two levies payable by all employers, whether state or private sector. In terms of the Regional Services Councils Act, priority in the allocation of this income had to be given to the areas of greatest need, which effectively meant the financially strapped BLAs. However, this assistance was only for capital projects and did little to alleviate the key reasons for the financial problems surrounding the BLAs.

These were the more immediate political goals, rooted in the politics of the period, which RSCs were designed to serve. At a more technical, local government level they were designed to facilitate the provision of certain local government services on a regional basis between local authorities within the area of jurisdiction of RSCs. These technical concerns had, in the late 1970s and early 1980s, provided the initial impetus to the RSC concept.[5] After their establishment, water and electricity provision and refuse removal were the major services they took up, although this varied from council to council, depending on a range of local circumstances.

Because of widespread fears by white municipalities that RSCs would usurp their most important powers and functions, government spokespersons characterized RSCs as 'horizontal extensions' of local governments and not as an additional tier of government superior to local authorities. They also stressed that RSCs would not be able to take over functions already performed by a local authority without its permission. Thus in the short term, RSCs were seen by the government as leaving the existing system of apartheid local government intact. Put another way, RSCs were not intended during this period to be metropolitan forms of local government. Metropolitan local government was rejected on the grounds that RSCs, by performing 'overlapping functions' between local authorities, rendered such a local authority system superfluous.

Yet there is some evidence that the government did view the introduction of RSCs in a longer term perspective against the unfolding of further reform measures. These perspectives, totally downplayed in official public justifications for RSCs, were revealed by a Progressive Federal Party (PFP) MP during debate on the RSC bill in 1985. The comments of Andrew Savage are quoted extensively:

> One must ask oneself what the main reason is behind this Bill. One has irresistibly to toy with the thought that it might be part of some hidden agenda. One can indeed imagine a scenario where local authorities, having become more and more debilitated, had begun to wither away, and where there was a multi-racial regional services council which expanded its operations, where discrimination did not apply, where people voted as one would like them to vote, that is, solely according to the fact that they were representatives of a community, and where the Group Areas Act had disappeared ... the hon Minister, however, has got himself such a reputation as a brilliant constitutional fiddler that even when one speaks to the members of his own party, they put this scenario forward to one as the reason why one should support this Bill.[6]

What is interesting in Savage's account of private NP agendas is the central role allocated to RSCs in a future local government system in which conventional apartheid measures did not exist. The logic of this scenario would have given to RSCs the most important role in local government and one which is close to that of a metropolitan authority. Besides Savage's analysis, there is other evidence from the same period which is also suggestive of a similar longer term perspective by the NP government towards RSCs. This emerges in the response by a former senior government official closely involved in the RSC initiative, Dr Fanie Cloete, to an academic analysis of the proposed councils. Cloete defended the RSC act from charges that it, in itself, relied on the provisions of the Population Registration Act of 1950. This latter act is generally seen as having provided the cornerstone of apartheid legislation by distinguishing between various ethnic or racial groups. Cloete essentially argued that the RSC act was colour-blind:

> The Act must of necessity take account of existing local government institutions, however 'inadequate' or 'limiting'

they are with regard to less than acceptable 'discriminatory' legislation. If the discriminatory aspects of primary local government institutions were to fall away, or their composition was to change, then no change would have to be brought about to the Regional Services Councils Act of 1985. The Act differs drastically in this respect from the 1983 Constitution in that the statutory definition of population groups in the RSA is not a prerequisite for the implementation of regional services councils.[7]

In other words Cloete was arguing that the legislative framework which governed RSCs could, in its own right, largely survive the demise of apartheid local government. There is nothing inherently surprising in the idea that the NP or certain senior government officials held such views towards RSCs. All governments, or at least sections of governments, undertake long-term policy planning projections. In this specific case, impetus for longer term projections and scenarios was aided by the reform process being undertaken by the NP government, limited though it was.

This brief analysis suggests thus that the RSC initiative was a multi-faceted one, serving and pursuing various objectives and purposes within the context of the politics of the 1980s. It had an element of local government service delivery about it; a further element was the extension of the principles underpinning the 1983 constitution to the local arena; all of these were combined in the latter half of the 1980s with what might be called an attempt at local government crisis management, designed essentially to rescue the crisis-ridden BLA system from total collapse.

The future of RSCs

Since the introduction of RSCs alongside local authorities in the late 1980s, there has been a reasonable amount of speculation as to how RSCs would evolve over time. This speculation centred around their relationship to local authorities, particularly since the RSCs would gradually assume a greater role in providing bulk services within their areas of jurisdiction. Debate about the future role of RSCs has stemmed primarily from three sources: local authorities, especially white municipalities; the RSCs themselves; and more recently from the publication of the Thornhill Committee Report into local government options. These are examined in turn. This debate is no new development within municipal ranks following the release of the committee's report. The debate followed more naturally upon the establishment of RSCs, but it has certainly been sharpened by the report of the Thornhill Committee.

Since the concept of new regional institutions at the local government level was first mooted, WLAs have been an important interest group with which the government has had to interact. Besides the predictable opposition which the initiative faced from municipalities controlled by political parties to the left and the right of the NP, NP-controlled municipalities did also tend to have some initial doubts about the proposed councils. But from about 1983 and 1984 onwards they did come round to accepting them, while still retaining a careful watch on the ways in which the RSCs would function.[8] Much of this, of course, stemmed from municipal self-interest and a desire to protect their own interests from newly established institutions whose functioning held the risk of overlapping with their own activities. Much of this concern does seem to have disappeared, partly because RSCs have not involved themselves so far in many of the activities and functions which the RSC act mentioned as possible spheres of involvement.

Nonetheless the nature of the relationship between RSCs and local authorities generally is one which leading municipal officials have speculated upon. For example, the former town clerk of Johannesburg, Manie Venter, has proposed a rather new and wider role for RSCs in local government. In an address to a Department of Development Planning conference in Pretoria in October 1989, he sketched a 'possible new form of administration and management' for local government.[9] Venter's proposal was aimed at achieving two things: securing a more efficient utilization of municipal personnel; and a greater degree of autonomy for local municipal officials from municipal councillors.

Venter argued that local authorities, 'especially developing and smaller ones which have limited financial means'[10] — a clear reference to BLAs — had to compete with one another for skilled personnel which was, furthermore, in short supply. WLA officials have always tended to point to the lack of expertise among BLA-employed bureaucrats; some have argued that this is one of the key reasons for the political crisis which has constantly surrounded the councils since their establishment. Venter thus suggested that RSCs take over the equipment and personnel of local authorities in their area of jurisdiction. RSCs, in terms of Venter's suggestion, would become super administrative and technical bodies providing services in their entire region of jurisdiction. He did, however, qualify his proposal by arguing that 'stable' local authorities who were prepared to accept full responsibility for conducting their 'own affairs', and who had the necessary resources to do so, could continue to exist in their own right. WLAs would thus have retained their autonomy.

By elevating RSCs into the administrative fulcrum of local government, Venter hoped also to achieve his second goal of greater autonomy for municipal officials from local government councillors. He sketched an option whereby RSCs remained indirectly elected bodies, but that decisions about the day-to-day functioning of staff would seemingly be channelled through the RSC and through a newly created state-appointed executive board or body. Directly elected councillors would continue to set policy for municipal functions in their area of jurisdiction, but the executive board would ensure and monitor the implementation of these decisions.

In the wake of the Thornhill Report, the importance of Venter's model lies not so much in its suggestions for the mutation of RSCs, but in its acceptance that greater centralization of staffing and a corresponding reduction in duplication were needed among local government bodies. It is also instructive for its attempts to secure more autonomy for officials from municipal politicians.

The committee's report, and its recommendations for possible future local government models, has decisively influenced the debate about the future of RSCs. Although the preliminary report of the committee, published in May 1990, made no reference to the future of RSCs, its second and final report, published in October 1990, did so. The importance of this report for the future direction of RSCs lay in its discussion of a possible metropolitan local government form for the metropolitan areas in South Africa. Government policy had previously ruled out any such development.

Before this report, discussions within RSC ranks about their future accepted the constitutional niceties of government policy between own and general affairs. RSC spokespersons argued, for example, that RSCs in no way occupied any position of authority over local authorities, and that 'they ought not to do so'.[11] On the other hand, RSCs were autonomous authorities who were not subject to the authority of one or more of their constituent primary local authorities. In short, according to G. Bornman — the then chairperson of the Central Witwatersrand RSC and president of the RSC Association of South Africa — RSCs were a 'separate co-operative authority for, and on behalf, of local authorities, bodies and communities of a region'.[12] This somewhat convoluted description of the status of RSCs accepted the boundaries of government policy towards local authorities but did appear to want to reserve, if not develop, an independent right and standing for RSCs.

The particular role which Bornman wanted to carve out for RSCs was that of co-ordinating developmental assistance to local authorities. Besides the more obvious functions of co-ordinating transport and regional land use and planning issues, Bornman appeared determined to secure a greater role for RSCs in the townships. This fell under the broad rubric of assisting in the development of BLAs, besides the already established RSC function of providing capital finance. Bornman advocated RSC involvement in developing new residential areas for Africans and of supplementing the sources of revenue open to BLAs, particularly in the metropolitan areas where they struggled with enormous deficits on their current accounts. These possible additional roles for RSCs were clearly also aimed at shoring up the politically and economically embattled BLAs during the state of emergency.

The importance of the Thornhill Committee for the future of RSCs lay in its rather obvious statement that 'when a new system of local government for South Africa is under consideration, it is essential to give attention to the role and place of RSCs in a new dispensation'.[13] It argued in favour of a continued role for RSCs but did propose certain changes to their functioning in certain areas. It argued that RSCs 'must continue ... to play an essential role as extensions of local government' in those areas where a metropolitan authority was not the product of local-level negotiations. In these areas their responsibilities and sources of income would be transferred to the new bodies. In areas where other forms of local government structures were negotiated, RSCs would have to adapt from their present race-based primary local authorities to the new non-racial authorities. The committee went further in these cases to propose, without giving any examples, that it might be appropriate to grant specific interest groups representation on the adapted RSCs. This elusive reference might have been aimed at securing the representation of business groups on the councils. In another rather cryptic reference, it proposed that RSCs could serve as a channel for the distribution of transfer payments from higher levels of government.

Thus the Thornhill Committee, in effect, distinguished between RSCs which function in the large urban areas, and between RSCs whose areas of jurisdiction include largely rural or small town areas. This urban/rural distinction is an important one since RSCs in rural areas are effectively precluded, by the large distances involved, from assuming responsibility for bulk services. Instead, they give much greater attention to their role in allocating levy income to local authorities within their area of jurisdiction.

In the wake of the Thornhill Report, government policy towards RSCs seems to have accepted that RSCs in urban and metropolitan areas will have to undergo potentially far-reaching changes. Both the Minister of Planning and Provincial Affairs, Hernus Kriel, and Dr Chris Thornhill in their addresses to the Regional Services Councils' Association conference in October 1990 stressed this point. Kriel noted that although he thought RSCs would remain a form of local authority in a new dispensation, it would be necessary to draw a distinction between urban and rural areas.[14] This point was elaborated upon by Thornhill. He argued that where metropolitan authorities were introduced, the *raison d'être* of RSCs would fall away. The levies at present payable to RSCs would accrue instead to the metropolitan authorities.

Rurally-based RSCs would be subject to potentially fewer changes than their urban counterparts, Thornhill argued. The major change would be that the participating local authorities within the RSCs would not be constituted on a racial basis. In addition, these changes might necessitate an amendment to the way in which voting strengths of participating local authorities were calculated.[15]

For their part, RSC spokespersons seem to have accepted that metropolitan forms of local government will entail a fundamental transformation of RSCs. They do, however, seem determined that in this process RSCs, and the principles which underlie them, should not be summarily abolished but rather transformed. For example, Len de Wet, chief executive officer of the Central Witwatersrand RSC, has argued that:

> While new structures for the metropolitan area are being considered the benefits of Regional Services Councils, in providing regional services, its wide tax base providing revenue to the local level of government, its ability to assist with the upgrading and development of infrastructure in the lesser-developed areas and the joint decision-making and co-operation established between various race groups should be retained and transferred to any new structure. Regional Services Councils in the metropolitan areas are a form of

metropolitan government and could easily form the basis of any future metropolitan structure.[16]

In effect, De Wet argues that the functions entrusted to any future metropolitan authority, within a two-tier local government structure, will not be far removed from the present functions of RSCs. Their major functions would be to co-ordinate functions within the wider metropolitan area and to provide bulk and other services of a regional nature in order to achieve greater efficiency and cost benefits. In addition, De Wet said a wide range of functions currently performed by the central government, or the provincial administrations, could be devolved to metropolitan governments provided fiscal autonomy was granted to these authorities in order to fund these functions. These functions could include education, hospital and health services, passenger transport, housing, and infrastructural provision. Similar sentiments have been expressed by the chairperson of the Pretoria RSC, Piet Delport.[17]

There does seem little likelihood that the functions currently performed by RSCs will be abandoned in any new dispensation. The small steps at present being made towards a regionalization of municipal services under RSCs will obviously be speeded up through metropolitanization. Certainly, the financial underpinnings of RSCs will not be abandoned in a context of enormous demands for infrastructure and services in urban areas.

Yet any discussion about the future of RSCs has to take account of at least three variants or models within the RSCs already established. In the first place, RSCs in the Cape are very different institutions to those functioning in the Transvaal and the OFS. Their distinctive features — a large personnel corps and a wider variety of functions — are the consequence of the Cape's system of rural, if not regional, local self government established in divisional councils during the 1800s. In other provinces these functions were vested chiefly in the provincial administrations. When the divisional councils were abolished in the late 1980s, their functions were mostly transferred to the RSCs. In other words, transforming the RSCs in the Cape would be a more complicated procedure.

In the Transvaal and the OFS, the already mentioned distinction between urban-based and rural-based RSCs has to be taken into account. In the latter case, the primary function is to allocate the income derived from RSC levies between their member authorities. RSCs in these two provinces do not possess a large staff complement. In theory, this makes it easier to transform RSCs into other structures.

Conclusion

In a very real sense RSCs were a product of the Botha era and its distinction between own and general affairs. Now that De Klerk has so significantly stamped his own dynamic upon South African politics and declared that local government structures cannot be based upon racial distinctions, the future of RSCs has to be reconsidered. Given that the debate about local government restructuring is still in its infancy, the RSCs are unlikely to be affected during the immediate future. Clearly they will be affected, but the continuities between the present structure and functioning, and possible successor institutions might be generally greater than expected, given their controversial past. In this debate the views of extraparliamentary organizations and movements towards RSCs will assume a greater prominence and importance than they have in past debates. This debate has probably been facilitated by the government's acceptance that RSCs in metropolitan areas will have to be fundamentally transformed; in short, there is a convergence of views on this point which is certainly a new development.

Notes

1 Dr Chris Thornhill was chairperson of an influential investigating committee, set up by government, to look into a system of local government for South Africa. His report was published in 1990.
2 Heunis C. 'Bekamping van die Revolusionere Klimaat', unpublished speech (Cape Town: 1986).
3 Heunis (1986).
4 Bureau for Information *The Regional Services Councils* (Pretoria: Government Printer 1988) 17.
5 Humphries R. 'Regional Services Councils', unpublished paper (Johannesburg: University of the Witwatersrand, Centre for Policy Studies 1991).
6 House of Assembly debates (1985) col. 7921.
7 Cloete F. 'Kommentaar' *Journal of Public Administration* (Pretoria: South African Institute of Public Administration 1986) 21 ii 61.
8 Humphries (1991).
9 Venter H. H. S. 'Local Government Administration: the Financial Implications', address to a Department of Development Planning symposium (Pretoria: 1989).
10 Venter (1989).
11 Bornman G. Presidential address delivered to the first annual congress of the Regional Services Councils' Association of South Africa (Port Elizabeth: 1988) 14.
12 Bornman (1988) 14.

13 Thornhill C. (chairperson) Report and recommendations of the investigating committee into a system of local government for South Africa, Council for the Co-ordination of Local Government Affairs (Pretoria: 1990a) 59.
14 Kriel H. Address to the second annual conference of the Regional Services Councils' Association of South Africa (Port Elizabeth: 1990).
15 Thornhill C. 'Regional Services Councils in a New Local Government Structure', address to the second annual conference of the Regional Services Councils' Association of South Africa (Port Elizabeth: 1990b).
16 De Wet L. 'Bulk Services for Metropolitan Areas', address to an Institute for Housing of Southern Africa conference (Johannesburg: 1991) 11.
17 Delport P. 'Metropolitan Development for the Future South Africa', address to an Institute for Housing of Southern Africa conference (Johannesburg: 1991).

7 Greying and free settlement

Fanie Cloete

Introduction

One of the most lasting legacies of apartheid in South Africa will probably prove to be the racially segregated nature of its towns and cities.

The pattern of residential settlement was directly shaped by the prevailing value systems and the resulting political and social relationships among the respective communities since the establishment of the first 'temporary' European settlement in 1652 on what later became known as the Cape Town beach front.

The largely informal, segregated settlement pattern which has since developed, was gradually formalized by *ad hoc* pieces of legislation for a full century between 1849 and 1949.[1] In 1950, the statutory controls over residential settlement were consolidated in a comprehensive, very rigid and prescriptive way, by the promulgation of the Group Areas Act. In the ensuing 37 years, between 1950 and 1987, deliberate attempts were made, through the implementation of the act, to reverse the few cases of racial intermingling which had occurred up to that time (in some cases by force). A strict geographical separation between races was in this way introduced by statute. It endured on the statute book until 1987.

The policy of racially defined Group Areas had already started to erode in the mid-1970s, when 'illegal' residents increasingly started to occupy white Group Areas for various reasons, and to such an extent, that it was no longer feasible to attempt eviction. The government officially acknowledged the failure of its Group Areas policy by introducing the concept of free settlement areas in 1987, and by announcing in April 1990 its intention to abolish the Group Areas Act in 1991.

The following issues will be summarized, analysed, and assessed in this chapter:

- the considerations leading up to the government's policy change towards more integrated residential areas;
- the details of the government's response to the greying of the cities; and
- the local government implications of the new policy including some alternative future policy scenarios.

The greying process

In the mid-1970s, 25 years after the promulgation of the Group Areas Act, the cities and towns in South Africa were still not fully racially segregated despite strict enforcement of the act. Although in the minority, residential areas like Claremont and Woodstock in Cape Town were, for example, still in essence fully racially integrated.

Attempts by the government to redress this situation, by offering all sorts of incentives to 'illegal' residents to move to other areas, had failed. Attempts to remove and resettle communities forcibly had drawn such intense criticism locally, as well as internationally, that the government became increasingly reluctant to continue with this policy on a large scale.

Another explanation for the persistence of some racially integrated neighbourhoods, despite the Group Areas Act, was the fact that the prohibitions on inter-racial marriage and social relations only applied to the white community. It did not apply to relationships across racial lines in the African, coloured, and Indian communities. As a result, relatively free racial intermingling took place in those communities and led to the situation that virtually only white residential areas were fairly uni-racial.

Racially separate Group Areas formed the basis for racially separate local authority institutions for each group area, irrespective of the viability of the different communities and their preferences in this regard.

Where it existed or was created, residential apartheid was very difficult to maintain in the bigger cities, for reasons that include the following:

- The chronic housing and land shortage in African, coloured, and Indian areas which steadily worsened over the years.
- The availability of housing in the (white) centres of cities increased as a result of upwardly mobile white residents moving out of these areas to the suburbs and emigrating after the political shock of the Soweto uprising in 1976.[2]
- An economic recession caused numerous defaults on bond payments by owners of property at the lower end of the market, including the city centres, and caused middle-class and lower middle-class residents to give up flats and seek other, less expensive accommodation. This increased the availability of housing in these areas.
- The economic recession also prevented white buyers and tenants from utilizing these housing opportunities. Instead, it increased the migration of Africans from the rural areas to the cities. Here, no accommodation was available in the areas designated for them, and transport to the cities was expensive and not always readily available from locations in the rural areas.
- A system of illegal white nominees, acting as fronts for African, coloured, and Indian entrepreneurs, had already developed in the late 1960s to utilize commercial and industrial opportunities in white areas. This precedent, which could not be controlled by the government, was extended by the new immigrants to include residential properties.[3]

The migration to and illegal settlement of Africans in the inner cities were stimulated:

- from 1975 by exceptions, which were increasingly allowed by the government, to the strict racial separation effected by the 1953 Reservation of Separate Amenities Act;[4]
- from 1984 by increasingly open central business districts as free trade areas to all races;
- in 1985 by the repeal of the prohibitions on inter-racial marriages and social relations;
- in 1986 when influx control was abolished; and
- again in 1987 when expectations of the pending repeal of the Group Areas Act were created by the report of the President's Council.

Considerations like these led to a situation where African, coloured, and Indian residents gradually infiltrated certain suburbs like Hillbrow, Mayfair, and others as illegal occupiers of properties. The first wave consisted of middle to upper middle-class people of coloured and Indian descent who could not find accommodation in their own areas, and could afford to pay (sometimes exorbitant) prices for 'illegal' accommodation in the 'white' inner cities. Housing was available, affordable, and in most cases much nearer to their workplaces, shops, and other amenities than in their allocated Group Areas on the periphery of the cities.[5] Their quality of life was also much higher.[6] Nor did they create much of a stir among the legal white residents because of their middle-class culture.

The second wave of immigrants were, however, poor working-class Africans who started to overcrowd dilapidated buildings, drastically lowering the quality of life in those buildings and in the neighbourhood as a whole. A deterioration in health conditions, and an increase in the incidence of crime, accompanied this latest change in the composition of the residents in those areas. This led to increasing feelings of insecurity among many of the remaining traditional white residents. The issue then became politicized because the conditions that prevailed proved to be fertile breeding ground for right-wing political mobilization among whites.[7]

Despite increasing calls from right-wing political groups for the government to do something, the NP did not act purposefully against these illegal residents. This was in part a result of the following considerations:

- The numbers of people involved (e.g. between 8 000 and 12 000 in inner-city areas in Johannesburg alone in 1983).[8]
- A 'conspiracy of silence' between landowners and tenants which made detection difficult.
- Insufficient personnel to check complaints or initiate investigations.
- A weak economic climate prevented allocation of more funds for alternative housing.
- A strong and increasing domestic and international political resistance against attempts to evict illegal residents.
- An increasing number of government defeats in court cases in which the government attempted to evict 'illegals'.[9]
- Increasing doubts about the feasibility of these policies, as well as ideological changes in attitudes regarding residential settlement, occurred in the decision-making ranks of government élites themselves, as a result of the difficulties of implementing existing policies in this respect (i.e. a loss of will to follow through with these old-style apartheid policies, against the background of other reforms aimed at diluting apartheid).

In the early 1980s it became evident to the government that its policies and legislation could not be enforced in practice.

The President's Council on Group Areas

On 31 October 1984, the State President requested the President's Council to advise him, *inter alia*, on the desirability of consolidating the Group Areas Act with the Reservation of Separate Amenities Act, the Slums Act, and the Community Development Act.

The council interpreted its brief liberally and on 10 September 1987 it recommended that the respective acts should not be consolidated. Instead the council accepted the inevitability of the greying of the cities and recommended the following relatively drastic policy changes:

- The repeal of the Reservation of Separate Amenities Act.
- The retention and extension of the Slums Act in order to facilitate its application and co-ordinate it with other aspects of urban planning, and to involve local authorities and other expertise more effectively in slum prevention and clearance by creating measures to prevent urban decay and slum formation through better standards for housing, health, and infrastructure.
- Substantial amendments to the Group Areas Act, or its repeal and replacement with other (racially neutral) legislation.

The abolition or amendment of the Group Areas Act would provide for the following changes:

- The protection of existing racially defined residential areas.
- The creation of orderly procedures at the level of the local authority, management committee, and legal residents and owners in a municipality, to open existing Group Areas, and establish new open residential areas according to local needs and choices.
- The choice of alternative ways for residents in open areas to exercise their municipal franchise in local government elections, from no franchise at all, to full franchise irrespective of race.
- The right of appeal to the administrator-in-executive committee was recommended.
- The use of town planning ordinances, town planning schemes, township establishment procedures, and property title deeds to regulate human settlement.

- The opening up of all land used for industrial, business, commercial, professional, and religious purposes for all races.
- The provision of more land for urban settlement and expansion, and the upgrading of existing residential areas and facilities.[10]

The main objective of these recommendations was the gradual opening of Group Areas by local communities themselves, without the government having to become involved in this process. The discriminatory aspects of the Group Areas legislation would, however, have had to receive attention through the amendment of the existing act, or its repeal and replacement with something else. The council left open the difficult question of municipal franchise, probably in view of the government's strong stand on racially separate local authorities at the time.

If implemented, the end result of the President's Council's recommendations would have been the legalization of the existing position in the cities, and the creation of a process whereby other Group Areas could have been gradually opened after full community participation at local level. It did not guarantee the opening of areas, but created an instrument through which it could be done. At the time, the report represented a dramatic change in NP policy. It was a change which outside commentators, as well as some government élites themselves, knew had to come. Unfortunately not all political élites in the NP shared this realization.

The government response

The government response to the recommendations of the President's Council was threefold.

Firstly, it decided to accept the principle of some open residential areas, but to reject the 'bottom-up' procedure recommended by the council to achieve this goal in favour of a 'top-down' procedure established in the form of the 1988 Free Settlement Areas Act.

Secondly, the government accepted the principle of a common voters' roll for residents in open areas in the form of the 1988 Local Government in Free Settlement Areas Act, but it also left open the sensitive political question of how to accommodate these areas in the existing system of racially separate local authorities, which it at that time still refused to change.

Lastly, the government decided to retain the Group Areas Act in an amended form. The 1988 Group Areas Amendment Bill was intended to 'protect' those Group Areas which had not been opened, against the 'insidious' greying process which had occurred in some areas like Hillbrow.

These three pieces of legislation will now be briefly summarized and evaluated.

The Free Settlement Areas Act

The act provides for a board appointed by the State President to investigate, consider, and recommend the opening of existing Group Areas, or the declaration of new open residential areas. The board must be representative of all racial communities.

The board *must* act upon a request by the State President, a chairperson of an 'own affairs' Ministers' Council, or the Minister of Planning and Provincial Affairs, to investigate a certain area. It *may* also do so at the request of a municipality, a coloured or Indian MC or LAC which controls the land in question, or a property developer who already owns the proposed free settlement area.

It is therefore expected that prospective developers invest capital in the area concerned before it is declared a free settlement area. Another implication of the wording of the act is that it is at the discretion of the board to decide whether an area should be declared a free settlement area once it receives the request from a local government body or developer. The act further does not allow the board to initiate an investigation.

The board must follow a lengthy and cumbersome process of consultation with interest groups which want to present evidence to the board. This includes the condition that the local authority which controls the area in question must notify all municipal voters in that area (or, in the absence of a voters' roll, all lawful owners and occupiers of land in that area) four weeks in advance of the intended inquiry by the board. The act also restricts the board from recommending the opening of an area which was not included in the original application to investigate. These restrictions obstruct the effective functioning of the board.

When considering a request, the board must give attention to the following considerations:
- the existing and future socio-economic profile of the area concerned and its environment;

- the need for available land, housing, services, and facilities in that environment;
- the views of all local government bodies, organizations, and individuals concerned;
- the implications of the declaration of free settlement areas for the local authority and environment; and
- any other consideration which the board or the minister may deem relevant.

The board advises the State President about its findings and recommendations. The State President alone can decide to open an area. If such an area falls wholly or partially in a white, coloured, or Indian Group Area, the chairperson of the Ministers' Council concerned must agree with the State President's decision. He therefore has a veto over the decision by the State President.

The act was put into operation on 1 March 1989. At the end of July 1990 (17 months later) 54 applications for the declaration of free settlement areas had been received by the board. A breakdown of the applicants is shown in table 7.1. A geographical breakdown of the location of land involved in these applications is shown in table 7.2.

Table 7.1   Origins of applications for the establishment of free settlement areas

State President	2	(4%)
Ministers' Council: Assembly	15	(28%)
Minister of planning	7	(13%)
Local authorities	8	(15%)
Developers	22	(40%)
Total	54	(100%)

Source: Department of Planning and Provincial Affairs.

Table 7.2   Location of requested free settlement areas

Transvaal	21	(39%)
Cape	17	(31%)
Natal	15	(28%)
Orange Free State	1	(2%)
Total	54	(100%)

Source: Department of Planning and Provincial Affairs.

Of the 54 applications, a total of 11 free settlement areas has already been announced. Of these, 5 have been officially proclaimed as free settlement areas. Another 6 areas have been approved as free settlement areas by the State President, but have not yet been officially proclaimed as such. The remaining 43 areas are still under investigation. Most of these areas are currently classified as white Group Areas.

The cumbersome process prescribed by the act for the identification and eventual declaration of an area as a free settlement area, has drawn much criticism both from left-wing and right-wing circles.

The most influential argument from the left has been that the main aim of the act seems to be not to open up areas as non-racial areas, but to delay and hinder the opening of areas as far as possible. The basis of this argument is the fact that the Group Areas Act is still in operation, and that additional Group Areas are in the process of being planned and declared. Free settlement areas are further intended to be exceptions to the rule and will number only a few in comparison with Group Areas. The Group Areas Act will therefore remain in existence as the basic statute regulating human settlement in the country. These critics are unanimous that both acts should instead be repealed as soon as possible, and all Group Areas be opened for all races immediately.

From the right, the main argument is that the act erodes the provisions of the Group Areas Act and promotes racial integration by legalizing unlawful occupation and squatting by 'disqualified' people in traditional 'white' areas. Right-wing activists want a more active and rigid enforcement of the Group Areas Act, with fewer exceptions granted.

The governing NP argues that a need exists for open areas, where people who prefer to live there can do so. In addition, they want to grant other communities the right to live on their own if they prefer to do that. The opening up of existing closed areas, and the establishment of new open areas, must be done in an orderly fashion by means of which the rights of all affected parties will be protected. Hence, the retention of the Group Areas Act, and the addition of the Free Settlement Areas Act, with its prescribed procedures for consultation and the gradual opening of areas for all races.

After the release of some prominent political prisoners and the unbanning of the revolutionary resistance movements in the country in February 1990, the NP committed itself to the repeal of the Group Areas Act during 1991. This does not necessarily mean that the government has changed its goal of reserving some residential areas for

whites through legislation. It only means that the NP has conceded
that the Group Areas Act has become a liability, instead of an asset
to them. In the meantime, the government is investigating the possibility of alternative, racially neutral legislation to replace the Group
Areas Act. This exercise is probably politically futile in view of the
increasing resistance against the principle of racially reserved residential areas. It can realistically be expected that all Group Areas
will, in the near future, be opened to all races through the repeal of
the Group Areas Act and the Free Settlement Areas Act.

The Local Government in Free Settlement Areas Act

Free settlement areas have serious implications for the government's
system of racially separate local authorities. Probably exactly for that
reason, these implications were avoided, both in the President's
Council's report and in this act which was supposed to address the
problem.

The act provides for the creation of a common municipal voters'
roll for all residents who live in a free settlement area, and who
qualify to be municipal voters, irrespective of race. Those who prefer
to remain voters on the existing (normally 'whites only') voters' roll
can, within 90 days after the declaration of the free settlement area,
exercise a choice to remain on that existing roll.

The Administrator concerned can determine how the voters who
elect to remain on the existing roll will participate in local elections in
future. In the *Administrator's Notice of 1989*,[11] the Administrator of
the Transvaal ruled that they remain registered voters in the ward (if
any) where they had been registered, as if no free settlement area
had been declared. In other words, for purposes of their political participation in local elections, it is deemed as if free settlement areas do
not exist. The only implication of this fiction is that fewer voters will
remain on the voters' roll, necessitating a new delimitation of wards
when the time for that occurs and, where no wards exist, an adaptation to the quota of voters per councillor will have to be made.

These implications are not serious at all, and can easily be rectified
when necessary.

The new non-racial voters' roll created solely for the free settlement area, however, poses more serious complications. Its purpose

is to establish a second-class electorate which does not have the same political rights as other municipal voters because they will not be able to vote directly for members of the municipal council. They are only allowed by the act to elect a MC for the free settlement area similar in function to MCs and LACs established for coloured and Indian municipal voters living in their respective Group Areas within the boundaries of the municipality concerned.

These ethnic committees are subordinate to the municipal council in all respects. The council delegates to them some powers and functions restricted to their Group Areas, either for final decisions, or recommendations to the council itself. In terms of existing legislation, the Administrator concerned can unilaterally transform or 'upgrade' an ethnic MC or LAC into a fully-fledged independent local authority for the members of that racial group. This has the effect that the area concerned is taken out of the jurisdiction of the existing local authority, and a separate sphere of jurisdiction is created for it. In this whole process, the existing municipality does not have any legal say.

The proposed 'grey' MCs for free settlement areas differ only in two respects from the traditional apartheid committees: their voters and members can be of any race; and the MC has equal representation with the city council on a joint committee which is supposed to take final decisions about matters affecting the free settlement area. It is still unclear, though, how decisions will be taken in this committee. The Administrator concerned has the power, in terms of the act, to prescribe a joint decision-making procedure, but so far nothing has been done in this regard in any of the four provinces.

In all other aspects the 'grey' committees are similar to the ethnic ones, even to the extent that they may be made independent, through unilateral action, by the Administrator concerned. This result, as well as the second-class status of voters on that voters' roll, and the lack of clarity about the relationship between the committee and the council concerned, have precluded cities up to now from applying to the Free Settlement Areas Board to have parts of their areas (normally *de facto* grey areas in the central business districts) declared free settlement areas.

Another criticism which has been levelled from the left at this instrument to open Group Areas, is the fact that it uses the approach of, and is put on a par with, the apartheid 'ethnic' committees. The most important argument in this respect is that free settlement is therefore not an attempt to abolish apartheid. It is unacceptable because it is part of the apartheid system.

Even if these complications with the proposed system are overlooked, another serious weakness precludes the implementation of this act in its present form. That is the fact that the act does not provide specifically for the case of whole cities being declared free settlement areas. MCs and LACs can only be established within the jurisdiction of an existing municipality. In order to open up a whole city in terms of the Free Settlement Areas Act, the establishment of a 'grey' MC for the whole area of municipal jurisdiction, the abolition of the existing 'whites only' municipality for that area, and the transformation of the 'grey' committee into an independent, non-racial municipality, will therefore have to be done simultaneously. It is an open legal question whether the legislative provisions which have to be used to effect this result, have been intended for this type of case, and can therefore be used for this purpose.

Political resistance against the effects of this act, and doubts whether the act has been intended to, and can really be used to open cities as a whole, therefore seem to delay its full implementation. It will have to be revised before it can be used effectively to open up whole cities.

This act was the first policy instrument of the government which implied acceptance of the principle of non-racial local government. It was, however, done in a very circumspect way, and it is clear that the act was not really intended to be the final word on a new local government system. It was apparently intended only to open up portions of cities. The vagueness surrounding the second-class status of voters and MC members in free settlement areas, also indicates that the act is first and foremost a transitional measure, and an attempt to avoid taking a stand on these controversial issues.

The government recently announced a few alternative models for a new local government system. They include an explicit, fully non-racial model of local government which makes many provisions of the Local Government in Free Settlement Areas Act obsolete. The contorted procedure to allow some voters restricted political participation in free settlement areas is now clearly out of sync with the latest policy change of the NP. These implications will be analysed and assessed later.

The Group Areas Amendment Bill

The third part of the legislative trilogy constituting the government's reply to the President's Council's recommendations, has not yet been approved by parliament. Since its original introduction in parliament in 1988 it has lapsed. It is inconceivable that it will be resurrected and approved, and will therefore not receive detailed attention here.

The bill provides for the strengthening of existing measures against illegal occupation of Group Areas by people who are 'unqualified' to do so (i.e. who do not belong to the race group for which the area is reserved). It also facilitates procedures for the application of Group Areas policies. Its most important details are the following:

- Penalties for the illegal occupation of property in a Group Area by a member of another race are drastically increased from a maximum of R400 or two years' imprisonment to R10 000 or five years.
- Property which is illegally occupied in a Group Area by members of another race may be expropriated and sold.
- Illegal occupants in a Group 06rea may be evicted from the property after conviction under the act on the order of the minister concerned.
- Inspectors may be appointed to monitor the enforcement of the act and investigate complaints of illegal occupation.
- Areas reserved for black occupation will become Group Areas and will, for the first time, fall under the same legislation as other Group Areas.
- A depreciation contribution may be paid by the state to the owners of property who had to sell the property at a loss as a result of the declaration of the area as a free settlement area.
- Provision is made for the freezing of the value of land considered for the development of sub-economic housing in order to forestall speculation.

This bill was clearly aimed at entrenching existing and future Group Areas against 'greying'. It picked up tremendous political resistance in parliament from every political party with the exception of the NP and the Conservative Party (CP). The NP did not want to send the bill to the President's Council for a final decision and the bill lapsed at the end of the 1988 session of parliament because of the three houses of parliament, only the House of Assembly had approved it.

Since then, the government's announcement that it intends to repeal the Group Areas Act in 1991 has rendered this bill obsolete. It indicates, however, the NP's strong commitment to protecting some residential areas for those whites who prefer mono-racial neighbourhoods.

Alternative local government policies

The NP's latest policy position on local government is that all concerned local communities in a specific area should work out a preferred model of local government through negotiations at local level. The Minister of Planning and Provincial Affairs announced five alternative models for this purpose recently. They are the following:[12]

Model 1: the retention of the existing apartheid structure of racially separate local government bodies, with joint provision of certain services where necessary.

Model 2: the establishment of a special permanent body to provide joint services to racially separate local government bodies.

Model 3: a 'federal'-type arrangement between separate local government bodies which would exercise separate jurisdictions in their respective areas, but would participate in joint decision-making over matters of common concern.

Model 4: one non-racial local authority on a one voter, one vote basis.

Model 5: any other model or permutation negotiated locally and approved by the central government.

The open-ended nature of this range of models enables local communities to put forward a proposal for a new structure for local government suitable to their tastes and needs.

By adopting this policy position, the government changed its traditional 'top-down' approach to local government to a 'bottom-up' approach, where few if any non-negotiables still remain. The parameters for a new local government model are wide open. The structure of local government can now be different from community to community and from province to province. In theory it is ideal to reform local government on the basis of inputs from the communities concerned.

Given the need to break cleanly from the past, any future local government system will have to be based on the principle of non-racialism. This implies the integration of all ethnically separate local government bodies into racially unified local authorities. Therefore the NP's first two models are probably purely theoretical and politically unfeasible.

Judged on its past record, the NP would probably favour either model 1 or 2. On the other hand, it can be assumed on the basis of existing evidence, that the ANC is in favour of model 4. This makes model 3 a possible compromise choice, provided that the constituent units of such a model are not racially based. In terms of model 5, appropriate permutations can be devised by the communities concerned to suit their peculiar circumstances. Options for this purpose may include:

- a strong or weak mayoral system;
- an executive MC system or multiple committees;
- voluntary neighbourhood councils with some delegated powers;
- binding referenda on important issues;
- other measures to increase the accountability of elected councillors to their voters, including regular report-back meetings and a vote of no confidence at a special meeting, automatically vacating the seat concerned;
- electoral wards or a list system for municipal elections; etc.

Both the NP and the ANC are on record that they are in favour of effective decentralization of powers and functions to the local government level. This is necessary in order to maximize the concept of 'bottom-up' institutional development. It includes effective devolution of financial powers of not only expenditure, but also of income generation.

Conclusion

From the above analysis, it is clear that the government's original policy response to the greying of the cities was to devise a set of transitional measures to try to synchronize some elements of a new policy approach with its still existing, but outdated, apartheid policies in this respect.

This approach to social change failed because it was too short term and *ad hoc*. It lacked a principled, comprehensive, and longer term response to developments in society.

The NP misjudged the nature of the changes which started to occur in the inner cities in the mid-1970s. It tried to treat grey areas as manageable (pragmatic) exceptions to the (ideological) rule of separate ethnic Group Areas, while they in fact signalled a new ideology of non-racialism which started to establish itself despite official opposition from the government.

As a result of this miscalculation, the NP's policy failed because it was too incremental to accommodate all the demands for societal change. Instead of taking the initiative, the government waited until the pressure to react to developments became too great. It then used a crisis management approach which tended to address the symptoms, and not the causes of the perceived problems. That explains the contradictions and lacunae in the various acts which resulted from attempts to treat policy problems as minor, isolated cases which had to be treated on their own. In this way they tried to resist and prevent change spillovers to other policy arenas which would have forced a rethink on the apartheid policy in principle. In the end events overtook them, and reform attempts became outdated even before they were implemented.

Much human suffering, and delusions that unfeasible policies were feasible, could have been avoided if political élites in the NP had accepted at an earlier stage the advice of some of its own advisers and that of its political opposition about the inevitability of ideological change. Such resignation to the inevitable could also have saved money, improved human relations, and strengthened the NP's bargaining position in trying to shape future policies more in its favour. NP political élites, however, chose to learn the hard way, and failed in the end. History will probably deal harshly with them.

The latest policy position of the NP regarding local government was largely forced upon the party as a result of an increasing perception in its own ranks of the failure of its original policy. It has eventually caught up with a dynamic, changing society and is probably pragmatic and flexible enough to accommodate very diverse interests at local government level. The prospects for the 'normalization' of local government in the near future are, therefore, very good.

Notes

1 Omar I. 'The Group Areas Act: a Historical and Legal Review' *De Rebus* (July 1989) 515–22.
2 Pickard–Cambridge C. *The Greying of Johannesburg* (Johannesburg: SAIRR 1988) 3.
3 Urban Foundation *Tackling Group Areas Policy* (Johannesburg: 1990) 11–13.
4 Urban Foundation (1990) 11–13.

5 Pickard–Cambridge (1988) 14.
6 Urban Foundation (1990) 14.
7 Pickard–Cambridge (1988) 5.
8 Pickard–Cambridge (1988) 7.
9 Pickard–Cambridge (1988) 6; Urban Foundation (1990) 12.
10 President's Council *Report of the Committee for Constitutional Affairs of the President's Council on the Report of the Technical Committee, 1983 and Related Matters* (Pretoria: Government Printer 1987) 157–62.
11 Dated November 1989.
12 Thornhill C. *Report and Recommendations of the Investigating Committee into a System of Local Government for South Africa* (Pretoria: Council for the Co–ordination of Local Government Affairs 1990).

8 Cities straddling homeland boundaries

Simon Bekker

Introduction

During 1990, debates regarding the future of South African societies were dominated by four themes:

- Whether the political transformation of cities should accompany or follow national political transformation — in short, whether or not the process of national negotiations should be accompanied by a parallel process of city-wide negotiations involving, *inter alia*, existing local government stakeholders.
- How a democratic and non-racial city, and hence a democratic and non-racial city government, should be defined politically and spatially.
- What scope and level of public service delivery (together with appropriate infrastructure) should be established by city governments for city-dwellers, in particular for poorer urban communities.
- What financial arrangements, including both capital and running costs as well as cost recovery, should be associated with these public service delivery needs.

This debate, moreover, has been endorsed and amplified by spokespersons of the South African government and of the ANC, together with representatives of political bodies affiliated to the ANC.

Accordingly, the prevailing issues within the debate are firmly rooted in the nature of urban conflict, urban repression, and urban resistance as experienced during the 1980s. Collective action during this decade revolved around:

- the BLAs;
- the minimal legitimacy they had in the eyes of the residents they were supposed to serve;
- their financial unviability; and
- the fact that they, as 'own affairs' institutions, were intended by government to fulfil black aspirations outside the 10 self-governing and independent homelands for participation in the democratic process.[1]

It is therefore not surprising that the debate has largely ignored the particular conditions which pertain in cities which incorporate areas falling under the jurisdiction of both a provincial administration and a homeland administration.

This chapter will address the particular issues created by the existence of a provincial/homeland divide within such cities.

The separate histories of local government

Historically, local government has been the responsibility of white city and town councils, acting as 'guardians' of the urban areas demarcated for other population groups. It has thus been structured on racial lines.

White municipalities have essentially followed the British model and enjoy considerable autonomy, within the limits of the powers accorded them, and subject to the control of provincial authorities and the central state.

Coloured and Indian MCs and LACs are essentially advisory bodies (to 'parent' white municipalities) and have no decision-making powers. The promotion of the Local Government Affairs Act of 1983 enabled such committees to assume full autonomy, but autonomy has generally been rejected on the basis that it implies acceptance of racial separation in local government.

African local government can only be understood by reference to developments both within and outside the homelands. Outside the homelands, African local government is a recent innovation. Prior to the Black Local Authorities Act of 1982, such institutions that existed possessed essentially advisory powers to superior institutions: initially white 'parent' municipalities, and latterly administration or development boards. With the introduction of the 1982 act, BLAs were thrust into autonomy, with minimal experience and entirely inadequate financial resources. On paper, however, they were granted powers equivalent to those of white municipalities, including primary responsibility for township development. Accordingly, they were supposed to play a particularly important role in meeting the challenge of urbanization. Their essentially contested existence in 1990 points to their failure to meet this challenge.

In white-designated South Africa, the historical evolution of local government along racially separate lines was further entrenched by the Republic of South Africa Constitution Act of 1983. This established the principle of 'own affairs' and 'general affairs'. It further identified local government, within the context of this primary distinction, as an 'own affair'. A recent innovation in the structure of local government has been the introduction of RSCs. These are intended to act as an extension of existing third-tier institutions and are responsible for 'general affairs' — i.e. the bulk or 'wholesale' supply of hard services such as water, electricity, sewerage, transport, and planning, as well as the provision and maintenance of infrastructure in areas of 'greatest' need. The primary local authorities constituting an RSC remain responsible for 'own affairs', especially the reticulation or 'retailing' of services to the household level.

RSCs are intended to fulfil a three-fold function. According to the (then) Department of Constitutional Planning and Development, they promote efficiency and cost-effectiveness through the rationalization of service provision, provide a forum for multiracial decision-making, and generate substantial revenue (from two new levies on business) for the development of infrastructure in the areas of greatest need, namely the African, coloured, and Indian townships. A number of additional reasons underlie the introduction of RSCs. Firstly, they provide a mechanism for 'transfer payment' to African, coloured, and Indian local authorities, as recommended by the Browne and Croeser Inquiries into local government finance. Secondly, they extend the principle of 'own' and 'general affairs' from the national tier and the provincial level to the third tier of government. And, thirdly, they provide umbrella institutions at the local level intended to strengthen legitimacy and viability, and thus enhance the capacity of local government to meet the challenge of rapid urban growth.

RSCs have been established in the Cape, the Transvaal, and the OFS. These regional bodies fall squarely within these three provinces: no RSC operates within a homeland. In Natal, an alternative form of metropolitan authority called the Joint Services Boards (JSBs), which are intended to operate within both Natal and KwaZulu, will shortly be introduced.

In South Africa's self-governing and independent homelands, the development of local authorities has followed a different path from that devised for white-designated South Africa. This path has been a highly centralized one.

Urban local authorities were established predominantly in terms of Proclamation R293 of 1962, which provides for the establishment of township councils. Responsibility for the development and administration of most R293 towns has formally passed to the various homeland governments. However, self-governing homeland governments do not enjoy full autonomy over township councils within their areas. On the contrary, the Department of Development Aid shares responsibility for most service delivery functions in these towns, and has wide-ranging control over finance, often setting uniform tariffs for municipal services in R293 towns. The independence of the TBVC (Transkei, Boputhatswana, Venda, Ciskei) states has, with a few exceptions such as in Mafikeng, heralded little change in this situation. In short, with few exceptions, homeland township councils are severely strait-jacketed regarding functions, powers, and financial freedom.

Outside proclaimed urban areas, there are tribal authorities which reflect traditional forms of government as practised in the particular area, sometimes in the modified form of a community authority comprising tribal chiefs, elders, and elected councillors. In all cases, these tribal authorities have little real say over local affairs and are scarcely more than agents for their respective homeland governments. During 1990, after the fundamental change in political climate heralded by the State President's 2 February speech, two new governmental actions regarding local government transformation took place. Firstly, established local governments were requested to make a choice regarding the 'Kriel' proposals, defined by the Council for the Co-ordination of Local Government Affairs. These proposals included a list of five options for city government arrangements. The minister requested all interested parties in different South African cities to identify, by October 1990, which option they believed would be most suited to their city and their interests.

It is clear that this governmental action signals a preparedness on the part of the authorities to enter into city-wide negotiations on city futures. It is also clear that in the short-term, at least, this action is aimed at cities in white-designated, rather than homeland, South Africa.

Secondly, the establishment of JSBs in Natal and KwaZulu has been planned. Legislation is in place and the demarcation procedure has been completed. In this case, it is clear that the new regional bodies will encompass areas within both Natal and KwaZulu.

Cities which straddle a provincial/homeland divide

If viewed in functional rather than administrative terms, there are a number of South African towns and cities that find themselves fragmented by provincial/homeland boundaries. Some examples of these dual towns are: Pietersburg and Seshego (in Lebowa); Pietermaritzburg, Edendale, and Vulindlela (in KwaZulu); and King William's Town and Zwelitsha (in Ciskei). Queenstown (on the Transkei border) and Fort Beaufort (on the Ciskei border) may also be considered to belong to this category. At city level, there are three examples: East London, Pretoria, and Durban. Since Durban will be used as a case study and accordingly will be analysed in detail, the first two examples will be outlined here.

The city of East London is distinctly smaller than Mdantsane, a sprawling city within Ciskei which was established in the early 1960s as the homeland town to which African residents of East London (living mainly in Duncan Village) were to be resettled. Together, East London and Mdantsane form a conurbation along the banks of the Buffalo river. Workers living in Mdantsane typically have to commute daily to East London's industrial areas, a distance of some 20 kilometres. The distances to other industrial areas in the region are usually longer. City government in East London is fragmented into a series of white, African, coloured, and Indian 'own affairs' local authorities, all accountable to the CPA in Cape Town, while Mdantsane has its own town council accountable to the Ciskei government in Bisho.

The city of Pretoria, when viewed as an economic entity, includes over half a million people who live within Bophuthatswana. The towns of Mabopane, Garankuwa, and Winterveld, all three of which are located within the Odi Moretele region of Bophuthatswana, form part of the Pretoria Functional Region (PFR). These towns, situated as they are next to one of Pretoria's main industrial areas, Rosslyn, are managed by local or communal authorities accountable to the Bophuthatswana government in Mmabatho. Their neighbouring urban areas within the PFR (such as Attridgeville, Laudium, Pretoria, Verwoerdburg, Eersterust, and Mamelodi) each have an 'own affairs' local authority which is accountable to the Transvaal Provincial Administration (TPA).

The fragmented city of Durban

Durban, however, is a prime example of a city divided by a provincial/homeland border. Over the next decade, this city will grow from 3.5 to 5.5 million people, an increase of 2 million in 10 years. By the turn of the century, over half of all African residents of KwaZulu/Natal will be living in the Durban Functional Region (DFR). The informal or shanty settlements within which approximately one half of African Durban residents currently live will, in all probability, further expand, and will continue to accommodate no less than half of these Durban residents. Since the vast majority of African residents in Durban live either in KwaZulu or in settlements on released land owned by the South African Development Trust (SADT), well over two-thirds of the population of the DFR resides in dense settlements located outside the province of Natal. The DFR contains a diversity of local authority bodies. These are not only structured along racial lines but differ in size and in terms of the duties which they undertake. Local authorities under the control of the Natal Provincial Administration (NPA) differ in status. There are boroughs, town boards, town committees, health committees, and the city council. Two Indian areas within the region have obtained borough status. African townships under NPA control have not yet reached either town or city council status in terms of the Black Local Authorities Act of 1982. The Development and Services Board (DSB) is responsible for development and regulated areas. On trust land which is administered by the Department of Development Aid, there is a township committee and a non-operative advisory board. The Indian and coloured LACs are advisory structures. There are also certain urban areas with no formal representation, which are served by the NPA. Local authorities in KwaZulu are either urban authorities with local government functions controlled by the KwaZulu Department of the Chief Minister under Proclamation R293, or are regional tribal authorities with limited functions and services provided by the KwaZulu Department of Works.[2]

The extent of local authority fragmentation within the DFR is illustrated by listing the various local authority structures within the region. Firstly, within the adjoining parts of KwaZulu, which are intended for African Durban residents alone, there are four urban local authorities and 15 chieftaincies within four regional tribal authorities. Some of these tribal authorities, though, do not fall fully into the DFR. Six chieftaincies are found within the Ndwedwe Regional Authority, four within the Umbumbulu Regional Authority, and five within the Georgedale and Hammarsdale areas.

Secondly, on released areas and land owned by the SADT, one township committee and one advisory board have been established. This SADT land is intended for use by African Durban residents alone.

Thirdly, within Natal various local authority structures have been established which are intended to represent the four statutorily defined population groups. These structures include one city government, 11 boroughs, seven town boards, two town committees, 15 development areas, and three regulated areas under the control of the DSB. In addition, there are a number of dense settlements within the DFR where there is no formal local authority, and others where public responsibility is shared by a number of different authorities, often at different tiers of government. Accordingly, in 1990, the public institutional situation in the DFR reflected a mosaic of uncoordinated local authorities ('own affairs' local bodies within Natal and a variety of tribal and other bodies within KwaZulu and on trust land). As a consequence, the city endures a persistent fragmentation of service delivery to its various communities. Planning for the region, moreover, is highly centralized. It takes place in Pietermaritzburg, Ulundi, and Pretoria rather than, in devolved form, within the DFR itself.

The core city government of Durban, together with a few other white DFR local governments, do operate as effective service delivery authorities within their areas of jurisdiction. Virtually universally, other DFR local authorities, often through no fault of their own, are strapped by the twin weaknesses of lack of credibility and lack of viability (both in financial as well as human resource terms). These weaknesses are especially apparent in KwaZulu, where urban local authorities are defined as little more than agents for the KwaZulu government and for the Department of Development Aid, and where tribal authorities are faced with urban problems their institutions were not designed to handle. Given this division, what prognosis may be offered for the proposed Durban JSB, a regional body which may well be able to play the role of a much needed metropolitan authority?

Joint Services Boards

The KwaZulu and Natal Joint Services Act (84/1990) is closely modelled on the Regional Services Council Act of 1985. There are, however, two major differences. Firstly, the pivotal role played by the Administrator in the RSC system is instead assumed by the Joint Executive Authority (JEA) which incorporates representatives from both KwaZulu and Natal. Secondly, the new metropolitan authorities will include, from the outset, local bodies in KwaZulu as well as in Natal.

The history leading up to the promulgation of the JSB act is a long and complicated one.[3] Suffice it to say that the KwaZulu Legislative Authority, after years of opposition, has agreed to the act; that criticisms of the act have been voiced regarding, *inter alia*, the 'own affairs' local authorities underpinning the JSB, and its link to the JEA; and that the first JSB (one of which will operate in the DFR) will be launched in a period of change and transition politics, which will undoubtedly deeply affect its foundation.

The burden of fragmentation

During the period of political transition in the 1990s, it is useful to analyse the challenges facing South African cities — those which straddle a provincial/homeland divide in particular — along seven dimensions:[4]

'Own affairs' and 'general affairs' City governments will need to move away from their statutorily defined ethnic foundations. Policy and practice, which have evolved regarding separate Group Areas and regarding separate public amenities, are the two prime examples within this category. In the case of cities which straddle provincial/homeland boundaries, this process of change is complicated by the fact that homeland governments themselves — and hence the local authorities which are accountable to them — are defined as ethnic institutions. They may be conceived of as grand 'own affairs' bodies. Accordingly, it will only be once these governments have been functionally and democratically reincorporated into the wider South African body politic that such cities will shed their fragmented ethnic characters.

Areas of jurisdiction The spatial form of government is a second issue over which debate has revolved. Questions regarding the areas of jurisdiction — defined in functional rather than ethnic terms — of city governments dominate discussion. In the case of cities which straddle provincial/homeland boundaries, the critical issue concerns the criteria used to decide whether or not local authorities within the relevant homeland should, or should not, be involved in some way in appropriate city-wide governments. Should East London and Mdantsane form a single metropolitan authority? Do Umlazi and KwaMashu belong within the Durban metropolitan region? And so on.

Informal settlements South African cities already include large numbers of shack settlements and shack dwellers. It is well known that these urban dwellers create particular challenges for city governments, challenges regarding both service delivery systems, as well as appropriate forms of representation. In the case of cities which straddle provincial/homeland boundaries, shack settlements tend to be located on the homeland side of the divide. Both the heritage of influx control, as well as land close to urban centres which is more accessible to informal dense settlement on the homeland rather than on the provincial side of the boundary, are primary reasons. Accordingly, it is homeland authorities — those least capable of tackling the task — who are faced with the major shack settlement challenges in these cities.

Training and qualifications of officials and councillors African local government has only recently been introduced by the South African government. It has only been introduced in white-designated South Africa and participants in the process have experienced a trial by fire due to rent boycotts, threatening bankruptcy, extremely poor polls, campaigns aimed at creating 'ungovernability', accusations of corruption, service delivery crises, and recent calls for the total scrapping of BLAs. All have pointed to the failure of the government's strategy in the 1980s of reform from the 'bottom up'. Nonetheless, these experiences have developed a cadre of experienced councillors (and some administrators), a group who may well serve their communities to better effect under a better dispensation.

In the case of cities which straddle provincial/homeland boundaries, however, councillors and African officials have had no such responsibilities thrust upon them. They have operated essentially as agents of homeland administrations, and most often of inefficient administrations at that. Little similar experience will have developed in this grouping.

Local government finances It has become common knowledge that BLAs — which are expected to be financially self-sufficient in their current accounts — suffer from an inadequate revenue base. Revenue sharing via RSCs, moreover, cannot meet the fiscal crises of these authorities. Current debate on this issue focuses upon the principle of shared city-wide revenue bases.[5] In the case of cities which straddle provincial/homeland boundaries, local authorities located within homelands have received large annual subsidies from the Department of Development Aid to balance their current accounts. These authorities, moreover, are not responsible for their annual budgets, and rarely become involved in discussions regarding tariff adjustments. As a result, the costs of basic local authority services in homeland residential areas are typically substantially lower than their equivalents in provincial residential areas within the same city. Tariff harmonization, when and if it is introduced in these cities, will probably result in substantial intra-city migration. On the other hand, dense settlements which fall within tribal authority areas of jurisdiction are often not required to pay for services, and where such charges are levied, the responsible authority is typically far removed from the communities.

RSCs and JSBs Positive features of RSCs include their administrative and institutional capacities. They bring together different representatives of different areas of the larger metropolis, they engender recognition of the extent of mutual interdependence within each region, they highlight the shortcomings and needs in less developed African areas, and they raise and redistribute regional revenue. Their weaknesses include the reality that RSCs are based on 'own affairs' local authorities. They are not directly accountable to residents, they are in a cleft stick regarding their finances, and are torn between the need for revenue for capital projects and the realization that increased turnover and payroll taxes are likely to depress urgently required economic growth and development. They are undermined by deep-seated suspicion on the part of many residents in their areas of jurisdiction. In the case of cities which straddle provincial/homeland boundaries, RSCs exclude urban areas which are located within homelands. This is a critical weakness since it undercuts a number of the advantages listed above, i.e. the recognition of mutual interdependence within the city in particular. Accordingly, the prospective establishment of JSBs in the Natal/KwaZulu region should be seen as a significant step forward in this regard since JSBs will straddle the Natal/KwaZulu divide found in particular in Durban and Pietermaritzburg.

The process of local government transformation As stated in the introduction, the major issue of debate here concerns whether the political transformation of cities should accompany or follow national political transformation — in short, whether or not the process of national negotiations should be accompanied by a parallel process of city-wide negotiations involving, *inter alia*, existing local government stakeholders. In the case of cities which straddle provincial/homeland boundaries, it is clear that this issue immediately coincides with that concerning the future constitutional positions of the four independent and six self-governing homelands of South Africa.

Notes

1 Bekker S. and Jeffery A. 'Local Government in Urban South Africa: a Normative Approach' *Local Government Series* (University of Natal: Centre for Social and Development Studies 1990) Working Paper no. 1.

2 Evans R. 'BLAs — Bread–and–butter Politics' *Indicator SA* (1988) 5 iv 51–6. Pistorius R. *Governmental Institutions in the Durban Functional Region* Tongaat Hulett Planning Forum (Durban: 1989).

3 Bekker S. et al. 'Metropolitan Government in Durban' *Local Government Series* (University of Natal: Centre for Social and Development Studies 1990) Working Paper no. 2.
McCarthy J. 'The Last Metropolis: RSC Stalemate, Indaba Checkmate' *Indicator SA* (1988) 5 iv 45–8.

4 These seven dimensions are not intended to cover the present debate on local government transformation comprehensively. There are, for instance, issues such as the form of the franchise, which are of equal importance to all cities, whether they fall squarely within white–designated South Africa or not. Rather, the seven dimensions have been chosen so as to highlight those issues which need separate consideration in cities which straddle a provincial/homeland divide.

5 Phillips M. (editor) *City Futures: Workshop Proceedings* (Johannesburg: Centre for Policy Studies 1990) 3.

9 Local government finance and institutional reform

Nigel Mandy

Separate local governments for urban African communities are administratively ineffective, financially unviable, and politically of dubious legitimacy.

Today there is near-unanimity on the need to work out new models of non-racial and regional government, suitable to the needs of each economically-bound urban area. Government wants existing structures to be maintained during a period of transition; but civic activists seek to destroy them immediately through boycotting service charge payments and at times more robust actions. During 1990, encouraging progress was made towards resolving the crisis on the Central Witwatersrand, but elsewhere politicized confrontation is exacerbating financial and administrative problems.

Historical background

Each WLA used to administer African residential areas or 'townships' within its municipal boundaries. Thus, for example, on the Central Witwatersrand, Johannesburg was responsible for Soweto, and nearby Roodepoort for Dobsonville. A third township to the south-west, Diepmeadow, had been created by central government to accommodate people resettled from Sophiatown and other inner-city areas against the wishes of the Johannesburg City Council. Diepmeadow was run by the Natives Resettlement Board.

All fixed property was owned either by the central government or by the local authority. House rents were low, as were standards of housing, infrastructure, and services. Commercial and industrial activities were discouraged in this regimented environment. Consequently there was no base on which assessment rates could be levied. Revenue for the administration of the townships was largely dependent on a municipal monopoly of liquor sales, but Johannesburg and some other municipalities did cover annual deficits from their general rates funds.[1]

During the 1960s, government policy was based on two delusions: firstly, that the process of African urbanization could be halted by influx control; and secondly, that new economic opportunities to be created in the homelands would pull increasing numbers to return whence they had come. Consequently, it was believed that there was no need to upgrade the conditions in which Africans lived in the urban areas. Those municipalities which tried to help African residents to live normal lives were regarded as being wilfully obstructive of the government's grand design.

Great consternation was caused in official circles in 1967 when the Johannesburg City Council's planning department published a report which stated that the city's African population had evolved into a settled urban community whose numbers were expected to increase by 50 per cent by 1980. This approach was condemned by a government committee of inquiry whose report led to the enactment of the Bantu Affairs Administration Act of 1971.

Under the act 14 Administration Boards were created to administer African townships and to enforce influx control in all South Africa's African urban areas. Among these was the West Rand Administration Board (WRAB) with responsibility for Soweto westwards, and the East Rand Administration Board (ERAB) for African townships from Germiston eastwards.

The Central Witwatersrand

The Central Witwatersrand, with the city of Johannesburg at its core, is South Africa's largest metropolitan area. A review of the situation there will illustrate how the present crisis has developed, and how current problems might be resolved.

Until 1972 the three townships that comprise Greater Soweto were regarded as an integral part of Johannesburg for the provision of all kinds of services and for the purpose of forward planning. These advantages were lost when WRAB took over in 1973.

Excision of a large part of the Johannesburg City Council's responsibility explains its parochialism and declining vigour for many years, and the frustration of many of its ablest officials.

Greater Johannesburg's fourth African satellite is the township of Alexandra in the north, adjoining Sandton. Established in 1912, this township was controlled not by a WLA, but by the Peri-urban Areas Health Board, an organ of the TPA. Freehold rights were formerly available without racial restriction, but were expropriated by the government in 1963. Housing and services were in very poor condition when WRAB assumed responsibility in 1973.

Takeovers by Administration Boards were superficially conceived and incompetently executed. Subsidies from municipal rates accounts ceased, and other financial resources were lacking. The benefit of shared expertise with white municipal departments greatly declined. Costs increased while efficiency diminished. Every attempt to increase site rents or even recoup losses on services like electricity, water, and sewerage inevitably became an explosive issue, with the government finding itself in the embarrassing position of being the sole landlord. The will to tackle real problems diminished because residents were seen as problems to be controlled, not as constituents to be served.

The Riekert Report of 1979 compared the financial reports of the Administration Boards for 1973/4 with those three years later for 1976/7. Expenditure on general services had increased almost threefold, capital expenditure had doubled, and the levies paid by employees had nearly quadrupled; but services and the boards' financial positions were deteriorating.[2] The Cillie Commission of Inquiry into the 1976 riots in Soweto and elsewhere found that a contributing factor had been resentment of Administration Board actions and dissatisfaction with inadequate services and facilities.[3]

In an attempt to improve the situation, a system of African community councils was introduced in 1977. Various powers were transferred to them in theory, but in practice they were subservient to the Administration Boards. Inexperienced councils were expected to make good shortfalls incurred by Administration Boards over which they had no control, under a policy with which they disagreed. Rents and service charges had been kept at uneconomically low levels for fear of political consequences. Service levies payable by employers had been frozen.

A departmental memorandum pointed out that it had never been the policy of government to subsidize any local authorities. These were 'on their own' as far as collecting revenue for their functions was concerned. As long as a council was dependent on subsidies — outside financial aid — there could be no question of autonomy. Council bodies should be weaned from dependence on outside aid in order to attain real meaningful local autonomy.[4] This statement should rather have been turned the other way round: unless a community is properly endowed at the outset, and unless it is provided with adequate sources of revenue, any appearance of autonomy is merely an illusion.

In order to meet their financial responsibilities, there was heavy pressure on community councils to increase township rents. The term 'rent' is a misnomer which has given rise to much misunderstanding and friction. House rent constitutes a fraction of the monthly charge. The rent comprises a levy for general municipal services, and charges intended to cover the steeply escalating cost of utilities supplied.

Like tenants under rent control, township residents had no conception of the cost and economic value of the services which they were receiving. Once such a market distortion had been established, especially in the emotionally-charged field of housing, it was extremely hazardous politically to try to eliminate it. The unfortunate councillors were on the horns of a dilemma. One sharp point was the need to ensure that township services continued to function, and the other was the inevitable wrath of their constituents if 'rents' were raised.

The basic issues were encapsulated in a newspaper's interview with SCA leader, Dr Nthato Motlana:

> Imagine people who cannot afford it being made to pay about R40 a month for rent and an additional large amount for electricity. What is needed is a hefty amount from the government to uplift Soweto.
>
> If the whites want us to live 30 km away from them, then they must pay for that privilege. We did not ask to be put these long distances out of town so that services for transport, for lights and water are stretched.
>
> We should be near our places of employment as happens all over the world. The lower and labouring classes live next to the factories, not far away in the suburbs — that's for the rich.
>
> The Central Business District and the industrial areas of Johannesburg are common to all inhabitants of the city and

rates that everybody pays should serve all people.

You can't justify our high rates for transport and other things by saying it's high time Africans paid for their services. How do they pay when salaries are not governed by productivity and skill but by colour.

The City of Johannesburg has subsidised Soweto for many, many years. This was not out of philanthropy because we were entitled to our fair share of the cake. Our money is spent in Johannesburg.[5]

Inadequate finances, insufficient control

The government was prepared to do no more than to guarantee loans raised by councils for capital works, such as the electrification of Greater Soweto. Such loans, together with operating costs, would need to be serviced out of future revenues. Subsequent events have shown that expectation to be unrealistic.

The government should have been doing everything possible to strengthen its new creations. Instead, unrealistic financial policies discredited and destabilized the BLAs.

The Browne Committee of Inquiry into Local Government also reported in 1979. Appointed at the instigation of WLAs which thought themselves hard pressed financially, it suggested no new sources of revenue for them. At that time government policy still contemplated the conversion of coloured and Indian MCs into fully-fledged autonomous local bodies, but Browne's adverse report helped smother that misguided concept.

Browne rightly observed that reorganization in a local authority system was generally accompanied by substantial costs, and predicted that the shortage of skilled and experienced staff would cause problems.[6] Apprehension was expressed that in the new dispensation for BLAs, financial control would not be afforded its due recognition.[7] Despite this warning, their treasury departments have been understaffed, and especially in the lower grades, personnel have often been inexperienced and unmotivated.

In 1986 the dramatic step of abolishing influx control was taken. The Administration Boards (which in the mean time had been renamed 'Development Boards') were abolished. Their supervisory functions were transferred to the TPA. BLAs had more powers and responsibilities conferred on them; but they remained ill-equipped to manage the newly acknowledged process of African urbanization.

Some comparative statistics

The nature of the problem may be illustrated by some comparative statistics compiled for 1986, before the four-year rent boycott caused Greater Soweto's financial position to deteriorate still further.

Johannesburg's municipal area measures 45 591 hectares. Adding Randburg, Roodepoort, and Sandton, the 'white' local authorities of the Central Witwatersrand cover 86 645 hectares. Their estimated population in 1986 was 1 350 000, of whom about 60 per cent were white, 25 per cent African, 11 per cent coloured and 4 per cent Indian. (Since then the African component has grown very rapidly in Johannesburg.)

For Africans, the combined areas of Soweto, Diepmeadow, Dobsonville, and Alexandra cover only 8 468 hectares. Accurate population statistics are not available, but an informed guess is that these areas accommodate about 1 800 000 people.

Average population density in the four white areas combined was thus 16 persons per hectare. Subtracting the large areas covered by mines and industries, the actual density was probably about 25 persons per hectare, which equals the norm adopted for white residential areas in the 1986 Draft Guide Plan for the Central Witwatersrand.

For the much smaller combined areas of the four BLAs, population density was then in the vicinity of 200 per hectare — far more than the 97.5 regarded by the Draft Guide Plan as appropriate for African settlement.

For the sake of simplicity, further comparisons are made only between the two councils of the first magnitude in size, namely, Johannesburg and Soweto proper.

Johannesburg's operating expenditure for 1986 was projected at R786 million, Soweto's at R104 million. Johannesburg's income from rates, plus profits on services, was budgeted at R203 million; Soweto had no rates income and projected a loss of R26 million on services. Johannesburg's base of capital assets was of course far larger, and much had been acquired at historically lower cost. The ratio of annual income to total external debt was 120 per cent for

Johannesburg, but for Soweto (assuming no boycott) it was only 19 per cent. This was a sure sign of financial trouble to come:

Johannesburg budgeted for a deficit of R3.9 million, which did not eventuate. Soweto budgeted for a deficit of R25.9 million which proved to be over-optimistic, being based on the mistaken assumption that there would be no boycott of rents and service charges.

Compensation for lack of viability

By the mid-1980s, the government had come to realize that the BLAs' infrastructural installations were inadequate and deteriorating rapidly; also that their revenues were insufficient to cover operating expenses and loan service charges.

Attempts to address the first issue were made by the creation of RSCs, and the second by means of 'bridging finance' loans from the TPA.

Regional Services Councils

Under the Regional Services Councils Act of 1985, RSCs have now been established in all the provinces except Natal, where a variant is now being introduced to take into account sensitivities in the KwaZulu/Natal situation. In the Cape Province, the system has been grafted on to the existing Divisional Council bureaucracy, but in the Transvaal, much leaner new structures have been created.

African councillors represent BLAs on the councils and executive committees of RSCs. Disputes concerning the legitimacy of BLAs have spilt over on to the RSCs. Nevertheless a good start has been made with non-racial bodies at the regional level controlling substantial funds.

The guiding principle, as stated in section 12 (6) of the RSC act, is that in determining the appropriation of funds, each RSC should give preference to the establishment, improvement, and maintenance of infrastructure and infrastructural services in the areas where needs are greatest.

RSC funds are raised by means of two levies, namely, the establishment levy on turnover, and the service levy on the payroll of business activity. Each RSC may (subject to approval by the Minister of Finance) set its own rates of levy, but there are obviously advantages to minimizing divergencies from a nationwide norm.

Originally there were complaints from the private sector that these levies would be complex and expensive to administer. However, experience has shown that the great majority of businesses complete returns without difficulty, using existing accounting systems.

More serious are some criticisms which have been raised on economic grounds by David Solomon. The turnover levy could affect the profitability of different business sectors to a greater or lesser degree, dependent on customary markups therein. It does seem that commercial activities tend to bear a heavier proportion of their profits than does manufacturing. There is a possibility that some enterprises might resort to vertical integration in order to avoid the incidence of taxation. And it is contended that by affecting the demand for labour, the payroll levy might force immobile workers to accept jobs at wages reduced by the payroll tax.[8]

These theoretical arguments have little practical force at the currently prevailing rates which are a low 0.11 per cent on turnover and 0.25 per cent on payroll. However, the situation could change if rates of levy were to be multiplied several times in order to finance possible additional functions such as subsidization of BLAs' operating costs and/or urban mass transportation.

Solomon suggests that a preferable alternative might be a centrally-imposed tax, accompanied by a revenue-sharing formula.[9] Such a centralized system would, he says, introduce subjective policy consideration into the allocation of funds. The recent diversion of the fuel levy from the Urban Transport Fund to the general Treasury, highlights the great advantage of having a dedicated fund available within a region, under the control of that region's own representatives.

Another revenue-raising possibility is to impose levies on the cost of supplying electricity, water, and sewerage disposal. This has not yet been tried.

RSCs have considerable borrowing capacity, bearing in mind their relatively assured flow of future income and the fact that (unlike municipalities) their own operating costs are low. Until now there has been little need to resort to borrowing because levy income has been flowing in faster than funds could responsibly be expended on projects which first need to be selected, designed, and put out to tender. That situation is changing as projects are vetted, and as new demands arise to assist BLAs in meeting their operating costs. The East Rand RSC (ERRSC) has already approved a regional sewerage scheme to be financed by loans serviced from future user payments.

Metropolitan and country RSCs compared

At present the enabling legislation prescribes a uniform structure for RSCs. Thus, in the Transvaal, the same system applies for three divergent types:

- Firstly, a high-density metropolis having a single core city, typified by the Central Witwatersrand RSC (CWRSC) with Johannesburg at its core. This covers 1 045 square kilometres in which there are 14 local bodies, including the 4 BLAs and some coloured and Indian MCs.
- Secondly, a multinucleated and more spread-out metropolitan belt, typified by the East Rand, whose RSC covers over 3 000 square kilometres and contains 32 local bodies.
- Thirdly, a widely-spread country area, typified by the Oosvaal RSC, headquartered at Bethal. This covers 34 000 square kilometres and has 62 participating local bodies. Its area is 33 times larger than that of the CWRSC, revenues are far less, and overheads are proportionately far greater.

In this third category, issues should be seen as relating more to the interdependence of each white town with its African satellite, than to the regional situation. The urgent need is to develop shared financial and management structures in each urbanized entity. There the RSC could be a useful source of finance, more than a co-ordinating administrative body.

The Central Witwatersrand RSC

A metropolis may be defined as a large area which is integrated economically and socially, but within which local government has been fragmented into several bodies. In such circumstances unco-ordinated planning, execution, and management tend to waste scarce resources, including skilled workers, and to cause environmental errors. Residents naturally tend to identify with parts rather than the whole, and there is an understandable desire by the more fortunate to maintain their existing standards.

In South Africa, co-operation on the metropolitan level is complicated by major ethnic and cultural differences, and by racial segregation whose settlement patterns and consequent resentments will remain long after apartheid legislation has been repealed. Nevertheless, the recognition of metropolitan identity is growing fast among the councillors of the constituent members of RSCs, particularly on the Witwatersrand.

Despite the predominant voting powers enjoyed by the constituent WLAs, RSCs have consistently allocated the greatest part of their revenues for the benefit of disadvantaged African, coloured, and Indian areas. Thus in his June 1990 budget speech, CWRSC chairperson John Griffiths reported that since its establishment in 1987 (and including the 1990/1 provisions) an amount of R661 million had been provided to assist constituent local bodies. Of this, R465 million had been allocated directly to developing bodies, while most of the rest had been for regional projects from which they had benefited.

The CWRSC had become the major, and in most cases the sole, provider of finance for the capital programmes of the BLAs in its region. Outright grants (not loans) were financing sewerage disposal, electricity, water, roads, stormwater drainage, refuse removal, and the provision of community facilities such as halls, libraries, clinics, and sports fields. A new and much more efficient computerized billing system had been provided for the treasuries of the four BLAs.

These capital projects appeared on the budget of the individual local authorities, but the RSC supervised efficient tendering and contracting procedures, using private sector consultants wherever appropriate. Provision was also made for proper maintenance in order to prevent facilities provided from falling into disrepair.

Very significantly, Griffiths observed that it was evident that the RSCs would in future have to play a more important role in alleviating the pressure on the operating accounts of local bodies, and in particular of the BLAs.[10]

The CWRSC's own operating expenditure comprised a mere 3.27 per cent of anticipated levy income for the year.

Bridging finance from the TPA

The TPA has in recent years rendered assistance to needy BLAs in the form of so-called 'bridging finance' loans. Since the councils have insufficient revenue to cover current expenses, it is unlikely that these loans will ever be serviced.

This system of bridging finance has had several unfortunate consequences. It has postponed the moment of truth when fundamental issues of local government financing must be faced; and it has channelled funds to those BLAs where boycotts have been prevailing to the disadvantage of those whose residents were meeting their obligations to pay service charges.

The TPA's budget for the financial year April 1990 to March 1991 provided for R428 million in bridging finance, well up from the previous year's R322 million. In his budget speech, Administrator Danie Hough noted that one of the TPA's major tasks was to undertake an urban development support programme to eliminate the backlog that had accumulated over the years in respect of the African sector of the community. He anticipated intensification of the onslaught on African local government which was taking place on two fronts, namely, open intimidation of councillors to get them to resign, and encouragement of residents not to pay normal municipal tariffs.

Boycotts had deprived councils of operating funds. The councils then approached the TPA for assistance to pay for bulk services purchased and for normal operating expenses. Hough warned that the province had only limited funds at its disposal for this purpose.[11]

The boycott spreads

For some years the boycott had been largely confined to Greater Soweto and to the Vaal Triangle BLA of Lekoa. However, early in 1990, the ANC and various civic associations were successful in motivating a boycott of rent and service charges in BLAs throughout the Transvaal. Demands made included the immediate resignation of African councillors and the replacement of BLAs by vaguely defined, non-racial, combined municipalities; writing off arrear rental and service charges; the negotiation of more affordable tariffs; and the transfer of rented housing stock to occupants.

The percentage of charges collected, which had previously varied from 60 per cent to nearly 100 per cent in various BLAs, often dropped to under 20 per cent and in some cases far lower. Residents' motives for withholding payment included political conviction, apprehension of intimidation, and financial convenience.

For a municipality, it is easy to cut off the services of one defaulter. However, enforcement becomes very difficult when thousands are not paying, and when attempts at collection are frustrated by various forms of militant action. Compounding the problem was ineptitude, and in some cases even sabotage within the municipal administrations.

Repeatedly the TPA issued warnings that the boycott was depleting funds budgeted for bridging finance far more rapidly than had been anticipated. In August 1990, a series of advertisements appeared urging people to pay in order to ensure the continuation of essential services. From September onwards, the scale of bridging finance was drastically reduced, with priority being given to the payment of salaries.

A most unfortunate aspect was that well-run BLAs, where collection had until recently been good, were required to exhaust all their capital development funds and other reserves before qualifying for bridging finance.

Shack and informal settlements

As the urbanized African population has grown through natural increase and inward migration, so an additional dimension has been added to the problem.

The building of shacks in the backyards of many township homes has perforce had to be allowed. Usually these have accommodated additional people, but now increasingly there is a tendency for the density of occupancy per room in the main house to be relieved by movement to outbuildings. Either way, the additional demands on already overloaded service systems in the BLA areas have been severe.

Householders have not hesitated to charge their shack tenants substantial amounts for rent and for electricity and water consumed, despite the fact that they themselves have been boycotting payments to the BLAs.

In addition, many new informal settlements have sprung up. Some of these are inside existing BLA areas, while others are further afield outside municipal boundaries. Some are unauthorized (as at Phola Park in Tokoza, where thousands have settled on land intended for industrial development), while others (as at Orange Farm to the south and Ivory Park at Midrand to the north of the Central Witwatersrand metropolis) are being created with government assistance. Land has been purchased on which plots have been laid out systematically with rudimentary services, with formal land title obtainable. Signs of upgrading through personal initiative are apparent in some areas, while others are being crippled by internecine strife. In some peripheral areas, the number of squatters is overtaking and surpassing the number of residents in formal housing. National Housing Commission funds have been made available in substantial amounts to help in resettlement, but land invasion is also taking place on a large scale.

It seems clear that much of the urban increase can only be accommodated in informal settlements with lower overheads and fewer demands on organized services and maintenance. But if the cost of providing land and even rudimentary services is to be recovered, then quite substantial charges will have to be levied on the residents of such areas, and somehow be collected from them (to the extent that subsidization is not feasible).

Available inexpensive land is mostly situated on the periphery, far from the city centres and places of employment. Consequently, affordability of transport costs presents a further complication.

Just as residents of white towns are in a more advantageous position than those in BLAs, so the latter are now significantly better off than those in the new informal settlements.

Soweto's finances analysed

Initially the SCA on the one hand, and the Soweto City Council and the TPA on the other, had refused to speak to each other. During 1989 cautious talks and investigations commenced with the SPD representing SCA interests. By mid-1990 a process of negotiation had been worked out whereby the investigation and formulation of proposals would be done in a Joint Technical Committee (JTC). Its members would report to the respective principals who would meet in formal session as and when necessary. Soon the Diepmeadow and Dobsonville Councils were joined in the process.

During negotiations it was agreed in principle that services should be paid for, and that people should be willing to pay for whatever they received; also that in addressing the issue of tariffs, both affordability and the cost of providing services would be relevant.

Research done by the JTC provided, *inter alia*, the following facts.

Bridging finance provided by the TPA to these three BLAs from 1984 till July 1989 had amounted to R792 million. The current level of assistance at R28.6 million monthly by mid-1990 could not be sustained.

Virtually no payments were being made on the electricity account. Since metering discipline was no longer maintained, consumption of power had soared, greatly increasing the council's debt to Eskom and endangering the operation of the whole distribution network. Water consumption averages were also high. That was to be expected where metering was not being enforced. Refuse removal and sewerage costs were close to the norm for local authorities, but these services were generally inferior — partly because of inefficiency, but partly also due to abuse by many residents.

The provision of bulk services alone was costing R13.8 million per month in Soweto. If tariffs could be collected in full (and assuming an average electricity consumption of 600 kWh units per house) the potential maximum monthly income was only about R6 million, but in fact less than R2 million per month was being collected during the boycott period.[12] Table 9.1 shows that the cost per household of operating the Soweto BLA as at June 1990 was R330.47 per month. If there had been no boycott, the maximum that could have been collected would have been R72.50 per month. The gap was enormous, yet residents felt that they were paying too much.

The BLAs' financial disadvantages relate primarily to administrative and community costs, and to loan charges.

In the Johannesburg municipal area, businesses pay 70 per cent of service charges and 74 per cent of assessment rates. As the business core of the country and of the metropolis, it has an exceptionally high proportion of commercial and industrial properties. Soweto, by contrast, has a minute proportion of such properties, and for various reasons it is proving very difficult to add to their number.

The existence of such a large concentration of businesses paying rates and service charges undoubtedly keeps Johannesburg's charges to residents substantially lower than they would otherwise be. The call for a shared tax base is thus understandable. However, aspects to be taken into consideration include the substantial expenditure by Johannesburg on providing services to commerce

Table 9.1 Soweto City Council: cost of municipal services and charges per house as at June 1990

Consumer services (bulk purchase plus operating cost):

Electricity	R106.74
Water	R 31.23
Refuse removal	R 13.97
Sewerage	R 11.25
	R163.19
Administration and community services such as housing, health, roads, and stormwater drainage	R 92.92
Loan charges	R 74.36
	R330.47

Source: Memorandum dated 30 August 1990, submitted by the Joint Technical Committee to the joint meeting of the Principal Bodies which concluded the Greater Soweto Accord.

and industry and to people throughout the metropolis, its existing commitments which leave little leeway for redistribution, and the advisability of maintaining standards in the increasingly multiracial city.

Loans by BLAs have been incurred in a belated and expensive attempt to improve their infrastructure. The burden of interest and capital repayment ought logically to be a charge on the wider community. In practice that is happening: firstly, by the government paying up as a guarantor under old loans; and secondly, by the RSCs providing grants for new capital investments.

The Greater Soweto Accord

Following on intensive negotiations, the Greater Soweto Accord was concluded on 24 September 1990 between the councils of Soweto, Diepmeadow, and Dobsonville, the SPD, and the TPA.

The immediate importance of the accord was to be found in the agreement to end the rent and service charges boycott, and the confirmation that R516 million of arrear debts owing by residents to the councils were being written off. This implies that debts owing by the council to the TPA will probably also have to be written off.

The electricity metering system would be reinstated with co-operation from the SPD, in addition to which an interim fixed charge of R23 per month would be levied for other services.

The chairperson of the principals' meeting, Fanie Ferreira (a member of the TPA's executive committee), praised the spirit of conciliation and mutual understanding in which the parties had come together in the best interests of all the people of Greater Soweto. He emphasized that the cost of supplying services and of administering the three council areas greatly exceeded the amounts which were to be collected in accordance with these arrangements. Indeed, even after further negotiations had achieved more realistic, affordable tariffs, large operating deficits would still need to be made good from other outside sources. Moreover, there was no scope for servicing debts which had previously been incurred for capital expenditure and bridging loans.

In the short-term, approaches would be made to the CWRSC, the Development Bank of Southern Africa, Eskom, and the Rand Water Board for assistance. In the longer term, the situation required a more logical reorganization of local and regional administration and finance within the metropolis of the Central Witwatersrand. To that end, the parties had resolved to form a Metropolitan Chamber to include the city council of Johannesburg and possibly other nearby local authorities as participants. It would serve as an interim forum whose primary purpose would be to investigate and formulate the setting of regional, non-racial, and democratic policy approaches for implementation at the metropolitan level. The chamber would not aim to duplicate the work of the RSC or any other existing organ of local government, nor would it usurp the authority of any existing local authority. All its decisions would be taken on the basis of consensus.

The chamber would appoint working groups to investigate and make recommendations for implementing solutions to such issues as upgrading the services and infrastructure of Greater Soweto, affordable tariffs for services, transferring the rented housing stock to residents, and establishing a common fiscal base for the metropolis.[13]

At the end of November 1990, discussions were proceeding on the inclusion of other local authorities on the Central Witwatersrand (including Alexandra) before formally constituting the chamber.

Electricity

A particular cause of contention has been the supply of electricity. As a direct result of the boycotts, by the end of October 1990, Eskom was owed over R70 million by various BLAs to which it supplied power directly. Summons had been issued against several of these, but bankrupt councils were unable to meet the demands. In other areas electricity was supplied via the systems of adjoining WLAs, some of which resorted to switching off the supply as arrears mounted.

Prepayment meters were being installed successfully in some small areas, but the total installed cost of about R500 per meter made provision of these devices impractical on a large scale even though they improve cash flow, facilitate household budgeting, and reduce operating costs. Another factor to take into consideration is the need to invest large amounts in repairing and upgrading run-down and inadequate systems.

An alternative approach might be to supply power at a fixed monthly charge via limited-capacity circuit-breakers.

The possibility of Eskom undertaking to supply electricity directly to individual consumers is increasingly being canvassed. That would depoliticize part of the problem, but would leave unsolved many others which the beleaguered BLAs are facing.

RSC assistance

The various RSCs have been approached for assistance to supplement the TPA's bridging finances as an emergency measure till March 1991, and thereafter in some manner still to be formulated. Funds for this purpose have been found primarily through cancelling or postponing infrastructure projects in BLA areas which had not yet been committed contractually.

In the Central Witwatersrand, the investigation included the three councils of Greater Soweto and also Alexandra. In a dramatic move, the CWRSC agreed not only to reschedule funds allocated for capital projects for the improvement of infrastructure, but also to provide additional financial assistance for basic operating costs. In that manner it could help to ensure the uninterrupted supply and maintenance of essential municipal services.

In regard to the supply of electricity, the CWRSC would pay approximately one-third of Eskom's account to cover the proportion of power used by local authorities in respect of street and high-mast lighting, the pumping of water and sewage, and other municipal purposes. Eskom would carry the risk of supply and therefore it would decide at what point the supply might have to be stopped if residents and other consumers did not satisfactorily meet their electricity account obligations. Eskom would also consider introducing a new residential tariff, applicable to dormitory towns and cities, which could effectively reduce the tariff by approximately 15 per cent.

The CWRSC's investigation established that for the period September 1990 to March 1991, the four councils would require R172.7 million to enable essential operations to continue. Only R20.1 million of this was expected to come from the council's own sources (excluding electricity) and R25.8 million by way of bridging funds from the TPA. R86 million would be made available by rescheduling funds from projects intended for improvements to infrastructure. The balance of R41 million (plus the CWRSC's electricity contribution of R27.4 million) would be funded from income (R8 million) and from short-term loans (R60 million) to be raised by the four councils, with the CWRSC underwriting their interest and redemption responsibility.

The CWRSC would require the four councils to submit credible financial plans for increased income, a reduction of expenditure, and co-operation with neighbouring WLAs; action against illegal users of services and defaulters; and the development of a longer-term economic tariff structure with due regard to affordability and availability of bridging finance.

These arrangements would take up 56 per cent of the CWRSC's levy income. That figure is well beyond the 20 per cent to 25 per cent proposed by the TPA as the assistance level to which RSCs should commit themselves. From April 1991 the state would be expected to accept a greater responsibility in assisting and meeting the shortfall, so that the CWRSC would not be required to provide more than 25 per cent of its budget for operating costs, to enable funds to remain available for upgrading and improving infrastructure.[14]

In a similar fashion the ERRSC was able to make R27.6 million available to the 14 BLAs in its area. Those funds would be used for the bulk purchase of water and sewerage services, and as far as possible also for refuse removal. Nothing would be provided for electricity, which the ERRSC did not regard as an essential service. Furthermore, the ERRSC's financial assistance made no provision for repairs, maintenance, and operating expenses. The continuation of essential services could not be assured, so that negotiations for the payment of interim charges assumed an even greater urgency in BLAs there.

Conclusion

By the end of 1990, supplementary funding provided by the government through the provincial administrations had largely been dissipated in purchasing bulk supplies of essential services. Repairs and maintenance had perforce had to be neglected, leading to the imminent collapse of many services and greatly increasing the ultimate cost of their restoration. A cautious movement towards joint administration with adjoining white towns was starting, but white municipal electorates were uneasy at the thought of joint municipalities in which African residents might not be prepared to make appropriate contributions to the cost of municipal services.

The signing of the Greater Soweto Accord gave hope that a process of return to normality had started, but the six-year-old boycott in Lekoa continued unabated.

Negotiations with civic associations and other bodies of concerned residents were achieving limited results in some places where interim fixed charges were to be paid while talks proceeded. Even in these cases, the proportion of residents who were resuming payments was in general not satisfactory. Clearly it was easier to start a boycott than to end one.

In many other BLA areas negotiations were in a state of deadlock. In several places resort was being made to switching off electricity supplies, leading to great resentment from people who had been paying, or who had been prevented from doing so; and also from many who considered that electricity should be free. Factional violence and lawlessness were on the increase.

The newly formed CAST was demanding the disbandment of all BLAs, but the depth of its support by the individual civic associations and people of the various BLA areas was uncertain. At the same time it had commenced negotiations at regional level with the TPA.

One of the most serious problems to be faced in post-apartheid cities will undoubtedly be the desperate situation of disadvantaged areas which will of necessity continue to be inhabited predominantly by persons who are African. Financial and administrative assistance will have to be provided by metropolitan authorities, and by the central government.

Notes

1 Lewis P. 'A City within a City — the Creation of Soweto'. Unpublished lecture. (University of the Witwatersrand 1969) 19–22.

2 Riekert P. J. *Report of the Commission of Inquiry into Legislation Affecting the Utilization of Manpower* (Pretoria: Government Printer RP32/1979) paras. 4.387 and 3.23.

3 Cillie P. *Report of the Commission of Inquiry into the Riots at Soweto and Elsewhere* (Pretoria: Government Printer RP55/1980) para. 600.

4 Mandy N. *A City Divided — Johannesburg and Soweto* (Johannesburg: MacMillan and New York: St Martins Press 1984) 213.

5 *Rand Daily Mail* 10 August 1979.

6 Browne G. W. G. *Report of the Committee of Enquiry into the Finances of Local Government in South Africa* (Pretoria: Government Printer 1979) RP 51/1980 1, para. 11.7.2.

7 Browne (1979) 11.7.2.

8 Solomon D. 'The Financing of Regional Policy: the Regional Services Councils' *South African Journal of Economics* (1990) 58 ii.

9 Solomon (1990).

10 Griffiths J. Unpublished chairperson's speech on the 1990/1 budget of the CWRSC (1990).

11 Hough D. Unpublished Administrator's speech on the 1990/1 budget of the TPA (1990).

12 Greater Soweto Joint Technical Committee (1990).

13 Ferreira F. Unpublished chairperson's speech on the signing of the Greater Soweto Accord (1990).

14 Central Witwatersrand RSC resolutions (October 1990).

10 Autonomy in local authority finance

Gerhard Croeser[1]

Introduction

Throughout the contemporary world, there are increasing problems related to the effective control of state spending through existing budgetary techniques. Despite valiant efforts, budget deficits are tending to increase as a proportion of gross domestic product. This involves growing state debt and resultant state burdens.

One favoured method in recent times of reining in state expenditure is to focus more sharply on how the various spending units slot into the budgetary system and on how the financial relations between the national centre, or central unit, and the subordinate units are arranged. The government's policy objectives, as they surface in the budgets of these subordinate spending units, are measured in terms of inputs; but the problem is how to measure output and optimum performance, or, as the Americans would put it, how to get 'more bang for the buck'. The obvious answer of the market-oriented private sector would be: better management, more local decision-making, and a cost-centred approach to ensure that the work involved met predetermined norms. Such an approach, aimed at raising both the efficiency and the effectiveness of public spending, warrants more attention in South Africa where, as elsewhere, there has in recent years perhaps been too great an emphasis on the stabilization and redistribution functions of government, at the cost of greater efficiency and effectiveness in the expenditure process. This latter objective can be realized, *inter alia*, by way of fiscal decentralization.

Ever since Margaret Thatcher's views on public finance began to be given concrete form in the 1980s, the pursuit of economic efficiency, rather than a myopic concern with stabilization and redistribution, has been the focus of attention. This was the case not only in the United Kingdom but elsewhere too. Devolution of fiscal powers, deregulation, and privatization are, in fact, simply the means of moving closer to the market mechanism in the provision of public goods and services.

Against this background, and based on the host of writings on decentralized budgetary control, the emerging pragmatic budget model looks somewhat as follows:

- The central government's responsibility should be confined to a broader policy on stabilization and redistribution, plus a small number of policy functions of a national character.
- The subordinate authorities should handle regional and local functions of direct concern to the communities involved.

This model, then, envisages a limited role for central government, and an extended role for local government, in the provision of public goods. The successful implementation of such a model is in large measure dependent on local autonomy and decision-making, accountability and responsibility, as well as on tax effort. Fiscal discipline will in all probability be gravely impaired when regional and local spending units regard themselves as mere agents of the central government.

Viewed from the taxation angle, the public sector in South Africa emerges as one of the most centralized in the world: excluding the TBVC countries and the self-governing territories, some 94 per cent of the tax revenue is collected at central level, 1 per cent at provincial level, and 5 per cent at local level. (Local authorities do, of course, add substantially to their revenues by way of the profits derived from commercial services such as the provision of water and electricity.)

By contrast, 80 per cent of expenditure takes place at central level, 9 per cent at provincial, and 11 per cent at local level.

This fiscal structure manifestly has implications not only for the ability of particular authorities to function as autonomous units, but also for the establishment and maintenance of financial discipline. Decision-makers operating in such a climate can easily succumb to the temptation to view their activities as agency services for the central government, and can argue with equal ease that the funds involved (especially shortfalls) will always be forthcoming from the central exchequer.

Centralization versus decentralization

The high degree of centralization under the present constitutional dispensation in South Africa raises the question of the merits or demerits of a centralized, as opposed to a decentralized, approach to public finance.

The main advantages usually adduced for centralization are:

- In those cases where the services involved confer wider benefits than those for the direct users (i.e. where so-called externalities are present and no individual can be excluded from the benefits), the central government is better placed to ensure efficient allocation.
- Differences between the fiscal capability of authorities on the same tier (i.e. horizontal fiscal inequalities) can be meaningfully reduced only via centralized governmental measures.
- Greater efficiency and scale economies in tax administration can be achieved.

In contrast, the following are regarded as important advantages of decentralization (where in this context decentralization implies the devolution of powers and not merely administrative delegation to lower levels in a head office/branch office relationship):

- Where the benefit of the service can be confined largely to the direct users of that service, decentralization has the advantage that the cost of the service, and the price charged, can be more closely linked. Put another way, those receiving the benefit, those paying for the benefit, and those providing the benefit are brought nearer to one another. This means that the services provided will have a value determined by their market which, in turn, will ensure a more efficient allocation of production factors.
- Appropriate services can be provided for smaller and more homogeneous communities which, in turn, contribute to greater efficiency and effectiveness, as well as to the depoliticization of the provision of services at central level.
- Another advantage is a greater willingness by the community to contribute financially and otherwise to local projects, since it is itself involved in decisions in this regard.
- Lastly, decentralization has the advantage of a relatively smaller degree of monopoly power than in the case of centralized government, which again contributes to greater efficiency in the provision of services.

Centralization does, of course, labour under significant drawbacks, inasmuch as the central government is manifestly less knowledgeable and less sensitive to the needs of all the constituent elements of the community. As one writer puts it:

... if administration is controlled by a remote government ... either or both of two things often happen: 1. the people become apathetic, expecting the paternalist[ic] government ... to do everything for them. Moreover, they cease to observe the immediate connection between the taxes they pay and the services which the remote government provides; so they do not feel concerned to prevent waste or extravagance by officials, for they do not think of the government's money as in fact their own; 2. the people suspect that their own local needs are being neglected or that they are not understood.[2]

The drawbacks of decentralization are, to a great degree, the mirror image of the advantages of centralization, namely, the handling of the wider benefits (externalities) of services provided on a decentralized basis, differences in the fiscal ability of decentralized governments, and the duplication of functions (such as tax collection) where centralization offers many scale benefits. In the nature of things, moreover, decentralization has considerable implications for the training of staff at lower government levels and/or the transfer or secondment of staff from higher levels.

Where centralization or decentralization involves both advantages and disadvantages, a pragmatic approach that seeks to combine the best of each is obviously indicated.

The government's view on decentralization to local authority level is set out in the guidelines accepted in 1982 for a new constitutional dispensation. Its commitment was also reaffirmed recently by the State President who, when addressing the 1990 Congress of the Cape Municipal Association, said that the government sought 'the greatest possible devolution of power to the lowest effective decision-making level. This embraces, *inter alia*, the maximum shift of government functions to the local government level, and the minimum central administrative control'. He added that 'devolution of power is meaningful only if accompanied by the devolution of sufficient fiscal resources and powers'.

In line with this policy, various functions and powers have already been transferred from state departments to provincial administrations, while further such devolution is constantly under consideration.

A good deal of work remains, however, with regard to the devolution of powers and functions from the central and regional (or middle) levels of government to the local tier. There has, however, been good progress towards reducing the degree of control over local authorities.

Toward a definition of financial autonomy

If autonomy in the financial sphere were to be defined in the first instant as the ability to finance at least current expenditure from self-generated revenue, then the majority of local government bodies in South Africa would meet this criterion. This does not, of course, apply to the large number of BLAs that for various reasons (quite apart from the present difficulties with non-payment) are unable to balance their books. This is so because even though they are, for all practical purposes, regarded as autonomous or self-governing bodies, this has failed to make them financially viable. This raises a question mark over their survival in the absence of adaptations to the system as it now operates.

There is usually a definite link between the viability and the autonomy of a particular government body. Viability should be the basis for autonomy: the more viable a local authority is, the more autonomous it will be, until it reaches the stage where it is able to dispense with external help in the making and execution of its decisions.

The following minimum can be proposed for the powers needed by a public body to function independently or autonomously: namely, the body concerned should be able to exert its authority via:

- determination of activities, i.e. of objectives and policy;
- determination of the executive institutions (organization);
- personnel recruitment;
- determination of work procedures;
- generation of funds from available sources, and the utilization or allocation of those funds; and
- control measures.

Government bodies at executive level exist to promote the good of the communities they are accountable to. The crucial test of such bodies is thus the general welfare of the community concerned.

In this milieu, political office-bearers must decide which matters are so essential for the welfare or even existence of the community as to require that the authority concerned should itself handle those matters on the community's behalf. In so far as the rights and liberties of the members of the community may be infringed when authority intervenes, and since the community will be looked to for financial input, decisions of this sort are of critical importance; the matters to be so dealt with, and the extent to which this must be done, are normally embodied in legislation.

In most democratic states in which a three-tier structure of legislative institutions is in operation, each tier normally has the power to create executive bodies of its own. The basic prescriptions concerning the relations among the executive organs of the several levels of government are normally embodied in the constitution. The political superstructure covering all three tiers is likewise prescribed. An executive body thus has no powers of taxation, nor has it any funds at its disposal other than those with which the legislators have endowed it. By laying down how public revenue is to be raised and public expenditure to be incurred, the legislatures retain a vital prerogative: 'the power of the purse' is the ultimate veto of the legislature over the executive.

In South Africa, local authorities fall under the direct control of the central and the regional authorities; they operate on the one hand in terms of parliamentary legislation that charges them with certain functions, and on the other in terms of the provincial ordinances applicable to them. Their powers are also spelled out in the ordinances. But municipal councils also exercise a legislative function through the framing of by-laws concerning the matters assigned to them in terms of parliamentary statutes and provincial ordinances. These by-laws, however, have legal force only within the jurisdiction of the municipality concerned, nor may they clash with parliamentary enactments or provincial ordinances. As to BLAs, their functions and powers are laid down in the Black Local Authorities Act of 1982.

Further refinement of the definition

If, by way of a second approach, financial autonomy were to be so defined so as to embrace not only the capability of financing current expenditure from self-generated revenue, but also the power of choosing which revenue sources are to be exploited and to what extent, then no local government body in South Africa would qualify.

This would also be the case if, in a third approach, the definition were extended to encompass the power of freely deciding on how available funds should be utilized. The statutes and ordinances referred to above prescribe, in some detail, not only which revenue sources may be exploited by local government bodies, but also what funds may be spent on. In other words, all the possible functions that such bodies may perform are spelled out in the legislation.

In addition, prior approval must be obtained for certain tariff adjustments, and all local authorities are subject to macro-budgetary control by the Treasury over their annual expenditure. The budgets of RSCs must be approved by the Minister of Finance, while the provincial administration must approve the budgets of the BLAs.

Against the backdrop of the government's stated policy of decentralization, the question arises whether existing statutes and ordinances should be so adapted as to bestow a higher level of autonomy in accordance with the second or third approaches outlined above.

Policy execution and local authority spending

Although there is doubtless much room for a further relaxation of control over local authorities, there are certain spheres where the supervisory or monitoring function can never be completely abolished. These include the following:

- Since the government is responsible for the overall management of the economy, it must always monitor the magnitude of local authority spending, the quantum of borrowing by that sector, the total tax burden imposed at that level, and the range of those taxes. The current expenditure of local authorities, whether financed from local or national tax sources, impacts on the aggregate tax burden in the economy and also on the relationship between private sector and public sector production.
- Local expenditure is also important in the light of the central government's anti-inflation stance, which may involve attempts to restrict the rate of monetary expansion or constrain public sector

borrowing so as to reduce pressure on interest rates. The local government sector must share this responsibility.

• Containing inordinate growth in local authority spending also forms part of the ongoing effort to contain the size of the public sector as a means of both lowering taxation levels and giving the private sector greater choice in its use or provision of goods and services.

• The central government's right to involve itself in local level finance is not always easily accepted. It is maintained that local authorities possess independent taxing powers and that, should they decide to finance extra expenditure from this source, the central government has no say in the matter. According to this argument, the central government should limit its involvement to the overall contribution made by national taxation to the cost of local services. The argument against high levels of taxation is not, however, confined to national taxation but applies with equal force to local taxation. Only the central government is in a position to judge the competing claims on national resources. There can thus be no question of its being indifferent to the level of local authority expenditure and taxation: it remains responsible, after all, for maintaining broad economic stability.

From the foregoing, however, the impression should not be gained that South Africa needs more centralization — quite the opposite is true. A far greater measure of fiscal authority needs to be devolved to the local government level. This should then be coupled to an increased measure of voter control at local level. Revenue sources in turn need to be devolved, or at least shared on an unconditional basis.

As to whether there should be adaptations in the existing statutes and ordinances to provide local authorities with greater freedom in the raising and spending of funds, the emphasis should initially be placed on the removal, as far as possible, of micro measures of control. Local government is, after all, a part of the government hierarchy in any country, and it cannot be expected of the higher levels that they should altogether renounce the supervision they exercise at macro level through their powers to prescribe at least the nature and extent of functions to be executed at lower level, and the revenue sources that may be exploited in the process. Were they to do this, their own status, and thus the whole state system, would be impaired.

Guidelines for intergovernmental financial relations

The foregoing exposition leads to the conclusion, firstly, that the degree of financial independence or self-government, reflected in the second and third approaches to the definition of autonomy outlined above, is not fully attainable for local government institutions in South Africa. Secondly, a pragmatic approach requires a suitable mixture of centralization and decentralization. Given the present constitutional changes, and also the necessity for government services to reflect in greater measure the needs of the society as a whole, then far greater weight will have to be given to decentralization in the future constitutional/financial model for South Africa.

The question arises, however, concerning what guidelines are needed to facilitate devolution to the local authority level. Such guidelines could include the following:

- As regards the three primary government functions, the central government must retain responsibility for economic stabilization, while the allocation function should, as far as possible, be vested in the middle and local tiers. This will ensure that the greatest correspondence between services and their beneficiaries in a particular community is obtained. As to the distributive function, a distinction should be drawn between redistribution between regions, which should be a central government responsibility, and redistribution among persons, in which all tiers of government can play a role.
- As far as the rationalization and division of functions are concerned, government policy on the devolution of functions to the lowest possible level of government should be noted. Higher levels of government should thus be responsible only for the overall or macro formulation of policy and co-ordination, but not control.
- If, in accordance with the policy to devolve functions, greater decision-making powers are granted to middle and local tiers of government, this should involve greater responsibility, accountability, and reporting.
- Ideally, all government entities should be fiscally autonomous, i.e. they should both generate sufficient revenue to finance their current expenditure, and have powers of decision over their own revenue and expenditure. There should, therefore, be a direct link between the spending and taxation decisions of such entities. Inordinate access to intergovernmental transfers from the central

level is therefore contra-indicated.

- Decentralization of functions will thus have to be accompanied by a shift of revenue sources. Regard must be given to the implications that arise for efficient administration, and for the current national shortage of a skilled work-force.
- Intergovernmental transfers in a future dispensation must be strictly based on objective financial norms that take into account the fiscal capacity, the needs, and the tax effort of the various government entities, as well as of the country as a whole.
- Serious consideration must be given to establishing, or extending, fiscal discipline and public reporting on the part of government entities. Greater fiscal autonomy at middle and local level will have to be suitably balanced by adequate measures to ensure accountability and public reporting, failing which the control measures over activities at these levels will not be capable of being lessened as desired. Micro control by higher government levels over the activities of lower-level government should therefore give place as far as possible to more effective control by the voters themselves.
- In the allocation of functions to lower tiers, regard should be given to the common nature of the different functions, the geographical area the services cover, the nature of the product or service, the recipients of the service, and any externalities present.

A future dispensation

The foundation stones of any future system of intergovernmental relations should rest on the following principles:

- Firstly, the constituent government entities should each possess a degree of financial autonomy that, at the least, complies with the 'first approach' definition given above.
- Secondly, those government entities should possess an adequate institutional infrastructure.
- Thirdly, the broad public, and in particular the taxpayer, must be enabled to play a much more prominent role in the spending decisions (and thus also the taxation decisions) of the government bodies under which they fall. Public accountability and reporting at lower government levels must be greatly extended.
- Lastly, but perhaps most importantly, the system must permit any

right of recourse: every government body at the middle and lower levels must make do in each financial year with its available revenue and will, in no circumstances, be able to call upon a higher authority for assistance in the event of funds having become exhausted. This also applies to the question of guarantees, whether implicit or explicit, on loans raised.

In conclusion, a few additional comments may be made on each of these foundation stones. As to financial autonomy, it can be anticipated that in a new dispensation, not all local government bodies will be able to generate sufficient revenue to meet the minimum requirements for autonomy. Apart from the possible future necessity for sharing specific revenue sources at local level, this also raises the question of intergovernmental transfers, briefly referred to above. In particular, the sensitive matter of minimum standards emerges here. Such an approach means that a conditional contribution will have to be made by a higher government tier to the revenue of a lower tier, so as to ensure minimum standards of service in a limited number of high-priority areas. Communities desiring higher or other standards will then have to look to their own financing.

As to autonomy in general, the viewpoint of the Thornhill Report[3] is supported, namely that in a new dispensation, provision will have to be made for various degrees of autonomy, and preferably also for various degrees of control. A local authority would then have to earn greater autonomy on the grounds, *inter alia*, of efficient and effective provision of services, the degree of financial self-sufficiency, and the level of participation through democratic processes. The granting of such autonomy could possibly, as envisaged in the Thornhill Report, take place in accordance with a suitable categorization. This implies that initially only a very limited form of autonomy could be granted to local authorities in the lowest category: this would involve a limited number of powers and functions. The degree of autonomy would then be gradually adapted in the course of time in step with the progress made by the authority concerned in meeting the requirements for greater autonomy. An approach of this sort would presumably depend on the availability of the services of some other body, which would have to provide certain functions in the interim so that the community concerned was not denied them altogether. Such a body would presumably also have its own revenue sources. Regional entities, such as the RSCs, may be able to play a part here, at least as financier of some, or all, of the services involved.

An adequate institutional infrastructure is vital because without this, no dispensation has a hope of success, even if adequate arrangements can be made regarding financial resources.

This imperative is further enhanced if a new dispensation brings with it a shift to the local level of certain important functions at present being performed at middle level. Much thought will still have to be given to this subject, especially with regard to the possible role that can be played by single-purpose institutions at local government level in the provision of specific services, as well as to the possible creation of joint administrations supplying services to more than one local authority.

As to accountability and public reporting at local level, an investigation is already under way. This would seem to be one of the areas where the higher-tier authorities will have to make a special contribution to the implementation of a suitable system of control, and particularly voters' control. In general, it would seem desirable that a system should be pursued whereby micro control by higher-level authorities is increasingly phased out and replaced by voter control, in line with the progress made by a particular local authority towards full autonomy.

As to the last foundation stone, serious consideration should be given to whether a future dispensation should not embody a legal requirement that the annual budgets of at least middle-level and local-level government institutions must balance, or must comply with certain financial prescriptions, such as their debt ratios. Indeed, the idea of a 'fiscal rule' will have to be seriously considered at central government level too.

Notes

1 This chapter is based on a paper delivered by the author on 1 August 1990 at a seminar of the South African Institute for Public Administration.
2 Allen H. *Decentralization for Development: a Point of View* Planning and Administration (1987) 24.
3 Progress Report to the Council for the Co-ordination of Local Government Affairs, on the Investigation into Uniform Legislation for Local Government in South Africa (May 1990).

11 Privatization and municipal reform

Chris Heymans[1]

For some time now, the South African government has been saying that it might want to 'privatize' some local authority functions, and some municipalities have actually begun privatizing. This process has been met by fierce resistance from trade unions and community groups. Privatization remains, nonetheless, on the agenda and raises important questions both about reforms of the existing system, and about a future system of local government.

Some of its proponents see privatization as a means to address many of the current financial and administrative problems of local authorities. Others maintain that a post-apartheid government might fruitfully consider local level privatization as a way to reduce the burden on the central state. Critics say its social and economic implications would be disastrous and that it has no place in a fair and just South Africa of the future.

This analysis *does not* offer definitive 'answers' to the many questions at stake. It aims, rather, to contextualize the debate on privatization and to raise some issues which could be conducive to rational and informed debate, both about suggestions for privatization in the present system and in the future.

It defines 'privatization'; traces its ascendancy on to the international and South African political/economic agenda; briefly surveys privatization initiatives in fields other than local government; and then focuses on *local level* privatization, internationally and in South Africa, through some empirical observations and by highlighting a number of the functional and political complexities around the privatization issue.

What is privatization?

The South African government's White Paper on privatization and deregulation of 1987 defines privatization as 'a systematic transfer of appropriate functions, activities or property from the public sector where services, production and consumption can be regulated more efficiently by the market than price mechanisms'.[2]

In terms of this definition, privatization involves a changing relationship between the public and private sectors. Two changes stand out: first, the transfer of assets from government to non-government ownership, and second, the replacement of state management and planning by competitive markets. The presumed policy outcome is the gradual reversal of government control over economic production and service delivery. The latter aspect of privatization is particularly relevant to the local level. These three aspects of privatization — ownership, competition, and public policy — warrant specific attention, also in relation to a clarification of the methods of privatization.

Privatization as a public policy has its roots in attempts, mainly since the late 1970s, in various countries to reverse the growing state involvement which has characterized western political economies since the 1930s as a result of, first, Keynesian influences and secondly, the growth of 'welfare states'. Increasingly sceptical about the discretionary manipulation of an economy in pursuit of socio-political objectives, the protaganists of privatization seek to reduce the role of the state in economic management.[3]

Proponents of privatization argue that it opens the production and service delivery processes in the economy to private — and by implication more efficient — management. They say that it stimulates competitive efficiency and introduces market-orientated economic processes. These are contentious views. For example, whereas privatization could enhance competition by shifting control over services and production to a variety of economic actors, it is not inevitable. Many observers point out that private monopolies could merely replace public ones (hence, the putative competitive advantages would not occur). Furthermore, notions of 'efficiency' vary, and economists continue to debate the question of whether privatization would enhance efficiency. It is also possible that the benefits of privatization could be restricted to a limited part of the population, while the rest might suffer if they have to pay (higher) market-related prices for their services, etc.[4] It would therefore seem that a number of the putative advantages of privatization are dependent on the assumptions one makes about certain causes and effects and the meanings attached to a number of concepts.

Regarding ownership, Truu[5] asserts that 'fully-fledged privatization' is established by the sale of at least 51 per cent of the shares in a public entity to private shareholders; thus control shifts from the public authority to private shareholders.

However, this is but one of various means to achieve privatization. At least five measures can be identified in this regard:

- The first is the sale of public enterprises and assets to private companies and individuals.
- Secondly, it could entail partnership arrangements where the public retains an interest, while allowing greater space for private interests and for the utilization of private-style management.
- A third option is the leasing of business rights for the management of some traditionally public sector-managed activities (toll roads are an example).
- Fourthly, services can be contracted out to enable the private sector to undertake public services on behalf of the public sector.
- Finally, services previously provided by the public sector can be discontinued.[6]

The significance of defining privatization in a wider sense than a mere transfer of state assets to private control, will become apparent later in the analysis when the South African government's responses to fierce opposition to privatization are discussed. It could also have implications for intermediate and long-term strategies aimed at reconciling the demands and interests of supporters and opponents of privatization.

Some international trends

Margaret Thatcher's policies 'to reinforce the market principle' in Britain played a considerable part in placing the privatization option on the public agenda.[7] Thatcher's privatization initiatives resulted in the transfer of 15 large and numerous small state-controlled corporations to the private sector. By 1988, the British government had sold over £30 billion of public sector assets and by 1987 an estimated 600 000 posts had been transferred to the private sector.

The policy was not an obvious priority at the time when Thatcher came to power in 1979; in fact, the Conservative Party's agenda did not even refer to privatization. However, it followed almost logically from the Thatcherite emphasis on a reduced role for the public sector; and once it took off, the process gained considerable momentum. The first privatization steps took place only in 1981 when British Aerospace was privatized. Since then, however, the process has accelerated at a rapid pace. Between 1981 and 1983, privatization brought the treasury over £700 million. The step which most vividly placed the privatization strategy on the public agenda, was the privatization of British Telecom in 1985. This boiled down, effectively, to selling off the assets not merely of a utility, but of a government department. This was followed by the privatization of British Airways in 1987 and preparations are under way for similar steps in the sphere of electricity provision.[8]

In Britain, the key areas for public sector asset sales at local level have been housing and land. The Housing Act of 1980 requires local authorities to sell council houses and gave council tenants the right to buy council houses at up to 50 per cent discounts (increased to 60 per cent in 1984). In the light of the long-standing opposition of many local authorities to such steps, the act enabled the central government to take over the task from reluctant local authorities. If a local authority delayed the sale of housing units, the Secretary of State for the Environment could appoint a Housing Commissioner to administer the scheme. These powers were not used often. However, they inevitably held serious consequences for the autonomy of local authorities. Furthermore, they facilitated the sale of 750 000 housing units by councils within the first four years of the new dispensation. By 1987, the Conservative Party prided itself during the general election that 'more than a million council homes have been sold in Britain since 1979'; about two-thirds of which involved sales to sitting tenants under a 'right-to-buy' scheme.[9]

The principle of facilitating the sale of council houses was not uniquely Thatcherist; in fact, it was introduced first by the Heath government in the early 1970s. It was also implemented without great resistance by the Greater London Council when it still existed.[10] However, under the Thatcher government these actions assumed new priority, and since 1980 considerable increases in such sales have occurred. Within the first five years of Thatcherist rule, public sector house completions were reduced by 50 per cent from 108 000 to 54 000.[11]

Major sales of land assets also occurred. The 1980 Local Government, Planning and Land Act obliged local authorities to produce registers of unused or under-used land in their ownership, and the Secretary of State was granted power to release certain sites. This has had a particularly significant effect on the release of land for private sector building activities. Between 1979 and 1986, local authorities in England sold land to private developers for around 52 000 houses; 16 500 houses were built through joint ventures between local authorities and private developers; and local authorities themselves built 7 000 low-cost houses for sale.[12]

Local authority services are being contracted out to increase efficiency by placing these services under the control of firms with a profit motive, and which would, theoretically, be free from the limitations of state bureaucracy.[13] Privatization also aims to reduce the role of the public sector, enhancing that of the private sector. Local authorities invite bids or quotes from private companies to take over services, such as refuse collection. In theory, the local authority should benefit, as the contract is supposed to go to the lowest bidder.

British officials cite various success stories in this respect. They claim that many councils have been able to save at least 30 per cent per annum on their previous service costs for refuse collection. According to officials, the Wandsworth Council, for example, which has been one of the leading privatizing institutions at the local level, has been recording annual savings on service costs of up to £6 million per annum.[14]

Despite various central government measures to encourage privatization of services, the process has proceeded rather slowly. The efforts to 'encourage' this form of privatization included, firstly, the government's introduction of controls over works departments to ensure increased contracting out. The government also established an Audit Commission to stimulate cost-efficient service delivery. In 1987, a bill was passed enforcing the principle of 'competitive tendering' more forcefully: local authorities now have to compete with the private sector for the majority of their construction and maintenance work.

The British government has been consistent in emphasizing the need for private contracts as a means to enhance efficiency. The Urban Development Grant scheme provides central government finance for projects jointly prepared by local authorities and the private sector which involve 'significant' private finance.[15]

However, local governments have to date not responded to these incentives with any great dedication. Although privatization has taken place, the magnitude of the process has been markedly more limited in the local sphere than at national level. Officials in British local authorities ascribe this to various problems which have delayed the process. One of the most difficult areas was the specification of the work carried out in a manner which would enable the local authority to intervene in the event of the private contractor being unable or unwilling to provide the service at a sufficient level of quality.

Furthermore, a number of other steps are always necessary; if not formally so in a legal sense, then at least to succeed in mobilizing sufficient political support from various interest groups. Thus, officials say that feasibility studies, consultations with trade unions, information meetings with affected staff, public notices, etc. caused the process to be severely delayed.

In fact, senior local government officials in Britain persistently stress the politically sensitive nature of the privatization process. They point out that Labour Party-controlled councils in particular, as well as trade unions, have thus far opposed the programme vehemently. This has spurred the Conservative Party on to enhance the levels of competitive tendering; some observers, for example, argue that 'competitive tendering' can be traced back directly to the 'winter of discontent' of 1978–9 when municipal workers were in the forefront of numerous strike actions. Thus, control over services at local level became a key aspect of the conflict between the Thatcher government and unions.[16]

However, there is ironically an increasing meeting of minds on the matter emerging at the moment, albeit not specifically on the issue of privatization. The notion of 'enabling' local authorities has been gaining ground among a wide spectrum of interests in Britain. Traditionally, local authorities were viewed as service-producing agencies; hence they were supposed to produce the services which they delivered. Now, the emerging view is that they should merely be 'enabling agencies', making it possible for local residents to receive services as cost efficiently as possible. For conservatives, this includes, *inter alia*, privatization. From the Labour Party and trade union perspective, however, the idea is not entirely anathema, but they see in the 'enabling' notion the possibilities for greater control over services by neighbourhood groups, unions, etc. It could, some sources argue, reduce the distance between consumers of services and the origins and control of those services.

In New Zealand, privatization has been on the public agenda since the mid-1980s and has now been extended to the local level. The first step was to commercialize public utilities — first at national and now also at local level — by employing private sector management to manage them as autonomous business concerns. To ensure that the advantages of commercialization would be achieved, specifications have been issued with regard to rates of return, prices, and quality levels. Thus, the 'privatization' is not unqualified — the government watches over the process to ensure that it does not contradict the aims of the programme.[17]

The New Zealand case highlights an important conceptual issue: the distinction between *privatization* and *deregulation*. Continued public control over privatized ventures means that deregulation has not been fully introduced. This shows that privatization and deregulation do not necessarily go hand in hand; in fact, continued regulation could well be used as protection against the undesirable implications of privatization.

Local-level privatization in South Africa

It seems useful to reflect first on the present state of the debate about privatization and the process of its implementation in South Africa, before moving on to some of the functional and political issues relevant to this debate and process, as well as to suggestions regarding privatization in a future framework.

Privatization has been an item on the agenda in South Africa throughout the 1980s. It was highlighted in 1977 in a high-profile critique of growing state involvement in the economy in a book *Assault on Private Enterprise* by Dr A. D. Wassenaar, the former chairperson of one of the country's largest long-term insurance companies, Sanlam. Later, government inquiries indicated that the state's share in the financial resources of the country had grown from 20 per cent in 1950 to 30 per cent in 1978. The *White Paper on Privatization* stated that: 'In 1985 public sector expenditure amounted to 38.1 per cent of gross domestic product ...'[18] Hence, calls for a reduced state role, later billed under the terms 'privatization' and 'deregulation', became integral parts of the debate on the South African political economy.[19]

'Privatization' of local authorities has been the subject of much debate and investigation by various bodies representative of local authority interests since the mid-1980s. The government's key advisory body on local government matters, the Co-ordinating Council for Local Government Affairs, continues to pay specific attention to privatization.

The arguments for privatization at the local level in South Africa often resemble those in other countries. The core argument is that private companies are more efficient than governments or municipalities. Its protaganists also believe that privatization would facilitate major savings for public institutions; an attractive prospect for many local authorities caught in the midst of serious fiscal shortages.

This raises the question of the link between privatization and the problems of Black Local Authorities (BLAs). While many of the issues raised earlier are comparable to those which have been characterizing the privatization processes and debates in other countries, the BLA issue adds a particularly unique South African facet to the matter. Another set of reasons for and arguments against privatization are at stake here.

Since their inception, BLAs have been plagued with many mutually reinforcing difficulties: a lack of funds, skills, ill-equipped administrations, and political controversy. The roots of the problem go to the heart of the burden of racially-based local government.

In the 1980s, the government attempted to address these problems mainly through Regional Services Councils (RSCs) and the 'winning the hearts and minds' strategy of the National Security Management System (NSMS). However, both were politically controversial and could not mobilize sufficient resources to improve conditions in the townships to levels which would make township residents considerably more satisfied with their plight.

By 1990, it had become clear that these efforts had not steered BLAs out of their fiscal predicament. By then the NSMS network in its old form had been abolished and RSCs were increasingly shifting funds away from development projects to 'bridging finance' aimed at merely covering some of the current expenditures of BLAs. Yet, the BLAs were still not near financial self-sufficiency.

Hence, the notion of privatization entered the fray — albeit in a rather paradoxical manner. It is paradoxical because the very immediate pressure for a deflection of responsibilities by the state through, *inter alia*, privatization, is at its most overt with regard to BLAs; yet, nowhere are the commercial prospects as limited as in the townships which fall under the present jurisdiction of these authorities. Consumers here often either cannot, or will not, pay. Economic as well as political realities make an investment in townships a high-risk venture in the view of many entrepreneurs.

Moreover, the concept of privatization has fallen into even further disfavour among an already sceptical audience within the townships because it is often seen as part of the state's efforts to save the controversial BLAs.

In his report on the finances of Soweto, Development Bank chairperson Simon Brand points out that apart from political factors, there were also other causes behind the non-payment of service charges on trading services.[20] In his view, it is possible that even if the political issues were to remain unresolved, an improvement in collection could be achieved if these non-political causes of non-payment could be addressed.

Brand reasons that the lack of reliability of the service and inaccuracies in accounts rendered in their own right appear to be significant causes of non-payment of services such as electricity and water provision.[21] Although efforts have been initiated by the Soweto City Council to improve the reliability of the service and the accuracy of accounts, considerable doubt remains about the capacity of the municipality to achieve this.

He therefore argues for the utilization of the capacity and the application of 'the disciplines of the private sector'. He contends that privatization of services could achieve improvements in the efficiency and reliability of the service and the credibility of the collection system. Privatization could further assist in dissociating the rendering of and payment for trading services from the political context of BLAs. In his view, this would put the provision of these services on a commercial contract basis between consumers and a more impersonal, less politicized provider of the service.[22]

Brand made special reference to the possible privatization of the electricity distribution in Soweto.[23] He cited the privatization of the electricity supply in Kwanobuhle outside Uitenhage in the eastern Cape as a possible model for Soweto — and by implication other townships. In Kwanobuhle, the capacity and know-how of Eskom has been utilized to assist in setting up a utility electricity company with participation from a combination of stakeholders such as employers, employees, and residents. Brand argues that such a privatization approach could be introduced incrementally in a city like

Soweto, starting with certain suburbs and expanding as experience is gained and success demonstrated. He suggests that this approach could 'in principle also be considered in the case of other trading services and in particular in the provision of water'.[24]

However, it should be noted that the Kwanobuhle case has remained rather controversial among opposition groups and residents because they perceive it as part of a campaign to circumvent boycotts of service charges. Many have also objected to the involvement of the BLA, and although the electricity utility, Kwanolec, has largely excluded the BLA as the project evolved, it is still deemed by many residents as too close to the 'system'. It also differs from the Soweto case in the sense that very few Kwanobuhle residents had electricity before the project was launched.[25]

Brand has acknowledged some of the shortcomings of his proposed approach to the privatization of trading services.[26] He argues that it would not be viable for privatized suppliers to sell services on the basis of what amounts to a commercial contract between the suppliers and individual consumers in cases where 'non-performance' by either the supplier or the individual consumer could have serious implications for the urban community as a whole. He cites waste removal as an example of such services, where non-payment of accounts by consumers and the consequent termination by the supplier of the service to such delinquent consumers could constitute a health hazard for the community, or could at least impinge negatively on the quality of life of the rest of the community. But he maintains that such services could be privatized in a different sense, i.e. on the basis of a contract between the local authority and a private contractor to enhance the capacity of the former to render an effective and efficient service.

However, the physical capacities of BLAs have been only part of the problem. Political instability in the townships has not made it attractive to investors to become involved there. This problem is unlikely to disappear for as long as the present system of local government remains in operation. Opposition movements have made BLAs primary targets of their campaign against the existing order.[27]

For township groups, already sceptical about privatization because of the reasons unionists and other critics offer generally, the link to BLAs merely confirmed many of their reservations. Unions and civic organizations in the townships needed little encouragement to embark on a mass campaign to oppose privatization at the local level.[28]

However, the greatest advances with regard to privatization have often occurred in — mostly white — municipalities where fiscal problems have not been at their most critical. Some major municipalities have embarked on selective privatization ventures, often for reasons similar to those underpinning privatization in other countries.

The town clerk of Welkom, for example, insists that the city's drive since 1988 to privatize services has been worth the effort every bit of the way. Following the government's White Paper of 1987, the Welkom municipality decided to privatize what the town clerk described as 'our very costly bus service'. The town clerk pointed out that, apart from resulting in an annual saving of at least R1.4 million on municipal subsidies for the bus service, privatization also facilitated fourfold expansion of the local black taxi industry.[29]

Privatization affected some 41 traditional council areas of concern in Welkom, including street vegetation, the local airport, recreational facilities, the showgrounds, road services, auditing, clinics, and school bus services. The council maintained a co-ordinating role and, according to the town clerk, privatized only after consultation with experts and interest groups. But they made the transfer of services to private agencies a priority. The town clerk claims that no retrenchments resulted from the process and that: 'Everyone is a winner with privatization at local level — the taxpayers, commerce, industry, and entrepreneurs.'[30]

The Cape Town City Council provides some of the most advanced examples of local level privatization in South Africa. Contract cleaning in the civic centre has been privatized since the building was handed over for occupation in 1979. Municipal officials regard the privatization of the Cape Town Symphony Orchestra (CTSO) as 'one of the most comprehensive and successful areas of privatization undertaken by the Council'.[31] It involved transfer of the function and of staff without loss of their fringe benefits. The CTSO received a grant-in-aid spread over 10 years from the council to assist them towards independence. Security services at various locations within the council's area of jurisdiction have been contracted out for some years already. Like many other local authorities, Cape Town has also been discussing privatization of services and facilities like abattoirs, markets, sewerage treatment works, and waterworks.[32]

Similar processes of contracting out of services, or investigations into possibilities in that regard, have been undertaken by various local authorities in recent years. As far as white local authorities are concerned, many of the issues in this regard show similarities with the experience in other countries. They generally concern questions of efficiency, feasibility, and the politics around accountability of local authorities, union protests, and job security.

As has been the case in Britain and other countries, the opposition from trade unions and community organizations has been a key issue in the privatization process and debate. Unions oppose privatization, first, on the grounds of what they perceive to be the shortcomings of the market in South Africa. They argue that the South African economy is characterized by a concentration of economic power in the hands of a few large corporations. In South Africa, privatization would simply transfer wealth from state sector monopolies to private monopolies. They say that it is not the private sector *per se*, but the competitive environment, that leads to gains in efficiency. This would be enhanced by the fact that only very large companies could afford to purchase parastatals, and this would increase South Africa's already high levels of economic concentration. Unionists argue further that the profit motive would not necessarily cause prices to fall because of competitive pressure, because monopolies and cartels increase profits by driving up prices and tariffs.[33]

Union opposition to privatization is, however, also based on the real interests of union members. They fear that privatization is likely to be both preceded and followed by retrenchment of workers. The unions reject business arguments that in the long term, a leaner productive sector will sponsor growth and employment. They say that workers do not have the means to wait for this process to work itself out, particularly in the absence of a well-developed unemployment and social security system. Unionists also question claims that privatization has been successful in Britain and the USA. They point out that these countries are highly developed and embraced privatization only after a long period of state-led industrial growth and the creation of viable social security systems. They question, in any event, the assertions that these privatization efforts have actually impacted positively on efficiency and service provision.[34] Regarding the view that privatization has a positive 'trickle down' effect, they argue that because the poor have no 'economic votes', they cannot influence the market. Hence, they say that the net result of privatization would be that the poor get poorer and the rich richer.[35]

Against this background, unions and opposition movements have embarked on campaigns to oppose privatization. Some local authority officials say that they have become increasingly reluctant to initiate privatization because of union opposition. In some cases, the officials say, unions have even demanded that services which have hitherto been managed through sub-contracting private agencies, should now be managed by municipal departments. Unions and the ANC have also warned that they would terminate privatization arrangements if they were to come to power.[36]

The anti-privatization campaign has been under way for some time, co-ordinated by a coalition — the Public Sector Forum (PSF) — which consists of four public sector affiliates of COSATU. One of its concerns has been local government.[37]

The privatization process slows down

As a result of this anti-privatization pressure, public institutions at all levels of government, as well as the private sector, have become more reluctant about proceeding with privatization. A businessperson, Donald Masson, articulated this reluctance: 'Arising from the discussions with the ANC, it seems to me that any further moves on privatization might have to be suspended for the time being. No purpose will be served by privatizing, say, Eskom, and then having to backpedal at some stage in the future.'[38]

The government has apparently taken note of the reservations expressed by certain groups about privatization. A senior cabinet minister, for example, suggested that many of the state enterprises currently acting as monopolies might not be privatized at all.[39] On the other hand, a new bill in early 1991 provided for joint ventures between municipalities and private firms. The government also appointed a senior town clerk to lead the further investigations into privatization at the municipal level.

In October 1990, the government intervened directly in the internal pricing policies of the electricity company, Eskom, and the recently 'commercialized' transport giant, Transnet. Both cases are directly relevant to the local level. As part of a new anti-inflation and economic restructuring plan, the government announced that these two agencies would limit their tariff increases over the next years. This manipulation of individual companies' operations for macro-economic purposes has given rise to speculation that privatization has become a less urgent priority in these sectors, and perhaps more widely as well. The government was accused of giving in to pressure from the ANC and COSATU to delay, if not reverse, the privatization process.[40]

Government officials say that they had never expected privatization to occur overnight. They argue that commercialization was always envisaged as taking four years or more, and that the process must be viewed from a long-term perspective. Sources close to the Office of Privatization maintain that the principle of privatization still stands, but the time scale may be different. They argue that certain state corporations are not suitable for privatization, perhaps for social reasons, but that is still under investigation.

A 1980 progress report[41] of the National Privatization Committee — which has been investigating privatization at local level — states that privatization 'also suggests that sound private sector business principles, management techniques and work habits be introduced'. This view — that the process entails more than mere transfers of services to private concerns — is directly relevant to local level privatization. It raises the notion of 'commercialization' — a concept which once was closely associated with privatization, but which is now increasingly being used on its own. Whereas privatization seems to imply — at least in the perception of many observers — a transfer of ownership or control, commercialization points at methods of management. The difference could be politically highly significant.

The cabinet minister in charge of the privatization process, Dr Wim de Villiers, told *Leadership* that there are two key aspects underpinning commercialization. The first is that capital has to be raised in the capital markets 'rather than by way of government handouts', and it 'must be utilized in accordance with the discipline of a profit and loss account and balance sheet'. De Villiers said that management style is of more immediate concern to his department than the transfer of ownership which 'can be argued about endlessly'.[42]

It is therefore conceivable that future initiatives could seek to take the process further through changes in the management style of local authorities and through an increasing array of joint activities involving local bodies and private concerns. The ownership question would have to be handled with great caution so as to avoid further confrontation with the unions.

Another strategy, which the protaganists of privatization have suggested, is for the government to make a public pledge to devote *all* proceeds of privatization to achieve 'economic justice'.[43] The R2 billion Independent Development Trust, established in 1990 to finance urban development through the proceeds of privatization, is an illustration of such action.

It has also been suggested that privatization need not mean that a service is handed over to a company. Along the lines of the argument for 'enabling measures' in Britain — which have attained an interesting consensus from groups with different political perspectives — it has been argued that a service could be handed to a community group or to a co-operative. This idea was particularly prominent at the time of the negotiations between Eskom and the Soweto People's Delegation in 1989. Although it did not materialize, sources close to that process deem such arrangements as distinct compromise possibilities. They do not call it 'privatization', and argue that it would rather be aimed at ensuring that politically accountable local authorities manage services. They regard it as essential for local authorities to be responsible to residents and say that fully privatized companies would merely be accountable to their shareholders. The challenge, they believe, is to find institutions which would enable residents to control the way the service is provided. These need not be state-supported official bodies, but they need to be publicly accountable. They argue that if the service is handed over to the community — or to a company which is responsible to it — residents would largely control the service, and it would be more likely to meet their needs.[44] The mechanism that was proposed to facilitate this was an electrical co-operative modelled on the rural electrical co-operatives that supply most of rural America with electricity. Similar ventures have been established in 42 developing countries.

Privatization in a post-apartheid South Africa?

The functional and political questions which have emerged from the international and South African experiences are not only relevant to the debate on privatization at present. They could prove relevant to the question: would a post-apartheid government, or post-apartheid local authorities, have an interest in privatizing local authority functions? This matter is of vital concern to the whole debate, since the present system seems — by most accounts — due for fundamental change.

Does the fierce political opposition from key political actors not jeopardize the prospects for privatization under a post-apartheid government? This might, indeed, be the case, but there could be reasons why such a government might well consider this option once it is faced with the realities of resource constraints.

As pointed out earlier, many areas — especially African townships — suffer from such severe resource constraints that they are likely to remain burdens to the authorities. A post-apartheid government will experience numerous pressures for welfare spending and might well be looking for some assistance. Faced by the demands of its housing, educational, and other social priorities, it might conclude that some local authority activities should be allocated to other agencies, such as the private sector.

Furthermore, a future government is likely to be operating in an environment which would be no less politicized than the present one — even though it might enjoy greater legitimacy among the majority of the population. Given the variety of pressures from an expectant public, it is not inconceivable that such a government might also find it appealing to 'depoliticize' some aspects of administration. In some areas this might be well-nigh impossible — local government could be such an area which would be impossible to depoliticize — but the government might feel that some of the services at this level ought to be removed from the arena of political contestation. It might argue that there are other priority areas where the inevitability of politics has to be accepted, and that some services make good candidates for exclusion from that.

It is, at this stage, difficult to construct exact scenarios of what a future government would want and what it would not want. It seems certain that — for ideological and constituency-related reasons at least — it would proceed reluctantly along the path of privatization, if at all. But the possibility of it finding attractive some way to spread the burden of service provision, cannot be summarily excluded. Hence, privatization, in whatever form, inevitably becomes an option.

The functional and political issues around the privatization issue are neither merely relevant to Thatcherist Britain and similar cases, nor only to the present South African government's attempts to overcome the legacies of apartheid local government. The matter cuts through to some of the vital questions around the shaping of a new system at all levels.

Intermediate and long-term functional issues

Among the feasibility questions is that of legal and institutional constraints. Various legal constraints could obstruct privatization. One example has been that it has not been possible for a municipality to enter a joint business venture with a private company. Some legislative amendments have already been made to allow local authorities to transfer functions or services to companies, while retaining a major shareholding in that company with board representation.[45]

Another matter concerns the decision about which services actually could and should be privatized. Even after various national and local level investigations, there is little consensus. Decisions of this nature are mostly situation-bound and are affected both by efficiency and capability criteria of the specific agencies in a particular situation, as well as the interests which could be served or threatened by privatization.[46]

The selection of appropriate functions to privatize could also require some trade-offs between the various objectives of the exercise, especially as regards the distributional and efficiency criteria. This could hold severe implications for decisions about the matter in a post-apartheid society.

It would appear that some of the options exercised by, for example, Thatcher in Britain, would be extremely difficult to attain in South Africa. For example, it was mentioned earlier that the sale of houses and land played a considerable part in the British privatization campaign. In South Africa, the levels of poverty are so severe that the capacity of residents to purchase public houses seems considerably more limited than in Britain. Innovative options are constantly sought by the public and private sectors to address this issue. Such innovations could include adaptive financing schemes to limit the risk of loans for financial institutions; an emphasis on site and service developments, rather than the building of formal houses; and even the handing over of rental stock based on an assertion that the rentals have in effect paid for the properties.

Initiatives to allocate the proceeds of privatization to development projects, including housing development, could also fall under such innovations. However, while it has been argued that privatization could be so structured and managed so as to ensure that 'vulnerable groups' receive assistance in order not to suffer under its effects, the capacity to achieve this objective could be difficult to judge before-hand. Questions regarding the collective nature of services are also due to enter the equation: if consumers perceive the use and pricing of a service to be immeasurable, they will be less inclined to pay for it in the type of specific terms which private providers would find profitably manageable.[47]

The question of whether privatization would ensure greater efficiency concerns both the debate around the privatization of current local authority activities, as well as the long-term development of local structures. Critics of privatization point out that the South African economy is being dominated by a few major corporations, and that this inevitably impacts on the level of competition in the economy. Furthermore, in a relatively small economy, such as South Africa's, there is often not much room to introduce more than one supplier in each of the electricity, transport, and services spheres; these are, in a sense, areas for what one could call 'natural monopolies'. Hence, it is argued, with privatization, many of these conglomorates would merely establish monopolies, or near-monopolies, and little of the efficiency rationale would be actualized.[48]

The politics of privatization

The politics of privatization is no less complex in South Africa than it has been in Britain and other countries. Apart from the very obvious issues around union resistance referred to above, a number of other matters, and interests, are at stake.

Some of the 'political' matters at stake have a distinct 'administrative' dimension. They could especially carry — and have in fact already carried — considerable weight in the debate about gradual reform of the present system.

One of these is the question of safeguarding the salaries and fringe benefits, such as pensions, of employees affected by privatization. A major related issue which has led to some reluctance among municipal decision-makers about privatization has been the impact which it could have on the grading of municipalities. Aspects of municipal government in South Africa, such as the powers delegated to the local body and the personnel practices and salaries of officials, are managed in terms of a statutory grading system. The grades are based on the size of municipal areas of jurisdiction, population figures, spectrum of historical functions, etc. Were functions to be privatized, the grading of municipalities could be affected as their functions become contracted out to private firms.[49] Officials' interests are therefore under direct threat if privatization is to have this effect, and this could pose a definite obstacle to the entire privatization effort.

There are also concerns that privatization could impact negatively on the accountability of service providers to their clients. Municipalities as public institutions have structural accountability towards consumers of services. Hence, they often sustain certain services, even if those services are not profitable, simply because as public institutions they have an accountability relationship with the consumers. In contrast, private companies would merely base decisions about the provision of services on functional criteria, and are likely to suspend services once they prove to be unprofitable. This difference has led to arguments for either keeping services under municipal control, or for special measures in privatization packages which would ensure that essential services are maintained in the event of private agencies withdrawing their services.

Two of the earlier points, from empirical experience internationally as well as in South Africa, are particularly relevant here. The first is the distinction which the New Zealand experience draws between privatization and deregulation. If a South African government or local government of the future decides, for whatever reason, to privatize, it might want to ensure the nature, quality, and continuity of services. One way of doing this could be to maintain existing, or draft new regulations for the services. Thus, it might opt for privatization or commercialization, but not for deregulation. As pointed out earlier, a post-apartheid government is likely to be quite sensitive to anti-privatization pressures; hence, it might find this option of continued regulation with privatization or commercialization attractive.

The second point to be made in this regard concerns the example of privatization by the Cape Town City Council. It seems fair to argue that a society can function well (albeit perhaps culturally deprived) without symphony orchestras; however, discontinuation of water supplies, refuse removal, etc., could have dire physical and social consequences. Thus, it is one thing to talk about the 'successes' of privatization when the service is not essential; it is another much more serious matter when an essential service is at stake. It is in this context that the accountability issue arises and no government, now or in a post-apartheid South Africa, would find it easy to disregard this need for ensuring that some services are kept intact.

Furthermore, the political demands for socio-economic improvement, which a post-apartheid government is likely to face, are likely to impact on the extent of activities which would be deemed 'essential'. It could well be wider than what would usually be viewed as 'essential' in relatively developed societies like the United Kingdom, and might well include development of infrastructure. For a South African government simply to shift its responsibilities in local level communities to the private sector, could be politically very risky. Were it to pursue such a direction, the framework within which it did so would probably require meticulous attention.

Conclusion

Privatization of local government has raised emotions in South Africa no less intense than in many other countries. While the government has often stated its intention to 'privatize' some local authority functions, and a number of municipalities, white and black, have begun privatizing, opposition from trade unions and community organizations has often been particularly vehement.

The government continues to favour privatization for a number of reasons. Firstly, it is argued that private companies are more efficient than governments or municipalities. Secondly, the maintenance of some services has become very costly to the government and to municipalities. Privatization, it is believed, could result in considerable savings for the public sector. It is not entirely inconceivable that this consideration could one day also cross the mind of a post-apartheid government faced by resource constraints. For this reason, the privatization debate might well live on even after a major political transformation.

In the townships, other reasons exist for privatization. Residents often cannot afford to pay the BLA the full amount it pays to buy the service. Politically-inspired boycotts of rent and service charge payments have also reduced the capacity of BLAs to meet their obligations towards suppliers such as Eskom and others to cover the costs of services, such as electricity and water. Hence, in almost all townships — even those not affected by rent boycotts — BLAs run services at a loss. Privatization has been considered an option because if BLAs no longer provided these services, they might not lose as much money as they do now. Politically, the reasoning has been that if a private company ran the service, only the company could be blamed, and there would be less danger of protests or violence.

Critics of privatization argue that the profit motive of private companies would probably raise prices and lead to wide-scale retrenchments. They also argue that privatization would facilitate the entry of private monopolies at local level. They warn that services could break down if companies withdraw services because they are unprofitable. Furthermore, the lack of infrastructure and the political instability in many areas — especially those under the control of the most inefficient local authorities (in African townships) — have made the prospect of privatization even more unlikely.

There have also been calls for services to be provided by public bodies which are responsible to communities. This, it has been argued, would mean that the community can ensure that services meet their needs. In contrast, private companies, it is said, are only responsible to the people who own them. It has been suggested that privatization does not necessarily have to mean that a service is handed over to a company; but that it could be handed to a community group or to a company partly controlled by a community. Some community groups have begun to consider this option. They believe that it only makes sense for a local authority to run services if it really is responsible to the residents in its area. They believe that BLAs are not responsible to residents; this means, they say, that residents cannot really control the way the service is provided. They argue that, if the service is handed over to the community — or to a company which is responsible to it — there would be far more control by residents over the service, and it would be more likely to meet their needs.

Vehement union protests in 1990 seem to have caused greater caution in government and private sector circles in the pursuit of privatization. At a time when the political temperatures are high as the various political protagonists engage in negotiations and the associated political manoeuvres, the government might well decide to avoid unnecessary complications such as the pursuit of privatization.

However, the debate is likely to continue as some authorities in the public and private sectors argue for steps to·ensure the efficient provision of services amidst the persistent difficulties of some public bodies to secure that. Many local authorities fall squarely in the latter category and are therefore likely to feature rather prominently in the debate. And while it is unlikely to be pursued with any great ideological dedication, the issue of pragmatically involving some private concerns might well feature somewhere as a post-apartheid government starts to pursue its expected wide range of social priorities.

Notes

1 The author is solely responsible for the contents of and views expressed in this chapter. These cannot be attributed in any manner whatsoever to any organization which has either employed him, or sponsored this research.
2 Republic of South Africa *White Paper on Privatization and Deregulation* (Pretoria: Government Printer 1987) 8–9.
3 Truu M. 'Economics of Privatization' *The SA Journal of Economics* (1988) 56 iv 256–8.
4 Innes D. 'Why Trade Unions Oppose Privatization' *The Innes Labour Brief* (1990) 1 iv 8–12.
   McGrath M. D. 'Privatization: Background and Issues in the South African Context' (eds.) Mobil Foundation of SA *Proceedings of Seminar on Privatization* (Cape Town: 1989) 11.
   Truu (1988) 255–6.
   Walsh K. 'Competition and Service in Local Government' (eds.) Steward J. and Stoker G. *The Future of Local Government* (Hampshire: Macmillan 1989) 42–3.
5 Truu (1988) 254–5.
6 Brand S. 'Privatization: an Economist's View' *The South African Journal of Economics* (1988) 56 iv 241–3.
   Republic of South Africa (1987) 9.
7 Rhodes R. A. W. 'Continuity and Change in British Central-local Relations: the Conservative Threat, 1979–83' *British Journal of Political Science* 14 ii 272.
8 Green D. G. *The New Right: Counter-revolution in Political, Economic and Social Thought* (Brighton: Wheatsheaf Books 1987) 187.
   Rhodes (1984) 272.
   Stoker G. *The Politics of Local Government* (Hampshire: Macmillan 1988) 176–7.
9 Douglas J. 'The Changing Tide — Some Recent Studies of Thatcherism' *British Journal of Political Science* 19 iii 411.
10 Green (1987) 187.
11 Stoker (1988) 176–82.
   Walsh (1989) 39–40.
12 Walsh (1989) 31–4, 37–40.
13 Cape Town City Council *Report on Privatization, Office of the Town Clerk* (1987) 9–13 annexes. C, E.
14 Cape Town City Council (1987) 14–15.
   Municipal Review (August/September 1987) 58, 680.
   Rhodes (1984) 272–3.
   Walsh (1989) 36–40.
15 Cape Town City Council (1987) annex. C.
   Stoker (1988) 185.
   Walsh (1989) 31–4, 36–9.
16 Cape Town City Council (1987) 16.
17 Republic of South Africa (1987) 4.
18 Brand S. 'Privatization: an Economist's View' *The South African Journal of*

Economics (1988) 56 iv 236–8.
Republic of South Africa (1987) 2–6.
19 Brand (1989) 55.
20 Brand (1989) 55.
21 Brand (1989) 55–6.
22 Brand (1989) 56.
23 Brand (1989) 56.
24 Personal interviews with BLA councillors, Kwanolec officials, and community activists.
25 Brand (1989) 57.
26 *The Sunday Times* 12 November 1990.
27 *Business Day* 30 March 1990.
    New Nation 16–22 March 1990.
    The Star 29 March 1990.
28 *The Star* 18 January 1990.
29 *The Star* 18 January 1990.
30 Cape Town City Council (1987) 35.
31 Cape Town City Council (1987) 35–7.
32 Innes (1990) 7–10.
33 Innes (1990) 10–12.
34 *The Star* 14 March 1990.
35 *Business Day* 30 March 1990.
    New Nation 16–22 March 1990.
    The Sowetan 12 March 1990.
    The Star 29 March 1990.
36 *Weekly Mail* 23 March 1990.
37 *The Sunday Times* 27 May 1990.
38 *Business Day* 2 April 1990.
39 *Financial Mail* 5 October 1990.
40 Annex. 2.
41 *Leadership* May 1990.
42 Brand (1988) 249.
43 *Soweto People's Delegation News* 28 January 1990.
44 *Business Day* 26 March 1990.
45 Brand (1988) 245–8.
    Permanent Finance Liaison Committee 'Privatisering: Plaaslike Owerhede', unpublished report from the Co-ordinating Council for Local Government Affairs (Pretoria: 1988) 6–7.
    Van Rensburg E. 'Privatization at Local Level', paper presented at the regional congress of the Chambers of Commerce and Industries at Sandton in the Transvaal (March 1990).
46 Brand (1988) 245–8.
    Gildenhuys J. S. H. 'Privatisering van Owerheidsdienste' *Administratio Publica* 1 i 21–5.
    Private interviews with various local authority officials.
47 Innes (1990) 8–10.
    McGrath (1989) 11.
48 Permanent Finance Liaison Committee (1988) 7–8.

12 Finance, electricity costs, and the rent boycott

Mark Swilling, William Cobbett,
Roland Hunter

Introduction

This chapter reflects on themes revealed by the Transvaal boycott of rent and service charges which began in a few townships in 1984. By the end of the state of emergency in 1990, this boycott and the social movements associated with it had spread to around 50 townships in the Transvaal and many more in the Orange Free State, northern Cape, and eastern Cape. By the end of 1990, even the government had acknowledged that the rent boycotts had begun to threaten the viability of South Africa's black local government system.

The financial cost of keeping the BLAs afloat brought the TPA to the negotiation table, failing which the wide-scale bankruptcy of black local government was assured. The many local-level negotiations which have ensued have illuminated some key features of the system of apartheid local government finance.

The chapter opens with a brief examination of the basic system of local government finance in South Africa, particularly as it has applied to the BLAs. The next section highlights the critical role of electricity supply, which has not attracted much attention beyond the negotiation table. Thereafter some points about the nature of the current crisis facing local government finance are made before examining some implications for the future financing of democratic forms of local government.[1]

The financing of apartheid local government

The typical apartheid city, with separate local authorities presiding over what were meant to be racially separated towns and cities, reached its highest point of development in 1982 when the Black Local Authorities Act was passed. This act, which provided for the establishment of fully-fledged municipal authorities for the townships, was the culmination of two contradictory impulses that have co-existed within the apartheid administrative system.

The first impulse was the racial/ethnic logic of 'self-determination' that was applied at regional/national level. This was expressed most clearly in the Promotion of Bantu Self-Government Act of 1959 which paved the way for the homeland system. The aim was to de-urbanize the rightless African majority — the so-called 'temporary sojourners'. Eventually, African townships were removed from the control of white municipalities. The Bantu Affairs Administration Boards (BAABs) were established in 1971 and charged with the task of administering the townships on the basis of financial self-sufficiency. 'Representation' was via the Urban Bantu Councils (UBCs), Advisory Boards, and from 1977, the Community Councils.

The second impulse was the application of the 'self-determination' logic at local level. Although the separateness of the African areas within the cities had long been a feature of apartheid urban administration, it was only once the permanence of urban Africans had been accepted in terms of the Riekert framework that the logic of apartheid 'self-determination' could be applied.

The acceptance of the unviability of the 'temporary sojourner' policy, therefore, led to the attempt to extend the basic apartheid principle of separateness to the cities. The end result was urban permanence without reincorporation into the primary local government system and the white cities. Instead, the BLAs were established to give substance to the pretence of separate African and white 'cities'.

This complex process of functional inclusion, spatial separation, and political exclusion at the local level gave rise to the current local government system within the 'apartheid city'. In addition to the well-documented political consequences of this policy, it is the regressive fiscal arrangements and contradictions inherent in this system that deserve greater attention than they have received in the local government literature to date.

The divided local tax base

In April 1989 the Soweto People's Delegation (SPD) released a report ('The Soweto Rent Boycott') which empirically demonstrated how the apartheid local government finance system facilitated the redistribution of local resources from the poor African areas to the rich white areas. Official reports subsequently acknowledged this basic point. The 1989 Brand Report and the 1990 Thornhill Report both conceded that African townships are financially unviable. It is worth recapitulating the basic SPD argument here.

The SPD demonstrated that about 300 000 Sowetans worked in Johannesburg each day in 1987. During this year they earned approximately R2 billion, of which up to R1.4 billion was spent in Johannesburg. African expenditure in Johannesburg's central business district accounted for between 70 per cent and 80 per cent of all purchases. It was then demonstrated that the Johannesburg City Council (JCC) obtained about 30 per cent of its income from its central business district and 70 per cent of its income from industry and commerce in the city as a whole. Given that the JCC is not responsible for municipal services in Soweto, and given that industry and commerce in Johannesburg are heavily dependent on African workers and consumers, it was argued that a net transfer of wealth from Soweto to Johannesburg is taking place. It is worth noting that Johannesburg's financial situation makes possible a 55 per cent monthly rates rebate to its domestic ratepayers. In the 1987/8 financial year, this rebate totalled R38.7 million, which was easily financed by the net gain Johannesburg had derived from the commercial and industrial rate income which should properly have been allocated to Soweto.

The pattern described above, however, is simply one demonstration of the basis for the basic financial soundness of Johannesburg and the fundamental fiscal unviability of Soweto. The pattern is replicated in a number of other ways. For instance, upgrading and development programmes in Johannesburg are financed through its Consolidated Loans Fund. This permits a pooled rate of interest on loans obtained from both external sources and Johannesburg's own Capital Development Fund. Currently, the pooled rate of interest is 10.92 per cent. In Soweto, these arrangements do not exist, and currently, the local authorities must pay up to 16.02 per cent on capital debt. Even very old debt, such as that inherited from the West Rand Administration Board (WRAB), must be paid for at interest rates of 14.5 per cent.

The fundamental unviability of the BLAs can be further illustrated by expressing their operating deficits as a percentage of their operating incomes. Tables 12.1 and 12.2, which show a number of local authorities on the Witwatersrand, starkly illustrate the point.

The same point can be illustrated in another way. The figures in table 12.2 present the aggregate gross expenditure, gross income, and deficits for white and black local authorities in the three RSC areas on the Witwatersrand. These figures are based on the budgets for the various local authorities for 1990/1. It should be borne in mind that budgets make no provision for rent and service charge boycotts: the data therefore illustrate official, budgeted unviability.

While the figures illustrate the unviability of the BLAs, when combined with population figures they also illustrate the drastic inequalities in municipal expenditures between the black and white local authorities (WLAs). Were expenditures per capita to be made more equal, the BLAs would of course become even more unviable.

These vastly different financial situations, juxtaposed within the apartheid city, lead to a new demand emanating from communities on rent and service boycotts. The 'one tax base' demand, originally articulated by the SPD, became a national rallying cry in the townships because the same basic distribution of urban resources that applies in Greater Johannesburg is applicable in many other towns and cities.

The RSCs and bridging finance

Two measures were introduced to address the unviability of the BLAs while still retaining the basic framework of apartheid local government. These were the RSCs and bridging finance.

The establishment of the RSCs was an implicit acknowledgement of the financial unviability of the BLAs. It was evident that more finance was needed for capital projects in the African townships, but the government was unwilling to impose a new burden on the central fiscus. The solution was a new form of local tax, but one which was not levied on individual citizens because this would have contradicted the apartheid logic. The solution was a levy on business payrolls and turnover coupled to a denial of business rights to representation. However, rather than allocating these new revenue sources to existing local authorities, they were allocated to regional

Table 12.1
Operating deficits as a percentage of operating incomes

Surpluses:	Alberton:	3.8%	(1989/90)
	Johannesburg:	3.1%	(1989/90)
	Springs:	1.2%	(1988/89)
	Brakpan:	1.1%	(1987/88)
	Modderfontein:	0.7%	(1988/89)
Deficits:	Kempton Park:	0.2%	(1988/89)
	Sandton:	0.6%	(1988/89)
	Benoni:	0.6%	(1988/89)
	Midrand:	3.6%	(1988/89)
	Tokoza:	24.3%	(1989/90)
	Tembisa:	35.6%	(1988/89)
	Wattville:	37.1%	(1987/88)
	Daveyton:	45.4%	(1987/88)
	Tsakane:	45.3%	(1988/89)
	Duduza:	52.0%	(1987/88)
	Soweto:	55.6%	(1987/88)
	Alexandra:	199.0%	(1988/89)

Source: These figures have been derived from the financial statements of the local authorities referred to as well as supplementary documents provided by the local authorities where necessary to complete the picture.

Table 12.2
Aggregate local authority expenditure and income data

	Expenditure R m	Income R m	Deficit R m	Deficit %
ERRSC[2] area:				
10 white LAs:	1 316	1 315	1	0.1
10 black LAs:	348	237	111	46.8
CWRSC[3] area:				
4 white LAs:	2 197	2 169	28	1.3
4 black LAs:	531	200	331	165.5
WRRSC[4] area:				
5 white LAs:	289	289	0	0
7 black LAs:	57	47	10	21.3

Source: These figures have been derived from the financial statements of the local authorities referred to as well as supplementary documents provided by the local authorities where necessary to complete the picture.

bodies that could spend the funds in local authority jurisdictions other than those where the levies were raised. Essentially it was a way of ameliorating the consequences of the racially divided tax base. Even though it was not on the agenda at the time, the government would not have been prepared to contemplate creating single tax bases because of the political consequences within the white community. (The concept was, however, subsequently adopted and supported by F. W. de Klerk in December 1990.)

The RSC system, however, resulted in a new set of unintended consequences that effectively exacerbated the fiscal crisis of the BLAs. In line with government policy, the RSCs spent most of their funds on capital projects in the townships. This was all very well, but it was based on the assumption that the BLAs had the operating income and the administrative capacity to maintain adequately the new roads, sewerage systems, water towers, and electricity networks that were installed. Even without the rent boycotts, it is doubtful whether this assumption was valid. In the event, the boycotts ensured that it was totally impossible to maintain the new capital assets adequately.

Overwhelmingly, the BLAs had neither administrative capacity nor financial resources: for example, they did not have the income necessary to pay qualified personnel needed to maintain new assets, and relied on seconded staff from the nearby WLAs or the provincial administrations. This situation eventually forced some RSCs to accept the necessity of subsidizing the operating costs of the BLAs.

In summary, the inclusion of the BLAs into the RSCs, and the changing role played by the RSCs as a result of this decision, was one way that the government responded to the fiscal unviability of the apartheid local government system. The other way was through the 'bridging finance' policy.

From their inception, the annual estimates of BLAs showed budgeted deficits based on the difference between the expected revenue from promulgated tariffs and the actual total estimated costs of services, administration, and loan repayments. Initially, these deficits were accepted by government as a necessary step in the process of gradually making the BLAs financially self-sufficient. On these grounds it was agreed to balance the books during the interim. However, communities became increasingly well organized and responded to rent and service charge increases with a number of tactics, including the rent boycott.

It soon became apparent to officials that tariff increases to attain self-sufficiency would be self-defeating if this triggered more rent boycotts which merely confirmed and compounded the problem of the BLAs. This, in turn, finally resulted in the acceptance that townships could not be regarded as financially self-sufficient. This resulted in what came to be known as 'non-viability' bridging finance becoming a permanent fixture in the annual provincial budget. While this amounted to the *de facto* acceptance of the necessity for inter-governmental transfer payments, the *ad hoc* nature of the transfers was reflected in the retention of the term 'bridging finance'. Ultimately these various measures to ameliorate the fiscal crisis of the BLAs, while retaining the basic framework of urban apartheid, were unsuccessful because of the rent boycotts.

Before turning to a discussion of the rent boycotts and the subsequent negotiations, it is necessary to examine some of the links between the fiscal crisis of the BLAs and the financial viability of the WLAs. One of the most important of these is provided by the structure of the urban electricity system.

The role of electricity in financing local government

There are three key points to be noted about the role of electricity in financing apartheid local government:

- WLAs almost always show a surplus on electricity;
- that surplus is often a very important part of the general income of WLAs;
- BLAs almost always show a deficit on electricity.

Again, these points can be illustrated most easily from local authorities on the Witwatersrand. An examination of aggregate income and expenditure statements shows that the electricity trading services of the WLAs contribute significantly to overall income. In Johannesburg in 1987/8, for example, while assessment rates yielded R176.3 million, the electricity trading service contributed a surplus of R129.2 million. Although electricity is not the only trading service which contributes net income to WLAs, it is by far the most significant. In Johannesburg, the gas trading service also showed a surplus, but this amounted to only R5.5 million.

Table 12.3 illustrates the pattern by comparing the percentage of income which was contributed by assessment rates against the percentage which was contributed by electricity surpluses for the vari-

Table 12.3   Position of electricity in gross income of WLAs

	Gross income	Rate income	Income from electricity	Surplus on electricity
Johannesburg: (1989/90)	1 453.9m 100%	247.4m 17%	650.5m 44.8%	204.3m 14%
Alberton: (1989/90)	130.5m 100%	15.3m 11.7%	81.4m 62.4%	14.6m 11.2%
Springs: (1988/89)	103.9m 100%	14.2m 13.7%	67.4m 64.9%	10.7m 10.3%
Benoni: (1988/89)	145.9m 100%	25.2m 17.2%	83.7m 57.4%	11.5m 7.9%
Brakpan: (1987/88)	76.4m 100%	11.2m 14.6%	42m 55%	6.4m 8.4%

Source: These figures have been calculated from the information provided by these local authorities in their financial statements for the years cited.

Table 12.4   Position of electricity in gross income of BLAs

	Gross income	Income from electricity	Deficit on electricity
Tsakane: (1988/89)	7.5m 100%	1.05m 14%	0.36m 4.8%
Wattville: (1987/88)	3.37m 100%	0.92m 27.3%	0.37m 10.8%
Daveyton: (1987/88)	22.91m 100%	8.3m 34.7%	1.03m 4.5%
Tembisa: (1988/89)	33.4m 100%	10.9m 32.6%	0.4m 1.2%
Duduza: (1989/90)	2.22m 100%	0.16m 7%	0.3m 13.4%
Tokoza: (1989/90)	17.87m 100%	4.36m 24.4%	0.68m 3.8%

Source: These figures have been derived from the financial statements of the local authorities referred to as well as supplementary documents provided by the local authorities where necessary to complete the picture.

ous local authorities. By contrast, BLAs almost never show a surplus on electricity. On the contrary, although the pattern is not consistent, the electricity deficit is often a large proportion of the overall deficit of these local authorities, as shown in table 12.4.

Broadly speaking, there are two ways in which electricity is supplied to local authorities in South Africa. The first may be called the 'dual system', where the WLA and the associated BLA buy electricity from Eskom independently of each other. The second is the 'dependent' system, where the WLA buys from Eskom and then sells bulk electricity to the BLA. What both systems have in common is that they generally work to the advantage of consumers under the jurisdiction of the WLA, and to the detriment of the residents of the BLA. In what follows, Johannesburg and Soweto will be used to illustrate the 'dual' system, while the 'dependent' system will be illustrated by the example of Benoni, Wattville, and Daveyton. (There are areas where a mixture of the dual and dependent systems exists, such as Witbank/KwaGuqa and Krugersdorp/Kagiso, but these systems will not be discussed here.)

The 'dual' system of electricity supply

Johannesburg's electricity system, which is the responsibility of the Johannesburg Electricity Department (JED), is connected to the national grid at three main supply points. The JED sold 5.4 billion kilowatt hours (kWh) or 'units' in 1987, from which it received an income of R415.7 million; from this it made a surplus of R104.8 million.

Soweto's system is a quarter of the size of the Johannesburg system. It is connected to the national grid at one point and is the responsibility of the Soweto Electricity Department (SED). In 1987 the SED sold 806 million units, or 15 per cent of JED sales. During that year, Soweto budgeted for a deficit on electricity.

The JED sold 64 per cent of its electricity to non-domestic consumers in 1987, but these consumers provided 70 per cent of the JED's income for the year. Domestic consumers, on the other hand, consumed 36.4 per cent of the electricity sold by the JED, but accounted for only 30.8 per cent of the income of the department. Clearly an internal subsidy was at work here, and one that was not available to domestic consumers in Soweto. Soweto sells 96 per cent of its electricity to domestic consumers, and 4 per cent to the 'industrial and commercial sector'. What is more significant, however, is the effect that non-domestic consumption has on the bulk supply price paid by the JCC to Eskom.

The formula used by Eskom to calculate the bulk supply price paid by a local authority (tariff A) has three components:
- a basic charge paid by all bulk consumers irrespective of the amount of electricity purchased;
- a demand charge which depends on the highest electricity demand in any one half-hour period during the calendar month; and
- an energy charge per unit of electricity purchased.

This formula has great significance for the price ultimately paid by domestic and non-domestic consumers of electricity. The amount of electricity purchased by local authorities varies during the day. There is a peak in the morning as domestic consumers prepare for the day, and another when they return from work in the evening. If a local authority has a significant industrial demand for electricity, there will be a relatively constant 'base load' which does not fluctuate very much during the 24-hour period. Local authorities which do not have a significant industrial load will not have a significant base load. Figures 12.1 and 12.2 illustrate the point.

Figure 12.1
The daily consumption profile of the township Mabopane East

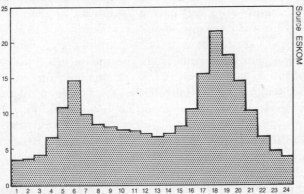

The effect of these patterns is that, because of the way the formula works, local authorities with a significant base load (and hence a low peak-to-base ratio) have a higher proportion of the electricity charged on the energy charge as opposed to the more expensive maximum demand charge, and hence pay Eskom less per unit of electricity than those without a significant base load and associated diversity factor.

Figure 12.2
The daily consumption profile of the municipality of Durban

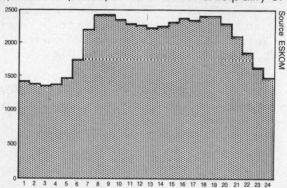

However, Johannesburg has another advantage over Soweto. Johannesburg has its own generating capacity (the power stations Kelvin A, Kelvin B, and Orlando, and five gas turbine generators). This capacity is used during periods of peak demand in order to reduce the extent to which Johannesburg must draw on Eskom's supply at these times. This practice of 'peak lopping' further reduces the expensive demand charge levied by Eskom.

Soweto does not have any significant non-domestic consumers; nor does it have its own generating capacity. The result is that in 1987 when Johannesburg was paying Eskom an average of 7 cents per unit, Soweto was paying 9.7 cents or 38.6 per cent more.

Soweto's morning peak demand occurs earlier than Johannesburg's, and its evening peak takes place later. This means that if the two load profiles could be merged, Soweto would incur lower bulk supply costs at no significant loss to Johannesburg. It has been calculated by Planact and confirmed by Eskom that if the Soweto and Johannesburg systems were joined, Soweto would save itself around R25 million annually in bulk supply costs alone. Other cost savings — for instance from amalgamating the JED and the SED — could also be expected, along with increased efficiency.

Residents of Soweto also bear another cost, however, and that is the capital cost of the electrical system itself. Johannesburg's system is established and mostly paid off. In Soweto the system was installed in the early 1980s in belated recognition that the urban townships are permanent and should be serviced. Although no accurate figures are publicly available, it is estimated that approximately R400 million is owing on the electricity system in Soweto. Residents were supposed to start paying this debt off in mid-1986. It was the electricity levy which was introduced to effect repayment, that triggered the Soweto rent boycott.

The 'dependent' system of electricity supply

Although the dual system described above exists in a number of other towns (e.g. Boksburg-Vosloorus), the dependent system is more prevalent. Benoni is a good example of the dependent system. Benoni has its own established and well maintained system that has been built up over the years. The systems in its two adjacent townships — Wattville and Daveyton — are connected to the Benoni system. Benoni's electricity department helps maintain the township systems.

Benoni purchases the bulk supply from Eskom and sells it to three basic consumers: its own domestic and non-domestic consumers, as well as to the Wattville and Daveyton local authorities in bulk. The Wattville and Daveyton councils then add on to the purchase price the cost of maintaining their own separate electricity departments.

A more detailed explanation of the unequal nature of this system is required. Six aspects are worth mentioning:

- Whereas Benoni supplies white domestic consumers direct, the township domestic consumers are supplied by a separate local authority which gets charged a bulk rate by Benoni, and then adds its own administration costs into the final unit cost carried by the consumer. If African consumers were supplied direct by Benoni, this additional cost could be carried by all consumers within the region. Instead, as the civics put it, the communities must pay for administrations created by apartheid, not by the people.
- Most of Benoni's consumption is non-domestic: commercial and industrial. This means that a surplus can be generated to allow the domestic price to enjoy the benefits of an effective subsidy. The townships do not have this advantage. Nearly all revenue needed to cover bulk supply purchases, repairs and maintenance, and capital upgrading (via levies to repay loan repayments) must come from domestic consumers.
- By selling electricity to the townships, Benoni is able to improve the level of its base load. In other words, whereas Johannesburg 'peak lops' to improve the ratio between peak load and base

load, Benoni achieves this by raising its base load by selling to the townships. This increased base load improves Benoni's load factor which is ultimately reflected in a reduced electricity cost per unit. This benefit, however, is not transferred to the accounts of the Daveyton and Wattville Councils.

- Most significantly, the townships — as bulk consumers of electricity — will be charged by Benoni according to the precise formula with which Benoni is charged by Eskom. By charging the townships, and other consumers of bulk electricity, for their own maximum demands, all of which happen at different times of the day and night, Benoni is able to generate a total in excess of the maximum demand charge for which it is liable to Eskom. It is this factor, above all others, that is most beneficial to the WLAs, and simultaneously most detrimental (and expensive) to the townships. The townships, of course, have no meaningful bulk consumers within their jurisdiction to effect the same result.
- Because the township consumers are the same people who work in Benoni's industrial and commercial areas, and given the contribution these firms make to Benoni's viability, this means that Benoni's surplus is effectively subsidized by the same people who are expected to pay for the full costs of their 'own' electrical systems.
- The costs of duplication due to the existence of three electricity departments to run a single electrical system are not carried by Benoni alone; they are effectively borne by all consumers, with the majority of domestic consumers living in the townships.

These inequalities could be largely done away with if there was a single non-racial electricity supply system for greater Benoni. This was proposed in a plan drawn up by the Wattville and Daveyton civics in October 1990. It was strongly supported by Eskom but, for obvious reasons, rejected by both the TPA and Benoni.

The case studies above underline why electricity has become such a critical issue in many of the local-level negotiations currently under way. It has also served to increase the importance of the role of Eskom in these negotiations. Whereas other parastatal bodies have, at best, enjoyed a peripheral observer status, Eskom officials are present at almost every negotiating forum, and have also been involved in facilitating actual agreements.

Eskom is quite keen for the issue of electricity to be deracialized and, thereby, depoliticized. As such, it often finds itself having to support civic-type positions and therefore, to some extent, comes in to conflict with the TPA, many of whose officials are still in an apartheid mind-set.

However, there can be no locally negotiated resolution to the enormous iniquities and inequalities that have been generated by the historic method of racially provided electricity. The depth of the problem and the size of the challenge — of providing electricity to 22 million (mainly African and poor) South Africans — strongly suggest that electricity supply and tariff can only be resolved at a national level.

The current crisis in financing local government

The civic associations

The rent boycotts were organized from below by highly effective local civic associations. Although a proper empirical analysis of the civic movement still needs to be done, suffice it to say that they are local social movements organized by an unpaid voluntary leadership who have succeeded in mobilizing their communities around the problems of daily township life. The issues around which they are organized are defined as 'civic' issues as opposed to (party) 'political' issues, i.e. housing, services, land, education, health, transport, and community facilities. Civics become involved in non-local political issues to the extent that they support national political formations. The ideology of the civics is shaped by the politicized leadership and immediate grassroots concerns of the rank and file who have considerable say in how the movements are run. The result is a radical conception of direct democracy, non-racialism, economic equality, and 'people's power'.

Some of the civics date as far back as 1979 (such as the Soweto Civic Association), whereas others were only formed in 1990. The newly formed Civics Association of the Southern Transvaal (CAST) has 50 affiliates in as many townships. In the highveld region, which is sandwiched between the East Rand and the lowveld, there are some 30 civics and the lowveld has over 50. It is significant to note that it has been accepted by all the liberation movements that civics, like trade unions, should be independent of the state and autonomous of political parties. This acceptance is going to have major long-term implications for both democracy and development.

The rent boycotts

The Transvaal rent boycott has gone through three phases. The first phase began in September 1984 and ended with the declaration of the state of emergency in mid-1986. During this period, some of the large-scale, long-term boycotts began such as the Vaal (September 1984) and Soweto (June 1986) boycotts. Smaller towns in the eastern Transvaal also launched boycotts during this period. According to the University of the Witwatersrand's Community Research Group, about 50 areas were participating in rent boycotts nationwide by mid-1986.

The second phase lasted from the beginning of the emergency to late 1989. During this phase many residents in the smaller towns, where rent boycotts had been launched during the first phase, began paying their rents and service charges because repression removed the civic from active community life. In some large areas, however, the boycott strengthened. This was particularly the case in Soweto, where activists were more able to disappear into a very large community.

The third phase began as the state of emergency ceased to be implemented towards the end of 1989. The release of detainees and De Klerk's 2 February speech spurred local activists into action. According to official figures, the rent boycott spread from a handful of townships in January 1990, to 35 in May, and to 49 in July.

In general terms the rent boycotts accomplished three things:
- They forcefully and aggressively shaped a policy agenda that revolves around what were originally the SPD's five 'policy principles' — namely, the write-off of arrears, the transfer of houses to residents, the need to upgrade services, affordable service charges, the creation of a single tax base and the establishment of a non-racial and democratic municipality.
- They exacerbated the fiscal crisis of the BLAs and critically exposed the fiscal unviability of the system.
- They prevented ad hoc amelioration measures, such as bridging finance and RSC levies, from rescuing the BLAs from fiscal collapse.

Instead, by mid-1990 all levels of government acknowledged that the local government system faced an immediate fiscal crisis that was beginning to result in service cuts, as well as a more fundamental structural crisis that called into question the viability of the system as a whole. This is what underlay a statement in May 1990 by the Minister of Planning and Provincial Affairs, Hernus Kriel, that the government was concerned about the effects of the rent boycott and was seriously considering a new local government policy based on the recommendations of the Thornhill Report. This report acknowledged the fiscal unviability of black local government and proposed that an alternative and potentially non-racial system was required.

It was in this context that local-level negotiations started across the Transvaal. The negotiation agenda was set by the 'policy principles' of the civics and was structured over time into two phases — the first dealt with measures to deal with the immediate crisis, and the second with long-term solutions to the structural crisis. The parties involved included the civics, BLAs, WLAs, Eskom, the TPA, the Rand Water Board (RWB), the Development Bank of Southern Africa (DBSA), and the various Transvaal RSCs. The negotiation format was conflictual, protracted, multi-layered, and came about with little or no mediation.

Before discussing the negotiation process itself, it is important to note why the TPA was brought to the negotiating table. On its own admission, it was forced to negotiate because it was running out of money to run the townships. The TPA budgeted R26 million per month for bridging finance for 1990. Because of the spread of the rent boycott, these funds were exhausted half way through the financial year: in some months, the TPA was paying close to R60 million in bridging finance. This direct impact of the rent boycott exemplifies most clearly the connection between the social movements, the failure of amelioration measures, and the final coming together of the parties to negotiate the possible parameters of a new local government dispensation.

The Greater Soweto Accord

The signing of the Greater Soweto Accord on 24 September 1990 marked a turning point in the urban transition. In terms of the accord, which was signed by the SPD, the TPA, and the three Soweto councils, it was agreed that Soweto's problems were both of a short-term and long-term nature. The short-term problems were the outstanding arrears, the boycott of rents and service charges, and the possible cutting off of services. The long-term problems were reducible to the apartheid city structure as analysed by the SPD in its 1989 report. The accord was, in essence, an agreement between the parties about how to resolve these short and long-term problems.

To deal with the long-term issues, it was agreed that a Metropolitan Chamber (MC) should be established whose mandate would be to design and implement a new 'non-racial and democratic' urban policy. It was agreed that the MC should comprise all the local government bodies and civic associations from the central Witwatersrand region. The policy fields that have been identified for investigation and design cover the entire spectrum of policy problems. The most immediate and pressing ones, however, were identified as the transfer of houses, the upgrading of services, affordability, and a single tax base. Some of the longer term issues that were identified included non-racial and democratic local and metropolitan government, industrial development policy, transport, the rationalization of administrations, social amenities, land use, and land availability.

As far as the short-term problems were concerned, the state agreed to write off the R500 million arrears amount 'owed' by Soweto's residents. In return the community agreed, via the branches of the civic, to resume payment of what was defined as an 'interim service charge'. This obviated the necessity for service cut-offs.

Until a new urban system is established, the SPD agreed on behalf of the community that the residents would pay an 'interim service charge'. This was a charge that would cover the cost of part of the bulk services or the equivalent of about one third of what it costs to run Soweto on a monthly basis. In terms of a separate agreement between the Soweto and Johannesburg local authorities and the TPA, the outstanding amount would be covered by the Central Witwatersrand Regional Services Council (CWRSC) until 1 March 1991, i.e. until the next financial year commences on the basis of a new national budget. This meant, therefore, that the bridging finance burden was transferred from the central fiscus to the RSCs. This is a major shift because it means that contrary to initial intentions to spend RSC funds on capital development, the RSC was brought directly into funding the operating account of the BLAs. Given that this money comes from levies on business in white Johannesburg, this represents the beginning of a metropolitan-wide redistribution process. The problem, however, is that the CWRSC had to stop a number of capital development projects to release these funds. It remains unclear where funds for future capital development will come from.

Other local-level negotiations in the Transvaal

The Soweto Accord set the framework for local-level negotiations in some 40 areas across the Transvaal. Although initial indications were that similar agreements to the Soweto Accord were a strong possibility in these areas, this looked increasingly unlikely as 1990 wore on. There were three reasons why towns outside the Central Witwatersrand found it difficult to come to similar arrangements to that reached in Soweto.

Firstly, there is no equivalent body outside this region to the CWRSC. The CWRSC has a huge income because of the rich concentration of economic activity in its area of jurisdiction and it is dominated by Johannesburg. All that was required was for Johannesburg to vote in favour of a motion that provided for the redirection of capital development funds to operating expenditure, and the Soweto Accord became financially viable. In the other areas, the RSCs do not have this kind of money. Furthermore, they are dominated by more conservative WLAs who refuse to allow 'their' white business areas and farmers to be taxed to subsidize the operating accounts of BLAs who cannot get their residents to pay for what they use.

Secondly, and more importantly, in most of the areas outside the Central Witwatersrand, electricity is supplied through the dependent system, i.e. via the WLAs. This meant that these local authorities needed to be party to the negotiations. In some areas this was possible, but in those areas where the CP controlled the WLA, this was impossible. This was why unilateral decisions to cut off services occurred in many cases before negotiations had even begun (e.g. Carolina and Bethal). The reluctance of the WLAs to participate in negotiations became increasingly more determined as civics came to the negotiating table armed with sophisticated analyses that demonstrated how the WLAs were benefiting financially from the way services were provided in the apartheid city. In other words, the rent boycott and the negotiation process began to reveal the underlying injustice of urban apartheid and underscored the necessity to dismantle it. Except for the local authorities in the Central Witwatersrand area who agreed in November to participate in the MC (i.e. Johannesburg, Randburg, Roodepoort, and Sandton), no other local authorities demonstrated a willingness to participate in the negotiated dismantling of urban apartheid. Instead, they were able to hide behind their constitutionally and legally defined position as separate local authorities with no responsibility for the African townships. In line with this callous morality, they were able to justify cutting off basic services to the townships. This, in turn, was the final blow to many already illegitimate BLAs. Councillors began resigning *en masse:* by mid-November, 237 of the 636 council seats were vacant, and 24 of the 82 BLAs were non-functional. In other words, as the crisis deepened, the apartheid local government system began destroying itself as the WLAs chose to defend themselves at the expense of their counterpart structures in the townships.

The third reason why local-level negotiations outside the Central Witwatersrand became increasingly difficult as 1990 wore on was a formula that came to be known as the 'TPA priority list'. In terms of a TPA instruction sent out to all BLAs in October, any incoming revenue from the residents should first be spent on salaries and then, in this order, water, sewerage, refuse, and electricity. If a given BLA spent its money on services before salaries, it would not be entitled to its share of bridging finance. This meant that where there were agreements that provided for flat rate payments to prevent service cut-offs, service cut-offs happened in any case because contrary to what the civics had agreed to, the money was spent on paying for what the civics perceived as apartheid administrations. This was another reason why councillors began resigning *en masse*. It was the primary reason for the resignation of Tom Boya from the Daveyton Council in October. He was one of the leading lights in black local government and was viewed, in some quarters, as a relatively credible 'moderate'.

By the end of 1990, it became increasingly apparent that until the constitutional and legal position of the WLAs is dismantled, local-level negotiations cannot proceed to their logical conclusion. Disempowering the WLAs, in turn, could only be achieved at the national level. It was this increasingly obvious and familiar link between the structure of political power and local conditions of urban existence that gave rise to renewed forms of mass mobilization. Under the leadership of the newly formed CAST, marches, consumer boycotts, and other forms of mass action were initiated from mid-November onwards to increase the pressure for urban and political change.

Financing local government in the future

There is one unfortunate consequence of the 'one tax base' demand and that is the assumption that a simple amalgamation of the white and African tax bases will resolve the problem. Although this may be true for one or two rich local authorities (e.g. Johannesburg and Durban), it is a mistaken way of posing the question. The basic problem is that under apartheid, local government has been steadily disempowered to a point where it is now responsible for only 10 per cent of public expenditure. Deracializing this small fiscal base will leave a future non-racial local government system without the resources it will require to meet the needs of the future non-racial towns and cities.

Obviously the starting point must be a non-racial, 'one tax base' approach. But from this point it becomes an extremely complicated exercise that involves variables that are way beyond the control of local interests and hence cannot be negotiated to conclusion at the local level.

The first task should be to define the functions that local government must be responsible for. Once this has been done, then it will be possible to calculate the appropriate expenditure levels that will be required for local governments to fulfil these functions. Obviously, the more functions local governments must perform, the more money they will need to spend. Once expenditure levels have been ascertained, then local fiscal capacities can be identified in order to determine the range of local taxes available to raise the revenue needed to cover the desired expenditure levels.

This sounds simple enough, but in reality is very complex. As far as functions are concerned, this is both a constitutional and policy issue because the functions that will be carried out by local government will depend on two related variables. The first is whether a centralized or decentralized system of government will be adopted. If it is a centralized system, then local government will have limited functions except to administer and apply nationally determined policies with nationally allocated resources. A decentralized system implies the existence of local governments that will be relatively autonomous when it comes to both policy formulation and revenue collection.

The second variable concerns the number of levels the future governmental system will have. If a basically three-tier system is adopted, this will mean dividing functions between the three tiers. There may also, of course, be divisions within certain tiers. For example, local government in metropolitan areas may need to have a metropolitan level and a local 'borough'-type level.

Clearly, the determination of functions cannot be done purely at the local level. Local and national negotiators will have to find some way of linking the local-level negotiation process to the national-level negotiation process in order to reach consensus on this matter.

As far as expenditure is concerned, it will be relatively easy to cost the local government functions once they have been determined. However, when it comes to ascertaining revenue sources, this again will depend on what the national taxation policy is going to be. At the moment, central government accounts for 60 per cent of all public expenditure, whereas provincial government accounts for 30 per cent and local government for 10 per cent. This expenditure profile leaves local government with no money to support an extension of its functions beyond the present level. By simply amalgamating the tax base without increasing the fiscal capacity of local government, all that will be achieved is the deracialization of a small section of the fiscal pie and, possibly, the inducement of another kind of local fiscal crisis as needs rapidly outstrip available resources. If, however, it is agreed that local government's functions should be extended and local government expenditure accordingly increased, the national taxation system will have to be tailored to meet the revenue needs of a democratic local government system. Ideally, if a decentralized system is preferred, local government should generate as much of its own revenue as possible in order to avoid controls from higher authorities. This, in turn, will mean investigating different types of local taxes. Four, in particular, are the most common: property taxes, sales taxes, a local income tax, and special taxes of various kinds (e.g. on enterprises or on consumers of certain products). At the moment, only the property tax and RSC levies are used at the local level.

Although the property tax is the most common local tax in non-commandist developed economies, it can give rise to three problems that will have to be faced. Firstly, the property tax is notoriously inelastic and clumsy. Fiscal gaps open between revenue and expenditure levels when inflation rises more rapidly than the municipal property valuation. Secondly, the property tax cements the individualized property relation into the foundations of the urban system. This could hamper a differentiated ownership system that may be needed to protect low-income areas from the market by way of mechanisms such as land trusts and housing co-operatives. Thirdly, the property tax effectively ties the interests of local officials and politicians to a defence of privately owned property and, to this extent, builds in a bias against public and collective ownership.

Conclusion

It has been argued thus far that the fiscal system of the apartheid town and city facilitated the net transfer of resources from the poor black to rich white areas. This helped the WLAs to be financially viable and enabled the white ratepayers to receive services at a standard that could be justified in a developed first world economy, but not in a middle developing economy such as South Africa's. This level of contrived privilege was only made possible by the structured extraction of resources from the politically disenfranchised, spatially marginalized, and coercively exploited urban poor. It was this basic inequality that eventually gave rise to the rent boycott.

The rent boycott movement has succeeded in creating the conditions where it was finally accepted that the entire local government system requires a complete overhaul, which will be predicated on the demise of the BLAs. This is why local-level negotiations broke out across the length and breadth of the Transvaal. However, as progress in these negotiations was made, so the WLAs began to hide behind their constitutional and legal status in a desperate attempt to protect the privileges of the white ratepayer. Until this status is dismantled, progress at local level is going to be limited. This much was recognized by the ANC at a national consultative conference on local government policy in October 1990.

When it comes to designing a new local government finance system, South Africans will be well advised to learn a lesson from Poland. During the so-called 'round table talks' in 1989 which resulted in a new constitutional order for that country, the only item the parties could not agree on was local government. The decision reached was that this would be left unresolved and would become a matter to be dealt with by the future government. Many of the people who were pushing during these talks for strong and relatively autonomous local governments eventually found themselves running the new democratically elected government. Not surprisingly, when it came to establishing a new local government system, they were no longer so keen on the strong decentralized system that they once called for from outside the corridors of power. This has become an important source of conflict between Polish communities and the new state.

It is a tremendous strength that the number of people involved in negotiating the new system of government is not limited to a handful of leaders at the national level. Local-level negotiations ensure that ordinary residents of communities are also involved in the transition process. However, the two levels of negotiation are going to have to be carefully co-ordinated so that the national level process does not undermine the local processes, and the local processes are not sabotaged by nationally protected special interests. This will, of course, also mean that the local negotiation process must not undermine the national negotiation process.

Notes

1   All three authors work for Planact, a non-profit urban development consultancy that works for the civic associations and trade unions. Much of the information and ideas presented in this chapter were obtained or collectively generated by Planact staff, its consultants, and civic activists engaged in grassroots organizing around these issues. The various reports by Andrew Nash of Kenwalt that Planact commissioned were particularly useful. The opinions expressed here, however, are those of the authors and not necessarily of Planact, its consultants, or its clients.
2   East Rand Regional Services Council.
3   Central Witwatersrand Regional Services Council.
4   West Rand Regional Services Council.

13 The housing crisis

Paul Hendler[1]

The reshaping of the South African polity and society in the 1990s is being refracted through the cities, where violent conflicts occurred during the 1980s. Social struggles have placed the questions of housing cost and location firmly on the agenda of change, alongside the national political and constitutional questions. The goal of this chapter is to assist in clarifying theories and deriving policy guidelines for altering material and social conditions of residents in South Africa's deprived townships.

Since the mid-1980s, there have been attempts to negotiate urban policies in some African townships. The major impetus for these initiatives emerged from the impasse between the state and the anti-apartheid community and youth organizations.[2] But prospects for local settlements promoting transition to more democratic and improved working-class living conditions depend on how major actors perceive the housing crisis, and not only on their political practices. Negotiators representing residents (i.e. 'the grassroots') need to understand mechanisms underlying the housing crisis so that they can frame demands which would alter the material and political conditions of township life.

This chapter aims to achieve its objective through exploring the interpretations of the housing question held by reputable urban scholars as well as major South African urban policy decision makers. Underlying assumptions about people and society form the basis for a wider rationale for comprehending causal relationships between contingent events in the housing field. Understanding 'homelessness', the enormous degree of overcrowding, as well as the patent inability of the majority to afford even the cheapest private market houses, is a matter of contention between antagonistic social actors. Each position's 'theoretical claims' can be tested against knowledge of empirical phenomena.[3] A rigorous comprehension of objective processes is one precondition for the development of sound negotiation and development strategics. Through analysing the advances and limitations of each standpoint, the chapter tries to articulate questions useful for progressive policy formulation during the 1990s.

Shelter: its shortage and cost

Regardless of their political conflicts, all major urban protagonists have agreed that there is an enormous shortage of affordable housing for the black — in particular the African — working classes. The old Department of Community Development's reports,[4] as well as the papers from the second Carnegie conference,[5] both pointed to the critical housing situation during the early 1980s. Historical figures gleaned from the Venter Commission of Inquiry (1980), the National Building Research Institute (NBRI) (1980),[6] the Department of Community Development (1981),[7] the West Rand Administration Board (WRAB) (1981),[8] the state's Department of Co-operation and Development (1984), and the South African Institute of Race Relations (SAIRR)[9] demonstrate that the housing shortage has been growing steadily. More recent NBRI research[10] has confirmed this trend.

Newspaper and other organizational and individual reports attest, independently of the state, to the critical accommodation shortage during the 1970s and the 1980s which resulted in illegal land occupations and the construction of squatter housing — the best known example of which was perhaps Crossroads near Cape Town.[11] By 1987, according to the UF, the Winterveld settlement (outside Pretoria) had approximately 600 000 informal settlers, while the urban periphery surrounding Durban had become the major growth point of informal settlements reaching a total of 1.7 million settlers.[12] During the 1980s, most African township residents were unable, at least in the view of potential lenders, to afford paying off loans over an extended period.[13] The frequent refusal by communities to pay monthly rental charges was a manifestation of their meagre financial resources.[14] Spontaneous defaulting on rent — characteristic, for example, of Soweto during the late 1970s — was overtaken by more organized political boycotts of payments to the BLAs during the 1980s.

Partly because of the inability of African workers to afford the cost of providing shelter, most township houses were built by the state during the 1950s and 1960s, but this did not satisfy the long-term need for shelter. This unsatisfied need — exacerbated by government reluctance to maintain relatively low rents — has fuelled the flames of revolt and thus turned the housing question into a conflict about costs and shortages. The turmoil and changing organization and administration of the townships during the 1980s and 1990s form the social background to this brief analysis of the housing debate.

Apartheid views

Between 1922 and the late 1970s urban and housing policies were justified on the assumption that Africans were the whites' wards, to be helped to develop in their own areas, and that the residential rights of Africans in white-designated areas depended on their ministering to white people's labour and other needs.[15] The positivist ideologies of state officials also assumed that township urban forms reflected the particular national consciousness and less developed needs of 'the natives'.

The reasoning was that Africans had themselves to blame for their endemic housing crisis because they had been expanding too rapidly without acquiring the resources to satisfy their most pressing needs; at the same time the state as trustee was perceived to have made enormous strides towards bringing the problem under control, if not solving it.[16]

Moreover, these views extended sometimes to parastatal technocrats charged with housing tasks. During the 1950s the NBRI — set up to research technical solutions for the housing crisis — accepted the state's ethnic categorization of African people as given.[17] During the 1940s and 1950s conservative liberals in the SAIRR expressed similar views, reflecting the growing impact of an idealist anthropology at the universities 'that was pliable to the needs of administrators'.[18]

During the 1980s and 1990s, as the NP moved further and further away from its traditional white support base, such views came to be seen as increasingly obsolete by upper echelon government officials. While the 'common sense' criticism of African population growth remains,[19] the apartheid interpretation of the housing question has become increasingly restricted to the CP and other right-wing elements. However the semi-autonomous BLAs have continued to rely on seconded white officials who are not used to accommodating residents' demands,[20] and have seen little need to negotiate with representative township groups. For instance during 1987 paternalistic white officials in the eastern Witwatersrand township of Tembisa were able to undermine emerging negotiations between the local councillors and community groups.[21] After the 1986 abolition of the Development Boards (which had 'run' the townships since the early 1970s) many conservative officials found a home in the provincial administrations' 'community services' sections, which during 1990 assumed municipal managerial roles in lieu of the increasing number of defunct local state apparatuses. While the liberalization induced by the NP's (post 2 February 1990) reform strategy has probably brought about a change of mind in some officials — there were during 1990 several significant local negotiation processes under way — the paternalistic views of local bureaucrats could, nevertheless, still critically affect the outcome of future bargaining processes.

Thus in addition to explaining very little, segregationist/apartheid views are an anachronism in an era during which negotiated incremental solutions to township housing problems are likely to be the order of the day.

Liberal and neo-classical views

In the 1950s, but more particularly during the 1970s, 1980s, and 1990s, the government's liberal opponents developed an alternative to the dominant racist interpretation. This was based on neo-classical economic theories, i.e. that the 'natural' relationship of individual consumers to individual suppliers and producers should not be tampered with by the state, and that individuals operating as 'homo economicus' would ultimately 'better themselves' and achieve parity through private markets and *laissez-faire* economic activity. The policy proposals emanating from this constituency emphasize the role of the housing market and technical and financial instruments in resolving accommodation problems.

This perspective stimulated important housing and urbanization debates by the more radically minded SAIRR liberals during the 1950s as well as during the heyday of apartheid. Since the 1970s these assumptions motivated the UF, which was established as a pressure group for big business, lobbying for a change in the direction of government practices.[22] By the mid-1980s, thinking in NP and senior civil service circles to a large extent reflected the liberal paradigm.[23] (The significant exception was the retention of racial land use planning.) The liberal point of departure also underlies the thinking of some constituencies in the African National Congress (ANC)[24] and the United Democratic Front (UDF).

Spontaneous migration by African peasants from rural to urban South African society[25] and migration as 'the push-pull mechanism'[26] emerged as the point of departure for the liberal urban studies corpus. Migration was accorded a determining role in the genesis of the housing crisis. But the implication was that in the long run, 'temporary' anomalies could iron themselves out through *laissez-faire* market processes. The UF — arguably at the forefront of liberal policy 'think tanks' during the 1980s and 1990s — has also based its policy positions on the assumption that a rapidly urbanizing society is a 'natural', spontaneous phenomenon, which requires creative management rather than control or resistance.[27]

A second major focus of liberal urban scholars was the South African state's interventionist policies and practices: 'temporary sojournership',[28] Group Areas Act population removals,[29] the prohibition of dwelling construction for Africans, and African home-ownership in South Africa's white-designated areas[30] during the late 1960s and early to mid-1970s, were seen to have brought about an acute housing shortage. The UF has also argued that notwithstanding the lifting of many of these constraints by 1990, shortages and relatively high costs have persisted due to the absence of clearly defined goals, objectives, and roles in current government housing plans.[31]

Migration, however, is hardly the spontaneous and 'natural' process which Maasdorp[32] and the UF[33] have implied, but since the turn of the century has been a response to social measures aimed at creating (and reproducing) a wage labour force in southern Africa — often through a violent process of land dispossession.[34] The conscious restriction of Africans to a relatively minute proportion of the land led to overcrowding and depleted the carrying capacity of the land reserved for African occupation, which increasingly became little more than labour reservoirs for industry located in the 'white' areas.[35] Thus the liberal paradigm's theoretical assumptions occlude a politicized perception of housing, the supply of which perforce is interwoven with social relationships of subordination/domination. Attributing the housing shortage to the relative absence of a private market — due to government policy — is equally limiting because notwithstanding its stated aim of restricting the number of houses for Africans, the NP government built the vast housing estates which constitute today's townships. Rather than being the villain of the piece, the NP regime appears to have played a contradictory role in the provision of shelter in the townships, a point acknowledged by Welsh,[36] himself a liberal scholar. Blaming the central authorities also does not adequately explain why, during the present 'individual-owner' policy (which commenced during the late 1970s), the short-age has persisted despite the lifting of restrictions on home-owner-ship and private provision of shelter. The importance accorded to the state stands in marked contrast to the omission to examine the way economic processes played a role in excluding people from accommodation. As with migration theories, social relations of power, embedded in the market, receive scant attention from within the liberal paradigm.

For instance, Dewar[37] and the UF[38] have addressed the access to fiscal resources issue, but not the question of why township dwellers did not have the money to house themselves. The type of approach adopted by Dewar, as well as by the UF, to low-income housing leaves serious political and economic issues unexplored.[39] The only power relationship considered worthy of central analysis is the oppressive role of the apartheid state. The logical progression from liberal and neo-classical assumptions is to overemphasize the removal of one form of political (i.e. apartheid) obstacles to the pro-vision of affordable, adequate housing, but to underplay other politi-cal and economic power relations which also stand between town-ship people and shelter. In a word, the housing crisis historically has been rooted in the land question, and remains to this day a political issue and one therefore which may not be resolvable solely through the removal of state intervention and the application of technical and financial stimulants to the housing market.

Negotiation demands which focus on removing apartheid regulations to the exclusion of examining specific social and economic processes which hinder the urban poor's access to and ability to afford residential shelter, are unlikely to lead to an improvement in residents' housing and living conditions. In this respect many of the assumptions underlying the UF positions on urbanization and regional development could be criticized for ignoring the 'hidden power' imbalances between (mainly African) working-class consumers and capitalist suppliers in the African housing field. Nevertheless, UF thinking has not simply been the outcome of logical deduction from underlying premises, but has also been shaped through its practice of reforming society, a mission prompted originally by the 1976 Soweto student protests and ensuing turmoil. Currently the UF has specific proposals for:

- public sector subsidization of land and 'first-time' housing;
- the urban poor's access to the private sector home loans finance market;
- public sector financing and cross subsidization for bulk infrastructure;
- land investment trusts to control speculation in land prices and to specify the type of improvements undertaken; and
- resolving conflicts over land (through proposed metropolitan land planning agencies) and consumer grievances (through a proposed housing industry ombudsman, licensed private sector agents acting for consumers, and an affordable legal aid system).[40]

Given the 'establishment' nature of the UF, it could be argued that the above mentioned proposals represent a necessary step towards securing an 'urban coalition'[41] on terms dictated by South Africa's ruling élites. Nevertheless, it might also be possible for residents and community groups to engage with the UF and develop the progressive content of these proposals, and thereby 'begin to make the exercise of grassroots community control over housing development a reality'.[42]

Clearly, the politics of community involvement and grassroots control requires an understanding of the complex power relationships and processes at work in the creation of the built environment and the reproduction of social life in the cities. Class relations and conflict — a glaring omission in the approaches adopted in the writings of Dewar,[43] Maasdorp,[44] Maasdorp and Humphreys,[45] Maasdorp and Pillay,[46] Morris,[47] and the UF[48] — remain an important component of such an understanding, and form the central concepts in a set of radical analyses of the African housing question in South Africa.

Neo-Marxist perspectives

Neo-Marxist theorists who perceived class conflict as the major process shaping township life, criticized both state as well as liberal policies, arguing that the social geography of the townships was a direct outcome of the conflicts waged over the distribution of the costs of reproducing labour power (i.e. reproduction being the replenishment of the physical capacity to work, and the control of the political/ideological processes which legitimate capitalist relations). This argument ironically also gave an analytical centrality to the state, and reflected the work of Castells.[49] Policy positions emanating from the neo-Marxist assumptions focused on popular, multi-class urban social movements and their resistance against the state, mainly around the issue of housing. It was argued that increasing state intervention in 'everyday life' (for instance as supplier of housing and subsidizer of transportation, i.e. the collective means of consumption) and the ensuing politicization of consumption issues, created a structural link with underlying capitalist production relations, on which urban movements might have a transformative impact. The implication was that a transition to a socialist society was the only guaranteed long-term solution to the housing crisis.

The milieu which produced these interventions contrasted sharply with the 1960s and the post 2 February 1990 dispensation. With the mass strikes in Durban during 1973, industrial conflict forcibly made its appearance in the 1970s, and dogged the ruling classes as the decade wore on. After 16 June 1976, the period was characterized by political conflicts in all the major African townships and, as far as the housing question was concerned, boycotts of rent increases. Due to the inability of many workers to afford even the basic rental payments, the housing issue had by the mid-1980s become increasingly charged with class conflict. This conflict reached its zenith with the burning of community councillors' houses and with the military occupation of the townships. In short, the period was characterized by new levels of resistance, as well as severe state repression.

The radical authors did not ground an explanation of urbanization and the African housing shortage on the ill-defined assumptions of 'the population explosion' and 'push-pull' migration, but analysed rather: the state's contradictory role in the reproduction of the relations of production;[50] the link between Group Areas legislation, influx control policies, and the history of capitalist development in South Africa;[51] the reproductive (and non-reproductive) aspects of urban planning undertaken by the administration boards;[52] and political conflict around the collective means of consumption.[53] As McCarthy[54] has argued, the urgent political crisis of the mid-1980s prompted radical analysts to focus on reproduction issues and the politics of collective consumption: in the radical paradigm, reproduction thus became the primary analytical category for making sense of the South Africa of the 1970s and the 1980s. The radical focus on the state differed, however, from the liberal critique in that government intervention was perceived not as an interference in 'natural' market processes, but as the wielding of ruling class power over the dominated classes of an essentially capitalist society.

With their focus on power relations, the radical concepts are useful tools for community groups that are engaging the state and local authorities in the 1990s. During the 1980s, however, policy guidelines emanating from the radical orientation were that housing should not be seen as an issue in itself which justified concrete development proposals, but as a means to be used to achieve the national political goals of anti-apartheid political movements. Indeed, in the absence of bargaining with the authorities (which has occurred with increasing frequency during 1990) there was no practical need for local organizations to frame substantive policy proposals for dealing with the problem. The apartheid state was seen as being responsible for the inadequate provision of shelter in South Africa,[55] and it was assumed that a new, nonracial, and democratic state would soon remedy the problem.

The state's actions, however, become too independent of economic costs and benefits in such accounts.[56] For instance, Wilkinson[57] addressed primarily the question of social reproduction and conflicts over the distribution of the costs of reproducing labour power, yet ignored the obvious, i.e. that the housing sector's capital accumulating imperatives were also reasons for changing housing policy.[58] Common to Ratcliffe,[59] Wilkinson,[60] Bloch,[61] and also to McCarthy and Swilling[62] was an absence of the potential effect on state policy and township politics of costs and profits in the housing, transport, and associated industries (i.e. the effect of capital accumulating activities on the shaping of the built environment). The same point can be made concerning the demands of trade unionists and community organizers during the 1980s. However, as housing policies during the 1980s came increasingly to reflect material conditions, the question arose of whether reproduction (i.e. in its political/ideological forms), or economic factors played the determining role in shaping urban processes.[63] Thus while class perspectives have made several advances in equipping urban movements with guidelines for understanding the complexities of the housing question, a fuller understanding of the townships' social geography requires an investigation of the cost and other factors involved in the production of the built environment.[64]

One key actor with an interest in the housing question is financial capital. This class interest has sought to expand itself through the creation of credit, and one of the principal means for doing this has been through home loan finance for low-cost dwelling units.[65] Large financial houses have become conspicuous by their presence in previously trouble-torn townships such as Alexandra, or in their vociferous support for an easing of traditional controls over their lending practices. As the liberalization of apartheid society has proceeded apace during 1990, it has become clear that the urban ghettos — once the stamping ground of the conservative Development Board officials — are becoming new sites for the investment of finance capital in South Africa. While the financiers remain adamant that theirs is the African community's path to a better future, at times they appear to be aiding and abetting a process through which the privileged few gain access to modern housing, while the unemployed, the homeless, and the aged are pressurized to relocate to site-and-service schemes on the urban periphery.

Thus for community negotiators (including squatter leaders) the question of democratic community control over the terms of finance and development in concrete projects, as well as over general processes of social reproduction and economic accumulation, are of crucial importance. The issue at stake is, however, not merely whether or not issues of production cost (and economic accumulation) or of immediate reproduction of the workforce have predominated in the decisions leading to the construction of particular townships, but rather understanding the complex interweaving of material and political factors. How the material becomes political and the political shapes the material, in the hands of individuals, political movements, and social classes, requires much more substantial research into urban questions and struggles in South Africa, as Mabin[66] has argued.

The nature of future local, incremental settlements to housing disputes, and their impact on everyday life in the townships, will depend to a large extent on how far the political actors are motivated to address these terms of the housing debate: class and social power, and the interweaving of economic accumulation and social reproduction. The relevance of urban studies to these urban political negotiation processes arises from the fact that a sensitivity to the complexities and nuances involved in the formation of class consciousness and the consolidation of urban political power is important for the development of democratic participation by working-class people in the running of their cities. Scholarly investigation can contribute to the development of an understanding which would serve to facilitate this process of democratization and empowerment.

Radical democratic views

A necessary (albeit not sufficient) condition for thorough-going social emancipation is active participation by literally hundreds of thousands of residents in urban development and housing processes. Despite their important contribution to the corpus of urban studies, radical South African theories are unable to theorize an empowered (albeit dominated) citizenry impacting on the politics of the built environment. Based on a neo-Marxist structuralism[67] which assumes that individuals are mere functionaries of society's structural network,[68] the radical analyses stress 'structural' class interests but remain silent about the concrete interests of, for instance, ethnic and language groups, women, the aged, and gays. Yet it is precisely the specific interests of strata within the working class, who are discriminated against, that are likely to provide the impetus for the mass participation necessary for real empowerment. These interests need to be translated into local demands (for instance, the provision of apartment accommodation for single parent mothers), instead of local agendas becoming merely ways of resisting accumulation/reproduction processes, still less as part of a national campaign for 'the transfer of power to the people'.

Since 2 February 1990, with the lifting of the proscriptions on the ANC, PAC, SACP, and other political organizations, there has been a surge of grassroots activity in townships as residents mobilized initially behind the ANC, but latterly increasingly independently in civic associations to improve their material lot. Concomitant with the emergence of grassroots power has been the outbreak of violence among residents in the African townships and informal settlements of the PWV region. The existing radical theories cannot provide a full understanding of these seemingly ethnic or cultural conflicts, precisely because of a reductionist emphasis on the logic of capital and class structures. Yet understanding the reasons for the mayhem is important to unite different township-based interest groups behind a progressive development strategy.

Concepts useful for interpreting current events have nevertheless been articulated abroad. Within left-wing urban sociology there has emerged a critique of structuralism by, among others, Castells[69] who has developed beyond the confines of 'social structure determinism'. In a shift from earlier positions, and reflecting more recent developments in western Marxist theory, Castells[70] maintained that:

- Cities do not simply reflect the logic of capital accumulation, but also the way conflicting historical actors assigned different meanings to the role and function of cities and citizens.
- There is a causal equivalence between the role of class, the state, gender relationships, and ethnic, national, and citizen movements.
- Urban protest-developed demands focused on state-provided goods and services as well as mobilization against local and central state authority[71] and the defence of cultural identity, organized around a specific territory.
- Grassroots mobilization resulting in urban social movements was necessary for city transformation.

In the post-structuralist vision, housing and urban political struggles have come to be seen as concerning the organization of experience and the production of personality systems and cultural values through gender and sexual relationships. Castells proposed that a combination of feminist and psychoanalytical theories could provide useful guidelines for studying the development of urban cultural identity.[72]

Castells's revised ideas may be useful for understanding the mechanisms underlying the 1984–6 popular resistance to the BLAs in South Africa, as well as the emergence of conservative ethnic-based vigilante groups (i.e. the 'witdoeke' of Crossroads, the Inkatha warlords in Natal, and the African vigilante forces which have wreaked havoc in the African townships of the PWV region during 1990). Popular township resistance and counter-revolutionary responses are clearly not reducible to conflicts over the reproduction of labour power and the distribution of the collective means of consumption; still less can they simply be read off from 'the logic of accumulation'.

Castells also developed his ideas on urban social movements and their production of 'new social effects'. He found that the movements were linked to three particular types of 'operators' who made it possible for them to have an impact on society: the media, technically competent professionals, and political parties. But he found that while being linked to these, urban social movements should remain autonomous in order to be able to change urban meaning. Any movement that was not autonomous became, according to Castells,[73] an appendage of the interests of these operators.

The above-mentioned redefinition of urban social movements may be useful for comprehending the new political practices which have begun to emerge in some of South Africa's largest African townships. In the PWV region, the impasse between the authorities and their township-based opponents has in recent years led to several negotiations over rent boycotts and illegal land occupation.[74] The emergence of large community organizations in the African townships has occurred because of the efforts of activists linked to the UDF and (to a lesser extent) the black consciousness-supporting National Forum Committee. More recently professional operators have also played critically important roles in enabling the negotiations to take place. But the danger exists that the practices of these operators could substitute for the much needed grassroots organization required by the fledgling urban social movements if they are to wring material concessions from the authorities. Yet while greater autonomy for these community groupings is required if they are to develop into grassroots-based urban social movements,[75] it would be a contradiction in terms to attempt to build community organizations which have no links with traditional political and other technical and media operators in South Africa.

Since 2 February 1990 — which marked the 'opening up' of political processes in South Africa — there has emerged a swell of grassroots-based civic associations in the PWV region as well as elsewhere in the country. It is at the grassroots of the cities that local community leadership is starkly confronted with questions about residents' material conditions as well as their power to control their lives. Besides the ANC, the NP government, the trade union movement, big business and other interest groupings, these local organizations have the potential to grow in strength and thereby could exert an influence over the country's future political culture and socio-economic development well beyond the confines of their particular built environments.

Conclusion

During the 1990s, changing political processes have placed the termination of apartheid racism firmly on the agenda of social change. Even the NP government — once at the vanguard of racial social engineering — has distanced itself from 'separate development' ideology and practice. The colour bar in sexual relationships fell away in recent years; currently the hospitals are being desegregated; the Group Areas Act will be abolished during 1991; and it is expected that within a couple of years the four-tier educational system will cease to exist. The sweeping away of residential, educational, and health segregation clearly offers potential for the release of enormous wells of creative energy by ordinary people living in the townships. From a liberal perspective, the removal of state controls will allow the full force of the market to direct the production and distribution of commodities — including housing — to satisfy popular needs, an assumption which underlies the argument for privatizing the use of society's resources. In the African areas, a private (albeit limited) housing market has been operating for the past decade.[76]

The problems experienced by Eastern Bloc economies in recent years, as well as the dramatic restructuring of those economies and societies during 1989 and 1990, indicate that for the users of goods and services, the market as a 'feedback mechanism' may in some ways be more equitable than centrally planned state control (of the socialist or apartheid variety), 'and more efficient than a system in which we all vote on the exact needs of our supermarket shopping basket in some popular forum'.[77] Yet while the housing market's mechanisms might have progressive possibilities as an index of social needs, the impact is always limited by the existing distribution of wealth and income. The liberal view that market-based social relationships are natural and equal (and hence just) often ignores the enormous inequalities of wealth in a country like South Africa, and tends to obscure the power imbalances between producers and consumers in the African housing market. If negotiated settlements to housing conflicts are going to lead to an improvement in the physical well-being of African working-class residents, the functioning of the private housing market needs to be channelled in such a way that it is not only the wealthy and the powerful who benefit: there is a real possibility that current high prices of land and housing will pressurize poorer residents to relocate to cheaper but disadvantaged regions on the urban periphery.

Clearly the market should be shaped to the advantage of working-class residents. Housing should cease merely to serve the narrow interests of the state and employers in the reproduction of workforces, and of developers in the pursuit of capital. The production of housing for maximum profit, the creation of home loan credit as a means solely for accumulating money-capital, and a fixation with private tenure and individual home-ownership as the *sine qua non* of development, are likely to pose serious threats to community attempts to rescue residents from further impoverishment and degradation. Understanding profit motives of developers and their capital accumulating imperatives could place community activists in a relatively strong position to wring certain concessions from them. A similar knowledge of the role of financial capital in the built environment could form the base for campaigns aimed at building societies and banks.

Social conflict around housing is increasingly being channelled through bargaining/negotiation processes, which require new forms of organization. Apartheid has produced passive township communities, many of whom have been denied the skills and confidence needed to challenge the apartheid urban system. This passivity is strengthened by a reliance on charismatic leadership figures who offer them deliverance by way of millenarian campaigns for unachievable demands whose failure strengthens a culture of powerlessness. Collective bargaining over housing is the antithesis of passivity, for it relies on residents winning gains through their collective efforts.[78] In order for local urban social movements to become more fully organized, they require greater autonomy from the national opposition movements and parties, as well as from a dogmatic fixation on past anti-apartheid strategies. Already this process is occurring in the Transvaal where a strongly organized, independent civic movement is emerging. Current ANC policy has also taken cognizance of this reality through stressing the need for independent community organizations. Through winning concessions from the authorities, financial institutions, and developers, the local associations could build grassroots organization as a basis from which to make further demands.

A more fundamental question concerns the structures through which residents can empower themselves and at the same time improve their material living conditions. While they lack the necessary resources, community organizations might have to be satisfied with joint ventures negotiated with developers and financiers. But in the longer term, the models of community-controlled development corporations, land trusts, and funds (which have been developed in other parts of the world), need to be examined for their application in the South African urban context.

Local negotiations have led to the crystallization of both establishment as well as progressive policy positions. The establishment parties generally tend to represent or be supported by the state and big business groupings, while the progressive sector includes the traditional anti-apartheid political groupings, the African labour movements, the emergent civic-based urban social movements (including representative squatter organizations), and a host of support agencies and organizations. In essence the establishment position rests on the assumption that private tenure should predominate as a means of holding and controlling residential shelter, and that technocratic 'experts' provided by the market should control the implementation of projects. By contrast the emerging progressive position is characterized by a willingness to explore seriously collective forms of tenure tailored to the urban poor's needs, and a principled and practical commitment to community participation at decisive stages of design and project implementation.

The challenge facing negotiation practitioners on both sides of the table is, at one level, the articulation of political and material demands (and concessions) in ways which do not fundamentally conflict with their respective interests. Thus there is unlikely to be a cast-iron distinction between establishment and progressive policy positions: it is conceivable that an establishment body might adopt aspects of a progressive position, and vice versa, despite the different underlying interests. The recently released UF position on housing (referred to earlier) is a case in point. The UF perceives land market regulation through investment trusts and individual title which can accommodate communal ownership, as a way to secure maximum private developer/contractor involvement in economic accumulation in the housing field. Yet simultaneously this position represents an ideological concession from the hegemonic 'individual tenure' position, which could be used to open up opportunities for community-based development corporations to secure housing on the basis of communal tenure. Community control over land could ensure relatively stable land and housing prices which would be more affordable for the majority of their constituency at future junctures.

Yet the question of popular participation in the design and implementation of housing projects appears to hold very little room for manoeuvre for establishment bodies. For some in the ruling classes and the state it is imperative to implement, as far as possible, a settlement between élites about the nature of the polity as well as the economy: the exercise of personal freedom is in any event meant to be experienced through 'the market' rather than through widescale involvement in the conscious building of political, economic, social, and cultural processes of everyday life.

Civic associations and community groups are arguably at a crucial stage of development where their organizational capacity needs to be significantly enhanced if they are to create the structures through which actual mass popular participation can be channelled. For example, paid, full-time community organizers, as well as ongoing education and training, are writ large as challenges for township organizations schooled in anti-apartheid protest action. Thus for the dominated classes, particularly the poorer strata of the working classes who objectively have only their own collective power to rely on, forging the necessary grassroots organization is an enormous challenge.

Notes

1 The author is grateful to Patrick Bond and Alan Mabin for their critical readings of this chapter.
2 Friedman S. 'Idealized Picture of Township Organization' *Die Suid-Afrikaan* (Cape Town: August/September 1989) 22, 27–9.
Hendler P. *Urban Policy and Housing: Case Studies on Negotiations in PWV Townships* (Braamfontein: SAIRR 1988).
Swilling M. 'The United Democratic Front and Township Revolt in South Africa' (eds.) Cobbett W. and Cohen E. *Popular Struggles in South Africa* (London: James Curry 1988).
Swilling M. 'The Powers of the Thunderbird' (eds.) Centre for Policy Studies *South Africa at the End of the Eighties: Policy Perspectives 1989* (Johannesburg: Centre for Policy Studies 1989).
3 Hendler P. 'Research Notes and Commentary: Understanding the Formation of the Built Environment — Methodology, Theory and the Interweaving of Capital Accumulation and Social Reproduction: Response to McCarthy' *South African Geographic Journal* (1990) 71 i 56–9.
Sayer D. *Method in Social Science: a Realist Approach* (London: Hutchinson 1984) 128.
4 South African Institute of Race Relations (SAIRR) *The Annual Survey of Race Relations 1984* (Johannesburg 1985) 374.
5 SAIRR (1985) 377.
6 SAIRR (1985) 375.
7 SAIRR *The Annual Survey of Race Relations 1981* (Johannesburg 1982) 243.
8 SAIRR (1982) 243.
9 SAIRR (1985) 374.
10 De Vos T. J. *The Black Urban Housing Market*, National Building Research Institute paper (August 1986) R/BOU 1419.
De Vos T. J. *Affordability of Housing*, paper presented to the National Association of Homebuilders conference (Pretoria: May 1990).
11 Cole J. *Crossroads — the Politics of Reform and Repression 1976–1986* (Johannesburg: Ravan Press 1987).

Evening Post 29 January 1982.

Kane-Berman J. *Soweto: Black Revolt, White Reaction* (Johannesburg: Ravan Press 1978) 51.

Morris P. *A History of Black Housing in South Africa* (Johannesburg: South African Foundation 1981) 54.

Sowetan 5 March, 11 August 1982.

12 SAIRR *The Annual Survey of Race Relations 1988/1989* (Johannesburg: 1989) 162.

13 De Vos (1986).

De Vos (1990).

Hendler P. 'Capital Accumulation, the State and the Housing Question: the Private Allocation of Residences in African Townships on the Witwatersrand 1980–1985', unpublished MA thesis (Johannesburg: University of the Witwatersrand 1986) 144–55.

Planact *Langa: the Case for Upgrade* (Johannesburg: Planact 1986) 16–19.

Webb T. 'Financing and Affordability, Case Study Analysis', Building Industries of SA Conference (Pretoria: May 1983).

14 SAIRR *The Annual Survey of Race Relations 1979* (Johannesburg: 1980) 422.

SAIRR (1985) 383, 385, 389, 393, and 395.

15 Stallard Report. Transvaal Local Government Commission report (TPI–1922).

16 Grinker D. *Inside Soweto — the Inside Story to the Background to the Unrest*, as told by the former secretary of the Diepmeadow Town Council (Johannesburg: Eastern Enterprises 1986).

Humphriss D. and Thomas T. *Benoni: Son of My Sorrow — the Social, Political and Economic History of a South African Gold Mining Town* (Johannesburg: Benoni Town Council 1968) 93–139.

Koornhof P. 'Urban Bantu Policy' (ed.) Rhoodie N. *South African Dialogue* (Johannesburg: McGraw-Hill 1972) 315–34.

Van der Wall G. 'Landelike Ontwikkeling in Suid Afrika en Verstedeliking', Building Industries of SA Conference (Pretoria: 1983) s312/13.

17 Welch C. 'Urban Bantu Townships, National Building Research Institute' *SA Architectural Record* (December: 1963).

18 Rich P. *White Power and the Liberal Conscience — Racial Segregation and South African Liberalism* (Johannesburg: Ravan Press 1984) 54–76.

19 Garbers S. *Keynote Address*, Innovative Building Technology Conference (Pretoria: March 1990).

20 Hendler (1986) 102–4, 131–4.

21 Hendler (1988) 12–15.

22 Hendler P. 'A Black Future for Free Enterprise — Urban Foundation Strategies for Change' *Work in Progress* (SA Research Service: October 1985) 39, 35–7.

Wilkinson P. 'Straddling Realities: the Urban Foundation and Social Change in Contemporary South Africa', Africa Studies seminar paper (Johannesburg: University of the Witwatersrand May 1982).

23 Departement van Staatkundige Ontwikkeling en Beplanning *Witskrif oor Verstedeliking* (Pretoria: 1986).

Knoetze J. 'A Positive Urbanization Strategy: the Phasing Out of Influx Control', Johannesburg CBD Association conference paper (1985).

24 Hudson P. 'The Freedom Charter and the Theory of National Democratic Revolution' *Transformation* (1986) 1, 6–38.

25 An early example is Franszen D. G. and Sadie J. L. *Inleiding tot die*

Bevolkingsvraagstuk (Stellenbosch: Universiteit Uitgewers 1950) 128.
26 Maasdorp G. 'Alternatives to the Bulldozer — an Economic Approach to Squatter
    Housing with Lessons for SA', occasional paper 6 (Durban: University of Natal,
    Department of Economics 1977) 2–8.
    Welsh D. 'The Growth of Towns' (eds.) Wilson M. and Thompson L. *The Oxford
    History of South Africa* (London: Oxford University Press 1971) 2, 175.
27 Urban Foundation (UF) *Policies for a New Urban Future — Policy Overview: the
    Urban Challenge* (Johannesburg: 1990a) 1–5, 47–50.
    UF *Policies for a New Urban Future — Regional Development Reconsidered*
    (Johannesburg: 1990b) i–viii.
    UF *Policies for a New Urban Future — Housing for All: Proposal for a National
    Urban Housing Policy* (Johannesburg: 1990c) i–x.
28 Welsh (1971) 195.
29 Maasdorp G. and Pillay N. 'Urban Relocation and Racial Segregation: the Case of
    Indian South Africans', research monograph (Durban: University of Natal,
    Department of Economics 1977) 7.
30 Morris (1981) 3.
31 UF (1990c) ii.
32 Maasdorp (1977) 2–8.
33 UF (1990a, 1990b, 1990c).
34 Legassick M. 'South Africa: Capital Accumulation and Violence' *Economy and
    Society* (1974) 3 iii 253–91.
    Van Onselen C. *Chibaro* (London: Pluto 1976).
35 Hindson D. 'The Pass System and the Formation of an Urban African Proletariat in
    South Africa: a Critique of the Cheap Labour Power Thesis', unpublished Ph.D.
    thesis (University of Sussex: 1983).
    O'Meara D. 'The 1946 African Mine Workers Strike in the Political Economy of
    South Africa' *Journal of Commonwealth and Comparative Politics* (1975) 13 ii
    146–73.
    Wolpe H. 'Capitalism and Cheap Labour Power in South Africa: from Segregation
    to Apartheid' *Economy and Society* (1976).
36 Welsh (1971) 235–6.
37 Dewar D. *Self-help Housing in South Africa: a Redefinition of the Problem*, South
    African Institute of Architects conference (April 1983) 2–4.
    Dewar D. *Urban Poverty and City Development: Some Perspectives and Guidelines*,
    second Carnegie conference into poverty in southern Africa (1984) 163, 1–6.
38 UF (1990c).
39 For a critique of the liberal position see Lea J. 'The New Urban Dispensation:
    Black Housing Policy in South Africa, Post Soweto 1976', the African Studies
    Association of South Africa and the Pacific conference paper (Victoria: La Trobe
    University 1980) 21–5.
40 UF (1990c) v–x.
41 UF (1990a) 50.
42 Hendler (1988) 40.
43 Dewar (1983, 1984).
44 Maasdorp (1977).
45 Maasdorp G. and Humphreys R. *From Shantytown to Township* (Cape Town: Juta
    1975).
46 Maasdorp and Pillay (1977).

216   *Paul Hendler*

47 Morris (1981).
48 UF (1990a, 1990b).
49 Castells M. *The Urban Question — a Marxist Approach* (London: Edward Arnold 1977).
    Castells M. *City Class and Power* (London and Basingstoke: Macmillan Press 1978).
50 Wilkinson P. 'A Place to Live: the Resolution of the African Housing Crisis in Johannesburg 1944 to 1954', Africa Studies seminar paper (Johannesburg: University of the Witwatersrand July 1981) 23, 39.
51 Ratcliffe S. 'A Political Economy of Housing' *Debate on Housing*, SA Research Service, Information Publication 4 (Johannesburg: University of the Witwatersrand 1980) 7–9.
52 Bloch R. 'The State in the Townships: State, Popular Struggle and Urban Crisis in South Africa 1970–1980', unpublished B.A. Honours dissertation (Johannesburg: University of the Witwatersrand 1982) 44–64, 69–79, 89–90.
53 McCarthy J. and Swilling M. 'South Africa's Emerging Politics of Bus Transportation' *Political Geography Quarterly* (1985) 4 iii 238–42.
54 McCarthy J. 'Paul Hendler's Rethinking of the Social Geography of the Black Townships: a Brief Reply' *The South African Geographical Journal* (1987) 69 i 86–8.
55 Hendler P., Mabin A., and Parnell S. 'Rethinking Housing Questions in South Africa' (ed.) SA Research Service *South African Review* (Johannesburg: Ravan Press 1986) 3, 195.
56 Hendler P. 'Capital Accumulation and Conurbation: Rethinking the Social Geography of the "Black" Townships' *The South African Geographical Journal* (1987) 69 i 60–85.
    Mabin A. 'Research Notes and Commentary: Further Notes on Material and Political Factors in South African Urban Processes: Response to Hendler and McCarthy' *The South African Geographical Journal* 70 iv 145–55.
57 Wilkinson (1981) 40–1.
58 Hendler (1987) 66–7.
59 Ratcliffe (1980).
60 Wilkinson (1981).
61 Bloch (1982).
62 McCarthy and Swilling (1985).
63 Harvey D. *Social Justice and the City* (London: Edward Arnold 1973).
    Harvey D. 'Class, Monopoly, Rent, Finance Capital and the Urban Revolution' *Regional Studies* (1974) 8.
    Harvey D. 'The Political Economy of Urbanization' (eds.) Gappert G. and Rose H. *The Social Economy of Cities* (Beverley Hills: Sage 1975).
    Harvey D. 'Labour, Capital and Class Struggle around the Build Environment in Capitalist Societies' *Politics and Society* (1976) 6, 265–95.
    Harvey D. 'The Urban Process under Capitalism: a Framework for Analysis' *The International Journal of Urban and Regional Research* (1978) 2, 101–31.
    Hendler (1987).
    Mabin (1988).
    McCarthy (1987).
64 Hendler (1987) 78–81.
65 Bond P. 'Township Housing and South Africa's "Financial Explosion" — the Theory and Practice of Financial Capital in Alexandra' *Urban Forum*

(Johannesburg: University of the Witwatersrand Press 1990).

66 Mabin (1988).

67 Castells (1977).
Castells (1978).
Engels F. *The Housing Question* (Moscow: Progress Publishers 1979).
Harvey (1973), (1974), (1975), (1976), (1978).

68 Hendler P. 'The Tyranny of Concepts: Assessing the Housing and Urban Political Theories of Manuel Castells' *The South African Sociological Review* (October 1989a) 2 i 30.

69 Castells M. *The City and the Grassroots* (Berkeley, Los Angeles: University of California 1983).

70 Castells (1983) 297.

71 Castells (1983) xviii.

72 Castells M. *From the Urban Question to the City and the Grassroots*, working paper 47 (University of Sussex: 1985) 5–6.

73 Castells (1985) 4.

74 Hendler (1988).

75 Hendler (1988).

76 Hendler (1986).

77 Landry C., Morley D., Southwood R., and Wright P. *What a Way to Run a Railroad — an Analysis of Radical Failure* (London: Comedia Publishing Group 1985) 90.

78 Hendler P. *Paths to Power* (Braamfontein: SAIRR 1989b) 40.

14 The commuting conundrum

Colleen McCaul

Historical overview

In apartheid's heyday, the state and the Department of Transport (DoT) took long travelling distances between home and work — created by the apartheid policies of homelands and Group Areas, as well as the low incomes of South African workers — as a necessary evil. They constructed their transport policies around these 'necessities'. Those being carried to work in the buses (mostly privately owned) and trains (state-owned) did not earn enough to pay their commuting costs at market rates and so the DoT, the South African Transport Services (SATS), and local authorities subsidized the cost of workers' transport. The DoT, since the late 1950s, has subsidized bus passengers by paying the private bus companies the difference, for each passenger they carry, between what his/her transport costs (including the bus company's profit) and what it believes the passenger can afford. SATS cross-subsidized some of the losses incurred carrying train commuters, and the state covered the balance. Municipalities subsidized their bus services from ratepayers' money. The cost of train commuter losses in 1988/9 was R813 million and the cost of bus subsidies in that year was R476 million, making a total commuter subsidy of R1.3 billion.[1] This figure excludes municipal subsidies and the subsidies paid by the departments of education for pupil transport. In 1988, bus subsidies averaged 55 cents a trip and rail subsidies 90 cents.[2] While subsidies were not provided out of generosity — they were to facilitate the apartheid arrangements of where people could live and to contain collective protests against paying market-related fares — they have in effect amounted to a social wage. Any future government has to take into account that a large number of people are dependent on this redistributive state assistance.

Passenger transport in South Africa since the 1930s has been a highly regulated affair, and the protected domain of the big bus companies and state-owned trains. No one could operate any form of public transport without a permit from 10 local road transportation boards, whose jurisdiction covered the whole country. New entrants in the passenger transport sector found these permits extremely difficult to obtain. This was so that the profitability of the bus companies could not be threatened because then bigger subsidies would be required. Private sector freight hauliers also experienced difficulty obtaining permits, as SATS needed protection from competition because it overcharged for certain freight transport to make enough profits to cross-subsidize commuter losses. As a result, much private sector freight traffic was kept off the roads through the permit system.

Because they were so protected from competition and had captive markets, passenger transport operators generally designed services for their convenience rather than the commuters': South African commuters have been faced with uncomfortable buses, overcrowding, crime-ridden trains, long walks to stations and bus-stops, and two to three transfers between modes on a single journey to work, because the vested interests divided up the turf between them.

The transition, however, from a highly state-regulated, inconvenient commuter transport system protected from competition, began from the late 1970s when African entrepreneurs, driving minibus taxis (kombi taxis) and carrying between nine and 15 passengers, made their appearance on the routes between townships and workplaces. (The new Road Transportation Act of 1977 allowed taxis to carry eight passengers instead of the previous four.) This was despite the difficulty in getting permits, and many operated illegally as a result. In the next 10 years, 30 per cent of the country's African commuters deserted buses and trains as their main mode of commuting and flocked to the taxis. Although they were not subsidized and their fares were therefore market-related and higher, these taxi commuters enjoyed a more comfortable ride to work: the taxi industry was largely responsible for cutting the average travelling time of African commuters from three hours a day in 1984 to two hours by 1989. They were also helpful in reducing the number of transfers from one mode to another on a single journey to work: by 1989 three out of four African commuters had no transfers.[3]

New policies, new problems

From the early 1980s the DoT set up a variety of commissions to sort out the transport sector because it found that no matter how much it was spending in ever-burgeoning transport subsidies, the trip to work was a volatile political issue, prey to boycotts and disruptions. It also needed a policy on the rising minibus taxi sector which, from the late 1970s, although operating often illegally because of the lack of permits, was increasingly threatening bus and train profits. This, in turn, meant more and more subsidies were required to keep the bus and train companies in business, even though proportionately fewer workers were benefiting from subsidies as they were travelling in the unsubsidized taxis. Furthermore, SATS's cross-subsidization of commuter losses was causing an outcry from the private sector because of its distortions of the economy. In general, the government was looking at ways of reducing the costs of the provision of all services and of depoliticizing state-provided services. Transport was no exception.

In 1987 after lengthy investigation, the government published a White Paper on National Transport Policy. This signalled the first real shift in transport policy since the 1930s. The recommendation of a previous commission in 1983, that minibus taxis be eliminated, was abandoned. (This was the notorious Commission of Inquiry into Bus Passenger Transportation in the Republic of South Africa, chaired by Dr Peter Welgemoed.) In terms of the White Paper, passenger transport was to be deregulated, privatized where possible, and responsibility for it transferred from the central state to the lowest level of government, namely the RSCs where they existed. The government decided to eliminate the permit system, and bus and taxi operators would in future have to comply only with stricter technical and safety requirements in order to be allowed to operate. SATS would also eliminate cross-subsidization of commuter services from its other services. The White Paper proposed that subsidies should be borne by RSCs — financed by levies on employers — and that RSCs should put bus routes requiring subsidies out to tender so that bus companies would have to compete for routes. It was believed that this element of competition would bring down subsidy costs. The White Paper expressed a goal of ultimately eliminating subsidies. Where rail services were needed, the RSCs would contract the railways to provide them.

Four acts to implement the new policy had been passed by 1990, but all hinged on a new Passenger Transport Act, which had been delayed because of substantial resistance: the organized black-owned minibus taxi industry — represented largely by the Southern Africa Black Taxi Association (SABTA) — was opposed to blanket deregulation on the grounds that there were inadequate facilities such as ranks, that there would be even more violent feuding between operators, that whites would take over the industry, and that, in general, there would be chaos. Local government was justifiably anxious about having to take over the huge bus and train subsidy burden. This averaged R604 per metropolitan commuter per annum in 1989 rand values, varying from area to area: in Pretoria, for example, it was R773 annually per commuter, and R319 in Port Elizabeth (the lowest).[4] Devolution of financial responsibilities, therefore, meant that employers in Pretoria would have to pay significantly higher turnover and employee levies than Port Elizabeth employers, for example. The Pretoria RSC was conducting an investigation into the effects on RSCs of taking over passenger transport responsibilities. The bus companies were worried about the insecurity of limited period contracts. The DoT, by 1990, had hoped that competitive tendering for contracts on bus routes would cut subsidy needs, but had conducted pilot projects with a tender system on some routes for four years and found that the level of subsidies required was not less than previously. The levels of competition envisaged in the White Paper were thought, by 1990, to be unattainable. One of the problems was that while subsidies were kept in check by cross-subsidization in a network of bus routes, competition creaming off the profitable routes in the network meant that greater subsidies were needed.

A task group representing all these interests under the auspices of the DoT finally came up with a draft Passenger Transport Bill in April 1990. In terms of it, the country would be divided up into passenger transport regions. Third-tier government bodies — envisaged as RSCs — would be appointed passenger transport authorities (PTAs) for the regions. They would have to formulate and implement regional passenger transport plans to co-ordinate passenger transport. The draft bill also provided for the establishment of a central passenger subsidization fund: it would contain all money appropriated by parliament for subsidizing passenger transport, and money would be allocated to the rail commuter corporation, and to regional passenger subsidization funds for each transport region. Regional funds were to be augmented by funds obtained from the RSC concerned. Subsidized passenger transport could be undertaken only in terms of contracts with a PTA, concluded after the acceptance of tenders in terms of regulations made by the Minister of Transport. The funds would also be used to pay the costs of transport facilities.[5]

All the details of the functioning of the act were left to the Minister of Transport to spell out in regulations. These could differ from one region to another. It was significant that the legislation was enabling rather than prescriptive, signifying the difficulties faced by the DoT in achieving the aims of the White Paper.

The government pressed ahead with the White Paper recommendations about SATS. From 1 April 1990 it became a public company called Transnet with five separate business divisions (for harbours, pipelines, road services, non-commuter railways, and airways). Its rail commuter services became the responsibility of the new South African Rail Commuter Corporation set up from the same date. This was to enable Transnet to compete with other transport organizations in the open market without the loss-making rail commuter services. The state is the sole shareholder in the corporation. Its budget for 1990/1 provided for a loss of R543 million, which would be borne by the state, using R150 million from the DoT and covering the balance from Transnet dividends as an interim measure. The state expected the corporation to do everything possible to become financially viable as it is keen to cut down on the amount of money being spent on commuter transport. To recover costs from tariffs, however, third-class commuter tariffs would have to increase by around 200 per cent. Because this is politically unviable it can be expected that many commuter services will be curtailed and commuters will have no choice but to use buses and taxis, or, in some cases, only taxis. In general the railways regard a commuter train service as viable only if it runs at 80 per cent capacity. In 1989 a train service between Hammanskraal and Pretoria was replaced with a bus service, for example, which led to violent commuter protests at the station. A R660 million rail link from Durban to the burgeoning informal settlements of Inanda, once a top priority in SATS's capital programme, was frozen in 1989 because of lack of funds. It would go ahead only if the private sector took over the financing and responsibility for charging higher fares. Major expansions to commuter rail services have been frozen because investments cannot be recovered at existing fare levels.[6]

The legacy for South African cities

The legacy for the apartheid city in transition is therefore a conundrum. A subsidy formula cannot be found because the DoT wants to limit its financial responsibilities, but this does not seem possible. The growth of the African taxi industry has meant that fewer African commuters use subsidized transport (subsidies, by 1990, reached only one in two commuters), and the DoT hoped that this would reduce subsidy costs. It has, however, in fact meant that more and more money has had to be spent on keeping bus companies in business in the face of strenuous competition. Between 1980 and 1989, expenditure on bus subsidies rose from R290 million to R570 million at 1989 rand values.[7] However, 28 per cent fewer passengers were carried by bus in 1988 than in 1980.

Minibus taxis occupy an interesting place in the new urban transport environment. They have the single largest share of the African commuter market, having rocketed from a virtually zero share 10 years ago. (The respective shares of the African commuter market of taxis, buses, and trains are 30 per cent, 27 per cent, and 24 per cent.)[8] In contrast to the DoT's view on taxis in the early 1980s when the big bus was seen as the answer to mass transport problems, the taxis, after a long struggle, have won acceptance as a major player on the transport scene. DoT officials defend the industry vigorously, make light of the sector's problems, and talk fondly of African small business. Despite having provided some solutions to historical transport problems (by cutting travelling time, transfers, and discomfort), they have resulted in many new ones. There is an optimistic view that because the taxi industry is African-owned, it will not run into the commuter resistance that has been a persistent feature of transport in South Africa. Already, however, there have been a number of taxi boycotts, similar to the traditional South African bus boycott, but with buses and taxis in reverse roles. Unionized taxi drivers (most minibus taxis are not driven by their owners but by badly paid employees) envisage using commuter boycotts as a bargaining tool and this could politicize the taxi industry further. SABTA's president, James Ngcoya, said in September 1990 that political groups were bringing too much pressure to bear on SABTA members by trying to 'politicize the taxi industry'. He said: 'Boycotts, stayaways, and other activities serving political purposes are seriously interfering with our right to make a living and, with the burning and stoning of our vehicles, involving us in huge and unnecessary costs.' Relations between taxis and commuters are, however, redeemed by some ambiguity. Commuters have suppported taxi operators in their struggles — such as by boycotting the midibuses that the bus companies introduced in 1984 in competition with the taxis. Civic associations have intervened to sort out violent feuding between taxi operators, and taxi operators have also assisted communities in their political campaigns at times (during a consumer boycott of white businesses in Boksburg in 1988, for example, taxi operators refused to transport black commuters to town to do their shopping).

Something of a time bomb is developing in the taxi industry in that the development of business skills has not kept up with its growth. Taxi operations are less profitable than is generally assumed. The informal transport sector's contribution to gross domestic product is quite impressive — 1.7 per cent or about R3.5 billion in 1989, according to the official Central Statistical Service. However, according to a 1990 study by Johannesburg transport consultants Bruinette Kruger Stofberg (BKS), a taxi operator owning one taxi has an annual expenditure of about R58 000 and income of about R70 000, meaning a profit of about R935 a month. According to the BKS study, the average number of taxis owned by each operator is 1.7, resulting in an average profit of R2 237 a month.[9] Once taxi operators get brought into the tax net, they are going to make even less. Low profit margins are because the costing of taxi fares has not kept up with inflation and has not effectively taken into account vehicle depreciation and future replacement costs. The outcome of this is violent feuding, as operators compete for business; demands that the government subsidize the taxi industry; poor wages for drivers (and consequent overloading and speeding, the main causes of the notoriously high accident rate in the taxi industry); as well as events like a collective protest by 400 taxi operators in Cape Town in February 1990 against high hire purchase repayments. Another alarming consequence is that the average age of the South African minibus taxi is six years — most are 1984 models — which is old for vehicles doing 12 trips a day on average.

A problem facing commuters is that as a result of the taxi industry and/or protest campaigns against bus services, buses are withdrawing from various areas completely. The bus service in Port Elizabeth (PE Tramways), for example, was in the process of being rationalized in 1990 with a view to possible complete closure.[10] KwaZulu Transport was curtailing services in the Pietermaritzburg (Natal) area as municipal subsidies were insufficient for it to afford to continue its service. In December 1989 the municipalities of Benoni and Boksburg phased out their bus services, leaving residents of the townships of Wattville and Daveyton to rely on taxis. The Ciskei Transport Corporation was closed in May 1990, apparently as a result of sustained boycotts by commuters.[11] As mentioned, the railways are now trying to make a profit, since commuter services are no longer cross-subsidized, and are also curtailing services.

As a result the minibus taxis have increasingly captive markets. This is ironic, since their advent meant that many commuters had a choice of transport modes. While only a quarter of all African commuters claimed in 1989 to have only one option of modes, this proportion is likely to increase. There has already been a hardening of attitudes to taxis — more than half of taxi users are dissatisfied with their safety standards, according to DoT surveys.[12]

Captive markets also mean that the taxis are under pressure to provide a service that commuters can afford, and this includes commuters who cannot afford to pay market-related tariffs for their transport. While growing class differentiation enabled relatively wealthier commuters to switch from buses and trains to taxis from the late 1970s, a failure to cost fares effectively has meant that taxis have become affordable to lower earners too, who will maintain pressure on taxi operators to keep fares unprofitably low, without subsidies.

The DoT faces a conundrum here in trying to sort out transport policy: it finally welcomed the taxi industry because it offered to take both the politics and the expense out of African urban commuter transport. It has done neither. Also, while the deregulation of passenger transport was aimed at reducing its cost, the DoT has found that bus companies managed to be more profitable in a regulated environment, as they could use their profitable routes to cross-subsidize their less profitable ones. Off-peak business was also important in maintaining bus companies' profitability, and the taxis have cornered most of that market.

The government responded to the subsidy crisis in 1990 by threatening that it could not continue to provide subsidies indefinitely at their current high levels. It was looking at ways of targeting subsidies specifically at long-distance commuters, so that they were not 'raided' by commuters who could do without them. The DoT regarded 5 to 10 per cent as an acceptable proportion of income for commuters to spend on transport. It had found that the mean percentage of income spent in 1989 was 8 per cent. Some 35 per cent of commuters, however, spent more than 10 per cent. The DoT has found through ongoing surveys by its 'National Black Panel' (set up to monitor commuters' problems with transport and the effectiveness of transport policy) that many commuters did not take advantage of subsidies — they bought cash tickets rather than season tickets, which are not subsidized. Adding to the DoT's frustration was its finding in 1989 that only one in five of all bus and train commuters was even aware that the government paid part of the cost of transport.[13] The bus companies have responded to threats of subsidy cuts by speaking the language of redistribution. In his chairperson's report in May 1990, Albino Carleo, the chairperson of the South African Bus Operators' Association (SABOA), representing most privately owned bus companies, said: 'Subsidies to mass transport, also referred to as redistribution of income and wealth, play a dominant role in the provision and operation of all [mass transport systems worldwide].' He said that in South Africa, millions of commuters relied on affordable, safe, and regular transport. 'To leave these commuters at the mercy of market forces where many of the services are clearly uneconomical and are of a purely social and political nature, is not acceptable and we run great risks in attempting to do so.' SABOA refers to the 'social responsibility' of the bus companies to keep regular schedules, even though meeting off-peak demand was uneconomical.[14] According to the executive director of SABOA, Professor J. Walters:

> In no cities in the developed countries of the world does unsubsidized or unregulated transport exist. The prospect of relying entirely on a free market and abolishing subsidies in these cities is never entertained, not because of ignorance of elementary economics or vested interests, but because of the fundamental principles of transport economics: that scheduled public transport services are indispensable to the urban economics and that such scheduled services are largely incompatible with competition.[15]

Workers in the transport industry are in agreement with the bus industry on the question of subsidies: protest marches took place on 1 December 1990 in Natal and the eastern Cape to government offices, to deliver memorandums demanding 'proper' state bus subsidies, taking into account average wages and the survival needs of bus companies. The memorandums also demanded the nationalization of the bus industry. Many planned marches in the Transvaal were not granted permission. The marchers included transport workers in trade unions affiliated to both the Congress of South African Trade Unions (COSATU) and the National Council of Trade Unions (NACTU), as well as members of ANC and SACP local branches, and civic bodies in the areas concerned.[16] Government at all tiers will, in the transition to a post-apartheid scenario, face the task of redressing historical socio-economic backlogs and inequalities for a growing urban population that, throughout the 1980s, made clear through campaigns in townships, its demands for better houses and infrastructure, lower rents, and affordable bus fares. Such campaigns are likely to continue in the 1990s. Demands for continued transport subsidies will be competing with demands for scarce state resources to be allocated also to health, education, housing, etc.

The future allocation of land for housing is an important consideration in finding ways of reducing the need for transport subsidies. According to the managing director of AECI and a member of the board of governors of the UF, Mike Sander,[17] meeting urbanization and housing needs will require the earmarking and allocation of 167 000 hectares (the equivalent of 20 Sowetos) in the next 20 years (i.e. to the year 2010). When racial zoning practices and deconcentration policies are abandoned, new homes will presumably be built on land close enough to the cities to obviate the need for large transport subsidies. Walters has pointed to one problem being that land currently identified for future development and housing is in most instances located at considerable distances away from job opportunities. For example, 13 506 hectares have been earmarked west of Soweto for African housing, while job opportunities are mainly on the East Rand and in the Vaal Triangle, putting upward pressure on transport subsidies.[18]

Of course the existing housing stock will continue to be where it is. Many people will still be housed at long distances from work: for example the 65 kilometres between Sebokeng/Evaton and Sasolburg, 65 kilometres between Atlantis and Cape Town, 39 kilometres between Khayelitsha and Claremont and Bellville, 76 kilometres between Pretoria and towns in Bophuthatswana, 68 kilometres between Botshabelo and Bloemfontein, and up to 190 kilometres between KwaNdebele and Pretoria.[19] Policies which open up the townships themselves for business development, and which encourage development in the buffers between townships and the white areas, would be helpful in providing employment closer to home.

A problem with continued transport subsidies to long-distance commuters is that they are encouraged to stay where they are. For example, the 20 000 or so daily commuters from KwaNdebele can afford to travel up to 300 kilometres daily because they are so heavily subsidized. The trade-off for them is that they live in an area where rents are nominal. If they lived closer to work, the state could save R40 million or so annually on their subsidies, which could be better spent elsewhere, but their rents would probably be higher.

Another of the challenges faced by South African cities is the state of the road infrastructure. By 1990 there was a backlog of R15 billion in expenditure on South African roads. Fuel levies paid by road users to the government were, until a few years ago, dedicated to road infrastructure. They now go directly to the Treasury. Although road users paid R5 billion in levies in 1989, the roads budget in 1990/1 was only R2 billion. The Southern African Bitumen and Tar Association described this as 'disastrous', and warned that South African roads were deteriorating to 'Third World standards'. It pointed out that expenditure on roads in real terms had declined by more than 30 per cent since 1975, while traffic loading had more than doubled in the previous 20 years.[20] Consequently, one of the challenges for urban public transport is slowing the trend towards the use of private vehicles through substantial improvements in the level of service, and developing privileged road space for buses and taxis. The DoT is also looking at ways of encouraging rail travel. It had approved in principle, for example, the allocation of R100 million to building a 15 kilometre light rail line linking Port Elizabeth's industrial areas with the African township of Motherwell. (Light rail, a tram system of electrically powered cars on rails, is far cheaper infrastructurally than heavy rail.) Three private consortiums were interested in constructing the infrastructure. Barry Lessing, the managing director of Spoornet (the Transnet company which runs the railways), said that Spoornet would welcome involvement in light rail transport if there were sufficient returns. It was highly unlikely that it would do so on its own, but a partnership with private companies would be one possibility. He believed that it would be relatively easy for the railways to attach light rail technology and operations to existing heavy rail capacity.[21]

Another infrastructural problem is the lack of taxi facilities, as the industry grew rapidly and unexpectedly. Ranking facilities are, however, seen as being profitable for private sector investors. Furthermore, taxi liaison committees are gradually being established in all major cities and towns to formulate solutions to taxi operators' problems. They discuss, *inter alia,* ranking and parking facilities.

They consist of representatives from the city/town councils, traffic departments, trade and commerce, and local taxi associations. By August 1990, 38 such liaison committees had been established. With a further 35 councils, negotiations were in progress for their establishment.[22]

Conclusion

For many users of South African public transport, historic transport problems were ameliorated by the birth of the minibus taxi industry in the late 1970s. This created many new problems, however, among them the consequences of captive markets, a bus industry in trouble but still needed by commuters unable to pay market-related fares, and rising subsidies reaching proportionately fewer commuters.

The continued subsidization of poorer and long-distance commuters is vital, but is under pressure. Transport subsidies will continue to be under threat as demands for their continuation will be competing in the 1990s with equally pressing demands on scarce state resources for housing, education, health, and other expenditure to redress inequalities.

One solution will be the elimination of racial zoning policies so that future land for new urban communities will be closer to where commuters work. Another will be the development of business and industry within or close to the existing townships.

The establishment of legitimate local government in South Africa's cities will also be part of the solution to passenger transport problems. Commuters will be able to participate more effectively than in the past in decision-making about their passage to work. Dissatisfaction with transport services in South Africa has historically manifested itself in knee-jerk reactions which have sometimes been counter-productive. Bus boycotts, for example, have sometimes resulted in the termination of services permanently, to the detriment of commuters. It is likely that as civic organizations become more sophisticated, transport problems will be tackled in a more concerted way, and in ways that vigilantly anticipate, rather than react to, changes. Their participation in the liaison committees that already exist may prove a useful forum for exerting such influence. In particular, where civic associations choose to remain independent of local authorities, they will be an important pressure group on transport issues.

Notes

1 Report of the Department of Transport and of the National Transport Commission for the period 1 April 1988 to 31 March 1989, RP90/1989; SATS 1988/89 annual report 33, 102.
2 Cameron B. 'The Question of Subsidy', paper presented to a DoT seminar on the National Black Panel (Johannesburg: February 1990).
3 Morris N. 'Black Travel Today — Some Facts and Figures', paper presented to a DoT seminar on the National Black Panel (Johannesburg: February 1990).
4 Cameron (1990).
5 Walters Professor J. 'A Review of Bus Transport Policy', paper presented to the Tenth Annual Transportation Convention (Pretoria: August 1990).
6 *Financial Mail* 24 March 1989.
7 Cameron (1990).
8 Morris (1990).
9 Gawthrop J. 'The Combi-taxi Databank', paper presented to the Tenth Annual Transportation Convention (Pretoria: August 1990).
10 *Infocom* 11 June 1990.
11 *Drive-on* June 1990.
12 Lombard M. and Morris N. 'Changing Attitudes to Transport', paper presented to a DoT seminar on the National Black Panel (Johannesburg: February 1990).
13 Van der Reis P. 'Image, Awareness and Communication: Black Travellers' Awareness of Deregulation, Privatization, Devolution of Power and Subsidies and their Image of Transport Operators', paper presented to a DoT seminar on the National Black Panel (Johannesburg: February 1990).
14 *Finance Week* 1990.
15 Walters (1990).
16 Information supplied by the Transport and General Workers' Union (9 March 1991).
17 Sander M. 'We Can Do It' *Leadership SA* (1990) 9 v.
18 Walters (1990).
19 Walters (1990).
20 *Engineering News* 27 April 1990.
21 *Momentum* 1990.
22 Information supplied by SABTA (12 September 1990).

15 Access to urban land

Tony Wolfson[1]

Introduction

To impact on the housing shortage facing the unemployed, those earning relatively low incomes, as well as economically better-off residents in South Africa, sufficient quantities of affordable, suitably located land will have to be identified and allocated for development. While unemployment and low wage earning pose priority challenges for reconstruction, urban land policy remains a vital ingredient of any future dispensation. This chapter concentrates on land provision for low-income housing as well as on the supply, price, and use of land.

Currently, the South African state acknowledges the urban problems created by apartheid. However, in response both to its fiscal limitations and in line with its recent policies of privatization and deregulation, the responsibility for housing has been passed on to the private sector. Since the enactment of the Black Communities Development Act 4 of 1984, the private sector's housing role has been facilitated. Nonetheless, the private sector is building houses in a market where 67 per cent of the population cannot afford a serviced site of R6 000, and an estimated 80 per cent cannot afford a low-cost formal housing unit (R20 000 including the land).[2]

Unemployment, low wages, and the private market prescribe land and housing affordability levels and, therefore, residential location and conditions. Much land allocated for low-cost housing remains unaffordable for the urban poor. Land which is affordable is subsidized by the state for site-and-service schemes, but is located on the urban periphery, at great distances from employment.

Affordability is not the only problem: the underutilization of prime urban land is exacerbated through its control by the private sector. Deregulation of the land market has not reversed the tendency of low-density land use. One of the determinants of residential land use is affordability. In the wealthy residential suburbs, extremely low building densities are permitted on land which is suitable for high occupation, building, and population density. In Bryanston, for example, the Sandton municipality permits a density of 2.5 to 3.5 units per hectare, and a maximum subdivision of 4 000 square metres.[3] Conversely, in Alexandra, which shares three of its boundaries with Sandton, unit densities per hectare (including formal houses and backyard shacks) have been conservatively estimated to number at least 160 units.[4]

A post-apartheid urban land policy should redress the current exclusion of many from access to affordable land and services. One approach might be for the state to intervene in land delivery and management. The possibility of private contractors being allowed access only to that land specifically set aside for private ownership, with the state ceding land to community land trusts for speculation-free lease to households, should be considered.

Under apartheid, the supply of state-proclaimed land has often been misconstrued as a land shortage. Current overcrowding in many African residential areas, however, may not be caused by a shortage of proclaimed land, but rather by a lack of affordable, suitably located land on which to build more housing stock.

The past and the present

A number of constraints affect access to suitable urban residential land in South Africa: the state's legislative land control mechanisms; the housing market's impact on land use; the low-income household's material limitations; and the unsuitable nature of geological sub-strata for housing in certain regions.

Apartheid laws created a large number of 'race zones' in which people designated as Africans, coloureds, Indians, and whites could acquire rights to land. In the allocation of rights, however, differences in terms of location, standards, and land use were created through racially conscious residential zoning.

Land segregation commenced with the 'scheduled black areas' or reserves stipulated by the Natives Land Act of 1913. The act formally dispossessed Africans of land they owned in the Union of South Africa and limited them to, in many cases, inferior land in a number of African reserves, which were already well populated. Hence, the overutilization and degradation of land in the reserves were caused by laws which disallowed the choice of and access to agricultural areas outside the reserves.

Two restrictions apply to the allocation of land situated in the self-governing 'homelands or reserves': first, 'non-blacks' are not permitted to acquire land in a 'scheduled black area'; and second, Africans are prohibited from acquiring land outside such an area. Rural land adjoining 'scheduled black areas' can be declared trust land and be released to the reserves.[5] Prior to the 1960s, most of the 157 000 hectares[6] of land owned privately by Africans within 'white' allocated areas, i.e. so-called 'black spots', was systematically appropriated and its occupants forcibly removed to trust land adjoining ethnically separate reserves.

Various influx control measures in the 1950s and 1960s stipulated the carrying of identity documents by Africans in 'white areas', thereby complementing residential segregation measures. In addition, the Group Areas Act, originally instituted in 1950 and subsequently updated seven times, provided for residential land to be set aside for coloureds, Indians, and whites.

In terms of the Group Areas Act, land falling outside Group Areas and the reserves is known as a 'controlled area', where rights to the land are 'frozen' in the hands of the race group having such rights. Due to past policies and laws aimed at forced removals, the controlled area is mainly in white hands, and comprises in the main agricultural land outside the cities.[7]

The Black Communities Development Act 4 of 1984 is the current legislation used to allocate urban land to Africans in 'controlled areas' or 'development areas'. Private developers, local authorities, and provincial administrations may apply, through procedures specified by the act, to develop townships. Section 33 (1) of the act directs that: 'The Minister may of his own accord or at the request of any interested person or body designate an area as a development area in which townships may be established.'[8]

Department of Planning and Provincial Affairs (DPPA) officials investigate the area concerned and make recommendations to the Administrator of the relevant province. Recommendations are based on the long-term development strategies of the DPPA, taking into account apartheid buffer zones, possible attached mineral rights, interested parties' views, and regional town planning guide plans. Newly planned, low-income areas usually occur adjacent to or within existing low-income settlements: none are to be found within white middle or high-income areas, even if land is available.

Applying for proposed development to be brought under local authority jurisdiction if the land in question is not within such an area is a highly sensitive political issue at present. If a community organization decided to develop sites, its application for land could in theory only be considered if the land were controlled by a BLA — a prerequisite unacceptable to many urban communities. Yet, as has been demonstrated in the case of Tamboville (a settlement adjacent to the township of Wattville on the East Rand), certain community developments in terms of squatting legislation have taken place under the jurisdiction of a white local authority (the Benoni Town Council). Thus there are loopholes in the present system which could be exploited by community movements.

All applications are evaluated by the provincial Administrator who assesses the attitudes of surrounding authorities and prevailing political circumstances. These criteria are responsible for the continued allocation of section 33 land as infill land between African townships, as well as on the urban periphery in areas which are not 'politically sensitive' for the NP, and until recently, in locations within the bounds of industrial deconcentration points.

For coloureds, Indians, and whites, there are four different land delivery procedures contained within the three houses of parliament as 'own affairs' matters and procedures for land allocation. African urban land issues are regarded as a 'general affair'. In reality, however, the four provincial administrations deal with African land issues,[9] especially in terms of residential land allocation.

The housing backlog in South Africa has been estimated at 1.8 million units, increasing at an average of 127 000 units per annum over the next 20 years.[10] The land shortage arising from this predicted backlog, given a density ratio of 28 (210 square metres) plots per hectare,[11] is 64 286 hectares. To accommodate the predicted increase in the backlog of 127 000 units per year, a further 4 233 hectares would be required every year. Urban residential land proclaimed for Africans has increased by 72 per cent between March 1989 and March 1990 (41 186 hectares to 70 936 hectares as shown in table 15.1 at the end of the chapter) and is quantitively ahead of the estimated need for land (64 286 hectares).

Thus far, the quantity of identified residential land has been evaluated against calculations using current town planning densities in African areas. This, however, is by no means useful for explaining the need for qualitatively suitable residential land in South African cities. The market and state planning bodies effectively determine land use and price. Prices are reflected by location, available quality services, prestige, neighbouring uses, and state decisions about zoning. 'Thus some land becomes expensive not because of its inherent qualities but because of decisions made with respect to it.'[12]

A legacy of low-density settlement (one plot, one unit), especially in white suburban areas (as shown in table 15.2), has meant that some of the most suitable land in our urban centres is grossly underutilized in terms of land use and use of services. For the wealthy, the market and local councils permit low-density land use and subsequent 'wastage' of space which could be occupied by the urban poor. In addition, market forces preclude the development of multi-storey apartment blocks because of the high building material, planning, and design costs involved in such projects, thus perpetuating low-density land use in poorer working-class areas as well.

For example, in Moroko and Killarney, similar sized areas (18 144 square metres and 18 626 square metres respectively) and numbers of dwellings (33) were investigated by Senior.[13] Vast socio-economic differences in terms of family size and income were evident in the amount of floor space individuals had in their respective homes. However, the most revealing evidence of the market's power to influence land use is in the comparison between the two areas' unit size and total floor space. Although the dwellings in the Killarney example were duplex townhouses, each unit had nearly four times the floor space of units in Moroko, suggesting that consumers could afford to buy more space and more expertise in terms of planning and design. Local council permission to build in certain locations at specified densities influences the price at which floor space can be purchased per square metre (in Killarney Village, one square metre cost R796 compared with R39 in Moroko). Obviously more floor space can be created by building upwards. However, the Killarney settlement's land use coverage (3 640 square metres) is almost double that of Moroko (1 782 square metres) and accommodates 62 per cent fewer people than the latter settlement.

Meadowlands Hostel and Melville also bear testimony to the way in which the valuable resource of land is underutilized. In Melville, an average of 39 people occupy one hectare of land compared with 690 per hectare in the Meadowlands Hostel. Even if Melville is examined alongside other areas with one unit per plot (Moroko), its density per hectare remains extremely low. Moroko accommodates 58 per cent more people on the land than does Melville, on similar sized developments. Melville's low-density land use can be explained by the size of its housing stock which is more than three times the size of stock found in Moroko.

Low-density land use seems unavoidable if the free market in land and housing is allowed to maintain unregulated control over the way land is used. Furthermore, the subjection of areas like Moroko to speculation in the future will no doubt force the poor out of these areas, unless the state assumes a more regulatory, protectionist role.

Geological suitability for residential development is a further constraint for land acquisition in South Africa, more especially in the PWV urban complex. The PWV region is the powerhouse and driving force of the South African economy, and probably will remain so in future years. It is also a major focal point for urbanizing communities, mainly because of the potential for employment. State reaction to the need for land in the PWV is evident in the amount of land currently under investigation in the Transvaal (as shown in table 15.1).

A geophysical investigation indicates that much of the state's proclaimed land for Africans in the PWV cannot be used for low-income housing. Near-surface dolomite underlies 14 per cent of the PWV area. It is inadvisable to build houses on such land because of the distinct potential for sinkhole and doline formation. However, geotechnical engineers are of the opinion that anything can be built on dolomitic surfaces or high-risk areas if cost is not an issue.[14]

Land allocation and constraints to land acquisition are major factors underlying the lack of access of the urban poor to residential shelter. Greater emphasis needs to be placed on more suitable locations, affordable pricing, and appropriate utilization, rather than simply on supply, as is the current practice. The origins of the current urban spatial form make it necessary to examine the state's current land policy and the problems emanating from the policy.

The perpetuation of low-density urban sprawl

Prior to 1985, direct state control of land use was manifest in forced removals and various anti-squatting laws. However, the state's fiscal crisis and the expense involved in monitoring and responding to continued defiance of the influx control laws made a revision of urban policy imperative — namely, the deregulation of access to urban areas.

Deregulation had its origins in the President's Council report on urbanization (1985) and the resulting White Paper on urbanization (1986) — the latter of which espoused the 'orderly urbanization' strategy. Currently, people are encouraged to settle in 'suitable' areas, places where the services and type of housing delivery is affordable to the household, rather than being forbidden to live in urban areas at all.[15] A hierarchy of 'suitable' urban services based on affordability is beginning to emerge.

The perpetuation of this hierarchy is supported by local state bodies. However, various state development agencies react differently. For example, BLAs are attempting to shirk attending to the needs of low-income communities in their jurisdictions, arguing that they lack financial resources and cannot encourage shack settlements. On the other hand, provincial administrations and some white councils are increasingly adopting a counter strategy. Prompted by politico-economic effects on their own agencies in the latter half of 1990, the TPA, which previously located site-and-service schemes in peripheral areas, set a precedent in the PWV municipal area of Midrand where a large scheme is being planned adjacent to existing wealthy suburbs. Nevertheless, many site-and-service schemes continue to occur at the urban periphery or within the bounds of industrial deconcentration points.

To cater for those people who cannot afford the costs of urban life, 'secondary' cities or industrial and residential deconcentration points[16] have been established by the state to provide cheap land for permanent settlement and employment for rural and urban surplus labour. Most deconcentration points, however, have not succeeded in attracting either surplus labour or labour intensive types of industry, mainly because of the recessionary economic climate and the closure of international markets to South African goods. The continued attraction of established metropolitan areas can be seen most dramatically in the massive expansion of informal settlements, particularly in the PWV, Port Elizabeth-Uitenhage, and Durban-Pinetown metropolitan regions.

A further economic strategy complementing deconcentration is deregulation. The effect of the privatization of the African housing market is causing those who cannot afford formal homes either to invade urban land, live in backyard shacks, or to resettle in areas such as deconcentration points where there may be work opportunities. Evidence from growing informal urban settlements and the expanding informal sector in South Africa's major cities suggests that land invasions and living in backyard shacks are the popular choice.

Development strategies, deregulation, and privatization do not address affordability, supply, or the underutilization of existing and/or future residential land. 'Orderly urbanization' has, therefore, arguably been a failure. Land invasions and backyard shack settlements contradict the intended aims of the policy. The following section will explore the urban land issues that would need to be addressed in a post-apartheid urban land policy.

Current urban land issues

The state policy of deregulating the housing market has resulted in an increase in the supply of land and housing for Africans who can afford market-related prices. With the state no longer providing housing stock for rental, low-income earners excluded from this market have had to pursue 'alternative' and 'illegal' forms of land and housing delivery. These have occurred in the form of land invasions and/or the building of backyard shacks within formal townships. Land invasions have occurred on a large enough scale to be considered an alternative form of land delivery.

When one tackles the issue of the various existing market segments, the Midrand example provides an insight into problems which could be encountered with regard to the establishment of low-income settlements in areas within or adjacent to wealthy suburbs. Recently, a situation arose in Midrand, approximately 20 kilometres north of Johannesburg, where the TPA proposed the development of a 'controlled', informal housing settlement on a site adjacent to a number of middle and high-income suburbs.[17]

Some residents of the suburbs concerned argue that the proximity of the proposed informal settlement will result in a decrease in the value of their properties. The residents are fearful that overcrowding, increased crime, health hazards, and a lack of infrastructure will be possible outcomes of such a project.

Counter to this argument is the need for low-income earners to have residential sites allocated for their use in areas which overcome the great distances from the workplace and the lack of access to efficient and affordable transport networks and urban services. Locations offering greater economic opportunity are not only a necessity, but could also lead to a reintegration of low-income communities into the central urban fabric, thus providing more permanent and secure access to urban services.

A proposed solution by the TPA and the Midrand Local Authority is a 'buffer zone' of middle-class (African) housing between the low-income (African) and middle and high-income (white and coloured) settlements. They believe this would prevent the middle and high-income properties from plummeting in value. Whether middle-class housing would be bought by Africans in such a racist context is debatable. An investment in a middle-income priced house in an 'experimental' area would most likely only materialize if purchasers were perhaps tempted with incentives.

In the Midrand situation, consideration needs to be given to not only the welfare of (a minority of) individuals, but also to the welfare of the large majority of people. Thus while people's investment in their homes is a planning concern, so are the rights of the homeless to appropriately located housing. This highlights the need for debate around future development principles which can give guidelines for community and individual rights to types of residential accommodation and location. At the root of this issue is the complex and contradictory relationship between housing as an exchange value and housing as a use value.

In addition to the principles about the right to housing, forms of tenure also need to be addressed as a policy issue. Private ownership of land and housing might not necessarily imply greater security of tenure than is obtainable either through the rental sector or collective tenure. A collective form of social control such as a Community Land Trust (CLT) could exist as an alternative to individual, private ownership. CLTs might be able to protect buyers against rising accommodation costs, and tenants or leaseholders against eviction through repossession. The emerging CLT strategy is also geared to contribute to improved utilization of urban land.

A third pressing policy issue is that of attending to the current underutilization of land, primarily through relatively low levels of densification. There are three interrelated and mutually dependent components of density: building density, occupancy density, and population density. Building density is measured in a floor area to site area ratio, determined by the space between buildings as well as building width, shape, and height. Occupancy density is measured in floor space per person and is directly related to income, the cost of floor space, and the need for space in terms of family size. A culmination of building and occupancy density is population density, determined by the number of persons per hectare.[18]

Low building and occupancy densities, such as those highlighted in table 15.2, are contributing to low population densities and hence to urban sprawl, wastage of facilities, and most importantly, underutilization of suitable land in some of the most accessible parts of the cities. Low-density settlements are, *per se,* relatively expensive, thus excluding cheaper housing from being developed in the most accessible areas of the city. Thus distant locations and related transport costs can also be seen as a consequence of low-density settlement, as can the intangible costs of social isolation.[19]

One way of developing policy on densification might be to challenge municipalities like Sandton that allow ratepayers to occupy space at a density of only three housing units per hectare. In the new spirit of reconciliation politics emerging in South Africa, it is a convenient time in which to intervene in the way land is used.

Existing land use zoning as outlined in the state's town planning guide represents a fourth area of policy assessment, especially since zoning is used to perpetuate separate racial and class development. Very seldom is land for low-income housing made available outside of existing low-income areas. Yet, proximity to established areas with tertiary educational facilities, proximity of informal sector trade to tap the financial resources of the wealthier areas, and more urban accessibility in terms of sophisticated transport networks are all vital to assisting the urban poor in improving the standard of their lives.

The last issue to be discussed is that of the geological suitability of land. In South Africa inexpensive, often geologically unsound land has generally been allocated to the low-income market to counter the affordability problem. Should not the land which warrants more expensive surveying and construction be allocated to the high-income market where these costs are affordable and manageable? Successful low-cost housing schemes are required to be as cost effective as possible. For example dolomitic land, because of its inherent instability, negates this process.[20] It is therefore suggested such land be avoided for cost effective schemes.

The issues that have been dealt with above point to the inability of market forces alone to address the ever increasing backlog of suitable land and housing. In future, the authorities as well as the urban poor themselves will be required to intervene in the allocation and management of land, in order for land and services to be delivered at affordable prices and to be used to their fullest potential.

Alternative land delivery mechanisms

There is a range of interventionary mechanisms that a future South African state, as well as organizations representing the urban poor's interests, might use to secure affordable land and services.

Land readjustment and cross-subsidization

In land readjustment schemes, the state temporarily expropriates and services unused (invariably peripheral) land from owners in order to initiate development. It is a useful way for the state to develop vast portions of land which it could not, ordinarily, afford to purchase at market prices. Land readjustment is particularly relevant when there is a large number of landowners, many of whom are reluctant to sell their land. In exchange for ceding their land to the readjustment scheme, owners receive a proportion of developed sites relative to a generalized value of the land in the area and the amount of land ceded to the scheme. This particular strategy has been used in South Korea, but as Lee Tae-Il[21] points out, assessing the value of land according to size and not location is problematic. Landowning participants in South Korean readjustment schemes claim that the distribution of betterment gains is unsatisfactory. If readjustment schemes are to be attempted in South Africa, addressing the 'betterment gains' aspect could be crucial to the success of projects.

Perhaps one of the most fundamental motives for landowners to participate in readjustment programmes is the prospect of increased values on their land being realized,[22] either through rezoning or as a result of the enhancement of the property through service provision. Doebele in Tomlinson[23] has estimated increases in value ranging from 300 per cent to 2 400 per cent in South Korea.[24]

The state profits from the scheme because it retains both the land designated for public use and as many of the newly created plots as are necessary to pay the cost of the planning and the infrastructure. However, there are numerous problems related to the increases experienced in land values. The greater the increase, the smaller the proportion of land that will be retained by the public authority to pay for the services. Furthermore, enhanced values are not likely to make such land affordable for the low-income earning bracket.

Land readjustment can also impose a betterment levy on landowners who, partly as a result of public sector investments in infrastructure and services, have realized capital gains on their land.[25] However, that property which is gained by the state usually has to be sold at cost-equivalent prices to recapture the costs of urban services.[26] In addition, administrative costs add to the cost of readjusted land, which inevitably makes land less affordable for the low-income sector. According to Hayashi[27] in Masser, a team of about 30 staff is needed to administer a typical project, with larger schemes requiring more staff for lengthy periods of time.

Cross-subsidization schemes can be used to combat the affordability constraint. In this process, the readjustment area is zoned for different land uses. Land can be sold or leased to commerce and industry in one portion of the scheme, and the revenue from these transactions used for reducing the price of land in the residential portion.

In the South African context, the difficulty of establishing land readjustment and cross-subsidization schemes would be largely due to race and class prejudice. In the latter case, landowners (mainly white) would not want to participate in schemes because of the argument that the presence of low-cost formal and informal housing affects the realization of profits from other forms of development, such as middle or high-income housing, commerce, and industry.

Notwithstanding problems experienced with the implementation of land readjustment elsewhere, this mechanism might operate successfully in South Africa if:

• each parcel of land were assessed in terms of location and other physical characteristics to ensure equitable distribution of development gains among participating landowners, through, *inter alia,* returning similar value land to that ceded;

- portions of newly developed readjusted land were structured to attract commerce and industry through, *inter alia,* appropriately designed transport networks, 'guidance' of 'big business' to these 'pre-selected multi-zoning areas', through incentives and/or direct guide plan interventions (similar to those used in the apartheid era, but with fundamentally different objectives), with revenue received for serviced commercial and industrial sites being used to cross-subsidize low-cost sites, services, and perhaps formal housing; and if
- land gained through the scheme were ceded to CLTs to ensure long-term affordability (preventing speculation by never allowing members to own their portion of land, but only the improvements which they make to their homes)

A further form of securing land for cross-subsidization techniques is through land banking.

Land banking

Land banking can occur either in the form of advance state acquisition of land or large-scale public ownership of undeveloped land for future urban use,[28] usually with the objective of making land more affordable. This is possible through stockpiling land and removing it from the property market, thereby preventing its price from increasing as a result of speculative dealing. The reservation of land for low-cost housing is a way to ensure the availability of suitable land in other areas besides the urban fringe or beyond.[29]

One of the essential prerequisites for land banking is the proper legal authority. The 'eminent domain' (priority land) principle or expropriation power is essential. In addition, the right of pre-emption (first refusal) must be in favour of the state in the case of real estate transactions in areas classified as 'eminent domain'.

How can land be banked? De Voy and Rodrunggruang[30] have outlined three methods:

- regulation and reservation;
- the use of state land holdings; or
- purchase.

Regulatory approaches include the zoning of land for housing with attached standards which only low-cost housing projects can meet;

and zoning and building codes, where a specified percentage of low-cost housing has to be provided for every percentage of a certain type of land use.

Reservation of land could occur through legal documents in the form of 'official mapping' whereby the state identifies specific land it wishes to reserve for various land uses.

Land banking through the transfer of state land into a land holding trust could only work if the South African state owned large portions of land in urban areas. It is doubtful whether there are sufficient quantities of state land to feed into a land holding trust: land annually being proclaimed and bought by the state for African development is mainly privately owned farm land. Land banking through the transfer of state land is not an appropriate mechanism in the present South African context. Neither is the purchase of large tracts of land for banking, when one considers the recessionary economic climate and the costs that would be incurred if land were to be held unproductive for lengthy periods. There are other means of obtaining affordable land without the necessity of large outflows of state capital — for example, the use of land taxes.

Land taxes

Various forms of land taxes can be used to promote certain land uses, to prompt decisions to sell, to lessen the price of land, and to discourage speculation. However, taxes only have a marginal effect on land use decisions. Land use is determined to a large extent by interest rates, returns on alternative investments, and direct interventions by the state in the form of land readjustment schemes. Nevertheless, existing urban land utilization in Singapore was improved through the use of specific vacant land taxes (VLT). Thus some limited impact can also be made on the price of land and to discourage land speculation.

Municipalities in the PWV region use the site value tax (SVT) system whereby 'Within each municipality, the tax rate (a proportion of the value of the land) stays the same regardless of the value of the land'.[31] The effect that this form of tax has on the decision to sell land is that land remains inactive for as long as the rate of appreciation and current rate of return are greater than or equal to the rate of return of alternative investments. SVT, therefore, does not induce certain land uses or prompt the owner to sell.

If an increase in SVT were to be implemented, all landowners would be affected. However if a VLT were used to reinforce the SVT, the cost of holding land would rise. Bahl[32] in Tomlinson explains how VLTs in Singapore operate in terms of low-building-to-land densities on vacated plots and properties. These properties are assessed at five per cent of their capital value, which is double that for improved properties.

Tomlinson argues that a post-apartheid future will be built on existing institutions and practices and that it makes sense in terms of land tax structures to continue with the SVT system. In addition, VLT should be added to the residential land tax structure. These two taxes could then raise additional revenue and encourage better utilization of the land (especially if a building-to-land-density ratio similar to the one in Singapore is employed).

As Tomlinson points out, vacant land taxes will be severely hampered in regions such as the PWV with its huge tracts of mining and agricultural land. Mining land is not taxed and the value of agricultural land is so low, that a tax calculated on the assessed value of such land would hardly impact on the increases in value that would result from speculative ventures.

Perhaps the way to combat speculation on land is to allow the landowner to determine the value of land for tax purposes, as is the method in Taiwan.[33] The value set by the landowner is also the price at which the land has to be sold to the state, should the state require it. The system can only work, however, if the state actually carries out its intentions and acquires land at landowner-set prices. There are of course, extra-legal means of acquiring land. The most effective from the point of view of the urban poor is land invasion.

Land invasions

In the latter half of 1990, the UDF proposed a campaign aimed at the occupation of unused land. The call by the UDF reflects a process which has been active in South Africa's landless communities for many years. Internationally as well as in South Africa, land seizure has been one of the most effective systems of accessing land for the poor.

In South Africa, the delivery of land through invasion or seizure has occurred either within the boundaries of townships or elsewhere, depending on the perceived viability of the area. Communities invading land are not only from existing townships; they are also refugees from the poverty-stricken bantustans. Over nine million people are said to be living in informal settlements (including backyard shacks) in and around South Africa's major urban centres.[34]

Survival on invaded land is dependent on the owners of the land and the development potential of the land. In Latin and South America, the most successful land invasions occurred on state land (trust or council land) or on land which was undesirable for development because of location and/or residential suitability. In many instances, informal settlers have been caught up in political struggles, and have pledged votes in return for formal recognition of their settlements and the upgrading of services. Could this legacy of patronage show itself in the present dynamics of South African political upheaval?

Although land has been gained time and again through invasions, the security of communities remains precarious, and this aspect, among others, highlights the negative implications of land seizure. The settlements that emerge through land seizures have proved to be very problematic when it comes to future upgrading or owner-builder home improvement. Services are difficult to install if dwellings are already well established. Furthermore, if households are never sure whether investment in the form of improvements made to their homes is worthwhile, then the settlement may never improve. Angel[35] argues further that even with tenure rights secured, this requisite still appears to be an insufficient condition for channelling people's resources into housing. A sense of security is more likely to be nurtured through an established and comprehensive housing policy. It is therefore likely that until South Africa has an unbiased and efficient housing policy, problems associated with land seizure will remain secondary to the primary goal of access to affordable land and to the city.

Land seizure is a viable alternative when formal mechanisms for land delivery are unsatisfactory or non-existent. However, because of the problems mentioned above, this form of accessing land can only be acceptable until such time as an affordable and efficient delivery system is set in motion.

This section has investigated alternative mechanisms for affordable land delivery. In order to establish a viable delivery system, the following aspects of the alternatives discussed above could be integrated for use. State regulation and reservation could be employed to 'map' out priority areas. Land readjustment schemes could then be used to obtain land for development without the state having to purchase land. SVTs, together with VLTs and the Taiwanese 'own assessment' taxing system, could play a minor role in discouraging land speculation.

The next section will address the system and structures needed for the distribution and management of land, taking into account the necessary protection of this land from the private sector.

A possible new approach

The delivery structure and process

The success of any future land policy depends on the committed intervention by a democratic government in the land market, in order to make it possible for those unable to compete in the formal land market to secure land for themselves in areas which would otherwise exclude them financially.

In a dual sector land structure (as shown in table 15.3), the first sector accommodates the private ownership of land and permits a regulated private sector land market to continue. The second sector consists of suitably located land which the state has secured through the processes of 'official mapping', land readjustment, and cross-subsidization programmes, and which could be controlled by CLTs.

A form of state land banking is envisaged to support the supply side of the public sector. However, it differs from the land banking objectives that occur in the private sector in that it is not guided by the 'investment' potential of the land, but rather by long-term objectives of access to 'suitable' locations. It therefore attempts to reverse the trend which Lojkine[36] described as occurring in Holland and Germany, whereby public land bank policy never applied to areas where the ground rent was greatest, i.e. central city areas. But with legislative mechanisms such as 'eminent domain' and pre-emptive real estate clauses, the post-apartheid South African state may be able to make positive interventions in this regard.

It is envisaged that landowners who own land in areas which coincide with that land which is prioritized by the National Housing and Land Commission (within the 'official mapping' exercise) should become participants in readjustment schemes. As already alluded to in the chapter, capital gains can be made from having one's land developed, therefore landowners would not lose capital as a result of a scheme.

The dual sector land structure also addresses the price and location of land. The objective of accessibility through affordability to viable urban locations should imply access to land in appropriate, safe, and non-polluted locations; access to basic infrastructure and to social services such as health care facilities, schools, and emergency services; and access to acceptable and appropriate building materials, technical expertise, and housing finance on reasonable terms. Accessibility also includes non-material elements such as the right to know about potential hazards, and access to legal assistance. In addition, access for groups traditionally excluded from housing plans, such as the disabled and elderly, is important.[37]

The crucial question, though, is does such land exist in South Africa's major urban centres or not? Previous land use density requirements in cities exclusively reserved for 'white' property ownership have left behind a legacy of low-density, underutilized residential space. The services provided in these areas such as schools, transport facilities, and recreation, to name but a few, are also underutilized. If the results of the 'official mapping' exercise indicate that a shortage of suitable land indeed exists in urban areas, a contingency plan could be the densification of existing low-density areas with the building of medium to high-density flats for sale or rental, with financial assistance from the state and/or the private sector.

With further reference to land availability, planners need to challenge the existing mineral rights legislation on land. The benefit of mining in certain marginal reefs should be weighed up against the benefit that could be realized if land of little mining value were to be accrued for residential purposes.

In the state sector, an annual amount of the state's financial budget would be necessary for the installation of bulk infrastructure and services on land earmarked for readjustment schemes.

CLTs could be used as a mechanism for the delivery, management, and control of public sector land. CLTs are non-profit corporations, rather than typical legal trusts. The use of the word 'trust' conveys a relationship between the members of the CLT and between the people of the community and their land. CLTs operate with an open membership, governed by an elected board that is typically structured to include leasing members, other community residents, and public authority representatives.

It is envisaged that through 'official mapping', land could be withdrawn from the private market temporarily. That land which, through the rules of readjustment schemes, is returned to its owner, should not be classified as public sector land. Nonetheless, land gained through the readjustment process could be divided up for multi-land use development. Some land could be set aside for CLT cross-subsidization purposes and be sold to commerce and industry at capital gains, and that which remains could be earmarked for ceding to public sector CLTs. Land donated by the state could be held in perpetuity by CLTs. As White and Matthei[38] explain:

> Through long-term lease arrangements, the land is made available to local individuals or organisations, who may own housing or other improvements on the leased land. Leaseholders' equity in these improvements is normally limited to the value they have actually invested (the purchase price and cost of major improvements), adjusted for inflation and real depreciation, so that when they move away and sell their property it will remain affordable for other residents of the community.

If the leaseholder's home improvements have been subsidized, the CLT may retain the value of the subsidy. Furthermore, if the value of the property appreciates because the community has become a more desirable place to live and work, the CLT should retain this appreciated value for the public benefit. Land is kept affordable for future leaseholders as a result of these measures. However, White and Matthei do point out that if price improvements on the land are not limited, CLTs may come to reflect the potential market value of the location, thus impacting negatively on affordability criteria.

The features of CLTs can be numerous. By controlling and managing land as a public resource, it is possible to remove land from the speculative market. In terms of land use, appropriateness can be determined by the governing board. Leases could be long-term, renewable, and inheritable, thus creating security of tenure for as long as the householder wishes to occupy the land. When land ceases to be used, perhaps by absentee leaseholders, the lease can be withdrawn and reallocated. The allocation of sites in a CLT should be through 'means testing' on a first-come-first-served basis, whereby access is granted to the poorest first. Lease fees can be used to acquire additional land, pay property taxes, and cover administrative costs.

CLTs can be used as efficient mechanisms for the supply of affordable land and the effective utilization of land and services. However, the most important feature of CLTs within the dual sector land structure is the community empowerment that can be achieved through suitable location and access to high-level infrastructure and services.

Conclusion

This chapter argues that despite the current emphasis on the shortage of allocated land for low-cost housing, this issue is not the most significant. Rather, the emphasis should be on the location and geological suitability of residential land. In addition, a more regulated rather than deregulated residential land structure is required to counter the material constraints that privatized land delivery imposes on people's access to land.

The problems that the state's policy of 'orderly urbanization' encounters are elaborated upon, the most significant being the continued growth of informal settlements in all of South Africa's major urban centres. This development on its own makes a mockery of the so-called strategy of 'controlled orderly urbanization'.

Future land policy issues are discussed. The most problematic issue here is the existence of a well-developed real estate market and established class interests. It is unrealistic to have booming property markets in South Africa's major cities when the economic status of the majority of people does not warrant such a market. Planning decisions in the future will have to prioritize development in favour of the majority where the most benefit can be achieved. Nevertheless, as the Midrand example illustrates, one cannot simply ignore the rights of existing property owners.

Alternative proposals of land delivery and control are evaluated. It is suggested that 'official mapping' should be used to identify available land. Thereafter, land readjustment schemes could occur, resulting in original landowners receiving developed sites as payment in exchange for land which the state gains through the process. Minimal capital outlays will be necessary if the state is able to sell portions of the acquired land to commerce and industry. There are ways of encouraging 'big business' to purchase sites in these areas; either through incentives (which can be costly) or through certain development regulations (e.g. for every X number of industrial sites developed in Midrand, X number of sites have to be developed in a specified readjustment scheme). Lastly, as well as readjustment schemes, land banking is required to support the supply side of the public sector. In addition, cross-subsidization is useful in the above processes because of the very costly exercise of buying, developing, and/or holding land for long periods of time.

A dual sector land structure is recommended in which the private market functions in one sector, while public sector CLTs lease land to individuals or organizations in the other. Within the public sector, the envisaged National Land and Housing Commission's 'official mapping' land identification exercise could address the problems of viable locations, and CLTs could tackle the issue of affordable land in perpetuity. However, a number of problems could be encountered. In terms of allocation of sites in the state sector, determining the criteria for selection would be difficult, as would be the choosing of beneficiaries.

Furthermore, speculation has increased the price of land substantially. If a future government hopes to bring down the price of land for those choosing to remain in the private sector, some form of financial disincentive would have to be legislated, which discourages the holding of vacant land for speculative purposes. A continuation of SVT as practised in the PWV, as well as VLT and 'own assessment' tax is advocated.

Table 15.1 The identification of section 33 land for African residential development, March 1990

Stage of identification	Province	31/03/89 (ha)	31/03/90 (ha)	% incr/decr
	Cape			
(a) land proclaimed		11 043	12 738	+15
(b) land approved but not yet proclaimed		3 810	3 367	−12
(c) applications under consideration		1 300	900	−31
(d) land being investigated *		0	0	0

* henceforth referred to as a, b, c, and d.

	Province	31/03/89	31/03/90	% incr/decr
	Natal			
(a)		1 310	2 765	+111
(b)		91	91	0
(c)		303	261	−14
(d)		0	0	0
	Orange Free State			
(a)		4 054	5 006	+23
(b)		733	27	−96
(c)		510	606	+19
(d)		0	0	0
	Transvaal			
(a)		24 779	50 427	+104
(b)		19 845	608	−97
(c)		12 546	5 441	−57
(d)		250	24 444	+9 678

Total national land identification as of March 1990 is indicated below. March 1989 figures appear in brackets.

Total land proclaimed for African township development (ha): (41 186) 70 936

Total land approved for proclamation (ha): (24 479)   4 093

Total area of applied for land under consideration (ha): (14 659)   7 208

Total land being investigated for township development (ha): (250)   24 444

Total   (80 574) 106 681

Source: Department of Planning and Provincial Affairs: Voorsiening van Behuising; Kwartaallikse Statistiek, March 1990.

The following assumptions can be made from table 15.1:

(a) Land proclaimed for African township development in urban areas has increased by 72 per cent per annum. Much pressure from political quarters, the media, and a general crisis in the reproduction of the labour force could have been responsible for the increase. In addition, the various provincial administrations have been reacting to 'squatting' within and outside of formal African townships and also to growing backyard shack settlements in the townships. Much proclaimed land, however, remains undeveloped because the market to which the private sector delivers housing is decreasing in size.

(b) Land in the process of being approved for proclamation has decreased by an average of 83 per cent per annum. Although an increase in gazetted land proclamation has occurred, private sector applications to develop land could have lessened over the period under investigation because of the steadily saturating private housing market for Africans.

(c) Land being considered for African housing has decreased by an average of 50 per cent between March 1989 and March 1990. This drop could also be attributed to the falling rate of private sector applications for development.

(d) According to table 15.1, only land in the Transvaal is being investigated for residential use. Land that is undergoing investigation is not necessarily linked to private sector development activity. The Department of Planning and Provincial Affairs (DPPA) can itself carry out land investigations. In 1988, for example, the DPPA commissioned a consortium of town planners to compile a report on land availability in the PWV. This would explain the lack of correlation between the decrease in applications for land and the increase in land being investigated.

Table 15.2   A cross-section of residential densities in Greater Johannesburg, 1984*

Settlement name	Soweto Meadowlands Hostel	Hillbrow —	Township Parktown Majestic Towers	Soweto Moroko	Killarney Killarney Village	Melville —
Total site area (m²)	22 742	9 373	15 015	18 144	18 626	18 312
Number of units	308	386	203	33	33	23
Area of units (m²)	18	96.5	161	54	201	188
Total floor area (m²)	5 544	37 249	32 683	1 782	6 633	4 324
Coverage in area (m²)	5 544	3 495	1 980	1 782	3 640	4 324
Family size	5.1	1.7	2.2	5.1	2	3.1
Total population	1 571	656.2	446.7	168.3	66	71.3
Unit price (R)	1 164	26 000	85 000	2 100	176 000	85 128
Breadwinners' annual income 1982/3 (R)	3 120	19 476	44 116	8 374	44 116	32 145
Building height**	1	10.7	16.5	1	2	1
Persons per hectare	690	700	447	92.8	35.4	39
Household density*** (m² per person)	3.5	56.7	73.2	10.6	100.5	60.6
Purchase price (R/m²)	65	270	528	39	796	453

Source: Senior B. 1984.

Table 15.2   Notes

*   The settlements outlined in the table above are in some cases representative only of selected study areas within the townships mentioned.

**   Building height refers to the average number of floors vertically above one another.

***   Household density is measured by dividing the area of the dwelling unit in square metres by family size. The resultant figure is the amount of floor space in square metres that each person has in the dwelling unit.

Table 15.3 A dual sector land allocation structure

NATIONAL LAND AND HOUSING COMMISSION

OFFICIAL MAPPING

national executive committee made up of professionals in the land field, politicians, church leaders, civic movements, labour union officials, and 'big business'

SERIES OF PUBLIC MEETINGS

LAND ALLOCATION

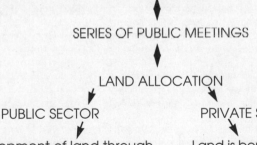

PUBLIC SECTOR

Development of land through land readjustment and cross-subsidization

PRIVATE SECTOR

Land is bought by the state, developers, local authorities, parastatals, and regional administrations for the construction of housing or development of site-and-service schemes to be sold on the private market

Land ceded to CLTs for leasing to members

Notes

1 The author would like to thank the Labour and Economic Research Centre (LERC) and Planact for the opportunity afforded during work hours to research and write this article. Much appreciation is forwarded to those individuals in these organizations who exchanged ideas and commented on the chapter. Special thanks to Paul Hendler and Karen Miedzinski for much encouragement and editing assistance.

2 De Vos (1987) in Tomlinson R. 'Land for Housing the Poor in the PWV' *Urbanization in a Post Apartheid South Africa* (London: Unwin Hymin 1990a).

3 Interview with the Director Town Planning, Sandton Municipality, November 1990.

4 A Markinor study of Alexandra (May 1990) estimated approximately seven backyard shacks per backyard. This figure has then been multiplied by the author with the average formal housing density of 20 units per hectare in African townships.

5 Latsky J. 'The Legal Challenge of Undoing Apartheid — Reflections on the Enormity and the Enormousness' *South Africa International* (July 1990) 21 i.

6 ANC *Policy Options on the Land Question for a United, Non-racial, Democratic South Africa*, ANC Land Question Seminar (17 February 1990).

7 Latsky (1990).

8 Planact 'The Black Communities Development Act 4 of 1984' *Planact Memo* (29 May 1990a) 2.

9 Latsky (1990).

10 *Weekly Mail* 6 October 1989.

11 Density ratio used by ORMET (East Rand Metropolitan Transport and Advisory Board) in Timmermans G. V. F. 'Commuter Transportation by Road and Rail: the Problems, Issues, and Opportunities Created by Development in the East Rand', paper presented at the Witwatersrand Chamber of Commerce and Industry (WCCI) and the Johannesburgse Sakekamer Conference (JAS) on the Future of the Witwatersrand (Johannesburg: June 1989).

12 Gilbert A. and Ward P. M. 'Access to Land' *Housing the State and the Poor; Policy and Practice in 3 Latin American Cities* (Cambridge: Cambridge University Press 1985) 70.

13 Senior B. 'Factors Affecting Residential Density: a Search for the Zen of Density', unpublished Ph.D. thesis (Johannesburg: University of the Witwatersrand 1984).

14 Planact *Memo on the Conceptual Context of the Land Market* (Johannesburg: March 1990b).

15 Republic of South Africa *An Urbanization Strategy for the Republic of South Africa*, a report of the Committee for Constitutional Affairs of the President's Council (Cape Town: Government Printer 1985) PC 3/1985.

16 Examples of deconcentration points in the Transvaal are Rietfontein, approximately 35 kilometres south of Johannesburg; Bronkhorstspruit, 40 kilometres east of Pretoria; and Brits-Roslyn, 40 and 20 kilometres respectively west of Pretoria.

17 *The Daily Mail* 16 July 1990.

18 Senior (1984).

19 Wolfson A. C. *Land for Low-income Housing in the PWV: Patterns of State Allocation and Prospects for Change*, unpublished M.Sc. dissertation (Johannesburg: University of the Witwatersrand 1989).

20 Brink A. B. A. et al. *Soil Survey for Engineering* (Oxford: Clarendon Press 1982).

21 Lee Tae-Il 'Land Readjustments in Seoul: Case Study on Gaepo Project' *Third World Planning Review* (1987) 9 iii.

22   Archer R. W. 'The Possible Use of Urban Land Pooling/Readjustment for the
     Planned Development of Bangkok' *Third World Planning Review* (1987) 9 iii.
     Lee Tae-Il (1987).
23   Doebele (1979) in Tomlinson (1990a).
24   Tomlinson (1990a).
25   Masser I. 'Land Readjustment: an Overview' *Third World Planning Review* (1987) 9
     iii.
26   Doebele (1982) in Lee Tae-Il (1987).
27   Hayashi (1978) in Masser (1987).
28   Shoup (1983) in Tomlinson R. 'Land for Housing the Poor in India and South
     Africa: a Study of the Delhi Development Authority and the Role of a Land
     Development Corporation' *Urban Forum* (1990b) 1 ii 146.
29   De Voy R. S. and Rodrunggruang C. 'Basic Land Banking Concepts and their
     Application to Low-cost Housing in Thailand' (eds.) Angel S., Archer R. W., et al.
     Land for Housing the Poor (Singapore: Select Books 1983).
30   De Voy and Rodrunggruang (1983).
31   Tomlinson (1990a) 103.
32   Bahl (1979) in Tomlinson (1990a).
33   Harris (1979) in Tomlinson (1990a).
34   *The Weekly Mail* 27 January 1989.
35   Angel S. 'Land Tenure for the Urban Poor' (eds.) Angel S., Archer R. W., et al.
     Land for Housing the Poor (Singapore: Select Books 1983).
36   Lojkine J. 'Big Firm's Strategies, Urban Policy and Urban Social Movements' (ed.)
     Harloe M. *Captive Cities* (London: Wiley and Sons 1977).
37   Leckie S. 'Housing Rights: Some Central Themes', presented at the Conference for
     Sustainable Habitat on an Urbanized Planet (Berlin: March 1990).
38   White K. and Matthei C. 'Community Land Trusts' (eds.) Bruyn S. T. and Meehan J.
     Beyond the Market and the State: New Directions in Community Development
     (Philadelphia: Temple University Press 1987) 41.

16 Class, race, and urban locational relationships

Introduction

The existing spatial forms of South African cities have been shaped by many forces, but state intervention to ensure strict urban racial segregation has been an especially significant factor. Indeed analysis of the processes shaping the development of apartheid urban forms provides important insights into the politics of urban development generally in South African cities. Specifically, the role of relationships between race, class, and locational relationships in the politics of urban development is thrown into sharp relief by a consideration of the history of efforts at forging patterns of urban apartheid.

Such insights, in turn, are useful within the context of contemporary debates on the prospective nature of post-apartheid society, and the post-apartheid city. By understanding the means by which locational relationships were manipulated so as to facilitate the consolidation of local, segregationist power blocs, for example, the prospects for undoing such alliances and promoting new ones, based upon post-apartheid urban visions, are enhanced. This brief contribution, therefore, sketches some of the main elements of a basic theory of class, race, and urban locational relationships as it is relevant in the South African context. These elements of theory derive on the one hand from a study of one history of South African urban planning and land use, and on the other from speculation on principles which may be relevant to the negotiation of South Africa's post-apartheid urban future.

The paper is structured so that, first, a broad historical overview and interpretation of the political economy of urban apartheid is provided. The central proposition here is that, historically, local political alliances based upon race and class have cohered, at least partly, around differing assessments of the relative costs and benefits of alternative patterns of locational relationships within specific cities. It is noted that these local alliances, in turn, in many respects prefigured the thinking behind the national segregationist planning practices of the 1950s and 1960s; that is, practices centred around the application of the Group Areas Act (1950). The paper then assesses the main contradictions of the urban planning strategies of the national apartheid alliance, and suggests that it is out of these contradictions that new, local political alliances have been, and will be, forged. The strategic opportunities that are raised by such considerations are discussed in conclusion.

Segregation and domination

The urban geographical literature is replete with different interpretations of the historical origins of racial segregation in South African cities. Davies[1] first referred to the 'colonial' origins of urban racial segregation in South Africa, and this theme has subsequently been echoed by Christopher,[2] Cook,[3] and Lemon[4] among others. Essentially, this school of thought has argued that, wherever colonialism has developed, the master-servant format of colonial social relations has required 'spatial distancing' of the residential settlement patterns of the colonizer and colonized. Residential segregation, in this view, becomes a necessary, symbolic demonstration in urban space of 'otherness': an otherness that is central to colonial systems of political domination.

However, as Abu-Lughod[5] and Findlay et al.,[6] among others, have pointed out in relation to patterns of residential segregation in post-colonial Africa, colonialism *per se* does not appear to be a political condition that is fundamental to the maintenance of patterns of urban racial segregation. In their studies of pre-colonial and post-colonial racial segregation in Rabat, Morocco, for example, substantial continuity in urban racial segregation was revealed, with one ethnic élite replacing another in the segregated residential space of the city in the post-colonial period.

Other students of the history of urban racial segregation in South Africa — such as Mabin[7] and Torr[8] — have located the origins of urban apartheid in the economic sphere: specifically in the social relations of production that developed with the establishment of the first industrial capitalist enterprises in South Africa. Mabin,[9] for example, has argued that the labour compound system in South African cities had its origins in the demands of mine-owners in Kimberley for controls over the labour process. Similarly Torr[10] identifies the rationale for the establishment of the first formal African townships — such as Lamontville in Durban — in the designs of industrialists to secure a cheap and divided labour force: divisions that would allegedly assist in reducing labour militancy.

The problem of specificity

While there can be little doubt that broader class struggles have played a significant role in the development of patterns of urban racial segregation in South Africa, the analytical problem remains that the system of class relations that is emphasized in the works cited above has hardly been unique to South Africa. And whereas it is of course true that urban racial segregation has not been unique to South Africa, it remains clear that urban residential segregation has assumed a specific form here.

This specificity became particularly evident in South Africa during and after the 1950s, when the Group Areas Act was implemented. This act required the strict residential segregation of the four 'groups' recognized in terms of the Population Registration Act (white, coloured, Indian, and African). As Davies[11] has observed of the period, what emerged was an urban form that was more structured and quartered than anything that had preceded it in either colonial or early industrial capitalist times.

The development and application of the Group Areas Act have, however, themselves been subject to various interpretations. Western,[12] for example, interprets the act as a grandiose demonstration of white political power at the national scale, following the rise of Afrikaner Nationalism that was politically founded in the assertion of racial privilege. Western[13] records, for example, the hostility of the Cape Town City Council to the 'intervention' of the act which, in his view, amounted to the superimposition of the political designs of those in control of the central state (the racially minded NP) over the political designs of those in control of the local state (in Cape Town, liberal integrationists in favour of a racially open class élite).

In essence, then, Western's[14] view was similar to those who emphasized the colonial origins of urban apartheid, in so far as he recognized a necessary relationship between the politics of racial domination at a national level and the local urban symbolism of distancing and segregation. For Western,[15] however, it was the appropriation of the organs of central state power by a post-colonial, ethnically based political élite that determined the centrally imposed patterns of segregation in the 1950s and 1960s. In this sense, Western's[16] analysis hinged upon a specific proposition on the nature of central-local state relations in the determination of urban policies and urban outcomes: that is, the proposition of central state determinism.

The role of locality

Despite the intuitive appeal of Western's[17] analysis within a context of liberal theories of the South African state, there is considerable evidence from cities other than Cape Town that local initiatives actually preceded and partially informed centralist approaches to urban apartheid. In English-dominated Durban, for example, many of the precedents for the Group Areas Act were developed prior to the ascendency to national power of Afrikaner ethnicity and the NP in 1948. These precedents are described in some detail in the now classic monograph of Kuper et al.[18] on the 'racial ecology' of Durban.

It would appear that during the 1920s and 1930s, local class alliances developed between business groups and the civic associations and local trade unions representing white working classes in Durban, and other cities. These coalitions received political expression through the local state, particularly that faction of it that was constituted by the city engineers, city health, and city estates departments. Such locally dominant class alliances had interests at variance with black traders, other entrepreneurs, and the working classes in general. Specifically, a major component of white workers sought relief from competition with black workers in access to housing; and several white-dominated business organizations sought protection from competition with growing numbers of black traders and other entrepreneurs.

The political manipulation of spatial relationships by local bureaucracies, under the influence of both white working-class organizations and businesses, was subsequently invoked to override the economic forces generating the competition.[19] In Durban, for example, white civic associations in coalition with the Durban Chamber of Commerce lobbied for a judicial commission of inquiry into 'Indian penetration' into inner city areas. These local inquiries, in turn, culminated in parliamentary legislation such as the Trading and Occupation of Land (Transvaal and Natal) Restriction Act of 1943 and the Indian Representation Act no. 26 of 1946 — both of which effectively froze the racial distribution of land in Durban, and other Natal and Transvaal towns and cities.

Central-local relationships

Moreover, at the level of local politics, the Durban city estates manager in 1943 produced a race-zoning map that not only proposed distinct racial 'group areas' for the city as a whole (down to the level of a detailed map), but also identified areas of Indian and African shack settlement 'suitable for future industrial development'. These proposals served as a basis for local state negotiations with the national state after the Group Areas Act was passed in parliament in 1950 (with open support, incidentally, from Natal 'opposition' MPs), and the pattern of land usage and racial settlement that exists in Durban today almost exactly mirrors these 1943 proposals of the local state bureaucracy.[20] This remarkable congruence of local state designs with ultimate land use and segregation outcomes, serves as a reminder that it was not simply a coalition forged at the level of the national state that realized patterns of urban apartheid. On the contrary, the very conception of such patterns and their final, local configuration depended upon local political and economic initiatives.

It should be clarified that Durban's local state structures did not of course single-handedly pioneer urban apartheid. The historical record suggests that local initiatives towards urban apartheid were afoot in several localities during the 1940s; and that local and national state structures did not act independently of each other in arriving at the urban apartheid 'solution' to the interests of power bloc alliances forged during the 1940s. There is a considerable literature on the historical development of racial segregation in Johannesburg, for example, that indicates how sometimes local and national state initiatives coincided, while at other times they were in conflict.[21]

A detailed literature on the various facets of the historical emergence of urban apartheid on the Witwatersrand can be found in several contributions to the University of the Witwatersrand's History Workshop series, and in the collected papers of the African Studies Institute Seminar.[22] One of the most apt characterizations of the politics of the local implementation of urban apartheid in Johannesburg, however, is to be found in the chapter on the destruction of Sophiatown in Lodge's *Black Politics in South Africa Since 1945.*[23] Here Lodge shows how a popular class alliance of workers, small traders, and professionals congealed around a local branch of the ANC during the early 1950s, in defence of their mutual material interests in the neighbourhood of Sophiatown — a racially mixed (but predominantly African) inner suburb that was widely regarded then as a convenient and urbane community.

Lodge[24] suggests that Sophiatown posed an obstacle to the designs of white property developers who, in turn, had influence on politicians and bureaucrats within the local state. At the same time, local and national politicians who were pursuing a strategy of patronage politics with the white working classes could point to the area as both a potential threat (in terms of competition for access to scarce urban land and housing resources) and a potential prize (in terms of its being a convenient site for 'upgrading' for white working-class habitation). Not surprisingly, therefore, the area ultimately became a symbolic battleground in early contests of national power between the NP and the ANC. After blacks had been evicted from the area in terms of Group Areas legislation, it was redeveloped into a white working-class suburb named, with appropriate symbolic resonance and pathos, Triomf (in English 'triumph').

Class, race, and locality

Implicitly, therefore, Lodge[25] identifies Group Areas as one of the key axes of national power bloc versus popular class alliance formation during the 1950s. Furthermore, both Lodge[26] and his political scientist colleague Stadler[27] have consistently identified problems of locational relationships within Johannesburg — conflicts over the presence of informal housing in certain areas, transport systems, the costs of the journey to work, etc. — as primary issues shaping popular versus power bloc class alliance formation in Johannesburg and, indeed, nationally during the 1940s and 1950s. This point has also subsequently been appreciated in the geographical literature on South African cities.[28]

It should be noted, however, that it is not simply conflicts between residential groups which have been the basis of both political mobilization and local state intervention over human settlement patterns, or 'who lives where' in the South African city. Often the central conflicts have been between the urban poor and those seeking to convert urban land to higher, non-residential, economic uses. As Parnell[29] observes of the Johannesburg case during the 1930s, programmes of 'slum clearance' were partly about industrial expansion:

> In instigating slum clearance projects in the 1930s, the Johannesburg Council had set three objectives. First, to ensure industrial expansion, second to guarantee the removal of any menace to public health, and finally to enforce residential segregation ... [As such] under the jurisdiction of the local state major initiatives to regulate the location of African, Indian and coloured residence were implemented.[30]

The coincidence of 'slum removals', racial segregation plans, and the expansion of industrial areas during the 1930s and 1940s was by no means restricted to Johannesburg, as research on Durban has recently shown. For instance, efforts to remove low-income, Indian-occupied settlements to the south of Durban in the 1940s were partly motivated along 'sanitation syndrome', racist lines,[31] and partly in terms of the need for further industrial land.[32] In short, simplistic notions of the actual formulation and implementation of urban apartheid as the product of an ethnically based, national political strategy should be viewed with some circumspection. While the Group Areas Act of 1950 was a major symbolic and legal instrument for the achievement of the aims of Afrikaner Nationalism, the local political and economic preconditions preceded the act in time, often by decades. These preconditions were largely the products of complex local political and economic alliances forged around 'urban planning' and 'local economic growth' strategies, often orchestrated by the local state.[33]

'City formalization'
and post-apartheid prospects

There can be little doubt, of course, that the structured racial ordering of residential areas, and the forced removals of urban communities on the basis of race, reached their most vigorous and ugly expression during the 1950s and 1960s. The tragic proportions and consequences of this period are well catalogued and illustrated, for example by Western.[34] It should nevertheless also be recalled that the 1950s and 1960s were a period of other significant urban transformations which might be collectively described as those of 'city formalization'.[35] The effective elimination of informal settlements, the construction of extensive state-run suburban housing estates, and an orientation towards grand, 'blueprint' urban planning generally, were all part of this pattern. The 'city formal' pattern as a whole, of course, led to a significant restructuring of the basic locational parameters governing urban development.

In practice, as several observers have noted, the main rearrangement was that affecting the residential location patterns of blacks.[36] Areas that were previously occupied mainly by blacks were recurrently earmarked for formal residential habitation by whites, or for commercial and industrial usage. A study by Kuper et al. in 1958,[37] for example, indicates that whereas 60 per cent of Durban's black population would be displaced in terms of Group Areas plans eventually agreed to by the council and the Group Areas Board, the equivalent figure for whites was 10 per cent. Similarly, the Durban Housing Survey of 1952[38] noted how an unequal exchange of property would occur in Durban if the council's technical sub-committee's proposals were ratified (as they largely were). Forty per cent of Indian-owned lands (by value) were to be set aside for white use, and only five per cent of white-owned land was to be set aside for Indians.

Such unequal exchanges, in turn, inevitably increased the price of property remaining in Indian landowners' hands and made property available for the white working class at a discount rate. There are few published analyses of the exact size of price inequalities caused by such differential supply constraints, but a recent multiple regression analysis performed on a sample of Cape Town's homes indicated that 'coloureds' are paying up to 90 per cent more for similar houses than are whites, owing to the inelasticity of supply caused by Group Areas.[39]

Racial structuring and 'city formalization' not only impacted upon the residential property market in a distributional sense; it also undermined the overall efficiency of the urban land market. For example, as a result of the application of the act in several cities, thousands of hectares of centrally located, formerly residential land were left sterile for decades: District Six in Cape Town, South End in Port Elizabeth, and Cato Manor in Durban are examples of this. In the last mentioned case, it has been estimated that the opportunity cost of leaving the lands idle up to 1984 was R1.5 billion (at 1984 prices).[40] Indeed, the rigid, central planning orientation of the 1960s soon became so entangled in economic contradictions and inefficiencies that substantial 'reforms' were required in the 1970s and 1980s, and these operated mostly as guarded, *post hoc* responses to changes that had already emerged on the ground.[41] The government's 'free settlement' response to the *de facto* breakdown of Group Areas in the 1980s is one example of this reactive style.[42]

In consequence, by the mid-1980s, it was possible for more left-leaning planning specialists and political groupings to take the initiative and conceptualize alternative, comprehensive, class-race-location relationships that might operate within South African cities during a truly post-apartheid era.[43] Some of these concepts were quite sweeping, and amounted to design-orientated 'replies' to the highly structured and quartered pattern of urban segregation and inequality that had arisen during the 1950s and 1960s. Others were more incrementalist, and envisaged targeted development programmes directed at the physical and symbolic reintegration of South African cities. In general, both types of post-apartheid urban vision were directed towards national policy debates.[44]

'Disjointed incrementalism' and post-apartheid prospects

The critical issues that await those who aim to influence the concrete realization of post-apartheid urban policy and development patterns are, however, likely to be only partly national in scope. There are dangers in making inferences about the process of urban politics and planning from South Africa's segregationist past towards its (hopefully) post-apartheid future. Nevertheless, if South

African history and, indeed, that of world urban experience is anything to go by, it is likely that much will depend upon local urban development initiatives taken in specific cities, and upon the roles played by various class and political groupings in relation to the local state.

The concepts of 'local-level negotiations', 'local state restructuring' and/or 'local government reform' are, of course, now central to the political nomenclature of both popular political organizations and civic associations on the one hand, and the state on the other.[45] This new fluidity with regard to the potential form and character of the local state, when combined with the extraordinary urban planning contradictions and inefficiencies deriving from the apartheid era, provides the principal raw material out of which newly dominant configurations of class-race-location relationships are likely to emerge. In particular, it would seem that loose alliances between local business groupings and local representatives of major black political groupings are beginning to make significant bids to influence the direction and outcome of either local government reform, or the future form and character of urban development, or both. Such efforts are still embryonic, and vary in their relative scope and ambitions, but what many have in common is that they are new attempts to forge local alliances around a 'culture of developmentalism'.[46]

It is still too early to tell whether such initiatives will have a determinate impact upon future urban development and local governmental outcomes, but reformist elements within the state by late 1990 were both providing the space for their effective operation, and even encouraging them to make formal proposals on local governmental outcomes. In the jargon of planning theorists, therefore, the South African urban policy arena appears in 1990 to be shifting away from 'blueprints' towards 'disjointed incrementalism'. If the record of the 1930s and 1940s is relevant to the future, the consequences of this shift may be rather more significant for national outcomes than they may at first appear. Those who, at local level, are most convincingly able to show, in practical terms, how race-class-location relationships both can and should operate in the post-apartheid era, could have a significant impact upon South African history.

Notes

1 Davies R. J. *Of Cities and Societies: the Geographers Viewpoint*, University of Cape Town Inaugural Lecture Series (1976).
2 Christopher A. J. 'From Flint to Soweto: Reflections on the Colonial Origins of the Apartheid City' *Area* (1983) 15 ii 145–9.
3 Cook G. P. 'Khayelitsha — Policy Change or Crisis Response?' *Transactions of the Institute of British Geographers* (1986) 11 i 57–66.
4 Lemon A. 'Imposed Separation: the Case of South Africa' (eds.) Chisholm M. and Smith D. M. *Shared Space, Divided Space* (London: Unwin Hyman 1990).
5 Abu-Lughod J. *Rabat: Urban Apartheid in Morocco* (New Jersey: Princeton University Press 1980).
6 Findlay A., Findlay A., and Paddison R. 'Maintaining the Status Quo: an Analysis of Social Space in Post-colonial Rabat' *Urban Studies* (1984) 21 i 41–51.
7 Mabin A. S. 'Labour, Capital, Class Struggle and the Origins of Residential Segregation in Kimberley, 1880–920' *Journal of Historical Geography* (1986) 12 i 4–26.
8 Torr L. 'The Founding of Lamontville' *South African Geographical Journal (1987) 69 i 31–46.*
9 Mabin (1986).
10 Torr (1987).
11 Davies (1976).
12 Western J. *Outcast Cape Town* (Minneapolis: University of Minnesota Press 1981).
13 Western (1981).
14 Western (1981).
15 Western (1981).
16 Western (1981).
17 Western (1981).
18 Kuper L., Watts H., and Davies R. J. *Durban: a Study in Racial Ecology* (London: J and J Gray 1958).
19 Kuper et al. (1958).
    Purcell J. F. H. *Durban, South Africa: Local Politics in a Plural Society* (Ann Arbor: Michigan University Microfilms International 1974).
20 McCarthy J. J. and Smit D. P. *The History of the Urban Land Use Process, Urban Planning and Urban Social Movements in South Africa*, research report to the Human Science Research Council (Pretoria 1988).
21 Lupton M. 'Class Struggle Around the Built Environment in Johannesburg's Coloured Areas: a Study in the Formation of Consciousness', unpublished M.Sc. thesis (Johannesburg: University of the Witwatersrand, Department of Geography and Environmental Studies 1990).
    Mandy N. *A City Divided: Johannesburg and Soweto* (New York: St Martin 1984).
    Mather C. 'Residential Segregation and Johannesburg's "Locations in the Sky"' (1987) 69 ii 119–28.
    Parnell S. 'Racial Segregation in Johannesburg: the Slums Act, 1934–1939' *South African Geographical Journal* (1988) 70 ii 112–26.
    Smit D. P. 'The Political Economy of Urban and Regional Planning in South Africa 1900–1988: Towards Theory to Guide Progressive Practice', unpublished Ph.D. thesis (Durban: University of Natal 1989).

22 Bonner P., Hofmeyer I., James D., and Lodge T. *Holding Their Ground: Class Locality and Culture in 19th and 20th Century South Africa* (Johannesburg: Witwatersrand University Press 1989).

23 Lodge T. *Black Politics in South Africa Since 1945* (Johannesburg: Ravan Press 1983).

24 Lodge (1983).

25 Lodge (1983).

26 Lodge (1983).

27 Stadler A. W. 'Birds in the Cornfields: Squatter Movements in Johannesburg 1944–1947' (ed.) Bozzoli B. *Labour, Townships and Protest* (Johannesburg: Ravan Press 1978).
    Stadler A. W. 'A Long Way to Walk: Bus Boycotts in Alexandria 1940–1945' (ed.) Bonner P. *Working Papers in Southern African Studies* (Johannesburg: Ravan Press 1981) 2.

28 Dauskardt R. P. A. 'Local State, Segregation and Transport Provision: the Atteridgeville Bus Boycott, 1947' *South African Geographical Journal* (1989) 71 ii 109–15.
    McCarthy J. J. and Swilling M. 'South Africa's Emerging Politics of Bus Transportation' *Political Geography Quarterly* (1985) 4 iii 235–49.

29 Parnell (1988).

30 Parnell (1988) 123–4.

31 Swanson M. 'Reflections on the Urban History of South Africa' (ed.) Watts H. *Focus on Cities* (Durban: University of Natal, Institute for Social and Economic Research 1970).

32 McCarthy and Smit (1988).

33 McCarthy and Smit (1988).

34 Western (1981).

35 McCarthy J. J. and Smit D. P. *South African City: Theory in Analysis and Planning* (Cape Town: Juta 1984).
    McCarthy and Smit (1988).

36 Maasdorp G. and Humphries A. S. B. *From Shantytown to Township* (Cape Town: Juta 1975).
    Maasdorp G. and Pillary N. *Indian Relocation and Racial Segregation* (Durban: University of Natal, Department of Economics 1977).
    Western (1981).

37 Kuper et al. (1958).

38 Durban Housing Survey *Durban Housing Survey* (Pietermaritzburg: University of Natal Press 1952).

39 UF *Tackling Group Areas Policy* (Johannesburg: UF 1990).

40 Davies R. J. and McCarthy J. J. *Residential Growth in the Durban-Pietermaritzburg Planning Region* (Pietermaritzburg: Town and Regional Planning Commission 1985).

41 Lemon (1990).
    UF (1990).

42 Bernstein A. 'Free Settlement or Free Cities?' (eds.) Bernstein A. and McCarthy J. 'Opening the Cities: Comparative Perspectives on Desegregation' *Indicator SA* (Durban: University of Natal 1990).
    Schlemmer L. and Stack L. 'Black, White and Shades of Grey' (Johannesburg: University of the Witwatersrand, Centre for Policy Studies 1989).

43 Smit (1989).

44 Smit (1989).

45 Heymans C. and Tlotemeyer G. *Government by the People* (Cape Town: Juta 1988).

46 I am indebted for this observation to Mike Sutcliffe, who is Associate Professor of Town and Regional Planning at the University of Natal, Durban, and a southern Natal ANC executive committee member.

17 One-city initiatives

Doreen Atkinson[1]

There is no strong tradition of city-based politics in South Africa. National political issues since 1910 have concerned the central structures of government, and the ethnic ownership of the state. Until the mid-1980s, city residents were too concerned with their identity within nationwide movements to give their identity as city-dwellers much thought.

In the latter half of the 1980s, two extraordinary things happened that require explanation. The first phenomenon was a series of local urban initiatives, intended to restructure the urban political order on a non-racial basis. The second remarkable fact was that none of these initiatives were successful in producing a lasting negotiated settlement between African leaders and the local white establishment in the cities. The first phenomenon is a triumph for human creativity and innovation in a culture of governmental centralization, and the second is a consequence of the pervasive ramifications of precisely these problems of centralization and polarization. It is a tragic political irony that these problems have engendered sufficient local support to make local negotiation processes possible, but have created sufficient obstacles to render effective settlements difficult to attain.

This chapter will explore the roots of this irony, and the ways in which it has played itself out in several different communities.

The problem of political synchronization

Since 1985, different kinds of city initiatives have taken place in Cape Town, Port Elizabeth, East London, Port Alfred, Swellendam, Soweto, Sandton, and Pietermaritzburg. These involved various combinations of local white, African, and coloured leaders, belonging to a wide variety of interest groups and political traditions. These initiatives have encompassed many forms of political action, ranging from boycotts and popular mobilization to negotiations, petitions, and shuttle diplomacy. They have all had broad goals of redesigning local government on a non-racial basis, and redrawing municipal jurisdictions to include all racial groups within a single municipality. These initiatives were remarkable, given the pervasiveness of racial divisions, the institutional separation between different race groups, the underlying class divisions, the militaristic paranoia of the central government, and the historic lack of meaningful city-wide solidarity in South Africa.

Since 1910, three main policies have had the effect of dismembering the city. First, the strict application of the Stallard Doctrine of 1922 prevented wealthier white urban communities from subsidizing black townships, with the result that wealth differentials grew even more stark. While white communities increasingly enjoyed social mobility and middle-class respectability, African townships declined into poverty-stricken slums or unattractive monotonous housing estates. Producing an overarching city loyalty in such conditions of inequality and diversity of experience would be a hazardous task in any country. In South Africa, where class and race boundaries overlap significantly, such an endeavour will require extraordinary political ingenuity.

Second, the Group Areas Act further insulated the different races and classes from each other. It became normal for whites to live in neighbourhoods that were exclusively white (except for the ever-present black domestics, gardeners, and other menials). At the time of writing, the imminent abolition of the Group Areas Act is viewed with anxiety and alarm by whites. The prospect of a mixed neighbourhood is experienced by whites as a breath-taking step into the unknown, especially because they intuitively associate African residential areas with poverty and crime. The principle of Group Areas has reinforced class divisions, and has insulated whites in modern urban enclaves, untouched by the urban slums and squatter settlements on the peripheries of the city.

The third step was the introduction of the Administration Boards in 1971. Until then, the African communities were administered by the white local authorities, on behalf of the Department of Bantu Affairs. There were wide disparities between the administrative styles of the white local authorities, ranging from fairly benign to relatively authoritarian. The municipalities generally treated the 'locations' with a combination of benign neglect, severity, and paternalism. For example, local officials often subsidized the 'Native Revenue Account' from municipal funds. Furthermore, despite the unambiguously unequal relationship between white and Africans, longstanding contact and familiarity tended to produce a fragile sense of belonging to the same city.

The Administration Boards removed the African communities from the jurisdiction of white local authorities, and incorporated them into highly authoritarian, regional, white-staffed bureaucratic empires. In effect, an institutional 'Berlin Wall' had descended on towns and cities, so that Africans' geographical proximity to the white city became dissociated from the white patterns of administration, political participation, and urban identity. Africans were *in* the city, but they were not *of* the city. There was no institutional channel for political or administrative contact between local Africans and whites. This division was reinforced by the creation of Africans Local Authorities (BLAs) whose councillors had a strong material interest in maintaining a separate institutional power-base.

It was precisely the ruthless totalitarianism of the Administration Boards that engendered its opposite — the development of militant African civic associations, unambiguously local in character, who initially defined the urban area as a site of struggle, and who subsequently began to postulate the city as the prize to be won. It can be said that the Administration Boards had produced the 'comrades'.

After 1983, the civic associations directed much of their energy against the Administration Boards and other government departments. By means of rent boycotts, education boycotts, and attacks on black councillors, the civic associations challenged the central state. These methods were sufficiently dramatic to signal to neighbouring white communities that something was horribly amiss in the townships. In the eastern Cape, it was the consumer boycotts that jolted the white business establishment and city councils into action, and in the Transvaal, it was the rent boycott that brought the provincial administration into negotiations. The political agendas of the civic associations penetrated right into white institutions for the first time. Needless to say, very few white élites were prepared for this.

The subsequent history of local initiatives was characterized by extraordinary diversity. When white city councillors were confronted by the alarming results of urban apartheid, they found that there were no public institutions in existence which could deal either with the issues raised by the black civic organizations, or with the methods they used. There was no precedent for dealing with the widespread and dangerously effective African mobilization after 1985. This meant that individual initiative and creativity inevitably played a very big role.

On the whole, African mobilization did not find a sympathetic response from whites. It required a councillor, municipal official, or businessperson with unusual courage and imagination to risk making contact with the unknown menace on the other side of the fence. While the security forces battled to subdue 'unrest' using the time-honoured methods of repression, local white civilians in certain towns began to consider the townships in a new way. An unprecedented concern for African living conditions, combined with a new calculation of material interests, propelled some white leaders to make contact with 'radical' African leaders in their communities. And it required black activists with a keen sense of opportunity and strategy to respond positively.

One of the first local negotiations took place in Port Alfred in 1985; then followed East London and Port Elizabeth in 1986, before the declaration of the state of emergency. In other cities, the future of the urban political order was also put on the agenda. Cape Town, Pietermaritzburg, Grahamstown, Swellendam, and Sandton all addressed the issue in different ways. Given the depth and complexity of the problem of urban apartheid, and the many ways in which it can be perceived, it was inevitable that there would be a wide variety of types of city initiatives.

The actors within these initiatives were subjected to a range of contradictory pressures. African organizations and white establishments had to respond to one another in new and untested ways. The central government and the Development Boards were unambiguously hostile to white municipalities' 'interference' in black townships, causing great anxiety among some white councillors and officials. Other actors, such as the Security Police, often intervened unexpectedly, producing confusion and setting into motion disorienting new ripple-effects.

Furthermore, because local white and African leaders always have to respond to different dynamics in their respective constituencies, it has been difficult to reach an historical moment when they have sufficient overlapping goals and shared perceptions to enable a negotiated agreement on the future of the city to be reached. Civic associations are constantly torn between local and national priorities; municipal elections can remove key councillors and produce a realignment of party-political positions; and the content of African demands can shift over time. In addition, institutions and organizations often contain within themselves different factions who interpret events and problems differently, and cause ambiguous signals to be sent to allies and opponents alike.

It is the lack of appropriate and shared institutions and procedures to deal with urban restructuring that has, thus far, prevented a synchronization of the agendas, priorities, and perceptions of African and white leaders within a single city. Not only are there no generally legitimate institutions for governing the cities, but there is also little agreement on the procedures required to establish such institutions. The political order, the economic structures, and the social fabric of South African cities have to be remedied. This is a task of extraordinary complexity, especially since the respective urban visions of the participants in local initiatives are often vague and even contradictory. Local actors are groping in the dark, as they seek to conceptualize and implement a satisfactory urban order.

This chapter will consider four types or urban initiatives, before returning to the question of defining an appropriate vision of the city.

Cape Town

In Cape Town, the main protagonist for municipal reforms has always been the city council itself. Of all cities in South Africa, Cape Town's council has the longest tradition of opposition to segregation, and is unique in that its position was not the result of direct African political pressure. It has always objected to the removal of coloureds from the municipal voters' roll. Its report to the Theron Commission in 1974 showed that the disruption of communities produces hostility to the council[2] which has to act as agent for the government. The city council always opposed the Coloured Management Committee system because it was associated in the minds of the people with the denial of civic rights. The Bloomberg Committee argued for the amendment of the municipal ordinance in such a way that all residents of Cape Town could vote.[3]

Yet the city council's standpoint has always been viewed with scepticism by African and coloured opposition movements in the Peninsula. Cape Town's Charterist organizations, as well as the strong Unity Movement presence, have always refused to form political alliances with elements of the white establishment. The council's 'Call for Dialogue' in 1985 received no response from extra-parliamentary constituencies. In 1986, the council employed Dr van Zyl Slabbert as facilitator to bring about a 'Peace Conference', but he was told by community organizations that the national political climate was too unfavourable for such a venture, especially due to the state of emergency.

Since 1988, the council has embarked on another initiative, called 'Goals for Cape Town'. It is intended to design an appropriate negotiating process around Cape Town's future, and only includes the official municipal area.[4] Key stakeholders in the city were identified, and organizations representing them were approached by means of a delicate and unpublicized process of shuttle diplomacy, to hear their views on the future of Cape Town. The council approached, among others, the business sector, political parties, extra-parliamentary groups, churches, the media, trade unions, and women's organizations. It is significant that the white establishment in Cape Town realized that the initiative depended on the participation of extra-parliamentary organizations for its success.

These organizations still saw many difficulties with the 'Goals for Cape Town' idea, because they felt that urban issues were not part of their national political agenda, and that the city council still had to remedy too many grievances before it would be taken seriously.

It is clear that the council and the community organizations do not, as yet, have sufficient common ground for negotiations about the city. However, in 1990, the council's longstanding interest in the issue was gradually being reciprocated, although there are significant differences in the visions of the city. To the extent that they are interested in urban issues, civic associations are advocating metropolitan non-racial local communities across municipal jurisdictions. This would be a 'one city' in the most inclusive sense of the term.[5]

This is not quite what the council envisages. It advocates, at most, the extension of the urban franchise to the whole municipality (thereby including the coloured areas). It may also consider including the townships of Nyanga, Langa, and Guguletu. It would be difficult to persuade the council of the viability of a metropolitan 'one city'. The financial burden of many poor townships, as well as the political intransigence of conservative white local authorities in the Peninsula, would make the council reluctant to envisage such a single metropolitan city government. While both the city council and the civic organizations have at least some interest in the 'one-city' concept, they give it quite different content. It is extraordinary that the most progressive city council has made so little progress in attracting the interest of opposition movements to negotiate about the urban order.

Port Alfred and East London

Unlike Cape Town, these councils were relatively conservative and apolitical until the white communities were jolted by the consumer boycotts of 1985–6. The white establishment had presumably been aware of poverty in the townships, but in both towns, a legacy of municipality-Administration Board hostility had prevented any involvement in township affairs.[6] Ironically, this hostility provided some common ground between the councils and the civic associations.

The subsequent negotiation processes were characterized by several unusual and innovative leaders. Men such as Gugile Nkwinti of the Port Alfred Residents' Civic Organization (PARCO) and Port Alfred councillor Dave Hanson, and Donald Ntintili of the Duncan Village Residents' Civic Association (DVRA) and East London councillors Donald Card and Gwyn Bassingthwaite, did accept each other's bona fides. In Port Alfred in June 1985, and in East London in December 1985, the respective white councils took the unprecedented step of inviting African leaders to a meeting to discuss grievances. There were several points of agreement between the councils and the civic associations:
- they objected to the activities and the existence of the Development Boards;
- they respected each other's economic and political power;
- they agreed on the principle of a single municipality (although not necessarily non-racial local government) in their respective towns; and most importantly

- the councils recognized the civic associations as the legitimate representatives of their black communities.[7]

In Port Alfred, two additional factors contributed to the uniqueness of the subsequent negotiations. First, there was extensive participation by the white business sector, which saw African prosperity and individual liberties as part and parcel of an economic revival in the town.[8] In addition, the Development Board supported the negotiations and made information available to the participants.[9] The board eventually reconciled itself to a municipality-controlled upgrading of the township, although it envisaged that the board would be the funding conduit.

Both negotiation processes were strengthened by interim successes. By the end of 1985, the Port Alfred negotiations had achieved co-operation between town and township on the spending of unemployment relief funds,[10] and a joint committee was established to plan the upgrading of the township.[11] In June 1986, the East London City Council and the DVRA agreed that the council would use its technical team to build 150 houses in Duncan Village, and the council also agreed to meet with the defence force to discuss the behaviour of troops in the townships.[12] It is significant that the respective civic associations turned to the white councils as a possible ally against the Development Board and the security forces. In both townships, there seemed to be a nostalgic memory of the pre-1971 period, when the townships were administered (by no means democratically) by the white municipalities. In comparison with the neglect, arrogance, and authoritarianism of the Administration Boards, the previous era seemed to represent a more benign order.[13]

Another factor which facilitated negotiations was the moderate demands of the civic associations. Their immediate priorities were an urgent improvement in living standards, and relief from the excesses of the Security Police and army troops. Unlike the Cape Town civic associations, PARCO and the DVRA wanted to put themselves under the wing of the white municipalities, as protection against the Development Board and the Security Police. Although the civics demanded a united municipality, they did not explicitly address the political question of a future non-racial local government. The mere involvement of the white municipalities in the affairs of the township was seen as such as a direct contravention of central government policy, that a single municipality would have been a significant victory. Political non-racialism was not as yet brought on to the agenda. This meant that local white leaders were not really pushed further than their political consciousness could allow, and thus their interest in negotiations was sustained.

Yet these fragile negotiations could not survive the strain caused by the broader political context. This had the effect of simultaneously undermining whites' courage to continue with negotiations, while intensifying the African leaders' frustration with the lack of progress. Unlike Port Alfred, East London's BLA clung tenaciously to power, backed by the Development Board. As time wore on, the city council became more and more aware of the risks it was taking by intervening in the jurisdiction of the board. Simultaneously, the DVRA became even more sceptical about the central government's intentions[14] and consequently the prospects of successful negotiations.

Other government agencies were even more intransigent. The Port Alfred City Council's letters to the Department of Constitutional Development requesting permission to administer the township, were met by bland reiterations of the government's BLA policy.[15] Events in East London were more dramatic: a council delegation to the Minister of Constitutional Development and Planning on 31 July 1986 was scolded for its audacity to question government policy, and sent home with a warning not to negotiate with radical organizations.[16] The government at that time still intended removing Duncan Village to the Ciskei.

In addition, the wild card in local politics was the Security Police. In both Port Alfred and East London, they constantly harassed the civic associations,[17] causing frustrating delays and awakening suspicion between the negotiation participants. The prospect of being detained contributed to African leaders' unwillingness to attend meetings with white councillors, and continued harassment caused suspicion. The state of emergency of June 1986 effectively removed the African leadership, and negotiations ended soon after in both towns.

Yet even the negotiations themselves were fraught with tension. In each case, the difficulties of local negotiations in a very centralized political system became evident. When it became clear that neither white local authority would be allowed to administer 'its own' township, it created confusion among participants about the future role of the city councils. In Port Alfred, the council found itself becoming an increasingly frustrated 'messenger boy'[18] between PARCO and the Development Board, as the latter remained the real source of legal and financial power. In East London, the knowledge that it was acting 'illegally' caused divisions on the council.[19] The mid-1980s were the heyday of militaristic centralization in South Africa, and city councillors were frail allies for African organizations. By July 1986, the brief moment of political synchronization between town and township had passed.

In both towns, no further negotiations took place, and the emergency ended. The business sector, in the meantime, had formed a strategic planning initiative, called 'East London 2001',[20] which was tentatively interested in negotiations about local government. The local ANC branch in 1990 began consolidating community organizations in a campaign for one non-racial, democratic local authority in East London, as well as the large Ciskei township of Mdantsane.[21] Its demands are much more extensive, both in political content and geographical boundaries, than those of the old DVRA in 1986. The council (largely new councillors after the 1988 municipal elections) has shown an interest in holding a non-racial, democratic forum, where the future of local government could be discussed. The mayor has advocated a single council, representing all ratepayers;[22] but it is unlikely that he envisaged the inclusion of Mdantsane. He was also anxious about the effects of a single local authority on a not very affluent white rates base.

In late 1990 the local political situation in East London seemed fluid and full of promise. There continues to be much interest in local government issues, but it is unlikely that the ANC's political agenda will easily be synchronized with the city council's political consciousness.

Pietermaritzburg

Since 1984, Pietermaritzburg has attempted an ambitious restructuring of the city's administrative and planning agencies. This project was the brainchild of the then City Engineer, Graham Atkinson. In October 1986, the concept of 'strategic planning' was introduced to the city council, which entailed the inclusion of a wide variety of interest groups in the planning process. Action groups, covering different issue areas, were formed, backed by the technical assistance and information resources of the City Engineer's Department.

The action groups developed an extraordinary range of objectives. For example, the 'housing' group considered acquisition of land, minimizing housing regulations, reviewing the standards for infrastructure, and self-help housing. The other groups were the 'employment' group, 'city finances', 'quality of life', and 'human relations'. While all these groups showed remarkable ingenuity in addressing difficult problems, it is the last one which confronted the real controversial issues of local government.

One of its main objectives was to promote 'appropriate representation on local government structures'. In February 1987, the group suggested holding a Greater Pietermaritzburg Conference[23] to discuss the nature of a single metropolitan council for the Greater Pietermaritzburg metropolitan area. The conference would be non-racial and widely representative, with an open agenda.

The conference never materialized because the organizers had not fully confronted the complexities of the political environment. First, 'Pietermaritzburg 2000' had largely drawn business and other establishment white leaders, thus offending the more populist style and anti-capitalist reservations of the UDF leaders in the township. The prospect of business funding of the entire strategic planning initiative further strengthened the ties between local government and business. UDF leaders were also suspicious of the council's motives, as well as the participation of the NPA and the discredited LACs in 'Pietermaritzburg 2000'.[24] While the organizers certainly wanted to include township leaders, their open invitation was not sufficient to attract interest. It would have required a long and delicate process of negotiation about negotiations, the examination of preconditions, the identification of participants, and the construction of an appropriate agenda, to have convinced the township leaders of the bona fides of the council. It is ironic that the Cape Town City Council's more politically sensitive methods and in-depth consultation about the negotiation process itself (hitherto fruitless in Cape Town) would probably have matched the demands and expectations of the Pietermaritzburg left. The synchronization of political processes between town and township remains a problematic endeavour.

Soweto

The impressive Soweto negotiation process is very different from the other initiatives, for it is the only one which has run its full course and achieved a negotiated agreement. However, its very success indicates the numerous preconditions that were required. The constellation of relevant political actors in urban politics is so complex that the recognition of the pre-eminence of some of them, and their subsequent alignment through a process of negotiations, simply cannot be taken for granted. Like East London and Port Alfred, the Soweto negotiations grew out of the protest politics after 1983. The Soweto rent boycott was part of a larger country-wide rent boycott movement since September 1984. The Soweto Civic Association (SCA) demanded that all councillors resign; that pensioners should not pay rent; that services be improved in the townships; that soldiers leave the townships; and that rents be lowered to affordable levels. These were later expanded to include demands to lift the state of emergency.[25]

The SCA was an unusually inclusive organization, encompassing Pan-Africanist, Black Consciousness, and ANC support. These groupings were united by 'civic problems', i.e. the problems of everyday urban living. As Swilling and Shubane note: 'The logic of the national struggle for state power, therefore, was not simplistically replicated at this level.'[26] This characteristic contributed greatly to the SCA's success in negotiating an urban transition — compare, for example, Cape Town's highly fragmented opposition movements, and the Inkatha-ANC tension in Natal.

The SCA placed a high value on local democracy and the need for legitimate local state structures. Its emphasis on the problems of daily life meant that deep-seated hostilities could be reduced, at least for the purposes of negotiation, to technical questions of service provision. Leadership tended to be drawn from older people, so that street committee meetings could be run in measured and consistent ways. The SCA also had an impressive array of resources, including an advice office, full-time employees, office infrastructure, and technical support. This helped to allay the usual fears of co-optation by white officialdom.

The SCA's mass base had two other important implications. First, the leaders were obliged to deliver victories. They could no longer rely on abstract promises of fundamental change at some point in the distant future. Secondly, the assurance of loyal support made tactical flexibility possible.

In December 1988, the SCA formed the Soweto People's Delegation (SPD) to negotiate an end to the rent boycott. The composition of the SPD was decided from a list of names that the SCA branches had been requested to discuss. The formation of the SPD also helped to remove the anxieties of certain supporters, since failure at negotiations would not affect the prestige of the SCA. The Soweto negotiations were crucially affected by the popularity of the Soweto City Council (SCC) among the business community, as well as squatters. The council had made land available for squatters in return for political support. This popularity encouraged the council to see itself as an independent political actor, and it unilaterally broke its rent agreement with the TPA in April 1989. By the end of 1989, both the TPA and Eskom were ready to meet the SPD and to bypass the SCC. Once again, a typical difficulty in local negotiations had been bypassed — in the absence of a pliable BLA, the authorities were free to look around for more effective and trustworthy negotiation partners.

The pioneering talks between the SPD and Eskom lasted about four months. The SPD used the opportunity to introduce revolutionary concepts in urban management, such as the non-racial and non-profit provision of services, and that state provision of electricity be replaced by community control, instead of private enterprise. It was also agreed that the Johannesburg and Soweto electricity systems should be linked. The SPD and Eskom issued a joint policy document on the parameters of future electricity supply policy.

The TPA was ready to enter negotiations by October 1989. Again, its involvement took place because of several important environmental preconditions: the financial crisis in Soweto; the effects of De Klerk's liberalization programme; the decline of influence of the 'securocrats'; the obvious ineptitude and illegitimacy of the SCC; the influence of crucial, innovative individuals within the TPA; and the intervention of the British and American embassies. It was also clear that the SCC had failed to secure payments from the community.

After several months of formal information exchanges between the TPA and the SPD, the TPA commissioned the Development Bank of Southern Africa to consider Soweto's difficulties. The Brand Report conceded some important principles: that Soweto should never have been created as a separate city; that Soweto could never have an autonomous economic base; and that a separate administration was too costly. However, the report stopped short of proposing that Soweto and Johannesburg share a single tax base and local government. Although the limitations of the bank's approach prevented further co-operation with the SPD, its report was crucial in articulating a new reformist vision of the city. In this way, it prepared the ground for the agreement of August 1990.

Yet another event took place, which promoted negotiations on Soweto's future. In April 1990, the Democratic Party took over the erstwhile NP-controlled Johannesburg City Council (JCC). The new chairperson of the management committee called for the 'reunification of the city', and organized a special committee to consider appropriate options for the Central Witwatersrand region. He initiated contact with the SPD.

On 30 August 1990, an agreement was reached between the SPD and TPA that an all-party metropolitan forum be established to supervise the transition to a new local government system. The JCC and SPD were key participants.

During 1990, two events took place to equalize the power balance between the SPD and the TPA, and to increase the TPA's willingness to negotiate. First, in May, the Minister of Provincial Affairs, Hernus Kriel, released an important report on possible local government options. He envisaged, *inter alia*, that non-racial local governments with common tax bases could be created, via a process of local-level negotiation. This strengthened the demands of civics everywhere that the apartheid city be dismantled. Second, the rent boycott in the Transvaal increased in intensity as a result of the lifting of restrictions on civic associations, and the TPA threatened to end bridging finance to townships. This meant that services would have to be cut off. Solving the rent boycott now became top priority.

In July 1990, the SPD and a top-level delegation of the TPA met in Johannesburg. A large delegation from the SCC attended the meeting. Both sides had formidable research and technical back-up; both sides could effectively employ sanctions (a boycott versus the cutting of services); and both sides could gain from an agreement. Both parties agreed that the arrears problem should be linked to a long-term programme to dismantle the apartheid city and create a new one. A Joint Technical Committee was established to work out how this principle should be pursued.

After several deadlocks, the parties agreed that an interim rental structure should be implemented, until an entirely new system is worked out. The TPA would write off all the arrears (R515 million) on condition it was directly tied to the acceptance and implementation of the rest of the agreement. There were also two long-term provisions: the establishment of a Metropolitan Chamber with representatives from local authorities and civic associations in the whole metropolitan region, and the creation of the Greater Soweto People's Fund, to raise capital for development in Soweto. The Greater

Soweto Accord was signed on 24 September, after cabinet approval and after the SPD received a mandate from the community.

Reconciling fractured visions of the urban local order

The announcement by Kriel in May 1990 that local communities could choose their own 'local option' has shifted the political terrain completely. If the government is to be believed, it will no longer be an obstacle to local negotiations. While this improves the prospects of local negotiations considerably, it will direct people's attention to another range of thorny political questions. No longer will civic associations and white local authorities be able to find common ground simply because of their shared hostility to central government policies; no longer can either conservative white communities or radical black organizations argue that central government intransigence makes the restructuring of local government premature.

Case studies show that the diversity of responses to urban problems, and the consequent difficulties of synchronization of agendas, may haunt city politics for a long time to come. The cities are simply too fragmented and polarized in too many ways for there to be any 'normal' or 'typical' way to proceed with restructuring. The urban agenda is radically unclear, and will have many unforeseen consequences. The rest of the chapter will outline only four aspects of the restructuring process which will be complicated by these difficulties.

The process of negotiation

What should the process of urban negotiation be? Should each town have a constituent assembly to draft its institutions? Who should be present? How should political influence be weighted? It is quite possible that different constituencies will have different ideas about an appropriate process of local government restructuring, ranging from a willingness to negotiate, to a dogmatic desire for total victory. Even if all (or most) parties in a city are prepared to negotiate, they may not be prepared at the same time — by the time one organization has prepared its constituency for negotiations, events within other constituencies may have taken a different direction.

Reaching agreements

Second, although there is by now some experience of urban negotiations in certain cities, there is very little experience of actually reaching agreement. South African interest groups are not accustomed to the anxieties of deciding when to compromise on what, and how to explain to their followers why their opponents and enemies still seem to be flourishing the very next day after signing an agreement. There is very little tradition in South Africa of win-win solutions, where victory does not imply the capitulation of the other side. So far, African organizations have been able to demand victory without seriously expecting to get it (the phenomenon of the dog who caught the bus), and white élites have been able to discuss issues with African leaders without having to deliver or implement a commitment to genuine political non-racialism.

It is also quite possible that, as the bogey of the central government retreats from the urban stage, the local white establishment will bear the brunt of African grievances. Ironically, it is also possible that whatever willingness white élites evince to remedy these grievances, may itself be cause for suspicion: 'What are whites' hidden agendas or concealed power resources, if they are so willing to meet our demands?'

The nature of the urban political order

At this stage, it is totally unclear which parts of the old urban order will have to be tolerated in the new. Political actors hold very different, and largely unexamined, notions about the most just urban order, ranging from total (utopian) restructuring of urban society, to a mere tolerance of non-racialism alongside a basically conservative life-style. It is likely that concealed but fundamental philosophical differences between relatively wealthy white communities and militant, deprived townships are likely to emerge.

For the first time, the future political ethos of the cities will be on the agenda. For example:

- Jurisdictional questions will influence conceptions about the nature of the urban community, e.g. is Mdantsane part of East London? Is Crossroads part of Cape Town? How will the presence of thousands of African working-class or traditionalist residents affect the political ethos of the city?
- What is the nature of the urban political community? Should all residents have the vote, or only ratepayers? Should voters be organized collectively, as in street committees, or should the city foster an individualistic liberal political ethos?
- What should the nature of urban administration be? To what

extent could and should urban officialdom encourage participatory planning?

- What kinds of redistribution are appropriate and feasible? Can the white sector carry the financial load of underdeveloped townships? If central government aid is required, how will it affect central-local power relations? What concessions will need to be made by wealthy white sectors to prevent them from leaving the city or from emigrating?
- What should be done about conservative white towns? What should be done about recalcitrant BLAs? Should they be coerced into a new urban order?

The nature of the actors

Negotiations in future will be complicated by the emergence of new actors and interest groups, and by internal changes within existing organizations. New dynamics within each community will be set in motion. In fact, the cultural and class dimensions of urban segregation may only now really become evident. New alliances may assist negotiations, or may undermine them. African organizations will have to decide how they will respond to business interests: does their shared identity as residents of the same city outweigh their different class interests? How should African organizations respond to the inevitable growth of class differences within their own ranks, especially between residents of the 'formal' city and those in the informal settlements? If participatory planning is a good thing, how will it affect the egalitarian nature of civic associations? Will their leadership have to acquire technicist skills? Will white and African residents of the same neighbourhood develop shared political interests? How will white élites respond to right-wing ratepayer associations and interest groups?

In sum, the process of negotiations, the reaching of agreements, latent normative differences, and the reconstitution of political actors mean that the future of urban politics is radically uncertain. A generation of political leaders, schooled in a polarized and centralized political culture, will have to fly in the face of all their political instincts, if a consensual urban order is to be reached. There is a great need for neutral third parties (universities, mediation agencies, and research institutes) to provide safe forums for discussion, as a possible precursor to eventual negotiations.

City issues are attracting widespread interest at present, and leaders are showing an extraordinary willingness to discuss issues creatively. This is highly encouraging, especially given the extreme fragmentation of our cities. However, it will be necessary to create some viable channels of contact between the leaders of the various communities within each city, to harness the diversity of local endeavours and thereby work towards synchronizing urban political agendas.

Notes

1 The author gratefully acknowledges the assistance of the Jill Nattrass Rotating Research Fellowship provided by the Centre for Social and Development Studies at the University of Natal (Durban).

2 City of Cape Town *Report to the Commission of Enquiry into Matters Relating to the Coloured Population Group* (February 1974) 27.

3 City of Cape Town, Bloomberg Committees *The Municipal Franchise* (July 1981) 10–11.

4 Zille H. 'City Futures Conference', address (Johannesburg: University of the Witwatersrand 5–6 June 1990).

5 Members of the Mass Democratic Movement 'City Futures Conference', address (Johannesburg: University of the Witwatersrand, Centre for Policy Studies 5–6 June 1990).

6 From an interview with a Development Board official (Port Alfred: 1 December 1987).

7 For example, East London City Council minutes (27 February 1986).

8 Chamber of Commerce memorandum (October 1985).

9 Interview with a Development Board official (December 1987).

10 Council minutes, and correspondence between the town council and the Regional Development Advisory Committee (15 July 1985).

11 Council minutes (18 November 1985).

12 Council minutes.

13 Interview with a DVRA member (10 February 1988); *The Weekly Mail* 29 November 1986.

14 Council minutes.

15 Correspondence between the town clerk and the Department of Constitutional Development Planning (23 January 1986, 7 March 1986, and 2 April 1986).

16 Council minutes (31 July 1986).

17 De Villiers M. 'Detaining the Peacemakers' *Sash* (August 1987) 40.

18 Minutes, Joint Working Committee (13 March 1986).

19 *The Daily Dispatch* 4 April 1986, 23 April 1986, 26 April 1986.

20 Bassingthwaite G., unpublished paper (Cape Town: University of Cape Town 1989).

21 Pobana M. 'City Futures Conference', address (Johannesburg: University of the Witwatersrand 5–6 June 1990).

22 Badenhorst M. J. 'City Futures Conference', address (Johannesburg: University of the Witwatersrand 5–6 June 1990).

23 *The Natal Witness* 11 February 1987.

24 Irvine D., address at a Centre for Policy Studies seminar (Johannesburg: University of the Witwatersrand 8 July 1988).

25 The analysis of the Soweto negotiations is based on Swilling M. and Shubane K. 'Negotiating Urban Transition: the Soweto Experience' *Transition to Democracy: Policy Perspectives 1991* (Cape Town: Oxford University Press 1990).

26 Swilling and Shubane (1990) 236.

18 Township resistance in the 1980s

Jeremy Seekings[1]

During the 1980s political protest in South Africa's townships, factories, and rural areas propelled the state towards unprecedented policy reforms. Township protests not only provided an impetus to limited constitutional and national political change, but were also a major factor underlying the extensive reforms of urban policy examined elsewhere in this volume. Growing numbers of state officials correctly recognized that such policy reforms were necessary to remove or diminish key grievances and hence defuse widespread discontent. This chapter examines township resistance in the 1980s, assessing the factors underlying protest and conflict, and the ways in which these changed during the course of the decade.

The first section briefly overviews the major events and themes in township politics during the 1980s. The middle section examines the ways in which these have been analysed. Existing general studies tend to emphasize either the structural context of the political economy or national political organization and leadership. Township politics needs to be understood in terms of the combination of these, focusing on the ways in which these were actually experienced by or affected township residents. The third section of this chapter explores how political organization, protest, and conflict at township level were shaped by broader economic and political factors, which imposed pressures and provided opportunities for action. But the section emphasizes the importance of local factors in determining the ways in which these led to resistance and to its form and duration. The paper discusses neither rural struggles nor the labour movement (although the latter played an increasingly important political role in South Africa).

Township politics in the 1980s

Four broad periods stand out in the development of township struggles in the 1980s. These differ primarily in terms of the scale, intensity, and form of protest and confrontation. From 1980 to mid-1984, township protests were generally limited and localized, involving diverse and disparate grievances. From late 1984 through to mid-1986, townships erupted in widespread and intense conflict. The imposition of a nationwide state of emergency in June 1986 ushered in a period of severe state repression that substantially constrained the level and especially form of township protests. During this period violent conflict in Natal and KwaZulu escalated. From early 1989 there was a resurgence in township protests.

Township resistance in the early 1980s was characterized by struggles that were limited and local in terms of both the nature of the motivating grievances and of the organization and leadership involved. The principal grievances underlying protests included rent increases, busfare increases, evictions, influx control, the housing shortage and inadequate township infrastructure, corrupt or unaccountable local township councillors, and conditions in the schools. These gave rise to discrete protests such as bus boycotts, campaigns against rent increases, and short class boycotts, and to broader struggles such as the proliferation of illegal backyard shacks and squatting. In many cases the leadership of these struggles was remarkably conservative: dissident or opposition township councillors, or conservative members of extra-state township civic organizations.[2]

During 1984 these protests were transformed into intense, extended, and bloody confrontations. The single most visible event in 1984 was the Vaal Uprising. Protests against rent increases culminated in a stayaway from work and protest marches on 3 September. The combination of isolated attacks on councillors — who were deemed responsible for the increases — and intolerant and brutal policing transformed a peaceful protest into a violent confrontation in which over 30 people were killed, including four councillors. The Vaal Uprising was, however, just the most visible of a series of escalating protests and confrontations. In early 1984 chronic protests had begun in schools, especially in Pretoria's Atteridgeville township. In mid-1984 there were rent struggles in the northern Orange Free State and East Rand, and school boycotts in these areas and parts of the eastern Cape. These led to violent confrontations from late August.[3]

One factor in these escalating struggles was the increasing national political organization and activity over primarily national and constitutional issues. In 1983 the UDF had been formed as an umbrella body for diverse organizations opposed to the proposed constitution and new urban policy legislation. The UDF was closely, if covertly, linked to the banned ANC, and the UDF's leading affiliates were explicitly 'Charterist' in that they endorsed the Freedom Charter, drawn up by the ANC in 1955 and subsequently seen as a statement of its aims and principles. A number of non-Charterist or anti-Charterist organizations, led by the Azanian People's Organization (AZAPO), formed a rival umbrella organization, the National Forum. In August 1984 the UDF and its affiliates, and to a much lesser extent the National Forum, organized successful boycotts of the elections to the new Indian and coloured houses in the tricameral parliament.[4]

During 1984–6 township resistance intensified and spread across almost the entire country. Among the proliferating forms of protest were rent, consumer and school boycotts, stayaways from work, and direct action against the security forces and symbols of authority. An important factor was state repression, which created an atmosphere which encouraged political violence. Specific incidents often produced reactive violence from residents, most visibly at funerals.[5] The escalation of repression following the confrontations of late August and early September 1984 in the Transvaal was, together with the schools crisis, the major issue underlying a Transvaal regional stayaway in November 1984. This two-day stayaway, probably involving about half a million workers and slightly fewer students,[6] was the first of a series of major protest stayaways. Township resistance also spread around the country. The protests of mid-1984 and late 1984 were largely confined to the Transvaal. Protests began in some townships in the eastern Cape and northern Orange Free State, but really only extended to these areas in early 1985. Protests escalated in the western Cape and Natal in the second half of 1985, and in the northern and eastern Transvaal from late 1985.[7]

During this period discontent and protest were increasingly focused on regional or national, rather than local issues. This provided the basis for two parallel developments. First, it provided a potential popular base for radical political organization. This culminated with the tentative organization of structures of 'people's power', i.e. principally street committees and people's courts which played limited administrative and judicial roles. These were most advanced in parts of the eastern Cape,[8] but were beginning to be developed elsewhere also.[9] Radical township organizations became involved in negotiations with employers and state authorities over a range of issues.[10] Secondly, however, opportunities opened for the proliferation of violent protest over immediate goals, bypassing formal organizational procedures and planning, and stifling debate and the possibilities for negotiation. The so-called 'youth' became prominent in protest. While posing an unprecedented challenge to the security forces, the violent and direct action of the 'youth' was widely regarded with wariness and even opposed by other township residents.[11]

In many townships the protests of the mid-1980s brought residents into common appreciation of and support for each other's concerns. In some townships, however, township residents came into conflict with each other. In the eastern Cape, for example, tension between UDF-aligned 'youth' and trade unionists led to incidents of violent conflict in 1984–5.[12] Reactionary township residents, supported by the police, formed vigilante groups which harassed and killed local radical activists.[13] In the sprawling squatter settlement of Crossroads, outside Cape Town, the 'witdoeke' of Old Crossroads, led by Johnson Ngxobongwana and supported by the police, razed the surrounding camps and violently evicted their residents.[14] In Natal and KwaZulu this period saw the first indications of the growing conflict between Inkatha and non-Inkatha groups.[15]

The imposition of the nationwide state of emergency marked the end of the second period of township politics. The state of emergency involved unprecedented levels of repression. Over 20 000 people were detained in 1986 alone. Political organization was largely paralysed.[16] The security forces were not the only repressive state institution. Students identified as 'comrades' were in many townships systematically excluded from school, and local administrators were reluctant to continue to negotiate with radical township organizations. But repression served to change the form of protests rather than simply suppress them. Attendance remained low at school. Rent boycotts — including from June 1986 in Soweto — continued, and were indeed reinforced by the state's attempts at suppressing them.[17] Trade unions became increasingly involved in political protests, and there was a series of major protest stayaways. The state's response to resistance did not involve repression alone, however. The state embarked on a much publicized selective upgrading of townships which it regarded as particularly volatile.

One crude indicator of the level of conflict is the monthly death toll in political violence. This fell during the second half of 1986 and remained relatively low until September 1987, when it rose massively. Almost as many people died during the first two years of the nationwide state of emergency (that is June 1986 to June 1988) as in the preceding two years of conflict. But the pattern of fatalities during 1986–8 was very different to the earlier period. While most deaths before about March 1986 were the result of security force action, during 1986–8 the overwhelming majority were the result of internecine violence within townships and rural areas. Deaths thus arose, not so much out of protests against the authorities, as of conflict within townships. This change was linked to another, in the geographical incidence of fatalities. While the death toll fell from mid-1986 in most regions, in Natal it rose rapidly.[18] Underlying the terrible death toll in Natal and KwaZulu was the escalating conflict between Inkatha and its opponents, which Kentridge describes as 'an unofficial war'.[19]

Only from early 1989 was there any revival of township organization and overt protest. Even when many detainees were released during 1987–8, township organizations often remained inactive, in part because of divisions between ex-detainees and those who had fled into 'exile' in (especially) Johannesburg, where they secured control of the allocation of resources. In some townships activists' concern to maintain their control of leadership led to violent conflict within organizations.[20] More commonly, however, activists lapsed into chronic, disillusioned inactivity.

The revival of civic protest began with defiance campaigns against social apartheid and the 1989 tricameral elections.[21] The state slowly grew more tolerant, permitting action which it hoped might help resolve the continuing rent boycotts and deepening catastrophe in the Department of Education and Training's schools. The amorphous Mass Democratic Movement (MDM) arose as an umbrella for broadly Charterist organizations, combining the former

UDF with the Congress of South African Trade Unions (COSATU). A plethora of new civic and youth organizations were formed, and existing organizations were imbued with new impetus and direction. The revival embraced townships which had hitherto remained largely unorganized, including many bantustan townships in Bophuthatswana, Ciskei, QwaQwa, and Venda. Consumer and rent boycotts spread, and meetings, demonstrations, and marches were held again. Squatter struggles proliferated with land invasions. Organization and protest were fuelled by the release of ANC leaders and the unbanning of the ANC, together with the South African Communist Party (SACP), and the Pan Africanist Congress (PAC).

The analysis of township politics

The township struggles of the 1980s have generated an extensive and varied literature.[22] Studies have differed according to their authors' ideological biases (that is the identification of the good and bad guys), methodologies (in particular the extent and type of empirical research undertaken), and the questions asked in the analysis. Besides detailed case-studies, two broad approaches predominate in the general explanation of township protests. These can be crudely labelled 'structural' and 'conspiratorial'. The structural approaches tend to focus on the material conditions within which action occurs. Township struggles are, in the cruder versions, 'read off' the structural context of the political economy, with limited consideration of the importance of specifically political factors. Conspiratorial approaches focus on the role of national political organization, and in particular the ANC and UDF. Township struggles are attributed to the machinations of activists (or 'agitators') working within a supposedly close-knit conspiracy.

Structural approaches to township resistance have focused on residents' material grievances and the causes of these. Structuralist and strongly materialist general explanations of political protest blossomed inside and outside South Africa in the early and mid-1980s, and were widely reproduced in sections of the left or alternative media. While there were great variations in astuteness, the common theme was that protest in South Africa was straightforwardly explicable in terms of the political economy. Oppression under apartheid, or exploitation under capitalism, or more often a combination of both, were seen as sufficient explanations of protest. The contradictions within apartheid and/or capitalism 'inevitably' led to overt struggle. This description is something of a caricature, but underlies accounts such as Saul and Gelb.[23]

Case-studies of particular protests explore the structural context in greater detail. Bus boycotts in particular were analysed in terms of the political economy of passenger transport. Studies typically outlined the structural context (state passenger transport policy), indicated the material grievances (rising busfares), and then documented the struggle itself.[24] Protests by the 'youth' have been analysed in terms of broad structural factors such as the extent of unemployment and the inadequacies of the education system.[25] For the most part little attention is paid to organizational issues. Some studies reduce political issues to the stark working-class or petit-bourgeois class character of the struggles. Others, acknowledging the complexity of urban politics, draw on international studies and analyse township resistance in terms of 'urban social movements', i.e. cross-class movements struggling over issues of 'collective consumption' such as housing and transport.[26]

Conspiratorial approaches, in contrast to structural approaches, placed their emphasis on issues of political leadership and downplayed the importance of material grievances arising out of the structural context. The primary source of conspiratorial interpretations of township politics was the state. Rarely did state accounts of township politics involve significant analysis, and it is therefore probably more accurate to refer to state 'narratives'. The key features of state narratives, as repeatedly propounded on SABC news during the 1980s, were that agitators, organizationally or intentionally part of a nationwide conspiracy based around the then banned ANC and SACP, roused numbers of township residents (especially the so-called 'youth') into violent protest.

This interpretation was presented most fully in the state's evidence in court, and was widely reported in the press.[27] National and local political leaders were charged in a series of cases with being party to an ANC-planned national strategy of challenging and subverting state authority, leading to the violent overthrow of the state. The state's evidence generally comprised three broad strands. First, expert witnesses demonstrated that there was an ANC/SACP conspiracy by drawing on ANC and SACP publications in which they called for (at different times) mass popular protest, the formation of township organizations, ungovernability, and the establishment of structures of 'people's power'. Secondly, expert witnesses showed that township 'unrest' occurred similarly across many townships. Thirdly, witnesses gave evidence that the accused were prominently involved in political organization and protest in the areas concerned. The state's argument was broadly that there was a conspiracy, that this explained the coincidence of geographically widespread protest, and that local political leaders (that is the accused) provided the link. Little or no evidence was presented, however, demonstrating any concrete links between the trial accused and either their alleged co-conspirators in other townships, or their co-conspirators in the ANC or SACP. The argument rested on unsubstantiated assertions regarding the intentions or actions of local level actors. There are clear problems with the logic of this analysis.[28]

During the later 1980s growing numbers of state officials recognized the importance of material grievances. The Van der Walt Commission, *de facto* an inquiry into the Vaal Uprising, noted the role of agitators but also recognized that residents had very legitimate grievances concerning local government and living conditions.[29] This shift of emphasis in state interpretations was increasingly reflected in NP rhetoric and policy. Nonetheless, an underlying concern with the importance of national level political leaders remained widespread in state-based circles throughout the 1980s.[30]

The conspiratorial approach, based on an underlying 'leaderist' conception of politics, was not confined to the state. The ANC often subscribed to a similar view in its own propaganda, attributing to itself the key role in the escalation of protest. This view was often shared by sympathetic analysts. Like the state, these conflated the intentions and activities of the ANC or UDF, on the one hand, with local level protest and organization, on the other. The increasing range of contacts between state officials or advisers and ANC/MDM leaders in the late 1980s probably served to reinforce leaderist views on both sides. The release of political prisoners and the unbanning of organizations thus represented in part the belief that the ANC-led conspiracy (embracing the UDF and MDM) needed to be taken on board somehow rather than suppressed. The underlying political analysis had not changed.

The conspiratorial approach pays attention to the issue of political organization and leadership but only, for the most part, at a national level. Even when state officials have recognized the legitimacy of certain material grievances, they have generally dismissed local protest and leadership over these as simply part of the national political struggle. Local or 'low' politics is thus collapsed into the 'high' politics of national organizations, especially the UDF and ANC.

In general, the conspiratorial approach predominated among national political organizations (the state, the then banned national liberation movements), while the structural approach characterized academic perspectives.[31] While the former were directly aware of the importance of choices they made, the latter recognized the constraints and pressures within which choices were made (generally by individuals who remained largely anonymous). Neither approach is adequate on its own, but both comprise elements of the whole picture. Some accounts of protests simply combine both approaches into a shopping-list of factors.[32] While such accounts usefully demonstrate the diversity or multiplicity of protests and their causes, they often fall prey to their own eclecticism. Protests and conflict are not located in an adequate analysis of either the political economy or of national or township politics.

A full account of protests and conflict needs to locate the choices regarding political action made by individuals at the local level — leaders, activists, and other township residents — within the context of constraints, pressures, and opportunities set by both the political economy and the actions of national political organizations. The growing number of case-studies of specific townships, organizations, or forms of protest provides a rich empirical base on which more general explanations can be developed.

Structural context and political organization

The structural context is the best place to begin an exploration of township protest. But township residents did not simply experience apartheid or capitalism as monolithic and overall phenomena. Rather, residents experienced specific features of these, and it was in changes in these features that protest was rooted. The three key features of the political economy which underlay urban protests in the 1980s were economic recession, the system of local government financing, and the system for political representation.

The South African economy slid into a deepening recession from 1981. Certain regions were especially hard hit, including the Vaal Triangle, East Rand, and eastern Cape — that is, where protest and confrontation first escalated in mid-decade. Despite the recession, real wages paid to African workers, and real average household incomes, continued to rise in most areas (the Vaal Triangle was one exception). But there was growing *inequality* in the distribution of household incomes, with the proportion of households with incomes below fixed poverty datum lines rising. Thus, while the recession did not bring general urban impoverishment, it did involve severe hardship for many township residents.[33]

The recession alone did not lead to protest or confrontation. But the second key feature of the political economy, namely the system of local government financing, served to exacerbate the material squeeze on township residents. Central state policy required township administration and development to be largely financed out of revenues raised within the townships, which necessitated repeated rent increases (and the eviction of rent defaulters). Rent increases were particularly severe in the Vaal Triangle — hard hit by the recession — rising over fourfold between 1977 and 1984. The one area where development in the early 1980s was, in practice, subsidized by the central government was Soweto, and rent increases were therefore less controversial than in the Vaal Triangle.[34] Elsewhere, however, the need to finance development through rent increases constrained development. The housing shortage grew and infrastructure remained poor. Protests against rent increases and evictions for arrears were accompanied by a proliferation of backyard shacks and squatting.

Protests against rent increases were central to township politics in the early 1980s, but they were not simply a spasmodic response. The importance of rent increases was bound up with the role of township councillors, and hence the more general issue of political representation. The political system denied township residents avenues through which their grievances could be taken to the central government. Elected township councillors had very limited powers, and were unable to redress residents' principal grievances. Councillors' hands were tied on the issue of rents, for example. Because development was dependent on rent increases, the 'price' of restricting rent increases was no development. Councillors — encouraged by the central state and tempted by the prospect of increased opportunities for corruption — preferred both development and rent increases to neither. The only avenue through which township residents could express their discontent was open protest and demonstration, and support for extra-state civic and political organizations.

The role of councillors in township protests was more complex than simply a failure to communicate residents' grievances. Protests against rents were also a protest against councillors and the changing role they played in township politics. The state's reform of local government between 1977 and 1983 gave township councillors few new powers but greatly extended responsibilities. Councillors were increasingly seen as responsible for a range of unpopular state policies, including rent increases and evictions. Furthermore, councillors were also seen to be using their limited powers to enrich themselves at their supposed constituents' expense. Township residents sought alternative channels through which their grievances could be redressed, turning to dissident or opposition councillors, and increasingly to extra-state civic organizations such as the Soweto Civic Association.[35]

What was the role of national political organizations in this? Most detailed case-studies of township protest have adopted a local focus and ignored national organizations such as the ANC and UDF. Studies of the national organizations themselves provide little discussion of their role or impact at the local level, and unfortunately there has been almost no analysis of the clearly important Congress of South African Students (COSAS, banned in 1985). The existing literature tentatively suggests that the impact of national political organizations in the first half of the 1980s was indirect rather than direct. In large part this was the result of their organizational shortcomings and their tactical weaknesses which arose from their particular priorities. Barrell's study of the ANC's military wing, Umkhonto we Sizwe, touches on the weakness of the ANC's political structures within the country and the constraints that this imposed on its military operations.[36] The UDF was preoccupied during 1983–4 with its campaigns against the tricameral parliament, and was involved in little campaigning or organization-building in African townships. Ironically, national political organizations sometimes had a counterproductive direct effect at the local level. The local strength of civic organizations rested primarily on their campaigning over locally and immediately important grievances, and their appeal diminished when they neglected this. Involvement in national campaigns thus sometimes exacerbated existing organizational weaknesses.[37]

Indirectly, however, national organizations such as the ANC and UDF had a major and growing impact. The main effect in the early 1980s was in terms of the recruitment and interaction of local activists, and the increased linkages of disparate local struggles with each other and with national politics. Charterist ideology became hegemonic among political activists.[38] In 1985–6, the impact of national political organizations in local politics grew. To some extent this was because the UDF and ANC responded positively to the rise in township protest, which had initially concerned local grievances. In 1985 there were major changes in the regional and national leadership of the UDF. Some national and regional leaders sought to broaden township protests by extending campaigns into townships that were hitherto quiet. Consumer boycotts were used in this way, with mixed results.[39]

More importantly, local struggles brought township residents into growing contact with each other and into direct conflict with the repressive state. Activists were therefore increasingly attracted to the ANC and UDF's national critique of and opposition to the state. The so-called township 'youth' were also attracted by the militancy of the ANC, and its calls for insurrection, people's war, liberated zones, ungovernability, and people's power. The importance of national and regional political factors was evident in the development of so-called 'people's power'.[40] Our understanding of the links between the UDF and local level activities remains constrained, however, by the relative lack of research in the regions where the UDF was most coherent (the eastern Cape, and possibly the northern Transvaal), providing a structure within or below which numerous affiliates undertook their activities.

The national political impetus to protest during 1985–6 should not be overstated, however. Local civic dynamics were behind rent and consumer boycotts and 'people's power', sometimes carrying along but at other times stalling, the explicitly political issues. Rent boycotts offered immediate material gains as well as the opportunity to challenge the state.[41] 'People's courts' offered practical ways of settling local disputes, and often drew on pre-existing structures of dispute resolution.[42] Negotiations between civic organizations and state structures reflected real attempts at tackling urgent problems, as well as a mechanism for further sidelining official township councils.[43] There were thus immediate and material as well as national political reasons for participation in protests or in 'rebellious' structures.

There was a similar combination of national and local, material and political factors underlying the upsurge of township struggles in 1989–90. While the return of the ANC to legal activity was very important, the major impetus came from local factors: housing, rents, services such as electricity, and busfares. As in mid-decade, the interaction of national and local struggles involved some tension. This was reflected in debates about the appropriate relationship between civic organizations and local ANC branches, the continued status of the UDF, and the formation of regional umbrella organizations for civic associations. The political consequences of these tensions were exacerbated by structural changes that had taken place in many townships during the decade.

The state's urban policy reforms, together with broader economic change, led to increasing differentiation within townships and their political fragmentation. State and private sector investment in township infrastructure and housing mostly provided for the growing numbers of relatively high-income township residents (see the chapters in section three of this volume). Boraine[44] argued that state strategy was aimed at creating 'divisions between middle-class home-owners in new élite suburbs and working-class residents of council housing and backyard shacks, as well as a separation between formal black townships (the new insiders) and the burgeoning peri-urban shack settlements (the outsiders)'. Upgrading, he argued, was 'deliberatively selective', producing new lines of cleavage in the townships.[45] Notwithstanding the undoubted pressures towards political fragmentation, struggles continued in both the established townships, especially though rent boycotts,[46] and in squatter areas.[47]

The squatter and backyard shack issue became a serious organizational problem. During the protests of the early and mid-1980s, backyard shack residents marched alongside their landlords, who were themselves usually council tenants. In the later 1980s backyard shack rents rose sharply, and this generated tension particularly where the 'landlords' were boycotting their rent and service charges to the council. Land invasions by backyard shack residents, who occupied land around townships, were a response not only to the housing shortage, but also to the political tensions which had emerged within townships and within township political organizations.

When bitter conflict broke out in townships on the Witwatersrand and Vaal Triangle in 1990, however, it was not between squatters and township housing residents, but rather between all of these and hostel-dwellers. The 1990 conflicts were largely an outgrowth of the chronic war in Natal/KwaZulu. The latter had a strong party-political dimension, arising primarily from the political ambitions, historical appeals, and organizational character of Inkatha.[48] But the Natal violence also involved a 'socio-economic' dimension: 'The political determinants of the violence are rooted in and sustained by underlying social and material conditions.'[49] What made the conflict especially bitter was the way in which economic and social struggles on the ground became inter-meshed with the political struggle.[50]

The same was true in the Transvaal in 1990. Inkatha leaders appear to have played a major role in precipitating and directing much of the violence, but the extent of the conflicts reflected broad political and material factors beyond the scope of any single political party. Conditions in the hostels were generally appalling. In some (but not all) areas there were long-standing hostilities between residents of the hostel and the townships. Civic or other township-based organizations had rarely organized among hostel residents, and the latter had often been alienated by the way in which protests such as stayaways had been planned and conducted. Economic, social, and political factors enmeshed on the ground.[51]

Conclusion

From the protests against the state in the early 1980s through to the violent conflict between township residents in the late 1980s, township politics involved a combination of political, social, and economic factors. The relative importance of these factors varied between townships and over the course of the decade. But it was *local* factors, or at least the *local* aspects of national factors, rather than those national factors themselves, which provided the impetus to protest and conflict. While South Africa's political and economic system produced widespread discontent in the townships, it did not inevitably give rise to protest. It was local conditions which sometimes made it rational for township residents to protest, and at other times promoted quiescence.

Township residents generally protested over local and immediate grievances. During the early 1980s these arose, for the most part, out of discontent with material conditions such as rent increases. But protests occurred when there was an immediate focus and framework for action. That focus was initially provided by the unpopular role of councillors and the organization provided by the emerging civic associations. The township 'revolt' of 1984–6 involved the politicization of township protests, with the issues of local and central state power becoming increasingly important. But protests continued to be rooted in local and immediate concerns. Party-political competition grew in importance during the decade, directly informing violence particularly in Natal and (in 1990) in the Transvaal. But the scope of this violence reflected the continued importance of local political and socio-economic factors.

National constitutional change will clearly not itself resolve these local factors. But a transformed national political context will produce changes in the local patterns of political organization and conflict. Notwithstanding major changes in state policies, many of the underlying material grievances will persist — including inadequate housing, urban infrastructure, and educational facilities, and rents (or bond payments) that many households regard as too high. It is to be hoped that struggles over these will largely be waged through democratic and non-violent processes. The experience of popular struggles against the state and civic organization gives much cause for hope. But the legacy of apartheid and of violent internecine township conflicts will not make the transition to democratic and non-violent urban politics easy.

Notes

1 I am grateful for comments made when part of this paper was discussed at the Contemporary South African Research Seminar at Stellenbosch University. This paper also draws on work done jointly with Matthew Chaskalson.
2 Cole J. *Crossroads: the Politics of Reform and Repression* (Johannesburg: Ravan 1987).
   Seekings J. 'Quiescence and the Transition to Confrontation: South African Townships, 1978–1984, unpublished D.Phil. thesis (Oxford: University of Oxford 1990a).

3 Chaskalson M. 'Sharpeville', unpublished paper (1988).
Seekings (1990a).

4 Barrell H. 'The United Democratic Front and National Forum: their Emergence, Composition, and Trends' *South African Review 2* (Johannesburg: Ravan/SARS 1984).
Collinge J. 'The United Democratic Front' *South African Review 3* (Johannesburg: Ravan/SARS 1986).
Dollie N. 'The National Forum' *South African Review 3* (Johannesburg: Ravan/SARS 1986).

5 Seekings (1990a).

6 Labour Monitoring Group 'The November Stayaway' *South African Labour Bulletin* (May 1985) 10 vi.

7 Indicator Project South Africa (IPSA) *Political Conflict in South Africa, 1984–1988* (Durban: University of Natal 1988).

8 Swilling M. 'UDF Local Government in Port Elizabeth' *Monitor* (October 1988a) 1 i 44–9.

9 Boraine A. 'Mamelodi: from Parks to People's Power', unpublished Honours dissertation (Cape Town: University of Cape Town 1987).
Burman S. and Scharf W. 'Creating People's Justice: Street Committees and People's Courts in a South African City' *Law and Society Review* (1990) 24 iii.
Jochelson K. 'Reform, Repression and Resistance in South Africa: a Case-study of Alexandra Township' *Journal of Southern African Studies* (March 1990) 16 i.

10 Hendler P. *Paths to Power* (Johannesburg: South African Institute of Race Relations 1989).
Swilling M. 'Beyond Ungovernability: Township Politics and Local Level Negotiations' (Johannesburg: University of the Witwatersrand, Centre for Policy Studies 1988b).

11 Burman and Scharf (1990).
Seekings J. 'People's Courts and Popular Politics' *South African Review 5* (Johannesburg: Ravan 1989b).

12 Adler G. 'Uniting a Community' *Work in Progress* (October/November 1987) 50, 67–74.

13 Haysom N. *Mabangalala* (Johannesburg: University of the Witwatersrand, Centre for Applied Legal Studies 1986).

14 Cole (1987).

15 Haysom (1986).
Sitas A. 'Durban, August 1985: "Where Wealth and Power and Blood Reign Worshipped Gods"' *South African Labour Bulletin* (February/March 1986) 11 iv.

16 De Villiers M. and Roux M. 'Restructuring Apartheid: Terror and Disorganization in the Eastern Cape, 1986–88' *South African Sociological Review* (1989) 1 ii.
Webster D. 'Repression and the State of Emergency' *South African Review 4* (Johannesburg: Ravan 1987).

17 Chaskalson M., Jochelson K., and Seekings J. 'Rent Boycotts, the State, and the Transformation of the Urban Political Economy' *Review of African Political Economy* 40 (1988).
Shubane K. 'The Soweto Rent Boycott', unpublished B.Hons. dissertation (Johannesburg: University of the Witwatersrand 1988).
Siyotula N. G. 'The Tembisa Rent Boycott', unpublished B.Hons. dissertation (Johannesburg: University of the Witwatersrand 1989).

18 IPSA (1988).
19 Kentridge M. *An Unofficial War* (Cape Town: David Philip 1990).
20 Morris A. 'The Complexities of Sustained Urban Struggle: the Case of Oukasie' *South African Sociological Review* (1990) 2, 1.
21 Collinge J. 'Defiance: a Measure of Expectations' *Work in Progress* (September/October 1989) 61, 5–8.
22 Seekings J. *South African Townships in the 1980s: an Annotated Bibliography* (Stellenbosch: University of Stellenbosch, Research Unit for Sociology of Development 1991).
23 Saul J. and Gelb S. *The Crisis in South Africa* (New York: Monthly Review Press 1981), republished with a new introduction and conclusion (London: Zed 1986).
24 McCarthy J. and Swilling M. 'South Africa's Emerging Politics of Bus Transportation' *Political Geography Quarterly* (July 1985) 4 iii 235–49.
25 Bundy C. 'Street Sociology and Pavement Politics: Some Aspects of Student/Youth Consciousness During the 1985 Schools Crisis in Greater Cape Town' *Journal of Southern African Studies* (April 1987) 13 iii.
    Woods G. 'Rebels with a Cause: the Discontent of Black Youth' *Indicator* (1989) 7 i 62–5.
26 McCarthy J. 'Progressive Politics and Crises of Urban Reproduction in South Africa: the Case of Rents and Transport', seminar paper presented at the African Studies Institute, University of the Witwatersrand (September 1986).
    Reintges C. 'Urban Movements in South African Black Townships: a Case-study' *International Journal of Urban and Regional Research* (March 1990) 14 i 109–34.
    Swilling M. 'Urban Social Movements Under Apartheid' *Cahiers d'Etudes Africaines* (December 1985) 99.
27 Most notably in the 'Delmas Treason Trial' (of national UDF and local Vaal Triangle leaders concerning the Vaal Uprising and other protests of late 1984 and early 1985) and the 'Alexandra Treason Trial' (of Alexandra civic leaders concerning the period of 'people's power' in Alexandra in early 1986).
28 This was recognized by the judge in the Alexandra Treason Trial who acquitted the accused.
29 South Africa *Report on the Investigation into Education for Blacks in the Vaal Triangle Following Upon the Occurrences of 3 September and Thereafter*, the Van der Walt Commission (1985).
30 Cloete F. 'Prospects for a Democratic Process of Political Change in South Africa', paper presented to the Conference on Perspectives on the South African State, Centre for Policy Studies, University of the Witwatersrand (February 1989).
    De Kock C. P. 'Revolutionary Violence in South Africa: 1 000 Days after 3 September 1984' (ed.) Van Vuuren D. J. *South Africa: the Challenge of Reform* (Pinetown: 1988).
31 Among academic analyses there seems to be a tendency to explain protest by 'our side' in structural terms, but by 'the enemy' in conspiratorial ones, that is denying them any significant social base. Thus ANC-aligned scholars view Inkatha and vigilanteism in conspiratorial terms, just as the state viewed township resistance. Inkatha-aligned academics, by contrast, now emphasize socio-economic factors.

32 Schlemmer L. 'South Africa's Urban Crisis: the Need for Fundamental Solutions' *Indicator* (1985) 3 i.

33 Seekings (1990a).

34 Seekings J. 'Why Was Soweto Different? Urban Development, Township Politics, and the Political Economy of Soweto, 1978–84', paper presented to the African Studies Institute seminar, University of the Witwatersrand (May 1988).

35 Seekings J. 'Political Mobilization in Tumahole, 1984–1985' *Africa Perspective* (October 1989a) new series 1 vii/viii.
    Seekings (1990a).

36 Barrell H. *MK: the ANC's Armed Struggle* (Johannesburg: Penguin 1990).

37 Evans M. 'The Emergence and Decline of a Community Organization: an Assessment of PEBCO' *South African Labour Bulletin* (September 1980) 6 ii/iii.
    Seekings (1990a).

38 Carter C. '"We are the Progressives": Alexandra Youth Congress Activists and the Freedom Charter, 1983–5' *Journal of Southern African Studies* (forthcoming).

39 Obery I. and Jochelson K. 'Consumer Boycott: Driving a Wedge Between Business and the State' *Work in Progress* (October 1985) 39.
    Seekings J. 'Organization and Repression in the Transition to Confrontation: the Case of Kagiso, 1985–1986', paper presented to the African Studies Institute seminar, University of the Witwatersrand (February 1990b).

40 Boraine (1987).
    Jochelson (1990).
    Swilling (1988a).

41 Chaskalson et al. (1988).

42 Burman and Scharf (1990).
    Seekings (1989b).

43 Hendler (1989).
    Swilling (1988b).

44 Boraine A. 'Managing the Urban Crisis, 1986–1989: the Role of the National Management System' *South African Review 5* (Johannesburg: Ravan/SARS 1989).

45 See also Jochelson (1990).

46 Planact 'Soweto's Three-year Rent Boycott' *Work in Progress* (June/July 1989) 59, 19–23.

47 Cole J. 'State Urban Policies and Urban Struggles in the Post-1986 Period: a Western Cape Perspective', paper presented to the Contemporary South African Research seminar, University of Stellenbosch (October 1989).

48 Aitchison J. 'The Civil War in Natal' *South African Review 5* (Johannesburg: Ravan/SARS 1989).
    Mare G. and Hamilton G. *An Appetite for Power* (Johannesburg: Ravan 1987).
    McCaul C. 'The Wild Card: Inkatha and Contemporary Black Politics' (eds.) Frankel P., Pines N., and Swilling M. *State, Resistance and Change in South Africa* (Cape Town: Southern Books 1988).

49 Hindson D. and Morris M. 'Trying to Piece Together Peace in Natal' *Work in Progress* (September 1990) 69, 21–3.
    Stavrou S. and Crouch A. 'Violence on the Periphery: Molweni' *Indicator* (1989) 6 iii 46–50.
    Stavrou S. and Shongwe L. 'Violence on the Periphery: the Greater Edendale Complex' *Indicator* (1989) 7 i 53–7.

Woods (1989).

50   See, for example, Gwala N. 'Political Violence and the Struggle for Control in Pietermaritzburg' *Journal of Southern African Studies* (April 1989) 15 iii 506–24.

51   Ruiters G. and Taylor R. 'Hostel War: Organize or Die' *Work in Progress* (November/December 1990) 70/71, 20–2.

19 The Conservative Party and local government

Louwrens Pretorius and
Richard Humphries

Introduction

One of the hallmarks of South African politics during the 1980s was the prominence which urban and local political issues occupied on the agendas and strategies of a variety of South African political parties and formations. In the case of white political formations, this was partially a result of the NP government's expressed preference for increased local autonomy. This provided the right-wing CP with a convenient strategic counter to the government's dilution of apartheid policies and practices: it would use local autonomy to prevent the scrapping of apartheid measures.

Within the narrow confines of white local government, the CP developed into an important political actor after the 1988 municipal elections. The party was committed to restoring white political supremacy and to undoing the generally limited reforms which the government had introduced during the decade. After the elections, CP-controlled local authorities began to implement a range of policies designed to secure 'whites only' facilities in areas where public amenities had previously been declared open to all races. Decisions by the Boksburg and Carletonville town councils and the consumer boycotts which black communities in these towns adopted in response, became synonymous with the intentions and consequences of CP policy. In response to these decisions the government initially argued that local government autonomy would have to be respected. Later government policies, however, emphasized and decreased the limitations of local autonomy and thereby the effective ability of CP councils to counteract government policy.

This chapter examines the CP's attempt to use control of local authorities to counteract policy changes at both the national and local level. It is argued that the attempt failed because local autonomy has always been strictly limited. It is also argued that attempts by the CP to prevent a new non-racial local government system will probably also fail since a standardized system can and most likely will be imposed before the next municipal elections, due in 1993.

The CP and the 1988 municipal elections

The October 1988 municipal elections firmly established the CP as a political force at the local government level. The party performed particularly well in the Transvaal, where it gained control of some two-thirds of the local government structures in the province. It performed less well in the OFS while making little inroad in the Cape and Natal. The elections were particularly important for the party for two related reasons. One was that they provided the opportunity to expand the party's organizational presence beyond its original Transvaal base. The other reason was the intention to use political control of municipalities to obstruct the government's reform moves.

The establishment of the CP in 1982 followed years of bitter infighting within the ruling NP over the terms of a proposed new constitution. The first real test of the party's appeal to white voters came only with the 1987 general election. In this election it had not only to establish its superiority over a longer-standing fellow right-wing political party, the Herstigte Nasionale Party (HNP), but had to undercut NP support, particularly in the Transvaal and the OFS. It succeeded handsomely enough in decimating the HNP but this right-wing rivalry still allowed the NP to win eight seats on a split right-wing vote. The CP triumphed in 22 constituencies. These constituencies were all in the Transvaal and were overwhelmingly rural farming constituencies. In the OFS, where it pinned most of its hopes for an advance outside the Transvaal, it captured a substantial portion of the vote. The combined right-wing (CP plus HNP) share of the vote served to predict the CP's 1988 successes in the province.[1]

In the light of this the CP regarded the municipal elections as a forerunner to the next general election — which was eventually held in September 1989. Party strategists accepted that the party had to overcome its established rural support base in the Transvaal and the OFS and develop increased support in urban areas.[2] In this respect the mining and industrial towns to the east and west of Johannesburg were crucial new avenues for the cultivation of support. Thus the CP's Cape provincial leader characterized the municipal elections as an opportunity for the party to 'score a try, which could be converted at the next general election'.[3]

Traditionally municipal elections in South Africa have seen minimal open or direct involvement by the major white political parties — although ratepayers' associations have often been sites for covert party-political activities. The reasons for this are varied but an important one must be the limited political autonomy enjoyed by municipal government. Local authorities have generally had to abide by the central government's policy decisions. Examples include policies with regard to access to public facilities and the racial zoning of residential and business areas.

However, overt party political involvement in municipal affairs began to change in the 1980s. NP policy began to emphasize the importance of political devolution and the deconcentration of administrative functions to lower tiers of government, especially municipalities. Although no new substantial powers were devolved to municipalities during the decade, the policy commitment did serve to increase the importance of local government among a wide range of political groupings. For the CP the challenge of the municipal elections, in this context, was to gain control of as large a number of municipalities as possible in order to obstruct the unfolding of reform measures by the government.[4]

The party's policy positions were predicated upon the assumption that political control of a municipality would allow it to undermine reform measures. Its municipal election manifesto was a mixture of local and national political issues; many of the latter were of little direct relevance to municipal affairs. The CP argued that it was not possible to draw any neat distinction between local and national issues because the election was ultimately about the political rights of whites. As one of its candidates in Pretoria put it: 'We are not fighting the municipal election on issues like pavements and roads, but for the fight for survival of Afrikaners and whites.'[5]

The party proposed, *inter alia*, to retain public facilities in white Group Areas for the exclusive use of whites, to prevent the erosion of apartheid measures in residential and business areas hitherto reserved for whites, and to prevent the use — through the medium of RSCs — of 'white money' for the improvement of infrastructure in the African townships. In short, the CP wanted to preserve the structure and fabric of the apartheid city.[6]

In many respects the outcome of the elections was very favourable to the CP. It won control of enough local authorities in the Transvaal to dominate the Transvaal Municipal Association (TMA). Some important large towns in the PWV region (such as Boksburg, Springs, Brakpan, and Vanderbijlpark) fell to the party, thus providing the beginnings of an urban base. Although the NP retained control of the OFS Municipal Association, the CP controlled sufficient rural towns to believe that it would be able to gain a number of parliamentary constituencies in the following general election. The municipal elections had thus indeed served to expand the organizational and support bases of the party but the strong test of implementing party policy still lay ahead.[7]

Discovering the limits of local autonomy

The results of two years of CP local government in a variety of towns have, however, highlighted the limitations rather than the opportunities of local power. Municipalities in South Africa have hardly any autonomy with regard to the enactment and implementation of the issues which divide and energize political parties. All the key so-called local issues are issues which reside squarely within the domain of national politics. This condition is of course variable rather than constant. During the period leading up to the municipal elections of 1988, and to some extent during most of the following 17 months, the CP could look forward to operating in an atmosphere of flux and uncertainty with regard to local autonomy. There existed at least the possibility that local preferences and decisions could prevail against central government policies. By late 1989 and especially since February 1990 it became certain, however, that the government would not permit the CP to conduct local government as it wished to do. Although government spokespersons — including the State President — maintained the intention of devolving power, the government made it quite clear that it would not tolerate public defiance of the repeal or modification of apartheid measures.

The period had also been marked by the substantive transformation of the nature of the political process. The formal and legalized entry of formations such as the ANC, PAC, and SACP accentuated the withering position of the CP in the South African political process even while its fortunes in white electoral politics were on the increase. Given the demands of 'negotiation politics', the likelihood of concessions to CP demands also seems to be decreasing.

By 1988, white party politics at municipal level revolved largely around four issues. These were the reservation of public amenities on a racial basis, RSCs, 'free trade areas', and residential Group Areas. Only in the case of separate amenities were disputes about reserving such amenities for specific population groups 'winnable' at the local level. This was because the Reservation of Separate Amenities Act enabled provincial and municipal authorities to regulate public access to certain amenities. As regards the other issues local authorities were able to articulate their preferences and attempt to influence decisions, but the final decision-making power rested with higher levels of government. Local authorities participate in RSCs and are an influence, but they cannot ultimately control budget and policy decisions. The power to decide on the location and the composition of residential and commercial Group Areas rested both formally and in practice with the central government.

Soon after the municipal elections, the CP-controlled councils of Boksburg, Carletonville, and at least six other major Transvaal towns resegregated previously desegregated public amenities. In accordance with party policy, a number of other CP councils in the Transvaal and OFS announced their intention to follow suit. The fate of Boksburg's return to strict segregation of public amenities serves to illustrate the limits of local autonomy and the consequent failure of CP attempts to implement its municipal manifesto. In 1988 the CP won 12 of Boksburg's 20 council wards. With a safe majority in hand, the executive committee immediately proceeded to reinstate apartheid measures — in the form of excluding black people from using the city hall and certain recreation facilities under the council's control. Consequently the town became a well publicized battleground between the right-wing council on the one hand and local black residents and business interests on the other.

Black reaction against the council's reinstitution of petty apartheid took the form of a seemingly quite effective boycott of Boksburg business by African and coloured consumers.[8] The battle between the CP and business interests was largely limited to outbursts of threats and counter-threats. The real effects of the year-long consumer boycott on the local economy is a matter of some dispute. The important fact is that the outcome of the battle was ultimately determined by the central government's decisions.

The CP justified its policy position and its actions in Boksburg in a way which, at the time, pinpointed the contradictions in government policy towards local autonomy in general and separate amenities in particular. According to Dr Andries Treurnicht, his party had a 'double mandate' to implement its policies: 'We have our own mandate and that of the NP which clearly states that it is up to each and every town council to decide whether or not certain facilities are to be declared separate amenities.'[9]

Some initial reactions from government spokespersons seemingly did not challenge this interpretation. The MEC for local government in the Transvaal, for example, said that in terms of the Separate Amenities Act, the Boksburg council was entitled to institute segregated public facilities. Furthermore, the council's actions conformed with the government's policy of devolving power to local authorities.[10] Other reports indicated that the government may have been considering the option of scuttling its declared policy of increasing local autonomy. It was also made clear that the government was seriously considering the repeal of the Reservation of Separate Amenities Act — as had been recommended previously by the President's Council.[11]

The matter was resolved some 12 months after the municipal elections — and soon after the NP won the 1989 general election by a comfortable albeit much decreased margin. The State President's post-election announcement that the Reservation of Separate Amenities Act would be repealed was followed by the voluntary termination of the consumer boycott in Boksburg.[12] The CP's reaction to the announcement, as well as to the proclamation of a 'free trading area' and of a 'free settlement area' in Boksburg, was to object that the government had 'no mandate' for such actions.[13] The firm intention of scrapping the Separate Amenities Act and the State President's clear directives about how municipalities should deal with segregated beaches during the 1989/90 holiday season, strongly indicated that the long propagated policy of devolution had suffered an important reversal by November 1989.

The extent to which the 'reintroduction' of apartheid measures in some CP-controlled municipalities in fact entailed effective resegregation of previously desegregated public amenities, is a moot point. It is not clear in which cases such measures had previously been formally — not to say effectively — abolished. With the (passive if not active) blessing of the central government, some NP-controlled councils had allowed the relevant measures to fall into disuse. In most of the towns which were won by the CP, such measures were still in place and stringently applied. The intensely contested and well publicized cases of Boksburg and Carletonville earned their status precisely because the deposed NP-orientated councils had followed relatively liberal approaches with regard to public amenities.[14] In many towns circumstances did not — from the CP's point of view — require action because the formal and effective pre-existence of reserved public amenities obviated the need for resegregation.

The limits on local autonomy — and therefore on successful local reaction against central government policies — were also illustrated in Pietersburg. There the issues of interest were the establishment of a 'free trade area' in the town's central business district and the CP-controlled council's announced intentions with regard to the Northern Transvaal RSC.

Approximately one third of Pietersburg's central business district was proclaimed a 'free trading area' in 1986. Although the surface area is substantial, the affected area is located on the perimeter of the civic and commercial hub of the town. The proclamation of the Free Trade Area was enforced by the central government. Although the CP opposed the proclamation in principle, the Pietersburg council went along with the government's decision. The reason for this 'compliance' was that the municipality wanted to retain what little influence it could possibly have, namely on the location of the area.

After the municipal elections, the CP announced its intention to test government policy, and no doubt its political will, by recommending the deproclamation of the area. But it did not act on the announced intention. The town's management committee knew, of course, that the government would turn down any request for deproclamation. It also did not act because of the relative weakness of its council. Although the CP is solidly established in the Pietersburg parliamentary constituency, it governed the town with a majority of only one councillor for the whole period of its municipal reign (from March 1982 to November 1989). This and the knowledge that it had to govern the town subject to central government policies and to pressure from local business interests, withheld the party from pursuing its intention.

The fact that decisions with regard to Group Areas rested with the government had somewhat similar effects on the post-election approach of other CP-controlled councils, notably that of the important West Rand town of Krugersdorp. That the government would not have been inclined to accept local petitions against free trade areas was made clear when it proceeded with the proclamation of such an area in Carletonville — in the face of the opposition of the CP-controlled municipality which came to power two months before the proclamations.

Although the CP vehemently opposed RSCs, it entered the municipal elections with the decision to 'use' RSCs for the benefit — as the CP sees it — of whites. After the elections, the CP held a veto in or controlled some two-thirds of the 12 RSCs in the Transvaal. The general expectation after the elections, based on this expressed intention, was that the party would attempt to channel RSC levy income into 'white' areas or, at the least, to delay budget decisions by employing a variety of obstructionist tactics.[15]

In the event, the budget processes in most RSCs were not unduly delayed, nor did allocations change drastically. Various problems did, however, arise. These pertained in particular to RSCs in the western Transvaal. In the rural Rustenburg/Marico RSC, a persistent dispute about the inclusion of black representatives on the executive committee arose. The West Rand RSC faced repeated difficulties with regard to the election of executive members. The Westvaal RSC experienced vexatious and often petty feuds about procedural matters. More importantly, it had great difficulty in passing its budget. The CP managed to delay approval of the budget for some five months. However, after 'encouragement' by higher authorities, the RSC did eventually approve the budget 'by consensus'.[16]

In the Northern Transvaal RSC, however, the CP was either unable or unwilling to pursue its intentions. Soon after the municipal elections, the Pietersburg town council decided that it would no longer negotiate with the Northern Transvaal RSC for the funding of projects. It also requested the RSC to vacate its offices in the Pietersburg municipal complex. But the Pietersburg council did not proceed with these resolutions. Instead it later extended the contract granting the Northern Transvaal RSC office facilities, and in May 1989 the RSC unanimously agreed to a 'record budget'. A senior RSC official in Pietersburg ascribed this outcome to the fact that Pietersburg's and other relevant CP councillors were, compared to say those of Boksburg, 'relatively experienced and hence responsible and aware of the contributions made by the RSC system to the general welfare'.[17]

Concluding comments

The cases described above suggest that despite government rhetoric about devolution and local autonomy, local government remained in its historical position, namely that of largely being a local administrative agent for the central government. This in turn implies that there never was much room for the CP to implement policies which ran counter to those of central government. But the CP was not only constrained by government policies and the lack of effective local autonomy. It was also hamstrung by the fact that its majorities in a number of towns were very narrow. The case of Pietersburg indicates that the CP, like any other party, had to conduct politics as 'the art of the possible'. In Boksburg (and in Carletonville) where the CP had relatively large majorities, the party felt strong enough to act affirmatively. It did so, however, in accordance with government policy and existing legislation — and on issues for which, in Pietersburg, there was less, if no need to act.

Once the government had formalized the desegregation of public amenities (which it did from 15 October 1990), the CP had to find ways around legislation which allowed it even less local autonomy. In Boksburg, for example, the council threatened to turn a newly proclaimed free settlement area in the town into a suburb for the council's African workers. This rather imaginative suggestion was never acted upon. But it was early warning of a variety of tactics being devised by CP councillors — often in partnership with conservative but nominally NP-oriented councillors — to deal with the post February 1990 era in SA politics. These centred mainly on attempts to amend municipal by-laws in ways which would limit the use of public amenities to whites — but without specifying racial categories. One popular device employed in the Transvaal was to attempt to charge 'non-residents' — a euphemism for blacks — for the use of town facilities in terms of a 1939 provincial ordinance. Such tactics, however, are failing because officials in the Department of Planning and Provincial Affairs — which has responsibility for supervising local by-laws — find reasons for rejecting the proposed by-laws on the basis that they are *ultra vires*. In this the government was strengthened by the decision of the Transvaal Supreme Court in the Carletonville case. Currently (mid-1991) the government is attempting to close as many legislative loopholes as possible. In the longer term, the CP tactics may well be responded to by anti-discriminatory 'civil or human rights legislation'.

Despite its failures in the area of policy implementation, the strong transformationist drive which has thus far marked the presidency of F. W. de Klerk has provided the CP with excellent opportunities for propagating its position and mobilizing support at the local level. At a CP municipal conference in Boksburg during January 1990, some 500 Transvaal CP councillors decided to resist the repeal of the Separate Amenities Act.[18] During a special congress of the TMA held in late March 1990, 150 of the 175 delegates voted in favour of a motion calling for the retention of separate amenities legislation.[19] Later, the annual TMA congress reiterated this position and also expressed itself strongly against the increased incidence of 'illegal squatting' and the government's 'laissez-faire policy with regard to the illegal occupation of non-Whites in white towns'.[20] At both the TMA congress and in some CP municipalities, the party gained a measure of support from nominally NP-oriented councillors — for example in Ermelo and Potchefstroom. However, in the NP-controlled municipality of Nelspruit, a CP motion in this regard failed.[21]

An important part of the CP's strategy in municipalities it controls has been to use the opportunities of political control to mobilize against further reforms by the NP government. It has actively encouraged the holding of referenda to consult white ratepayer opinion about the repeal of the Separate Amenities Act and the possible introduction of integrated municipalities. These were intended to demonstrate 'white rejection of multi-racial town councils and forced integration'. Party officials announced late in 1990 that such referenda had been 'successfully enforced' in a number of Cape, Transvaal, and OFS towns. This local mobilization is partly dictated, too, by the CP's belief that the post February 2 1990 reforms are not yet irreversible and that a return to a form of white supremacy rule and government is possible.

NP reforms have thus elicited quite strong reactions by the CP in various towns and, against the background of significant shows of unease by whites, the possibility of extra-parliamentary reaction by factions of the CP and portions of the broader white right-wing movement must still exist. However the government does not appear to have been swayed from its general policy direction by these developments. Reacting, for example, to a petition in favour of separate amenities in Mossel Bay, De Klerk replied that the government would no longer allow segregated amenities to be reintroduced in the town because a 'standardised policy' was needed.[22] Short of anti-discriminatory legislation, which the government has indicated it may have to consider if circumstances warranted it, there are a number of means which the government could use to discipline recalcitrant local authorities. These could include the withholding of public finances.[23]

This analysis has pointed to the inability of CP municipalities either to deflect or retard the government's gradual movement towards accepting the need for a non-racial local government system. Projected forward it would then suggest that they would also be unable to prevent the establishment of such a post-apartheid local government system. However, given the underlying trend in government policy of allowing a local option negotiating process to emerge, as opposed to a nationally imposed and standardized structure, at least for the foreseeable future, CP councils would obviously refuse to participate in such local negotiations. By excluding themselves, and thus the white local authority, they would make it very difficult for localized negotiation processes to develop meaningfully in CP towns.

There is one scenario in terms of which CP councils, or a minority of them, might decide to participate in local options — that is that if at a national level the party decided to participate in the negotiation process. Although the party has hitherto rejected such participation, it has been suggested that the CP parliamentary caucus is severely divided on this issue.[24] If the CP was to decide to participate in the negotiation process, then local councils might well also decide to participate in local options.

Yet any decision by CP municipalities to exclude themselves from local option negotiations would obviously create political conflict in cases where various civic, even business groupings in some of the towns were prepared to engage in a local process. This conflict would inevitably have to be dealt with by the government in one way or another. Already the Minister of Planning and Provincial Affairs has warned that there must be a time limit or cut off point to any local option process before the government imposed a standardized framework on councils and towns which had not completed any local option negotiations.[25] In this way the CP councils would be dealt out of the process. In any case municipal elections are scheduled for 1993; presumably the government expects to have consensus on a post-apartheid local authority system in place so that these elections would be for non-racial authorities. In this case history might well record that the 1988–93 term of office of the CP councils was marked by their general failure to prevent the final dismemberment of apartheid local government.

Notes

1 See Bekker S. and Grobbelaar J. 'The White Right-wing Movement in South Africa: Before and After the May 1987 Election' in Van Vuuren D. et al. *South African Election 1987* (Durban: Owen Burgess 1987).

2 Interview conducted by L. Pretorius with the chief information officer of the Conservative Party on 1 June 1989.

3 *The Citizen* 17 October 1988.

4 See Humphries R. *On the Beaches* (Johannesburg: University of the Witwatersrand, Centre for Policy Studies 1988).

5 Quoted in Humphries R. 'Showdown on Platteland and Rand' *Indicator South Africa* (Durban: University of Natal 1988) 5 iv.

6 See Pretorius L. 'The Conservative Party of South Africa and Local Government', unpublished paper (Johannesburg: Urban Foundation 1990).

7 For an analysis of the election results see Humphries R. and Shubane K. 'A Tale of Two Squirrels' in *Centre for Policy Studies: South Africa at the End of the Eighties* (Johannesburg: University of the Witwatersrand, Centre for Policy Studies 1989).

8 For an account of the boycott see Mashabela H. and Narsoo M. *The Boksburg Boycott* (Johannesburg: South African Institute of Race Relations 1989).

9 *The Citizen* 5 March 1989.

10 *Financial Mail* 2 December 1988.

11 *The Citizen* 25 May 1989; *The Star* 7 December 1988.

12 *Die Beeld* 20 November 1989.

13 *The Citizen* 17 November 1989; *The Pretoria News* 24 November 1989.

14 *The Star* 22 December 1988.

15 *Business Day* 13 February 1989; *The Star* 10 December 1988.

16 *Transvaler* 30 March 1989, 13 June 1989; *Western Transvaal Record* 24 March 1989, 28 August 1989.

17 The local authorities constituting the Northern Transvaal RSC had been dominated by the CP since 1983. In interviews RSC and provincial officials suggested that the problems experienced in specific RSCs may have been a consequence of the 'attitudes of individuals' rather than a coherent CP strategy. Some officials also expressed the opinion that events such as those in Boksburg itself may be ascribed to the 'relative inexperience of Boksburg councillors compared to those say of Pietersburg'. Interview conducted by the authors in Pietersburg on 18 August 1989.

18 *Die Patriot* 26 January 1990.

19 *Die Patriot* 6 April 1990.

20 *Die Patriot* 12 November 1990.

21 *Die Patriot* 9 March 1990.

22 *Die Patriot* 24 August 1990.

23 This was threatened by the Minister of Planning and Provincial Affairs when he said that local authorities which persist in the reservation of public amenities may have to forgo state aid in the development of such amenities (*Die Beeld* 17 November 1990).

24 *Rapport* 14 April 1991.

25 *Finance Week* 7–13 February 1991.

20 The challenge of the cities

Ann Bernstein

Introduction

South Africa today faces three major challenges. The first is the economic challenge to increase our rate of growth and development in such a way as to provide millions of new jobs for a large and growing population; and to redistribute access to economic opportunity and power. The second challenge concerns urbanization and the need for massive socio-economic development. Society must maximize on the dynamics of the (mainly African) urbanization process so as to make the phenomenon 'an instrument of national development and personal betterment'. The third challenge is a political one. It is the task of building a democratic political culture that encompasses black and white South Africans, where diversity and its corollary — dissent — are encouraged, and where the poor are not excluded from the social contract of a 'new South Africa'. It is only such a political culture that can create the institutions and processes able to facilitate the tough choices necessary to meet the economic development and distribution challenge, and at the same time provide the mechanisms to govern the cities, manage urban growth, and deliver on the scale required.

All three of these complex demands are highlighted in the challenges facing South Africa's urban areas. The three national demands — increased economic growth and massive job creation, rapid urbanization, and the challenge of building an inclusive democracy — all come together at the fulcrum of the nation: in the cities. The attention of the national decision-makers should now be turned to these cities, their place in the social structure, how they should be managed and governed, and the inter-relationship of sound urban growth with healthy rural and regional development. South Africa's keynote politics today are the politics of the city. Our dominantly urban economy cannot escape the effects of urban disorder. By the same token, however, our future prosperity also hinges on the management and development of our cities.

It is for these reasons that, during the period 1986–90, the Urban Foundation (UF) and Private Sector Council on Urbanization (PSC) engaged in an extensive research and policy development programme, resulting in comprehensive and detailed proposals for a new urbanization policy and strategy for South Africa. This chapter summarizes the key elements of those proposals, and explains how they are intended to further the causes of both democracy and development in a post-apartheid South Africa. In order to understand why such an effort has been necessary, it will be useful to reflect briefly upon the historic legacy of policy affecting urbanization and the cities in South Africa.

Historical context

For most of this century, official policy has been designed to prevent large-scale African urbanization. Over the past four decades, however, the South African government has created an increasingly explicit urbanization policy designed to affect the rate and patterns of urban growth. This policy included:

- homeland development and homeland urban growth supported by the industrial decentralization policy;
- the pass-laws — a pivotal component of the policy designed to control the movement;
- settlement and location of African people throughout the South African space economy;
- controls over the movement of TBVC citizens coupled with restrictions on the development of housing of scale in the white urban areas;
- constraints on the economic growth and spatial expansion of the large metropolitan and other urban areas, supported by politically based decentralization and urban deconcentration policies;
- statutory residential segregation, segregated amenities, facilities and institutions, and other discriminatory policies confining

African settlement, economic development, and use of facilities to restricted, isolated parts of all urban areas; and

• the forced removals policy, the land acts, and homeland consolidation, all of which combined to exclude Africans from ownership and occupation of large portions of the South African land area.

More recent government policy has influenced 'where' and 'how' African urbanization has taken place in South Africa. However, it has not been able on any significant scale to prevent urbanization. It has changed the natural course of urbanization, altered its form, influenced its location, and disguised its magnitude. Over time, these policies have generated far-reaching consequences.

The statutory segregation of races has created an ineffective structure in all South African cities. This has led to gross variations in housing and service provision, wasted costs in duplicated services, and negative race relations. The policy of restricting African urban development in the 'white' urban areas and rechannelling urbanization to the homelands has led to geographic and hence economic, social, and political marginalization of urban African populations.

The impact of rapid urbanization and population growth has been concealed behind the 'fences' of internal segregation and homeland borders. The increasingly 'Third World' character of South Africa's cities and towns has been disguised and denied, allowing local and central white decision-makers to ignore the implications and policy consequences of increasing urbanization in their areas.

As a consequence, present policy has the paradoxical result that the most recent, least experienced, and financially least viable authorities (homeland governments and BLAs) have to cope with South Africa's greatest management challenge — the restructuring of institutions and policies so as to meet the needs of millions of urban dwellers effectively.

Present policy conflicts with reality

In the past decade, apartheid ideology has inexorably come into conflict with the reality of modern South Africa. This reality is a single, interdependent economy; a growing and irreversible rate of urbanization; and an interdependence of black and white South Africans.

In the 1980s this conflict between traditional policy and economic reality led to a change in official rhetoric and some aspects

of policy. In brief, the decade saw the recognition of the permanence of African people in the South African urban economy and a
tentative exploration of the ramifications of that recognition.

As events since 1986 have shown, however, the full implications
of accepting African urbanization entail far more than a mere shift of
rhetoric, an acceptance of African population growth and migration
to the cities, or a new housing policy. What is involved is a fundamental reassessment of the way in which policy is formulated, power
is allocated, and development is managed.

Although there have recently been a number of important statements by senior government officials indicating a new and welcome
openness to rethinking some critical urban policy issues, there
appears as yet to be no comprehensive new policy framework, nor
principles to guide a new approach, or an identifiable process for
developing a positive urban strategy.

Rather, the authorities work with an outdated policy framework
which results in a national approach that can only be termed a failure, and which entails recurring 'crisis management' on urban issues.
It has the following main characteristics:

- The lack of a firm national leadership regarding the critical role of
  the cities in economic growth, and the equitable allocation of
  opportunities and resources.
- The exclusion of the relatively well-resourced white local authorities (relative, that is, to the other local authorities neighbouring
  them) from meeting the urban needs of African South Africans
  and the needs of the city as a whole.
- The *ad hoc* adaptation of old policies to try to cope with rapidly
  changing situations.
- Fragmented and confusing administrative and government structures at regional and local levels.
- An absence of any vision concerning where South African cities
  are going and how we intend to 'take them there'.

The PSC approach and policies

The PSC policy proposals on a new urbanization policy for South
Africa are intended to direct the country away from this inadequate
approach of *ad hoc* crisis response. A new urbanization strategy has
been formulated which is comprehensive in scope, balanced in its

attention to rural and urban sectors, but focuses on the management of urban areas.

The PSC policy proposals are detailed and comprehensive. It is therefore difficult to summarize them in a short analysis such as this. Ten substantial policy documents have recently been published which capture the detail of the PSC research and policy proposals, and there are approximately 500 independent research documents upon which the 10 policy documents are based.[1] Nevertheless, key elements of both the PSC approach and proposals can be identified here, specifically as they relate to the cities.

The PSC approach to a new urbanization strategy for the country begins with the recognition that previous policy for rural, regional, and urban development in South Africa has failed. Consequently, a new policy framework is required that can cope with the emerging political, demographic, social, and economic realities of South African cities, towns, and farms. The PSC concluded that a new urbanization policy must be based on sound demographic research, accurate analysis of international and local successes and failures, and a vision of a new, economically thriving, and democratic South Africa. The PSC policy proposals, while they are research-based and are the product of extensive testing and consultation with business and community-based leadership, should be seen as a contribution to a vigorous national debate, and not as a proposed 'blueprint' for unilateral imposition.

The PSC's broader policy framework comprises policies for regional and rural development, and policies for managing South Africa's cities. The latter are the emphasis of the present analysis, and they can be divided into five sections, including policies for the following:
- urban physical structure and development;
- urban finance;
- housing, informal settlement, and services;
- residential zoning; and
- urban government.

Regarding urban physical structure and development, the PSC concluded, *inter alia,* that racial legislation and thinking are the key obstacles to effective urban development. Not only must all racial laws be repealed, but the fragmented, inefficient, and inequitable development patterns of the past must be reversed by a new planning emphasis upon urban coherence, efficiency, and performance. However, a non-racial approach is a necessary but not sufficient condition for good urban development.

Growth-oriented inclusive cities will need to reintegrate African townships and core cities, and make maximum use of all existing investment and skilled personnel (e.g. existing schools, recreational amenities, technical training colleges, city engineers, town clerks, etc.). Moreover, there will need to be a national commitment to five nationwide priority action programmes with specified target goals to ensure:

• permanence, security of tenure, and opportunity to upgrade conditions where appropriate for millions of inhabitants of informal housing;
• security against crime for all urban dwellers;
• environmental protection and neighbourhood upgrading in the cities and towns;
• sufficient trained management resources (town clerks, engineers, community organizers) for the cities and towns; and
• sufficient finance, and appropriate new vehicles for urban development.

Regarding urban economics and finance, the PSC proposes not only that there should be more effective use of existing infrastructure facilities and amenities, but that central government should allocate greater sources of finance to urban development. These allocations should be directed to the key areas and sectors defined by the overall urbanization strategy. In this way, national expenditure can achieve maximum returns in development terms. The PSC therefore recommends that a broadly based, multi-party investigation into urban finance should be appointed to decide on the nature of central government funding.

As a contribution to this investigation, the PSC has developed the concept of a cities development fund (CDF). At various points in South African history, specialist institutions have been created by the state for particular development purposes (e.g. the Industrial Development Corporation in the 1940s). In these cases, seed capital (in a single sum or series of instalments) has been made available on concessionary terms on condition that the institution would operate on a commercial basis as soon as possible. It is proposed that this principle now be applied to urban development in the form of a CDF.

At the local government level, effective local government requires greater decision-making autonomy and increased sources of finance. Moreover, community participation and active involvement are central to effective urban and rural development policy. The UF and the

PSC define community participation as: democratic, representative local and central government; participation in key decision-making in-between regular elections; and participation of the relevant community in development projects.

With regard to existing forms of urban government, the UF and PSC's conclusions are that the present system is fundamentally flawed. Increasingly, the racial basis of present local government structures is at odds with the realities of economically integrated and growing cities. The major adaptation to the present system lies in the introduction of RSCs. These bodies, on which all local authorities are represented, are effecting a measure of infrastructural development and redistribution, but their composition is based upon racially structured institutions which are increasingly in conflict with functionally integrated cities, and which remain politically contentious. Moreover, the appointment and indirect election of RSC members undermine local accountability and democracy, and the RSC tax/levy form tends to inhibit investment in urban areas.

All of the UF and PSC's research into the experience of urbanization indicates that effective institutions are the key to good city management. Before this can develop in South Africa, however, what is required is an unambiguous government commitment to non-racial local government. Once this has been achieved, it will be possible to complement national negotiations with local level negotiations on functionally defined geographic areas for new non-racial local government institutions.

It should be clear that none of the above will be possible without the immediate repeal of the Group Areas Act. Indeed the UF and PSC have concluded that the abolition of Group Areas is only the first critical step that must be taken in the development of a new, non-racial urban policy for the country. It should also be clear that unless immediate steps are taken to resolve South Africa's pressing national housing crisis, the challenges of urban management will become less and less tractable.

South Africa has, at present, a shortage of some 880 000 urban housing units and this shortage is increasing in size as population growth and urbanization outstrip the ability of both public and private sectors to respond. In large part, this is because of the failure of present and previous housing policies.

The future

Urbanization is a fundamental process in any society. In South Africa, where for most of this century policy has been geared at preventing African urbanization, a positive approach to the process entails a fundamental reorientation. A new urbanization policy must therefore encompass policies that affect many of the economic, geographic, and political sectors of our society.

Moreover, the ascendant role of the cities in the life of the country demands that they play a lead role in change. This will require a major attitudinal shift by all South Africans in which it is recognized that South Africa today faces a stark choice. Either we will continue with a reactive, crisis-oriented, inevitably inadequate response to the phenomenon of rapid urbanization, or we can choose to direct this irreversible process and turn it into an economic, political, and development opportunity for all South Africans. All the research indicates that it is necessary to follow the positive, development management route and that success is possible. The following six dominant themes in our proposals support this conviction:

■ Urbanization must be managed. If it is, it can be an instrument for accelerated economic growth, national development, and individual betterment. The countries where urbanization has been successfully harnessed to ensure development have used this process
  • as an opportunity to implement national goals that include:
  ○ eradicating absolute poverty;
  ○ maximizing job creation;
  ○ reducing population growth;
  ○ restructuring access to economic opportunities; and
  ○ incorporating hitherto excluded sections of the national population into political and economic development.

At its best a positive urbanization strategy can be a vehicle for reconstructing a divided society and building a nation.

■ The cities must lead and show that a South African of all can work for all.

The ascendant role of the cities in the life of the country demands that they play a lead role.

The cities can:
  ○ spearhead economic growth and demonstrate the opportunities of an expanding domestic market, and the benefits of planning

for the present 35 million South Africans, and indeed the 60 million expected by the year 2010;

o constitute arenas for racial accommodation and new ways of living together; and

o provide the initial testing environment for democratic decision-making and nation-building through effective community participation and full citizenship.

In the cities, black and white South Africans can learn to live together on an equal and mutually beneficial basis.

■ There are costs if we do not act boldly and decisively in response to the urbanization challenge.

There are significant risks in a *laissez-faire* approach or negative response to the urbanization challenge. Inefficient cities, declining urban investment, environmental deterioration, mass unemployment, and continual instability and conflict are the inevitable results of attempts to avoid, prevent, or ignore urbanization.

Two potential nightmares threatening South African cities arise from present hesitations. The one nightmare is symbolized in violence and a terrible breakdown of normal life, that has become the recurrent reality of communities in Durban and Pietermaritzburg. The dense, unplanned informal settlements and overcrowded townships of urban South Africa, both of which lack adequate facilities and amenities, make this a potential outcome throughout the country. The second nightmare is the threat of administrative breakdown in the health, education, service provision, and other urban systems. This would also include the land ownership system increasingly under threat from the large numbers of homeless urban dwellers who see no other reasonable option but to occupy land not planned for low-income residential settlement. The conflict potential in this competition for resources will grow in scale and intensity so that it becomes harder and harder for anyone to govern according to ordinary rules of ownership and payment for services. We believe that these prices do not have to be paid. Sound policy, good management, and decisive leadership are needed to end present insecurities and avoid new ones.

The insecurity and conflict that currently characterize urbanization in South Africa are partly created and certainly exacerbated by a failure in the present policy initiatives and political leadership to provide city dwellers with confidence in the management of a difficult transition process which affects their daily lives.

■ A new urbanization policy requires political leadership of the highest order. The challenges that face the cities are essentially political in origin. Leadership is required that has vision, courage, and ability:

○ to see all the linkages in our present development crisis;
○ to develop, articulate, and market the comprehensive package of policies that will comprise the new urbanization strategy;
○ to move decisively and take the necessary bold steps;
○ to establish faith in the process necessary to sustain commitment; and
○ to achieve results.

National and local leadership must seek to develop popularly accepted and effective processes and institutions that will develop and then communicate a shared vision of the future. This vision must:

○ be inclusive of all citizens;
○ be built on democratic decision-making and participatory processes;
○ be realistic about the scale of the challenge to be faced;
○ focus on economic growth and on opening opportunities for the poor; and
○ provide permanence and security for all.

Above all, leadership is required that will take risks, have the strength to create 'space' for other leaders, and be able to build alliances across traditional, ethnic, and ideological barriers.

■ There is a broad-based spectrum of South Africans potentially ready to mobilize around a strategy that focuses on the cities and their future.

Black and white South Africans do have converging common interests in the urbanization process and in particular the economic future of the city, the provision of amenities, services and facilities, and the maintenance of reasonable standards. All urban dwellers have a common interest in security of tenure and person, and permanence in their city and neighbourhood.

The results of the 1989 general election give positive backing to the broad conclusions of our development approach. An analysis of the electoral trends in South Africa's five largest cities shows an overwhelming majority of white South Africans are committed to 'non-discriminatory' reform carried out through negotiation with Africans.

In the African community recent initiatives indicate increasing political support and demand for representative leadership to negotiate urban issues and achieve results.

These trends give convincing evidence of popular support for what we have been arguing on different grounds altogether. There are increasing signs of a growing convergence between the findings of our development-oriented research and the political mood of the country. All our work shows that given a credible policy package, principled leadership, and a commitment to a process of negotiation, a widely based, mainly urban 'coalition' can be realized.

The PSC's work provides the research foundation for such a working consensus, where cross-cutting interests in a particular city or town and across the nation could enable independent interest groups to work together on selected urban issues, while retaining their own constituencies for other areas of activity.

- The removal of all racially based legislation and policies is a prerequisite for a new urbanization policy.

Urbanization in the 1990s will be progressively dominated by the interests, needs, and numbers of African South Africans. As the central participants in the process, their views will be paramount in the acceptance and implementation of new policy direction. Their support groups, required within the coalition for city-led growth, will be crucial component bodies. The cities themselves will become an important arena of success for African interests — taxi owners, trade unionists, business people, sports administrators, and health workers.

Among these groups we have been unable to find a single African leader who does not advocate the removal of all racially based legislation. This involves a systematic programme to repeal:

- ○ the Group Areas Act (and related legislation);
- ○ the Separate Amenities Act;
- ○ the Land Acts of 1913 and 1936 (and related legislation);
- ○ racially based local government legislation;
- ○ legislation that prevents the acquisition of South African citizenship by putative 'homeland' residents; and
- ○ the Prevention of Illegal Squatting Act and its replacement with legislation that deals positively with informal housing.

While we have chosen to make the above point in a political context, the entire developmental thrust of our research also shows that segregation and statutory discrimination are the critical obstacles to the future development of the cities. However, the removal of racial discrimination alone will not provide a way of managing urbanization. That task, we believe, requires a new national development framework that is built on principles of non-racialism, democracy, and accountability; scale and affordability; and with a special focus on the poor.

The new national framework for development must include:

o An unambiguous commitment to non-racial local, regional, and central government and planning.

o A national strategy to break the housing crisis and provide secure and upgraded shelter for the vast majority of South Africans.

o An urban policy for post-apartheid cities that aims to manage large cities effectively and equitably, reintegrate the divided cities and towns, strengthen economic growth, and open access to the cities and all urban institutions.

o An effective urban finance strategy that encourages strong local government, new large-scale urban development, and equity in cost recovery.

o A rural development strategy that goes beyond the repeal of the land acts to expand South Africa's capacity to feed itself, provide new rights and opportunities for African farmers and workers, and provide a means of dealing with the historical legacy of forced removals.

o A new multi-sectoral approach to regional development that moves beyond a failed industrial decentralization policy.

The implications of changing policy in South Africa — of really accepting African citizenship — are immense. What is ultimately involved is a fundamental reassessment of the way in which policy is formulated, power allocated, resources distributed, and development managed.

Success in South Africa's cities is critical for the country's economic, political, and constitutional future. The UF believes we can 'win' in our cities. This will require courage, leadership, and the will to act on all sides. We will need to find the right balance between idealism and pragmatism, efficiency and equity; and most importantly, between democracy in its deepest and widest sense and the delivery of services, shelter, opportunities, and hope for the future on a scale that the nation requires.

Notes

1 See the *Policies for a New Urban Future* series, Urban Foundation (Johannesburg).

21 The role of the civic movement

Cas Coovadia

Introduction

During 1990 and into 1991, the crisis of black local government in the Transvaal intensified. At a policy level, this finally forced the government to admit that a new local government system was needed to replace the old racially based system. At the local level, however, this crisis led to a series of local-level negotiations, mainly between civic organizations and the TPA, but which also included a range of other actors.

Through these negotiations, civic organizations are beginning to establish a concrete link between fighting for new forms of non-racial, democratic local government, and new urban development policies that reflect the needs and demands of the urban poor, especially in the areas of land, housing, and services.

Local-level negotiations that begin on a specific local government issue, such as rentals and service charges, often evolve into broader negotiations around development issues, such as land, houses, and services. In some cases, these negotiations have extended to include the formulation of completely new local government structures.

Through both their mass struggles and their involvement in local-level negotiations, civics are thus helping to shape future local government and urban development policies in a way that actively involves urban communities.

It also means that individuals and organizations at a grassroots level are obtaining practical experience about the possibilities and problems of local government and development in a future South

Africa. If these processes only resulted in this educative process, it would be a significant achievement.

This chapter uses these experiences to raise key issues relating to local government and urban development policies. The emphasis is on the role of various actors during the current period of transition in the formulation of policy, particularly through the process of local-level negotiations. Urban struggles have become central in determining the formulation of future local government and development policies. The extent to which community-based organizations such as civics are able to participate in actively formulating their needs and demands during the transition period, will determine the extent to which they will be able to play a leading role in the implementation of future policies.

The paper also makes the point that a development strategy should be based on the building of community-based vehicles for development during the current period, rather than waiting for centralized technocratically conceived planning exercises and the intervention of some future democratic state to deliver goods and services.

Civics and the BLAs

Preceding chapters have provided detailed analyses of the crisis of black local government. What needs to be stressed here is that the emergence of the civic movement was inextricably tied up with the establishment of the BLAs. By granting 'self-determination' to black townships in the early 1980s, the government took the apartheid principle to its logical conclusion at the local level. This, in practice, had three consequences that help explain the emergence of the civic movement. Firstly, blacks were defined as a homogeneous group and located in geographically separate localities from those inhabited by whites. Instead of facilitating control, this separation became the social base for powerful movements opposed to urban apartheid. Secondly, instead of legitimizing the state, the BLAs were seen as the local extensions of white minority rule and rejected on these grounds. Thirdly, the financial unviability of the BLAs, the corrupt practices the councillors were renowned for, and the high cost of low standard services all forced communities to organize to secure for themselves what local government was failing to provide.

Civics are local social movements accountable to local communities. They have elected executives, formal constitutions, and their organizational structures are based on active grassroots participation by the membership. The extent of their support is dependent on their capacity to articulate the day-to-day grievances of the ordinary township resident. It is for this reason that they have had to perform a dual role. On the one hand they have mobilized and organized around basic socio-economic demands such as housing, services, and land. On the other hand, they have also been forced to link the resolution of these problems to the dismantling of apartheid. This is why they became part of national organizations that were part of the national liberation movement, such as the UDF.

Now that the dismantling of apartheid is a foregone conclusion, the political objectives of the civics have, in this sense, been achieved. Their development objectives, however, are a long way from being achieved. This is why, during the transition, civics are turning to these issues and formulating strategies to handle them. This, inevitably, is going to entail their becoming increasingly independent of the political formations they were once so closely allied to.

The local-level negotiation process

The main actors

Most of the negotiations have taken place between the civic organizations on the one hand, and the TPA on the other. However, other bodies have been present during the negotiations.

The TPA has always insisted that the BLAs must be present at the negotiations, and in fact must be the main negotiating partner for the civics. Civics have continued to insist that the councillors are unrepresentative and should resign. However, for progress to be made in the negotiations, many civics have permitted the BLAs to take part in the negotiations as part of the TPA delegation, and not as 'autonomous' bodies.

The negotiations have often been attended by bulk suppliers such as Eskom and the Rand Water Board. In some cases, civics have persuaded neighbouring WLAs (e.g. the Johannesburg City Council and the Sandton Town Council) to attend the negotiations, so that they can begin to assume some responsibility for the entire city. The

Development Bank of Southern Africa and some RSCs have also played a role during the negotiations.

Demands of the civics

The main interest of the TPA is to get residents to pay a flat rate for services in order to provide the BLAs with some form of income to prevent them from collapsing. The TPA's main weapon in this regard is the threat to cut essential services. In some cases, civics have only negotiated on the immediate issue of stopping service cuts through the payment of an interim charge. This is particularly the case of the civics that are inexperienced and not well organized.

However, many civics have responded that they would consider the payment of an interim service charge, provided that a number of short-term demands are met, and that satisfactory progress is made towards meeting certain long-term demands.

Short-term demands have included:
- the right to organize and to report back;
- no cut-offs of services;
- the writing off of arrears;
- the resignation of councillors;
- the appointment of an administrator acceptable to all parties involved in the negotiations for a specific period; and that
- WLAs take on certain financial and administrative responsibilities during the interim period.

Long-term demands have included:
- non-racial municipalities based on one tax base;
- the upgrading of services and conditions in the townships;
- the provision of more land;
- the provision of houses for low-income groups;
- the transfer of rented houses to the people;
- the upgrading and conversion of hostels; and
- affordable service charges.

Many civics have made it clear that these demands are linked, and are part of a single negotiated 'package'. An interim service charge will only be paid when the short-term issues are addressed, and when proper mechanisms have been established to deal with the long-term issues. The Soweto Accord signed in September 1990 was achieved by agreement on the short-term issues, a period during which an interim charge will be paid by the residents, and the establishment of a Metropolitan Chamber to negotiate the implementation of the long-term demands.

An affordable and permanent tariff will only be paid when there are definite moves towards the introduction of a non-racial local authority based on a single tax base.

Responses of the authorities

Writing off of arrears

Where the civic has proved to be a strong negotiator, the TPA has agreed to write off all arrears. This has been done in Soweto, and is being done in Alexandra. Arrear rentals and service charges can be written off on the basis of:

* prescription: debts older than three years old are not recoverable, if they have not been properly pursued by the authorities;
* validity: were the tariffs legally promulgated?
* enforceability: are the records of the council relating to rentals and service charges accurate?
* quality of services: discount for poor standard of services;
* meter reading/administration: are the meters accurate, read on regular occasions?

With reference to the point on validity of service charges, recent legal research indicates that due to a technicality, service charges of the BLAs throughout the country were promulgated in an invalid manner. This means that all service charges in black townships throughout the country could be illegal.

If the Ngakane versus the Town Council of Mohlakeng case is upheld, it would mean that the boycotts of rentals and service charges are in fact legal, and that the provincial and local authorities cannot legally cut services to the townships on the basis of non-payment of rent.

Resignation of councillors

The TPA has refused to encourage or endorse the resignation of black councillors in any way. The position of the government is that councillors must stay in place during the process of negotiations. It is clear that the government is trying to build up a set of black allies to use during the process of both local and national negotiations.

In some cases, it is clear that councillors have been turning to organizations such as Inkatha for support against the civic organizations which are perceived to be ANC-alligned. The civics have continued to demand the resignation of councillors. The Civic Association of the Southern Transvaal (CAST) resolved to engage in mass action to persuade councillors to resign.

Where councillors have resigned, the TPA has appointed administrators. While this is clearly an unsatisfactory form of local government, it has assisted the process of negotiations in that appointed administrators do not claim to represent a constituency. This solves the problem of having to deal with supposedly 'elected' councillors.

Many civics have made the point that while councillors should resign immediately, services should continue to be provided in the interim period by the existing BLA administration, while negotiations take place regarding new forms of non-racial local government.

Some civics are demanding that an independent administrator, acceptable to all parties in the negotiations, should be appointed during the transition period. For example, this demand has been agreed to in negotiations between the Atteridgeville-Saulsville Residents' Organization (ASRO) and the TPA.

Non-racial local government and one tax base

The government has accepted in principle the civic demand for a 'non-racial, democratic form of local government, based on a common fiscal system'. What this means in practice will be the subject of future negotiations and struggles at a local and national level.

In the case of Soweto, for example, the TPA has agreed to establish a Metropolitan Chamber. This is a forum with powers to negotiate a new form of non-racial metropolitan government for the greater Johannesburg region. All local authorities and civics within this region have been invited to join the Metropolitan Chamber.

Residents in Soweto regarded the establishment of the Metropolitan Chamber as sufficient progress towards non-racial local government for them to begin paying an interim service charge.

In Alexandra, a local government and finance sub-committee has been established under the Alexandra Joint Negotiating Forum, to begin working towards new forms of non-racial local government between Alexandra, Sandton, and the surrounding sub-region. Residents in Alexandra will only consider paying an interim service charge if satisfactory progress is made by this committee.

Land

In certain instances during negotiations, the TPA has agreed to begin identifying land for low-income housing on a non-racial basis, and providing civics with information on land availability. However, on the whole, government land-use planning is still following the apartheid model of locating poor people far from urban areas, as well as according to racial categories. This is also the practice of bodies such as the Urban Foundation.

In the case of Tamboville outside Benoni, negotiations on new forms of land use followed a land invasion. In this instance, the Wattville Concerned Residents' Committee (WCRC), assisted by consultants, mapped out a residential settlement on an area of land adjacent to Wattville township belonging to the Benoni Town Council. Five hundred families were elected by the community to 'invade' this land.

Following the land invasion, the Benoni Town Council agreed to assist with the development of the Tamboville settlement, and raised a loan of R2 million from Benoni's Capital Development Fund to service the land. This process is currently being supervised by a joint technical committee, representing both the Benoni Town Council and the WCRC.

In Alexandra, the Alexandra Civic Organization (ACO) won its demand that the Alexandra East Bank not be developed under the auspices of the Alexandra council. This agreement forms part of the Alexandra Accord that was signed in March 1991.

Another civic-controlled upgrading project that followed a land invasion is the case of Phola Park outside Tokoza.

Housing

In terms of housing, the government (assisted by big business) is still generally committed to the privatization of the supply of housing. This means that housing continues to remain unaffordable for most urban Africans.

However, there are indications that new forms of housing delivery that are being advocated by the civics, are being seriously considered. For example, in Alexandra, the ACO has put forward a multi-million rand development proposal for the Far East Bank, an area of land adjacent to Alexandra. This was in response to the TPA's call for development proposals to be submitted by private developers.

The ACO's proposals are based on the notion of community participation and control. The ACO has argued that the land, as a scarce resource, should not be given to private developers where it would be subject to speculation and the negative effects of the property market. Instead, the ACO has suggested that the land be administered by and developed through a non-profit Community Land Trust, a mechanism that is designed to protect the interests of low-income residents.

To this end, the ACO has launched a series of workshops in Alexandra around questions of design, density, and affordability, to try and establish the best way in which the Far East Bank can be utilized for low-income people.

These sorts of projects, while still in their infancy, have given many civics an understanding of a range of different approaches to development. They are seen as pilot projects where a learning process can take place, rather than as ready-made models of development that can be imposed anywhere else.

Hostels

The upgrading and conversion of hostels have become a priority for many civics in the Transvaal, given recent violent conflicts between hostel-dwellers and township residents. This issue has featured during some of the negotiations.

The TPA has responded that it agrees to the abolition of the hostel system in principle. However, this generally means selling the hostels to private buyers for purposes of converting them into family flats.

This has been opposed by civics for two reasons. Firstly, privatization of hostels will generally lead to increased costs for hostel-dwellers, forcing many of them to find alternative accommodation.

Secondly, it is clear that not all hostel-dwellers want converted family accommodation, either because they are single, or because they do not wish their families to come into the urban areas.

Some civics, such as the ACO, have launched an in-depth research project, in conjunction with hostel-dwellers in Alexandra, to establish in more detail the best way in which hostels could be upgraded and converted to new forms of accommodation.

Services

Many civics have got the TPA and some of the bulk suppliers to agree in principle to the provision of new services and the upgrading of existing services. However, there are different interpretations as to what this actually means in practice.

For the TPA, the provision of services is defined solely according to levels of affordability within any community. Thus, if a community is very poor, then the level of services will reflect this. For example, in site-and-service areas, services are limited to gravel roads, one water tap per 30 households, and weekly refuse removal. Residents dig their own toilets.

Civic organizations, on the other hand, are examining ways in which a minimum level of services to low-income communities can be provided at affordable levels.

Firstly, there is a debate as to what defines a minimum level of service. For example, does the definition exclude electricity as the Urban Foundation has suggested? If it does, should the electricity be provided underground (which is more expensive) or through overhead bundle conductors?

Secondly, civics are examining methods of subsidization of services. In the interim period, some civics are demanding that neighbouring white municipalities, because of their access to expertise, capital equipment, and resources, take over the provision of certain services, i.e. rubbish removal and the maintenance of roads and stormwater drains.

Where white municipalities are involved in the provision of water and electricity to black townships, they are being challenged to provide these services at a rate equal to, or below, the rate that applies in the white areas, thus effectively subsidizing costs.

In the longer term, civics are looking to the introduction of a single administration, based on an integrated local, metropolitan, or regional tax base, as the way in which the provision and supply of services to low-income areas can be cross-subsidized.

Success of local-level negotiations as a strategy?

There are many cases when civics have not succeeded in winning some or any of their demands. The TPA has successfully isolated some civics, particularly those that are not well organized, and has used the negotiations to impose harsh conditions of payment on certain areas.

However, civic organizations in the Transvaal have begun to establish a number of criteria for successful negotiations. These include:

* having a clear set of demands and objectives;
* having a strategy that distinguishes between short-term and long-term demands and that provides a way of linking them;
* the need for a mass base, well organized structures, and a regular process of reports to gain further mandates;
* full-time trained civic officials, with an office, a telephone, a fax, and other necessary equipment to facilitate rapid communication;
* training in negotiating skills;
* technical support and backup, including lawyers, town planners, accountants, engineers, and architects;
* the need for ongoing education and training within the civic;
* co-ordinating with other civics, through regional and national civic structures.

It is clear that civic organizations have gained an immense wealth of knowledge from the process of negotiations, including an understanding of the key actors in the development process, and the nature of state, parastatal, and private sector development institutions.

Many civics regard local-level negotiations as part of continuing mass struggles and mass action, and not as a substitute for them. Civics continue to organize mass protests against the BLAs and service cuts, and campaign for non-racial local government based on a single tax base.

Strategic issues for the future

From protest to development

For the past decade, civic organizations have been in the forefront of organizing and mobilizing communities around a range of both grassroots and national political issues. It is clear from the events of the past fews months that a shift is taking place, in that many civics now see themselves as involved in the process of development, addressing issues such as the provision of land, services, community facilities, and low-income housing.

This has led civics to begin emphasizing their autonomy from party-political organizations, and to build up strong organizational structures throughout the whole community. Many civics are attempting to move beyond being committees of activists, to become organizations which can represent as many residents as possible on issues of development.

However, it is important to assess carefully whether the civic organizations themselves should become development agencies, or whether civics should be part of a broader structure, such as a Community Development Trust, that takes on the task of development. In other words, should civics remain mass-based representatives of community interests, or should they become professional managers of development projects? If they become the latter, then the chances are high that no one will fill the vacuum they leave behind. This will, in the long run, not be in the interests of the communities.

Organization and management

As civics (and some trade unions) have moved towards the role of development agencies, they have realized that their organizational structures need to be altered. During the process of negotiations, the civics have had to work hard to build local structures at street level, in order to inform residents about the negotiations, and receive mandates before agreements are signed.

The complexities of the negotiations, including the work of the joint technical committees that are frequently set up by the principal parties to the negotiations, have prompted civics to establish their own technical, housing, and research committees. These committees, in turn, have established a wide range of links with professional consultants, so that civics can match the levels of information ranged against them in negotiations.

Some civic bodies have also begun to establish themselves on a professional basis, with offices, equipment, and full-time staff. It is no coincidence that the civics that have made the most gains are those that have had this kind of capacity (e.g. Wattville, Alexandra, Soweto, and Kimberley).

Training for capacity

Many civics have realized that they do not possess the necessary expertise within their own ranks to handle large-scale development programmes. Civics have tried to initiate various education and training programmes in order to:
- develop their own expertise;
- increase their capacity to manage projects and funding;
- achieve levels of community participation in the formulation of development strategies; and
- deal with consultants, private developers, and state agencies.

Sources of development finance

As project implementation has become a reality, civic organizations and trade unions have had to build up their understanding of sources of development capital, and the styles and methods of a variety of state, parastatal, and private sector development agencies. These have included the following groupings:
- RSCs;
- Development Bank of Southern Africa;
- National Housing Fund;

- state housing subsidy schemes;
- South African Housing Trust;
- Independent Development Trust;
- capital development funds and consolidated loan funds of white municipalities;
- Urban Foundation (loan guarantee fund, small group credit union);
- pension and provident funds;
- banks and building societies;
- funds controlled by insurance companies;
- company social responsibility funds; and
- international development agencies, including the World Bank.

Co-ordination and development of national policy

During the process of negotiations, civics have begun to see the need to co-ordinate regional strategies and policies, in order to avoid the situation where weaker civics are divided from the better organized areas. This has been a favourite tactic of the TPA, which has consistently refused to negotiate with groupings of civics, preferring to strike different deals with single civics.

Currently, civics are moving towards the co-ordination of policy at a national civic level through a series of workshops.

There is also a need to work towards common national policies on developmental issues. There are many cases where civics have found their strategies at a grassroots level contradicted by national statements and actions by political organizations.

For example, there have been occasions when a political organization such as the ANC has entered into negotiations about services on behalf of a community, but without consulting the civic concerned. There have been instances where rent boycotts have been called off by the ANC, again with no consultation with the civics. A recent ANC statement, which disavows boycotts of bond repayments, undermines the ability of grassroots communities to put pressure on financial institutions which are centrally involved in the provision of privatized housing.

There are clear indications that national-level negotiations between the ANC and the government can have adverse consequences for grassroots communities. For example, part of the ANC's national political strategy has been to win over homeland leaders to the side of the ANC at the negotiating table. In many cases, this strategy has succeeded in broadening the political base of the ANC. Yet this strategy has often been at the expense of civics and other community-based organizations in the homelands, that have been waging active struggles against the homeland administrations.

Civics rely on their ability to resort to mass action to strengthen their hand at the local-level negotiation tables. Yet the South African government is doing its utmost to separate the ANC and national negotiations from mass action which it characterizes as 'violent' and contrary to the spirit of constitutional negotiations.

Many civic organizations have firmly resisted this pressure and have, in fact, stepped up their campaigns of mass action. For example, CAST has continued to call for mass marches to protest the continued existence of the BLAs and the MCs, as well as the cuts to services.

Role of state and civil society

For many years, within the progressive movement, there has been a tendency to believe that the 'new democratic state' will provide for all. With the experiences of socialist states in eastern Europe, and post-colonial states in Africa becoming clearer, this view is beginning to change.

Civics continue to place a strong emphasis on the centrality and importance of non-racial and democratic forms of local government for the success of future development policies. In particular, civics are examining the possibilities of a future national state low-income housing programme, channelled through local authorities.

Civics are beginning to examine various financial systems for local government, taking into account the existing rates of local taxation and the availability of development capital within current WLAs, and the future needs of low-income communities. Civics are also developing ideas around new tiers of government, particularly within large metropolitan areas.

Despite this necessary emphasis on the future developmental role of local and metropolitan government, there has also been a growing debate about the need to avoid an over-reliance on the post-apartheid state for the provision of basic needs. In particular, the limitations of any state form is being recognized, particularly in terms of the limited size of the central fiscus and the competing demands for scarce funds, as well as the need to avoid bureaucratic and 'top-down' approaches to planning and development.

Many civics have begun to investigate and establish a range of community-based institutions that can carry out developmental work. These institutions, while controlled by a community and not the central or local state, are also very different to the individualized and privatized notion of development currently being promoted by both capital and the apartheid state.

Community-led development is seen as a process of development that allows for community mobilization and participation on a collective basis, avoiding both a 'statist' and a 'privatized' emphasis that has polarized the debate until recently. However, community-led development is not viewed as an alternative or a substitute to state development programmes, but rather as a necessary complement.

Forms of non-profit community development institutions under consideration include:

- community ownership systems, such as land trusts, electricity co-operatives, and housing co-operatives;
- non-profit financial institutions such as community credit unions and banks; and
- community-based development organizations, such as development corporations.

While these institutions are being initiated by the civic organizations, they are seen to be representative of wider community structures. In terms of developmental projects and programmes, many civics have tried to involve a broad range of community organizations, in different sectors, and in some cases representing different interests.

Within civics, there have been many debates about affiliation to political organizations, in particular the ANC. The general consensus that seems to be emerging is that while the process of development is political (as opposed to apolitical), it nevertheless should not be party-political. Civics should therefore be independent mass-based organizations (similar to trade unions), and development projects and programmes in any community should not be tied to a particular political party. Funds for development should not be used by any political party to reward supporters, or penalize dissenters.

Unity and division

Many civic organizations are now very aware of the way in which the provision of material resources to poor communities can have a very divisive effect. They have also seen how development projects initiated by the apartheid state have often had the effect of dividing communities, increasing stratification and the potential for conflict.

Civics are therefore trying to move in a direction where they increase their organizational capacity in the free-standing and the backyard shack settlement areas where developmental needs are often the greatest. This is not an easy process, because it is often resisted by the civics' traditional constituencies in the established townships and the matchbox houses.

What civic organizations are realizing is that 'communities' are seldom, if ever, homogeneous, and that while the anti-apartheid struggles of the previous decade were predicated upon unity within a community, development programmes have to recognize divergent and in many cases conflicting interests.

22 Challenges of process and policy

Lawrence Schlemmer

On 13 December 1990 the State President announced that his government had accepted the principle of 'one city, one tax base'. This goal had become one of the rallying calls of the extra-parliamentary civic associations, and was part of a more general demand for reunited, undifferentiated, and completely non-racial cities. Until recently this set of objectives was perceived to be fairly radically at variance with the government position. Hence there would appear to be considerable recent convergence between the basic thinking of the major protagonists in the arena of local government. Indeed it is this broad framework of convergence which has made it possible for the government and most major parties to endorse local negotiations on an interim restructuring of local government. The establishment in April 1991 of a Metropolitan Chamber for Johannesburg as a forum for such negotiations, involving the TPA, the civic associations, the BLAs, and the white city councils is a major breakthrough in the process. How enduring and resilient, however, is this early broad convergence likely to be?

Among people who are committed to the broad principle of a non-racial democratic South Africa, there are two major views about how the transition should, or might, occur. One perfectly understandable view is that the transition requires a fairly immediate and urgent elimination of all the features of South Africa's past policies and structures which are racially divisive. This view assumes that the main, and for some perhaps the only legitimate role of the present racially based authorities in the country is to negotiate and manage their own capitulation and withdrawal from power.

A second view, not necessarily held only by conservatives, is characterized by 'realpolitik'; this is that a successful transition requires a trade-off between existing patterns and the demands for their elimination. It assumes that if there were no expectation of some continuity with the past, the transition would not be occurring because white interest groups and most white constituencies would simply not permit it. While this viewpoint would not necessarily, and should not, endorse any maintenance of official racial discrimination, it acknowledges that certain vested interests and the administrative machinery which implemented previous policies require a 'buffer' period to adapt to open non-racial conditions.

This second view is easily confused with the motive of continued racial privilege (and indeed this would be the motive among some people who subscribe to the view). As already suggested, that is not the only motive, nor is it the most soundly reasoned. A more analytically based reason would be that certain existing structures of authority and management, in both the public field and the private economy, *relatively speaking*, have the experience, personnel, expertise, and financial resources to manage and maintain complex public organization and private investment, and that their summary removal would damage everyone's interests, not only their own. Hence the trade-off between transformation and continuity.

This view is not easily accepted outside of existing vested interests because to a substantial degree, the non-voters who aspire to full power and opportunity lack resources, experience, and expertise precisely because of apartheid. It is an unyielding fact at the present time nonetheless. There can be few people who could honestly point to any major examples of sound management and the development of complex social, political, and economic organization in the extra-parliamentary sector, aside from the trade unions which have particular roles not easily compared to other management tasks.

The conflict between the two views and the dilemmas involved are very aptly illustrated by current developments in our cities and towns. Underlying the textural detail in local debates, negotiations, reform, and responses to reform is this contrast between the politics of transformation and the politics of realistic compromise. This chapter will explore first the prospects for a reconciliation of such views, and second will examine some of the more specific issues which have to be addressed before South Africa's cities and towns will be able to become aligned with the emerging reality of the new South Africa.

Prospects for reconciliation and constructive negotiation

As outlined in much greater detail elsewhere in this book, there are a number of current initiatives aimed at negotiation between civic associations and the existing authorities over specific grievances and problems (like rent and service charges) and over a new and racially inclusive system of local government. Such negotiations are provided for in the government's Thornhill Report prepared at the request of the Council for the Co-ordination of Local Government Affairs. The government position, however, is that the outcomes are to be regarded as provisional pending negotiations at central level. As already stated, the most advanced initiative is in the Central Witwatersrand where, after a protracted rent and service charge boycott in African areas, the TPA, after negotiation with, *inter alia*, the SPD, has established a Metropolitan Chamber for Greater Johannesburg. The Johannesburg City Council has responded very positively to the opportunity and has begun preparing its position, as has the SPD, involving the major civic associations in the area. Other initiatives at earlier stages of progress include developments in Cape Town, Durban, Port Elizabeth, areas in the East Rand and the eastern Transvaal, and isolated examples elsewhere.

These developments parallel the negotiating process at central level and, in the case of the Central Witwatersrand, may even be in advance of national negotiations. These initiatives all tend to occur within the broad understanding that there will be trade-offs and compromises (the second view stated in the introduction) even though the rhetorical posturing does not always suggest this.

There appear to be over 40 rent and service boycotts in various townships, mainly in the Transvaal and OFS, which have led to the cutting of services in 23 townships over the past three months,[1] and where comprehensive and constructive negotiation has hardly started except over the boycotts themselves. These forms of action are based not only on grievances but are also aimed precisely at mounting pressure for local negotiations. Therefore, although they exact heavy penalties as regards public funds and painful sacrifices from residents where services are discontinued, they may in the end produce positive outcomes in the form of more urgent local negotiations. In fewer cases there are African consumer boycotts as well, launched in protest against various actions by white authorities, particularly where township services are discontinued.

At the same time there is an active commitment by both the ANC and CAST to a campaign of 'mass action' to demand the resignation of existing authorities. Although the stated aims are to use peaceful methods, it is impossible to separate this strategy from the record of the immediate past. Six councillors were killed in the first seven months of 1990. Two attacks on councillors were mounted daily, and 87 attacks on the houses of councillors occurred.[2] The pattern has continued. From February 1990 to April 1991, 324 BLA councillors resigned, 224 as a direct result of political pressure in the Transvaal. In that province 39 out of 78 BLAs have collapsed, and been replaced by appointed Administrators.[3] In the country as a whole well over 100 out of 258 BLAs have been replaced by Administrators. The testimonies of many of the councillors reflect fear for their lives and the safety of their houses, families, and businesses.[4] The campaign of pressure and mass action has most recently been extended to coloured, Indian, and even white town councils, although its prospects of succeeding are considerably diminished in these areas. CAST president Moses Mayekiso has said: 'We have to get rid of the structures ourselves. If we don't the process will take too long.'[5]

Mass action could be intended as a focused protest and power strategy aimed at alleviating specific grievances. It could also be a more extensive power strategy outlined by two senior SACP underground 'cadres'. Quoting Mao Tse Tung, 'You cannot win at the negotiating table what you have not won on the battlefield', their view of mass action is to 'open the doors to a transfer of power', to establish coercive leverage, and that 'the negotiations table is not the real battleground'.[6]

Mass action of the second type conforms to the rigid demands in the first view of transition outlined in the introduction. One of the reasons for confusion among political observers is that both mass action and a willingness to negotiate on specific grievances seem to exist side by side. It raises questions about the coherence of the process on the side of participants from African communities and extra-parliamentary movements.

Understandably, a combination of factors, including some bond payment boycotts and aspects of the mass action referred to above, have negatively affected housing development in the townships. Eight major construction companies withdrew from the townships late last year, and white trade unions are demanding increased protection for their members working on township projects. Certain banks and building societies are reluctant to make individual loans in a range of townships.[7]

Broadly, then, African community-based political action in urban areas has assumed a dual form. On the one hand there is recognition of the need to negotiate and find compromise solutions. The potential contribution of existing WLAs to the government and management of reunited, racially integrated cities is accepted, albeit reluctantly, by some of the township-based organizations participating in the negotiations.

On the other hand, at another level of majority-based organization, mass action appears to be aimed at forcing the pace of change beyond that which would allow for orderly negotiation at this stage. This political action appears to be aimed at alienating and weakening the strength and credibility of the very authorities with which negotiation will have to be conducted.

An additional issue is perhaps most disconcerting of all. Mr Olaus van Zyl, the Transvaal Provincial MEC in charge of local government, claims that 'Organs purporting to be representative of residents (in townships) have thus far been unable to fulfil agreements where such agreements have been reached' (i.e. boycotts have continued despite agreements).[8] Is this another manifestation of double-strategy, or is it due to lack of effective support and mobilization in the townships?

A further complication arises in that there is increasing uncertainty about the political location of the forces behind the mobilization in the townships. As indicated, both the ANC and CAST have called for intensified mass action and the participants in the action are frequently aligned with both organizations. Yet CAST has recently announced, through its Assistant General Secretary Cas Coovadia, that it was attempting to shake off its identification with 'congress-orientated' organizations like the ANC. The reason given is that the linkage prevents the civic associations, which intend to form a national body, from gaining the support and participation of all township residents across lines of political sympathy.

The argument at one level appears to be plausible. Urban grass-roots grievances cut across party lines. Yet if one considers two factors, the very same argument can be interpreted as an attempt by over-arching civic bodies to impose a disguised or an alternative political hegemony on the townships. The first factor is that, in its stated motivations for mass action, CAST is adopting a very clearly defined policy of power confrontation. Would all aggrieved township residents endorse this strategy? By presenting itself as the primary organization to articulate and promote 'grassroots' township interests, CAST is not exactly allowing residents the benefit of democratic choice of strategy.

A second factor is that CAST is not exactly politically neutral. In the words of the journalist Esmare van der Merwe, 'many of CAST's leadership are trade unionists, some of them with strong ... SACP ties ... This could mean that the SACP ... is focusing on civics to establish a separate power-base'.[9]

Perhaps the most disturbing feature of all is that in the ebb and flow of all this political action, the opinions and inclinations as regards strategy of the ordinary people themselves — the 'grassroots' — are not heard. Everything is filtered through what are mostly self-appointed organizations and activists. Not even opinion polls provide many insights because of the enormous costs involved and the fact that the commercial organizations which have the resources to conduct them persist in asking the worst and most vacuous type of pop survey questions that can be imported from the United States. This author, however, was able to undertake a modest survey recently which suggests that over three-quarters of ordinary residents in the metropolitan townships, while thoroughly disapproving of African town councillors, do not endorse power confrontation, intimidation, or attacks on white authorities.[10]

The comments made above on the extra-parliamentary movements are not to suggest that the current authorities involved in local political process are exempt from hidden political agendas and power strategies. There have been equivalent accusations of dual strategies directed at the state, and pointing particularly to possible covert stimulation of violence by undefined 'third forces', taken to be associated in some way with the state.

The danger, however, is that the political stresses and complexities will obscure some over-arching realities. The cities are precisely the place in South Africa's transition in which negotiated alternatives to divided local government, racial zoning, and segregation can combine the experience, managerial strength, fiscal resources, and technical expertise of WLAs with the development priorities of South Africa's long neglected townships. The quality of the new South Africa will be substantially determined by the quality of urban government. Negotiated local charters and new forms of integrated metropolitan government of high quality could emerge within one to two years if the type of negotiation which has begun to occur in the

Central Witwatersrand proceeds. Obviously, aspects of the mass action and reaction referred to above could place this outcome in jeopardy.

It is possible that the 'mass action' of the ANC and of CAST is little more than a symbolic display of leverage and influence which is intended to be brought to bear in constructive negotiations. Coovadia has qualified his initial threats.[11] Furthermore, in the case of Greater Johannesburg, the civics and the SPD have proceeded into initial meetings despite attempts by CAST to introduce issues which would have caused delays. The rhetoric employed, however, strains this generous interpretation. Even if it is merely pre-negotiation posturing, it could enormously strengthen the resistance of right-wing groups in urban politics, and may be discouraging even to non right-wing municipalities which are not as sophisticated as those in the Johannesburg area.

This raises the issue of white community-based politics. A process of reasonably orderly and constructive negotiations at local level could be threatened by white conservative interest groups which are at their most powerful in urban areas in the Transvaal. Three hundred CP councillors apparently met in January to discuss strategy to resist non-racial local authorities.[12] One must expect that the CP, which controls almost 70 per cent of WLAs in the Transvaal, will elaborate its strategies as the negotiation process gathers momentum and achieves greater visibility. In the case of white local politics, the attitudes of ordinary white voters and ratepayers are crucial. What does the available evidence suggest?

In late 1989, the author conducted an enquiry among white voters nationwide. A range of questions on residential desegregation and on alternatives to the present dispensation were posed. Among the 1 800 respondents, no more than 30 per cent welcomed or accepted the complete abolition of residential segregation. The basis of the sample was the nationwide white panel of Market and Opinion Surveys (Pty) Ltd. The same organization, using the same panel, has just published its latest poll in which comparable questions were posed.[13] From these results it would appear that the recent draft legislation intended to abolish the Group Areas Act and the Land Acts is supported by some 43 per cent and 39 per cent of white voters respectively — hence indicating what appears to be an increase in support for desegregation.

More significantly, however, the results indicate that opposition to the ending of residential, land, and educational segregation is still firm at roughly 35 per cent of the sample. The particular panel used as a basis for the sample has consistently underestimated support for right-wing political parties (as assessed against the outcome of national elections), and hence the opposition to desegregation is probably closer to four out of 10 whites.

More importantly, the whites who hold these opinions are likely to be concentrated in areas outside the generally more cosmopolitan metropolitan areas of Johannesburg, Cape Town, Durban, and Port Elizabeth. Indeed in smaller towns, the anti-desegregation viewpoint is likely to be held by a majority.

Therefore, once the process of statutory reform and negotiation for change in local government structures moves outward from the metropolitan areas to more conservative towns and cities, white opposition is likely to become manifest. One may even see sharply polarized civic action by community groups in both the African and white communities. While this kind of reaction may not derail the process, there are likely to be delays and disruptions from time to time and place to place.

One must therefore conclude that the process of pre-negotiation and early negotiation around the issue of change in local government structures, while extremely promising in certain major metropolitan areas, is likely to bring a great deal of conflict, controversy, reaction, and counter-reaction as it moves outwards to non-metropolitan areas. One might be inclined to considerable pessimism were it not for the over-arching effects of national negotiations. Conceivably, by the time the issues are on the boil in smaller towns, results from the proposed Multi-party Conference will have established a framework and a momentum of change which will over-ride local conflict.

Major constitutional issues facing non-racial cities

If the final assessment above is valid, one might make the assumption that the political process at local level will move through the current phase of pre-negotiation positioning, power play, and conflict and settle down to address the substantive issues of local restructuring and development. These issues are likely to create at least as much controversy and conflict as the current phase of pre-negotiation positioning. In the section which follows, some of the major issues and challenges will be reviewed.

In the opening paragraph of this chapter it was suggested that some convergence of thinking between major parties on the *broad* outlines of the post-apartheid local government structure was emerging. However, the apparent agreement on *broad* concepts of change may in many ways be misleading. The 'one city' concept may turn out to be a lure, drawing diverse interest groups into sometimes intense conflict over the precise implications of a reintegration of white and black municipalities. Similarly, the concept of a single tax base may prove to be a battlefield on which different communities may wage a fundamental fight over who should decide on how the local revenue should be spent, and even perhaps on levels of local taxation.

The scope of future consensus or conflict can only be assessed once specific parameters of change are debated. There is considerable variation in the intensity of perceived needs for change and in the levels of determination to sweep aside old structures. One does not know how serious this variation might be because up to now there has been less than adequate debate about mechanisms, boundaries, procedures, and powers in new forms of local government. It is perhaps appropriate, therefore, to raise some of the issues which need more debate from now on. Not all issues can be covered. Those selected stand out as the more problematic.

Phasing of levels of negotiation

Firstly there is the uneasy issue of the place of local negotiations in the wider context of national reconciliation. On the surface government appears to have endorsed local negotiation for interim structures. Most civic associations are clearly willing to engage in local negotiation. How meaningful are these moves, however? When the positions of government and the extra-parliamentary movements are viewed more closely, considerable ambiguity becomes apparent.

On the side of government what is not clear is how far it will allow local agreements to go. It has to be remembered that all local agreements will have to be approved by provincial administrations. While the government has stated that the current negotiations are open and unconstrained, it must be concerned about two possible kinds of outcome. One would be where local negotiations result in too few safeguards for minorities, setting a precedent which will complicate negotiations for final structures at national level. Another problematic outcome would be where local white minority interests demand and retain too much autonomy or a too manifestly racial basis, thereby bringing them into conflict with a more flexible and moderate government position at national level.

There is also a dilemma for extra-parliamentary movements. At central level some eventual compromise between majority and minority interests seems inevitable, although it may not have to take the form of very clearly defined constitutional 'group rights'. Given the fairly intense commitments which appear to be developing around the concept of the non-racial 'one city', how difficult will it be for the same kind of compromises to be accepted at local level? The dilemma may crystallize in the other direction. A group of municipalities and civic associations in a metropolitan region may hammer out a compromise between each other which could establish a precedent for the ANC at national level, cutting across substantive principles or a negotiating strategy.

One answer to the dilemma on both sides would be for the benefits of constitutional diversity to be accepted. Different cities and regions have different political dynamics. Varied local constitutions can be a way of resolving conflict. This would optimistically presuppose, however, that politicians at national level will accept the principle of pragmatism and trade-offs and relax the imperatives of their national 'charters'. Another option would be to attempt to complete either national or local negotiations first, but this is clearly impractical in the light of the build-up of political expectations.

There is no doubt, therefore, that the national and local dynamics of negotiation are going to complicate each other. This may be a good thing in some local areas and a bad thing in others. Whatever the case, it will be a great tragedy if local initiatives are usurped or undermined by national power play, or if the national resolution becomes mired in precedents set at the local level.

Local versus national negotiations

One encounters the optimistic notion that different political groupings at local and provincial level have experience of one another, know each other, have exercised leverage on each other, and for this reason will more readily come to terms with each other than national groupings. This may be very true in some cities and regions.

On the other hand, in other urban complexes, like, say, the East Rand, and particularly in smaller towns, different local communities may be more mobilized around deeply polarized objectives than is the case at national level. Relative to some local actors, De Klerk and Mandela and their respective senior colleagues are veritable states-men-politicians. One can see prospects of what has been termed an informal 'grand coalition' at national level. Could one conceivably imagine anything similar occurring between highly aggrieved and mobilized civic associations and deeply resistant CP councils?

Up to now most local negotiation initiatives have emerged out of specific problems to be solved — rent and service boycotts, con-sumer boycotts, and the like. Local electoral power has not yet been on the agenda in such negotiations, but until it is, the existing dynamic of negotiations will remain essentially a preamble.

Therefore as against the optimism referred to earlier, one must consider that the politics of territory, patronage, and vested interests are often at their most intense in local areas. At the same time it is inconceivable that national problems will be solved in a situation of hostile stalemate at third-tier level. The failure of African local gov-ernment to achieve legitimacy has a proven capacity to paralyse national politics.

Hence, even if local negotiation is going to be more stressful and complex than at any other level, it dare not be delayed. Conservatives and comrades are going to have to begin talking. Above all, it seems that it will have to keep pace with and remain broadly congruent with issues at national level. However, there can be no firm imposition of national blueprints. Rather, the emphasis will have to be on more and better ongoing communication between politicians at different levels.

Local 'federalism' or dual-level local government

This issue has certainly been implicit in the debate up to now and is referred to from time to time in the form of broad warnings and injunctions. It requires much more attention, however. One can pre-dict quite confidently that as the political interaction on the future of our cities progresses, the issue of local federalism will become the focus of sharply contrasting views. Perhaps some further comment is necessary. These comments, however, are made in the context that racial zoning or Group Areas will no longer apply. All people will be free to live where they like and where they can afford to live.

As already suggested, a very tentative majority consensus is emerging on the need to reintegrate divided metropolitan and urban administration and to restructure local government so that all communities may benefit from a single tax base. Some local political actors expect that this should lead to an undifferentiated municipal electorate for the spectrum of formerly separated local authority areas. This would produce an expanded single city or town council. An inevitable consequence would be that the electoral wards and councillors currently constituting the most highly developed core of mainly white municipalities would emerge as electoral minorities in a new ward system extending to the edges of the townships and perhaps beyond into informal housing areas.

This shift can be interpreted in more than one way. Firstly, it can be seen as what might be termed arithmetic or demographic legitimacy: the clear and untrammelled implementation of the principle of majority choice. Given the demographic ratios of the communities within our urban context, in most urban areas the former townships will control the central council. Conditions and policies determining how the tax base will be developed and allocated will in effect be determined by communities whose per capita contributions to the tax base will be lowest but who, through mass purchasing power and employee numbers, make a very substantial if not dominant indirect contribution to the size of the fiscal cake. Effective pressure for a redistribution of tax revenue from the core areas to the mass townships will be very great.

This view has many adherents, enjoys considerable legitimacy, and benefits from the frequent assumption that the power of numbers constitutes the essence of democracy. It would be unrealistic to expect that political spokespeople for the mass townships would willingly favour any other approach.

The issue can, however, be interpreted differently from an equally democratic viewpoint. This viewpoint would be that the essence of democracy is to include as many diverse interests in the system of government as possible. This implies that representatives of specific constituencies must effectively be able to articulate and defend the interests of the constituents to whom they are accountable. If an elected representative becomes powerless because he or she is part of a minority opposition party in the overall system, then one purpose of democracy — the effective representation of *variety* — is defeated.

There are other arguments similar to these which are relevant in our cities. The people who pay most in terms of local rates are likely to vote for minority parties. Their capacity to pay higher rates can be seen as an index of wealth, privilege, and material advantage.

One view would be that since this wealth is accumulated on the basis of the labour and purchasing power of the township masses, the latter should be able to demand and define the redistribution of that wealth through the local government. Another view might be that wealth is not only the product of labour and consumer expenditure, but *also* of initial risk capital, management skill, product development, and technical expertise. This view would suggest that the wealthy are also creators of wealth and should have substantial say over what happens to the taxes they pay. In particular, the argument would be that they should at least help to determine the conditions in which the local economy functions.

One can go on and on contrasting the two types of arguments. There are no logical absolutes; no correct and incorrect ways of understanding democracy. All so-called imperatives of democracy are in fact the products of one or another set of interests and ideology.

What is relevant to the future of our cities, however, is that the two major types of assumptions will resolve themselves into two views about a local 'constitution'. One view would favour the majoritarian principle of an undivided electorate; the numerical winner takes power principle. The other view is bound to favour various ways of effectively representing interest minorities and the diversity of interests.

The latter principle may emerge as one or more of the following arrangements:

- Wards of unequal size and demographic weight, so that the electoral leverage of minorities is increased; or voting systems which have a similar effect, such as the option to exercise a double vote provided the second vote is for a second party, thus probably increasing the votes gained by minority parties.
- The retention of existing municipal boundaries, or of wards, for a lower level of representation, and a city-wide or over-arching metropolitan level of representation to deal with issues of general concern, including fiscal redistribution. The two levels would bal-

ance each other's political power. This would be a typical form of local 'federalism'.

- The devolution of some municipal powers downwards to individual wards, so that ward or neighbourhood committees, burgesses' associations, or the like retain some countervailing influence relative to the overall majority-based dispensation. This author gains the impression from conversations that there is considerable support for this in government ranks.

As already suggested, each approach will have its fervent protagonists and there are no correct answers engraved in stone. The outcome will simply have to be determined by negotiation and compromise. The case this author would like to make is that of compromise. This is not simply because compromise is generally good or inevitable. There are more tangible advantages.

In regard to minorities in a new dispensation, it has to be pointed out that to insist too firmly or rigidly on the constitutional protection of minority interests would build chronic conflict into the system of local government. Minorities and majorities might consolidate behind constitutional rights and safeguards, doing their best to extract maximum benefits out of the system. The local 'constitution' will be born in conflict and will remain controversial. This will not be a recipe for civic harmony and investor confidence in our new cities.

As regards the 'majorities', however, there are also very considerable objective disadvantages in insisting on unqualified local majority rule. Experience has taught that majorities are too amorphous and general to take collective decisions. What happens is that a political élite within the majority party writes the agenda and prepares the policies. This élite responds to the most vocal popular lobbies and most muscular subgroups in the majority. Some categories of people inevitably lose out.

Therefore questions which local African community leaders should ask themselves are the following: Will undifferentiated majority party rule allow particular civic associations, especially smaller civics, to retain autonomy and a particular accountability to their constituents? Will relatively less sophisticated 'squatter' communities be able to compete in the arena of the majority party? This has not been the case anywhere in Africa, to this author's knowledge. More and more Africans will also be living in apartment house areas outside the townships. Their interests cannot conceivably be the same as those of township residents. Will they not become obscured in the tension between the middle-class suburban and the mass townships?

Another danger of smaller communities being eclipsed in the larger majoritarian process inheres in the local bureaucracy and planning establishment. As metropolitan areas grow in size, so the complexity of competing interests increases and the effective political distance between neighbourhoods and the city hall increases. Immediate political interaction becomes more difficult. In such situations not only does effective participation become more problematic, but the co-ordination and regulation of municipal affairs become all the more necessary. Inevitably, and without preconceived intention, planners and bureaucrats become more and more important in co-ordinating and regulating policy. Well organized lobbies can possibly have an impact on their decisions but it is much more difficult for small communities to understand and influence the process. In these complex situations is some provision for direct participation by local communities, irrespective of size, not an important corrective?

Even the issue of a single tax base becomes problematic in the light of the questions posed above. At the moment fiscal redistribution is taking place through the RSCs. The taxes (levies) which are redistributed are indirect, collected from employers and from the proceeds of commerce and industry. The very poor certainly make a substantial indirect contribution, but the indirect contribution of the unemployed and the people who consume little is modest. A single tax base, as the fiscal engine for development, usually requires that everyone pays direct rates and levies. With growing African property ownership, which is going to include even the ownership of sites in informal housing schemes, people will discover that power over a common fiscal base also involves the obligation to make direct payments to it. 'No taxation without representation' is no more valid than its obverse, 'no representation without taxation'. It is particularly in regard to the implication of a general rate base and general rates contributions that the smaller communities will be well advised to look after their specific interests.

Many other questions like these can be posed. The answers are complex but they all boil down to the fact that the representation of diversity will not only benefit the middle classes or the white minority. It will be equally salient for smaller, sub-metropolitan civics and residents' bodies.

Also important is the question of an economic development strategy. If the intention is to secure development and redistribution on behalf of the poor, there are more ways of doing it than by using majority leverage to force redistribution. Elsewhere in the world this, *inter alia*, leads to companies moving out of the cities and to the rich moving to semi-rural suburbs. In South Africa and anywhere else for that matter, development is the product of synergy; of co-operative endeavour to address problems. Municipal government, the private sector, voluntary organizations, and local communities will have to combine efforts to overcome our immense socio-economic problems in urban areas. City government which creates space for and confidence among all these varied agencies is necessary. Effective co-operation of resource-rich local interests in development programmes may yield more in terms of development than attempts to force them to pay for redistribution.

These are some of the reasons why it would seem to me that local political compromise which allows space for co-operation between diverse interests is essential. Compromise cannot be decided upon in advance. It can only emerge out of negotiation which should commence without delay. It goes without saying, however, that negotiation must involve the full diversity of types of communities and not only those political organizations which are currently mobilized to participate.

Inequality and socio-economic development

Very broadly speaking, there is a degree of duress on all political groupings to compromise on their political and constitutional demands. Without compromise, very little more than stalemate will emerge. There is a balance of power in South African urban areas — albeit power of different kinds — which might ultimately incline the protagonists to reasonable stances.

More intransigent, however, are the socio-economic issues. These issues have their effects beyond the control of politicians, and their solutions are often beyond the skills and resources of politicians. Yet these problems and issues, if unsolved, remain exploitable by activists in such a way as to place the entire democratic process at risk. A few selected examples of serious socio-economic problems are presented.

Urban unemployment and the challenge of development

South Africa's cities, like those elsewhere in Africa and the Third World, are going to have to cope with very great burdens of dependency due to unemployment, particularly African youth unemployment. Accurate estimates of African youth unemployment are not available, but this author's own survey evidence suggests that it varies between 30 per cent and 50 per cent or more, depending on the region of the country. It is particularly youth unemployment which contributes to the kind of petty crime and vagrancy that can make streets in certain areas of cities places to be avoided. In a valuable overview, the Paris-based Organization for Economic Co-operation and Development points out that:

> In recent years an increasing number of local authorities have become actively involved in business and job development ... [because of] High structural unemployment that is unlikely to diminish even if the general economic climate improves; disillusionment [exists] with national employment policies [and] the feeling that local authorities should not remain passive, that they should intervene, mobilise, 'do something', even if their resources and room for maneuver are limited.[14]

In South Africa, local authority intervention in the creation of employment is bound to have to follow these international trends. Local authorities have an established role in planning for serviced industrial and commercial land, and some local councils have achieved some success in attracting investment to their areas. It is likely, however, that pro-active intervention will have to go beyond this role. In future local authorities will have to consider assisting in the establishment of skills-training schemes, local employment bureaux, labour-intensive local upgrading projects, community-based job-creation programmes, and other ways of improving the conditions for job creation.

Perhaps the greater test for local politicians, therefore, will be the challenge of moving beyond political competition, into areas of co-operation with one another, across party lines, in seeking to address the detailed challenges of urban development. In this process politicians will also have to move beyond interest and grievance articulation. The short-run sentiments of their constituents will have to be counter-balanced by a concern with longer-run issues of development. All local politicians will have to develop an unaccustomed respect for an urban climate and urban planning which attract investment and encourage initiative and entrepreneurship.

Movement to the city centre

The history of ghetto formation in the USA is in substantial measure a history of movement from the rural south, and more recently Latin America, into inner-city rental accommodation which is or was cheap in absolute terms but expensive in terms of value for money. The underlying dynamic in the movement of people is dominantly economic in the sense of a desire to be close to sources of employment and cash income, often in the informal sector, which is usually at its most developed in dense urban concentrations of poor people. The South African situation is duplicating this process, possibly with a few intensifying factors to boot.

Around South Africa's major metropolitan concentrations there are at least between four and five million shack dwellers[15] who experience both poor physical living conditions and the disadvantages of being at a considerable distance from the concentrations of the inner-city. Added to this there is a substantial under-employed population in the African rural areas and to a lesser extent in the white rural areas. People in the African rural areas have the added freedom to move since the traditional land tenure system and extended family occupation of rural holdings mean that individuals can move to the city without placing their rural resources at risk.

Hence, the City Engineer of Cape Town has reported[16] that some 5 000 families per month are moving from eastern Cape rural areas into the shack belt of Greater Cape Town. For a possible substantial proportion of this large number of shack dwellers — not all of whom are without income (average incomes are well in excess of R300 per month) — opportunities to move into inner-city rental accommodation will be very attractive if cities become residentially 'open'. Even over-crowded slums could hardly match the density per structure in the shack areas.

A crucial question is whether or not cities contain areas of vulnerability; i.e. districts in which there are deteriorating apartment buildings with high vacancy rates and in which the profitability of the buildings will be increased or even simply maintained by landlords allowing multiple occupation of units. Some cities are more at risk than others — for example the Johannesburg areas of Joubert Park, Doornfontein, and Hillbrow have already illustrated the process in action. In certain circumstances there may not be residential movement as such but an oscillating movement into inner-city areas because of the presence of commercial and civic facilities.

It must be emphasized immediately that these new forms of utilization of inner-city resources can be a positive contribution to alleviating the resource constraints for South Africa's poor people. Part of the massive housing shortage for Africans could be addressed in this way. The important point to make, however, is that if the intensity of utilization leads to a deterioration of physical structures, condemned buildings, over-crowded and malfunctioning facilities, and a withdrawal of productive economic activity from centre-city areas, the process can be self-defeating. Resources will in fact be destroyed.

Recent estimates by the Bureau of Market Research at the University of South Africa are that, contrary to official estimates, virtually 80 per cent of Africans are already urbanized on a permanent or semi-permanent oscillating basis.[17] These figures accord with this author's impressions of very recent growth in shack settlement.

More broadly, the phenomenon of hyper-urbanization is likely to introduce a new and very heated polemic into the debate on urban development. On the one hand there are the protagonists of high-density cities, or higher-density compact cities. The Urban Foundation has taken the lead in arguing for an acceptance of density as a positive stimulant for development.[18] Certainly one can see quite clearly that the construction of bulk infrastructure and accommodation for rapidly increasing urban populations could be a short-run growth stimulus. Furthermore, an abundance of willing labour concentrated around key industrial areas is a positive stimulant for industrial investment, and the settlements associated with the labour will constitute highly accessible markets. New housing has spin-offs in stimulating the market for household goods which can help to sustain any initial economic stimulus.

All these positive factors presuppose, however, that the socio-political climate in high-density cities will facilitate investor confidence. This would appear to be uncertain at least. Against this argument in favour of high-density cities, one encounters equally convincing arguments pointing to the dangers of over-urbanization. Harvard University economist Jeffrey Sachs, for example, has been quoted as saying that *one* of the reasons for the superior growth performance of middle-level Asian economies over their Latin American equivalents is lower levels of urbanization in the former. Thailand and Malaysia, for example, with less than 40 per cent of their population urbanized, have been able to avoid heavy fiscal expenditure on relatively unproductive urban infrastructure and services, thus facilitating a higher rate of capital formation for more competitive industrial strategies.[19]

High-density inner-cities involve the danger that slum conditions and resulting social pathologies will co-exist with high land values, reasonable rentals, and adequate profitability for landlords in apartment house areas, secured through multiple occupation of units and overcrowding. The urban fiscus then has to respond by bearing the relatively high costs of services and the upgrading of infrastructure, which must involve rising levels of taxation and urban financial stresses. Given high land values, urban renewal is prohibitively expensive.

There is also the consequent danger that the middle-class consumer and investor, due to changes in the social character of the city and crime, will on an increasing scale leave the central city for the suburbs. This results in a further loss of revenue for the urban fiscus. For example, recent USA census results suggest that the white to black ratio of New York (a surrogate for socio-economic class distinctions) has shifted from 2:1 in 1980 to 1:1 in 1990.[20] A 1990 opinion poll in New York yielded the estimate that 68 per cent of residents perceived that the quality of life in the city had become 'worse' in recent years whereas only seven per cent felt that it had become 'better'.[21] This kind of problem appears to be endemic in cities exposed to high levels of in-migration of poor people without jobs and adequate resources.

The alternative of lower rates of in-migration is hypothetical in the South African case, however, unless positive measures are adopted to stimulate deconcentrated development. The earlier policy of ideologically based decentralization to so-called homelands and their borders was inefficient and a net drain on public resources. More rational, economically based attempts to stimulate decentralization have an almost equally poor track record.[22]

The policy dilemma can, however, be stated as follows. If in the future any tax or other incentives for capital investment and the establishment of industry are offered as part of government industrial development programmes (which are more than likely), the policies attached to those incentives will stimulate either increased urban density or some measure of urban spread, decentralization, or deconcentration. The choice is difficult and more complex than most of the arguments for or against urban concentration would suggest. This issue is likely to be one of South Africa's longer-run challenges and sources of debate, outlasting many of the current issues.

The danger of persisting effective segregation

The US Association for Urban Studies reported in 1987, over 25 years after the beginning of the US Civil Rights campaign, that:

> Our most basic conclusion is that none of the well-known economic, social and statutory changes have fundamentally altered the ghetto system. Ghetto expansion and the resegregation of integrated neighbourhoods are still taking place.[23]

An American author has described balanced integration as 'hard and expensive work'.[24] The USA experience — indeed the international and southern African experience as well — is not a basis for great optimism about the prospects for an easy and cumulative process of desegregation in South Africa, even without the Group Areas Act and minority rule. A common pattern in the USA is for city areas to 'tip', changing from near-white to near-black fairly rapidly once the proportion of new black residents reaches 15 to 20 per cent. This occurs despite a possibly superficial sentiment in favour of desegregation among 80 per cent or more of USA whites. The reasons for the pattern are frequently fears of a fall in property values, or active stimulation of white property sales by estate agents — a process called 'blockbusting'. This leads to a spread of resegregation, associated with white movement beyond the core city boundaries into satellite suburbs and towns in which similar processes are unlikely. The departure of whites often leads to the decentralization of companies and shopping centres, causing a relative decline in revenue for the core city. This pattern is particularly applicable to middle-class family areas.

The informal concentration of ethnic residence, if it becomes too obvious or visible, can be a source of continuing stress in race relations. An impression is created of continuing islands of (white) privilege and semi-exclusivity which could become explosive issues in the non-racial politics of our cities in the future. What are the prospects?

Under conditions of complete desegregation, a pattern will most probably emerge in which upper middle-class white areas will stabilize with a small to moderate proportion of relatively affluent African residents. Such areas will be unproblematic. Lower middle-class areas which have new or sound housing stock will become very attractive to whites leaving older lower middle-class areas which have integrated. These newer 'white' areas will become bastions of relative homogeneity, as in the USA, with relatively high property values and minimal integration. They are likely to upgrade spontaneously. On the other hand, areas in which most Africans live, for no reasons other than the fact that their lesser original quality and higher vacancy rates made an early integration possible, and the fact of inevitable crowding, will tend to deteriorate in standards. In this regard it should be borne in mind that the social activity at 'street' level is definitive. If crime, begging, and street youth formations become typical, an area will acquire a reputation determined by the street rather than the internal quality of dwellings and the social standards of residents.

The implication of these trends could mean that residential areas polarize in quality (as flat buildings tend to do in Hillbrow currently) and that the quality differential is superficially associated with race. If this occurs to a serious extent, a condition will emerge in which cities reassume an overt racial anatomy.

If a desegregation and informal resegregation pattern along these lines is to be avoided or minimized in South Africa, then particular attention has to be given to methods of protecting desegregating areas against a deterioration in physical standards. The normal health and nuisance by-laws, as currently implemented, are probably not sufficient. Special and very sensitive methods will have to be formulated by local authorities, in consultation with local residents' committees. In particular, steps might have to be taken to prevent a tendency among landlords to facilitate or encourage overcrowding of rental accommodation as a means of increasing or maintaining profits. At the same time, any undue artificial curb on the profitability of rental accommodation will also lead to physical deterioration. These are difficult challenges but they have to be faced lest the new African residents of open areas find themselves plunged back into informal variants of the socially 'disadvantaged' segregated conditions they have sought to escape from.

A very complex issue in this regard is schooling. If integrated schools change their educational character too markedly or rapidly, it tends to stimulate white or middle-class family flight more than any other single factor.

Pro-active steps may also be possible. 'Infill' developments in vacant or redeveloping areas might be planned as attractive and safe low-cost neighbourhoods dotted around the city, breaking the racial correlations. Furthermore, great attention should be given to maintain safe and clean streets in all areas, and for this reason local authorities must be prepared to expand their inspectoral, security, and cleansing services, studying the emerging problems and attacking each one timeously.

Furthermore, through the planned development of parks and other urban features, planning authorities should attempt to facilitate the emergence of 'enclaves' in which social, economic, and ethnic variety can be maintained in situations of close spatial juxtaposition.

Some of these issues are dealt with in a recent government White Paper on Land Reform.[25] Clearly there is concern over the maintenance of residential standards. A proposed Urban Environment Board and certain mediating agencies have been proposed. However, such provisions, enacted at this stage, are likely to be perceived by extra-parliamentary parties and policy groups as perpetuating privileges and racial exclusivity.

The proposed legislation will be opposed. For this reason it is perhaps urgently necessary for these socio-economic aspects of urban policy to be raised in local negotiations as soon as possible, irrespective of whether the central standards legislation is passed or not. An ideal situation would be if broad agreement on optimal approaches to protecting desirable elements in the urban fabric were to coincide with initial moves to establish non-racial local government.

Some concluding comments

This chapter has attempted an overview of three levels of challenge facing South Africa's apartheid cities in transition. The first is the current problem of political mobilization, conflict, and reaction as urban political interests prepare to negotiate future policy and structure for the cities. In discussing this process, relatively little attention has been given to the justifiable mass grievances and inequalities which previous policies have bequeathed to the cities. These problems are adequately covered by other chapters; suffice it to say that they are very serious and it would be illogical to expect a harmonious and crisis-free pre-negotiation phase. The brief discussion in this chapter suggests an ever-present risk of severe disruptions to the political process. Equally important, however, is the possibility that local and central negotiation politics can destabilize each other. On the other hand, the momentum of moves towards reconciliation in certain major cities, and at the national level, might facilitate solutions in difficult local situations. It is necessary to emphasize a point made earlier to the effect that effective and ongoing political communication between local political actors and between local regional and central political actors and agencies is essential if a constructive overall pattern is to be maintained.

A second level of issues concerns the substantive or 'constitutional' issues of future urban political structure. In the discussion offered it has been suggested that over-simple interpretations of the requirements and principles of democracy might prevent compromises being achieved which could ultimately benefit all urban interests. Attachment to the imperatives of the majority principle versus commitment to 'federal' forms of (non-racial) electoral differentiation need not be the polarizing commitments they currently appear to be. The principle of effective local community participation could invite the interests of both African township residents and white and other minorities.

A third level of issues relates to socio-economic problems and policy alternatives which will emerge more and more prominently as issues when the short and medium-term political issues are resolved. These ultimately may be the most difficult to resolve. It seems clear from an abundance of international evidence that interest-based and competitive political orientations have never distinguished themselves in bringing development and quality of life to Third World cities. This is a level of challenge which might indicate to political actors in South Africa the obligation to rise above immediate interest-based competition and to co-operate around longer-run policy challenges.

All told, South Africa's cities present a formidable challenge of policy substance and political process. The slum belts, the islands of privilege, the fiscal crises, and the political tensions of Third World and many rapidly changing First World cities reinforce that challenge. The minority fears and majority grievances in South Africa have also created fertile soil for the promotion of high-key ideologies which are wielded like clubs in the political debate. Perhaps the most important problem in the urban process in South Africa is the imperialism of conflicting goals and commitments. For this reason it is perhaps instructive for both majority and minority-based political actors to reflect on the fact that problems of urban development throughout the world, at one stage or another, have proved everyone wrong.

Notes

1   *The Star* 4 April 1991.
2   *Saturday Star* 15 December 1990.
3   *The Star* 28 March 1991.
4   *Business Day* 14 January 1991.
5   *Sunday Times* 20 January 1991.
6   Kasrils R. and Khuzwayo M. 'Voices from the Underground: Mass Struggle is the Key' *Work in Progress* (January/February 1991).
7   *Business Day* 1 November 1990.
8   *The Star* 28 March 1991.
9   *The Star* 15 October 1990.
10   Schlemmer L. 'Township Residents amid Violence and Negotiation', research brief (Johannesburg: University of the Witwatersrand, Centre for Policy Studies 1991). Detailed results are currently being computer-analysed.
11   *The Star* 24 January 1991.
12   Ibid.
13   *Rapport* 21 April 1991.
14   Organization for Economic Co-operation and Development *New Roles for Cities and Towns* (Paris: OECD 1987).
15   Cooper C. et al. *Race Relations Survey 1988/9* (Johannesburg: SA Institute of Race Relations 1989) 162.
16   In a personal communication to the author (1989).
17   *Business Day* 25 March 1991.
18   Haarhof E. 'High Density Cities' *Natal University Focus* (1991) 2 i.
     Urban Foundation 'Policy Overview: the Urban Challenge' (Johannesburg: Urban Foundation Policies for a New Urban Future, undated, *circa* 1990).
19   Quoted by Gail N. 'The Four Horsemen Ride Again' *Forbes Magazine* (July 1986) 95–103.
20   Reported, *inter alia*, in *The Star* 4 April 1991.
21   Attinger J. 'The Decline of New York' *Time Magazine* (17 September 1990) 46–54.
22   Urban Foundation (undated, *circa* 1990).
23   Quoted in *The Star* 16 February 1988.
24   Monti D. J. 'Residential Integration in the United States', report to the Urban Foundation (Johannesburg: 1989).
25   Republic of South Africa 'White Paper on Land Reform' (Pretoria: Government Printer 1991) 13–91.

Abbreviations and acronyms

ACO Alexandra Civic Organization
ANC African National Congress
ASRO Atteridgeville-Saulsville Residents' Organization
AZAPO Azanian People's Organization
BAAB Bantu Affairs Administration Board
BAD Department of Bantu Administration and Development
BLA black local authority
CAHAC Cape Housing Action Committee
CAST Civic Association of the Southern Transvaal
CC Co-ordinating Council
CCC Cape Town City Council
CDF cities development fund
CLT Community Land Trust
COSAS Congress of South African Students
COSATU Congress of South African Trade Unions
CoT Committee of Ten
CP Conservative Party
CPA Cape Provincial Administration
CPRC Coloured Persons' Representative Council
CRADORA Cradock Residents' Association
CTSO Cape Town Symphony Orchestra
CWRSC Central Witwatersrand Regional Services Council
DBSA Development Bank of Southern Africa

DFR Durban Functional Region
DoT Department of Transport
DPPA Department of Planning and Provincial Affairs
DSB Development and Services Board
DVRA Duncan Village Residents' Civic Association
ERAB East Rand Administration Board
ERRSC East Rand Regional Services Council
HNP Herstigte Nasionale Party
JCC Johannesburg City Council
JEA Joint Executive Authority
JED Johannesburg Electricity Department
JMC Joint Management Centre
JSB Joint Services Board
JTC Joint Technical Committee
kWh kilowatt hours
LACs local affairs committees
LP Labour Party
MC Metropolitan Chamber
MCs management committees
MDM Mass Democratic Movement
MEC Member of the Executive Committee
NAC Native Affairs Commission
NACTU National Council of Trade Unions
NALAC Natal Association of Local Affairs Committees
NBRI National Building Research Institute
NP National Party
NPA Natal Provincial Administration

NPP National People's Party
NRC Native Representative Council
NSMS National Security Management System
OFS Orange Free State
PAC Pan Africanist Congress
PARCO Port Alfred Residents' Civic Organization
PEBCO Port Elizabeth Black Civic Organization
PFR Pretoria Functional Region
PSC Private Sector Council on Urbanization
PSF Public Sector Forum
PTA passenger transport authority
PWV Pretoria-Witwatersrand-Vereeniging
RSC Regional Services Council
RWB Rand Water Board
SABOA South African Bus Operators' Association
SABTA Southern Africa Black Taxi Association
SACCOLA SA Consultative Committee on Labour Affairs
SACP South African Communist Party
SADT South African Development Trust

SAIRR South African Institute of Race Relations
SATS South African Transport Services
SCA Soweto Civic Association
SCC Soweto City Council
SED Soweto Electricity Department
SPD Soweto People's Delegation
SVT site value tax
TBVC Transkei, Bophuthatswana, Venda, Ciskei
TMA Transvaal Municipal Association
TPA Transvaal Provincial Administration
UBC Urban Bantu Council
UDF United Democratic Front
UF Urban Foundation
VLT vacant land tax
WCRC Wattville Concerned Residents' Committee
WLA white local authority
WRAB West Rand Administration Board
WRRSC West Rand Regional Services Council

Index

Index